Indian Subjects

Publication of this book and the SAR seminar from which it resulted
were made possible with the generous support of the Annenberg Conversations Endowment.

School for Advanced Research
Global Indigenous Politics Series

Indian Subjects

Hemispheric Perspectives
on the History of Indigenous Education

Edited by Brenda J. Child and Brian Klopotek

SAR
PRESS

School for Advanced Research Press
Santa Fe

School for Advanced Research Press
Post Office Box 2188
Santa Fe, New Mexico 87504-2188
www.sarpress.org

Managing Editor: Lisa Pacheco
Editorial Assistant: Ellen Goldberg
Designer and Production Manager: Cynthia Dyer
Manuscript Editor: Cecile Kaufman
Proofreader: Diana Rico
Indexer: Catherine Fox

Library of Congress Cataloging-in-Publication Data

Indian subjects : hemispheric perspectives on the history of indigenous education / edited by
Brenda J. Child and Brian Klopotek.
     pages cm. — (Global indigenous politics series)
  Includes bibliographical references and index.
  ISBN 978-1-938645-16-7 (alk. paper)
  1. Indians of North America—Education. 2. Indian students—United States—History. 3. Indians of North
America—Cultural assimiliation. 4. Indians, Treatment of—United States—History. 5. Off-reservation
boarding schools—United States—History. 6. Education and state—United States—History. 7. United
States—Race relations. 8. United States—Social policy. I. Child, Brenda J., 1959-
  E97.I44 2014
  371.829'97—dc23
                         2013034497

Library of Congress Catalog Card Number: 2013034497
International Standard Book Number: 978-1-938645-16-7
First edition 2014.

Cover illustration: Flor Ángela Palmar with her daughter, Anggie Hernández Palmar, on the occasion
of Flor Palmar's graduation Magíster Scientiarum in Basic Education Adminstration, Rafael María Baralt
Experimental University. Photo courtesy of David Hernández Palmar, 2011.

*The School for Advanced Research (SAR) promotes the furthering of scholarship on—and public
understanding of—human culture, behavior, and evolution. SAR Press publishes cutting-edge scholarly
and general-interest books that encourage critical thinking and present new perspectives on topics of interest to
all humans. Contributions by authors reflect their own opinions and viewpoints and do not necessarily express
the opinions of SAR Press.*

Contents

Figures

Preface

Brian Klopotek

Indian Subjects began with a conversation at a meeting of the American Society for Ethnohistory in Chicago in 2004. I had just presented an early draft of "Indian Education Under Jim Crow," a paper that would eventually become a chapter in this volume. At the time, I had only envisioned it as part of a story of Indian history in Louisiana, but Brenda Child, as a longtime scholar of Indian education, viewed it from another angle. She recognized that there were many other similar stories of Indian education that had happened outside the federal purview, but that they were scattered and never made it into the larger story of Indian education in the United States. Collecting these stories together would fill enormous gaps in our knowledge of Indian education in the United States and perhaps even change the most basic understandings of what that history looked like.

As the conversation proceeded, we thought more about what kinds of information were missing from the literature and what kinds of essays we would like to have available to use in our classrooms. We both teach classes on the history of Indian education, and while we had ample material available on boarding schools in the United States and Canada between 1875 and World War II, we had to search much harder to find material on education outside the boarding school walls, outside the area between Arizona and the Upper Midwest, outside the classic boarding school era, and outside of the English settler states. We had never found any material comparing indigenous educational histories in Latin American and Anglo North American nations. And while there had been significant analysis of gender in education, issues of sexual identity and issues of race outside of the Indian-white dyad were virtually absent, as well. We set out in search of scholars doing pathbreaking work that would begin to fill in some of these gaps and point to exciting new directions for future research. Some we found already doing this work, and others we cajoled into doing it.

Thus, *Indian Subjects: Hemispheric Perspectives on the History of Indigenous Education* brings together an outstanding group of scholars and professionals who we have asked to think historically about indigenous education. Trained in anthropology, history, law, education, and literature, and in interdisciplinary programs including Native studies, the chapters they have written are about indigenous education throughout different regions and eras, predominantly but not exclusively within the twentieth century. Most of the authors, including the co-editors, are indigenous scholars, a number of whom have chosen to write about the historical experiences of their own people and communities. In addition, Roy Huhndorf and Flor Palmar collaborated with two different authors in the volume to bring essential perspectives from their lifetimes of experience as leaders and professionals in indigenous communities.

The stories of Indian education that we are most familiar with are the boarding school histories; whether run by the federal government or religious orders, they dominate academic and community views of indigenous educational histories. The lessons learned from these histories demonstrate the devastating impact of Anglo settler colonialism and assimilationism, just as they document multiple Native responses. While recognizing the value of boarding school narratives and the lessons to be drawn from these histories in the United States and Canada, they provide a fairly narrow view of indigenous educational history. The chapters in this book push beyond those boarding schools, into an expansive range of indigenous communities, indigenous intellectual circles, and indigenous homes, to make a critical intervention into how we think about indigenous educational histories. Changing the historical narrative of indigenous education to be multisited and multiscaled—even just shifting the terms from *Indian* to *indigenous* and back again—reshapes the parameters of the discussion. When we envision this field more broadly to include Indian education in the southern United States under Jim Crow, indigenous education in Alaska, in California, in Hawaii and other Pacific Islands, and in Mexico, Peru, Venezuela, and elsewhere in Latin America, new information and new patterns come to light. Some of the chapters in *Indian Subjects* are about boarding and residential school history, but the book is designed to open new doors for conversations about less familiar subjects. The volume pushes toward more hemispheric and global conversations, fostering a critically neglected scholarly dialogue that has too often been limited by regional and national boundaries.

Because our goal was to create a broad collection of essays that cohered well around these themes, and because the scholarship of contributors to this volume was wide-ranging, we convened a short seminar at the School for Advanced Research in Santa Fe in the fall of 2009 to discuss and assess each other's projects and the collective stories they tell. During the seminar, unifying themes emerged that run throughout the volume. Readers might find it helpful to think about these threads of analysis as they read the chapters.

Thread 1: Education has consistently been connected to issues of land, economy, and autonomy in indigenous settings throughout the hemisphere. Dispossession, dependency, and attacks on indigenous sovereignty have all been facilitated by educational policies and practices. Education has indeed been a site where multiple political issues are negotiated and social worlds constructed, for good or ill, whether under the eye of national governments or carried out on smaller scales at the local level. Given the extensive interconnections of education to virtually every other issue facing indigenous communities and their relationships with the various powers that be, education must be understood as a critical indigenous political issue throughout the Americas and the English settler states.

Thread 2: Indigenous groups throughout the hemisphere have adapted to and selectively adopted educational and economic strategies from colonial nation-states, though such choices have always been mediated by the constraints of dominating power relationships. Such choices have posed enormous conundrums for indigenous peoples, who must seek education in languages of power, such as Spanish and English, in order to protect their communities from exploitation or to pursue economic opportunities or life interests. At the same time, however, such education in colonial languages has been a significant source of exploitation, and a means of eradicating indigenous cultures and languages. Many communities have found themselves asking questions about how to protect indigenous cultural and linguistic heritage in an age of global economies.

Thread 3: Just as indigenous groups have adopted elements from outside groups, so colonial educational institutions (defined loosely as educational systems imposed by external political and cultural groups upon indigenous groups) have selectively incorporated indigenous cultural practices such as arts, crafts, and even languages into colonial school systems. While seemingly benevolent, the political and cultural content of those practices has often been removed and replaced with colonial values in colonial educational institutions. Indeed, education throughout the hemisphere has consistently been a site of containment of indigenous political and cultural difference, and a site of transformation of indigenous peoples into loyal citizens of the state.

Thread 4: We have been left to wonder why indigenous education has generally been kept separate from other histories of racial segregation in education, though many of the same intellectual and emotional justifications informed them both, and many of the same social relations were reproduced with each system. Clearly, whites created distinct racial projects for land-based indigenous groups (e.g., Native Americans) and groups racialized solely to exploit their labor (e.g., African Americans), as Patrick Wolfe has discussed elsewhere.[1] Racializations of indigenous groups tend to protect white interests by pushing toward assimilation of indigenous peoples (or, more accurately, of their land) into the dominant society, while racializations of landless groups exploited for their labor protect white interests by keeping them excluded from equal access to various benefits of citizenship. Despite this distinction, there is significant overlap in these categories, as Native Americans have been exploited for their labor and historically enslaved, and historically racialized immigrant groups have been coercively assimilated into colonial societies, as well. The general failure to group these histories of segregated education together perhaps has to do with the invisibility of whiteness and white supremacy at the center of racial and colonial schemes. Whatever the reason, the time has come to examine these histories side by side.

Thread 5: By exploring these histories, we can reassess the central issues in indigenous educational history as well as the sites of intervention to create new trajectories and alternate futures for us all. Readers should bear in mind at all times that forces outside of educational policy impact the circumstances indigenous peoples find themselves in, and that educational policy must be connected to broader historical patterns.

This volume consciously builds on, rather than rejects, the scholarship that has come before it, and we extend our deepest appreciation to all the scholars and community members who have participated in these conversations to date. There is plenty more to say on indigenous educational histories, and we hope this volume pushes the conversation in productive new directions. We feel confident that readers will find much to engage with in the chapters that follow, as we have.

For helping to make the short seminar so productive and rewarding, we would like to express our gratitude to the staff at SAR and SAR Press, including James Brooks, Nancy Owen Lewis, Lynn Thompson Baca, Lisa Pacheco, Leslie Shipman, Carla Tozcano, Ray Sweeney, and Randy Montoya. We would like to thank the University of Minnesota and the University of Oregon for providing funds to support travel to Santa Fe for contributors. Our appreciation also goes out to two anonymous reviewers at SAR Press who provided helpful suggestions for improving this volume, and to our copy editor, Cecile Kaufman.

Note

1. See Wolfe, "Land, Labor, and Difference: Elementary Structures of Race."

1 *Introduction*

Comparing Histories of Education for Indigenous Peoples

Brenda J. Child and Brian Klopotek

One of the essays in this book tells the story of a remote Indian population living in northern Minnesota who, in 1900, took a radical position against the construction of a government school in their Ojibwe community. An important geographical feature in this region is a peninsula that divides a large lake into lower and upper bodies of water, and the peninsula was an excellent vantage point to observe any newcomers making their way across the lake. When workmen hired to build the school disembarked from their boat on the southern shore of the peninsula, onto a sandy beach lined with tall grass and towering hardwoods, they were immediately surrounded by a guard of armed Ojibwe men asking them to leave.[1]

This unexpected assertion of sovereignty, while common to this people and place, was not well received when agents of the US government learned of the event. For these Ojibwes, one of a number of small, self-sufficient villages on the reservation, each with a traditional governing system of hereditary chiefs, the indisputable reality was that only they had autonomy over their lands, water, and children's education. In contrast, the Indian agents assigned to administer Ojibwe reservations interpreted this episode (as they did in detailed reports) as an act of hostile Indian rebellion on American soil. In the end, there was a peaceful resolution. No blood was shed, the school was built after a great deal of negotiation, and Ojibwe children dressed in uniforms and attended the new school for many years thereafter. The community incorporated the school and the English language into their ongoing life, retaining their distinctive traditions of culture and spirituality while growing increasingly bilingual throughout the twentieth century. After a few decades, the school closed when the political winds shifted so that it was more practical for children to be bused to public contract schools on the reservation.[2]

It is intriguing to read official reports and try to interpret this small moment in history that was part of the founding of the Crosslake Boarding School in Ponemah, Minnesota, on the Red Lake Indian Reservation. Themes common to indigenous history and settler colonialism are immediately apparent. In 1900, the United States was still in the throes of allotting Indian lands and pursuing a policy of coercive cultural assimilation. Even the people of remote Ponemah had sent some young people to Carlisle and other Indian boarding schools. By the turn of the century, Indian people had enough experience with mission and government schools to view their establishment as threatening—either personally jeopardizing the health, well-being, and security of their children, or collectively endangering their political institutions and cultural survival. The Crosslake Boarding School is one tiny ripple in a sea of examples whereby indigenous people—communities, families, parents, and children—expressed autonomy even as others positioned them as dependent subjects to be controlled through education. This struggle—a contest over the position of indigenous peoples as *colonial subjects* versus indigenous peoples as *conscious subjects* striving to shape their own world— animates the histories examined in this book. *Indian Subjects: Hemispheric Perspectives on the History of Indigenous Education* delves deeply into how in the United States, Canada, and Latin America, education has been a central domain for the contestation of these issues of subjection and subjectivity.

Indigenous Education Before Colonization

Prior to the arrival of Europeans, the peoples of the Americas had their own educational systems, or ways of transferring knowledge from one generation to the next. While some peoples, such as the Maya, developed systems of writing, most knowledge was transmitted orally, most often from one family member to another. The language, of course, would be taught simply through speaking it, though at times individuals might specialize in oratory or story-telling practices if they had a particular talent, or they might be tasked with learning other languages for diplomatic purposes. Many kinds of knowledge would come through participation in a community of shared values, customs, kinship, language, and territory. Knowledge of gender systems would come from living them as well as from origin stories and other cosmological sources. Ceremonies might be taught through participation, or, for more elaborate ceremonies, a person or group of people might be apprenticed to a mentor or mentors who would teach them how rituals should be conducted, along with the religious justifications for them. Knowledge of food production, whether it be through agriculture, fishing, hunting, or gathering, would often be encouraged with celebrations of a child's first basket of berries or first buffalo kill. Knowledge of homebuilding, tool making, weaving, arts, and other kinds of manufacturing would typically come from participation in these activities with older relatives. Travel near and far provided knowledge of the land, its resources, its peoples, and its history, and groups developed deep and abiding ties between their land, their religion, their history, their values, and their culture, as Keith Basso documents so powerfully in his work with Western Apaches. Some people specialized in medical knowledge and would catalog the uses of herbs and minerals that would provide foundational knowledge for many modern pharmaceuticals. Knowledge of a community's political system and values, of clan and kinship, of stars and seasons, of heroes and tricksters, of laws and customs—all of this knowledge was passed down orally, through participation in community life.

One of the ways indigenous peoples have been able to retain significant amounts of knowledge despite lacking systems of writing has been through extensive use of mnemonic devices. In an early twentieth century Flathead story that ends with a tick being flattened in a comical way as the mouth of a volcano collapses, the tick becomes a mnemonic device for knowledge of a volcanic eruption witnessed centuries earlier. A Western Apache story about a geographical formation where a person acted foolishly in the past makes that place into a daily visual reminder not to behave in a similar way. A series of pictographs on a buffalo skin becomes a "winter count," used by Lakotas to keep track of the major events a community experienced every year. A person's name might carry knowledge of the migration of their ancestors from one area of the Americas to another, or it might evoke a memorable event in their lifetime. The thousands of individual beads of a wampum belt are used to recall the history of a treaty for the Haudenosaunee, with recitations of the history lasting several days in some cases. Quipus, or talking knots, could be used in the Andes for recording transactions or other numerical information. Mnemonic devices help people retain memory of events that have taken place over extraordinary amounts of time, as well, as in the case of the Klamath tribe, who retain a story of two volcanoes erupting simultaneously in their homeland at the time of the creation of Crater Lake. Their description of the event has been verified by geologists, who date the eruption to seven thousand years ago.[3]

Many of these knowledge systems have been destroyed or significantly interrupted through colonial educational institutions designed specifically to interrupt the intergenerational transfer of knowledge. A near consensus developed among Anglo-American policy makers in the late nineteenth century

United States that Native children must be removed from their communities entirely in order to effectively strip them of the ways of thinking of their parents and their communities. While Native students and families resisted these efforts, colonial educational institutions used every conceivable means to eradicate indigenous knowledge and lifeways, keeping children away from their families and communities during times of their lives when they would typically learn vital information about what it means to be Ojibwe, Mohawk, or Hopi. As the colonial takeover of Native lands progressed, many of the skills that used to provide food and shelter for people became obsolete, pushing indigenous peoples to seek out educational opportunities so their children could survive in the new world order, but even in these circumstances, the kinds of education Native people received in colonial educational institutions never matched their hopes.

Colonial Education and Indigenous People and Their Languages

Across the hemisphere, colonial education for indigenous people was initially designed to contain them, to make them into safe neighbors and subjects of the state, with the expectation that with enough effort on the part of pupils and their "superiors," they might eventually become integrated citizens in some degree. In the United States, the land policies of the late nineteenth century were the impetus for the establishment of off-reservation government boarding schools; it is doubtful that a national system of segregated, off-reservation schooling for Indians would have ever been considered, let alone actually built across the country, without this compelling interest. Assimilation, in itself, was the stated rationale, guided by naturalized assumptions of European cultural superiority, but the desire for unimpeded access to indigenous land and resources had always been the less obvious driving force.

At a time when Indian people in the western United States were still defending their homelands and moving to reservations, Indian education was drawn into the political process whereby the United States and its growing population gained access to Indian land, casting a long shadow over Indian self-sufficiency. Those who planned the new schools sought to actively produce new social, economic, and political worlds, not just prepare younger Indians for jobs and life in the English-speaking United States. *Indian Subjects* argues for a view of indigenous peoples, and often the students themselves, as understanding that Indian education was a fundamentally political process, which is why they participated in it, and in the end remembered it, in the extremely diverse ways they did.

Several of the authors in *Indian Subjects* address one of the most pernicious aspects of an education focused on spreading and upholding the colonial cultures, which is that schools emerged as primary sites for attack on indigenous languages. In the United States, Canada, and other countries in this hemisphere, Indian languages were regarded as a threat to Christianity and the security and unity of the nation, so schools effectively outlawed them and punished children for expressing themselves in their indigenous languages. In the United States, the Bureau of Indian Affairs only began to close boarding schools and promote public school education more widely for American Indians in the 1930s, by which time Indian people had lost most of their former lands and a great deal of autonomy. Following this vast dispossession, Indian languages were no longer so threatening, and the Bureau of Indian Affairs seriously considered for a time the practical benefits of bilingual education in their remaining Indian schools. Once Indian languages no longer posed any real threat to the land claims of the nation, bilingual reading materials could be prepared, as they were in some Navajo schools, and today, indigenous language revitalization is often funded by state and federal programs.[4] While the correlation is starkly evident, the eradication of indigenous languages was tightly linked to the dissolution of indigenous sovereignty and the assertion of colonial sovereignty over the land.

In Latin America, similar trends prevailed. Debates from the earliest years of conquest about whether to use Spanish exclusively or to allow the use of Native languages tilted toward the exclusive use of the colonial language at moments of political unrest in the Andes, for example.[5] Mandatory Castilianization was deployed as a weapon to undermine indigenous resistance and proclaim absolute Spanish authority. In later years, the predominantly Spanish creole elites who fought for independence from Spain also sought to distinguish themselves from local Native populations, leading to similarly assimilationist policies on indigenous languages.[6] As in the US, only after indigenous land tenure and political systems had been effectively contained was there a commitment from state actors to protect languages in any degree.

As a result, indigenous communities are trying to preserve or resuscitate their languages throughout the Americas and the Anglo settler states, but they face a dilemma: European languages are politically, economically, and socially empowered, while indigenous languages are consequently disempowered. In order to access power for indigenous communities in their relations to the state and to the global economy, indigenous people need to be educated in colonial languages. And yet education in colonial languages is the very problem they are fighting against, and there is considerable debate over the extent to which bilingual education (versus immersive education) defies or promotes assimilationism in different contexts. It is clear in all cases, however, that the economic, political, and social structures of colonialism place a significant burden on indigenous languages. *Indian Subjects* illuminates the multifaceted and changing history of language in indigenous education, and encourages comparative perspectives. Once linked solely to language decline and endangerment, educational institutions now appear to some to be a potential stabilizing force in the recovery of our languages.

Race, Segregation, and Indigenous Education

A core understanding within *Indian Subjects* is that race and the ideology of white supremacy are fundamental to indigenous educational history. Any story involving education that separated Natives from Europeans, African Americans, and others must involve a conversation about race, regardless of region or country. Some scholarship has already demonstrated the value of attention to racial thinking in comparative work on indigenous education. Margaret Jacobs reveals that although policies calling for the removal of indigenous children from their homes in the United States and Australia were remarkably similar, "it was the specter of 'miscegenation' between white and black Americans, not the American government's treatment of American Indians," that guided ideas about indigenous educational policy in Australia.[7] It is almost baffling that the influence of racial thinking beyond the Indian-white dyad has been so understudied in US Indian educational histories, as well. One of the strengths of comparative work is that it illustrates the complexities and contradictions of colonial education worldwide and allows us to draw new and larger conclusions about these projects.

While broader race relations are rarely discussed in histories of indigenous education, neither is the establishment of federal boarding schools for American Indians included in the historical narrative of segregated education in the United States. Rendering segregation as almost entirely a black and white story passes over significant opportunities to better understand how race functioned in conjunction with educational policy. For example, a significant court case in 1924, *Piper v. Big Pine*, illustrates the ways that Indian families undermined some local white supremacist educational policies, even as the courts confirmed the "separate but equal" doctrine. Alice Piper, an American Indian girl in California, fought for her right to attend the local white school instead of a nearby Bureau of Indian Affairs (BIA) establishment.[8] She had been excluded from enrollment on the basis of her race under the California separation of the races statute, which stated:

> *The governing body of the school district shall have power to exclude children of filthy or vicious habits, or children suffering from contagious or infectious diseases,*

and also to establish separate schools for Indian children and for children of Chinese, Japanese, or Mongolian parentage. When such separate schools are established, Indian children or children of Chinese, Japanese, or Mongolian parentage must not be admitted into any other school.[9]

Arguing that the state was obliged to provide education for all children, the California Supreme Court ruled that Indian students must be admitted to public schools in California, even if their parents lived on reservations and paid no taxes to the state, and even if there were a BIA school available to them. The court affirmed that the school district could set up a separate school for Indians, but ruled that unless and until that happened, Indian students were to be allowed to attend school with whites. While not exactly a crushing blow to white supremacy, the case did manage to integrate Indian students into some white schools, and established the right of Indian students to attend public schools in the state of California. Moreover, it stands as evidence of the ways in which Indians were grouped with people of other races in local (rather than federal) segregation policies, and the ways Indians fought against those policies.[10] Educational policy, in fact, was a central means of establishing, protecting, and contesting the privileges of whiteness throughout the country, so bringing these bodies of literature into conversation with one another will certainly prove fruitful for scholars of race and the history of education.

Exploring and Comparing Regional Histories

Perhaps because of the need to understand the complexity of indigenous experiences with boarding school education on the mainland of the United States, scholars have focused less on the broader history of public school integration, and excluded the fascinating development of indigenous education in Alaska and Hawaii until recently.[11] Any survey of colonial education systems demonstrates their similarities and differences, contradictions and complexities. In the United States, Canada, and Latin America, these educational projects typically began as mission schools or other proselytizing methods, determined to "civilize" children and often adults through religious instruction and other efforts to convince indigenous peoples to emulate European lifestyles. Unevenly, colonial state powers intervened to gain control of indigenous education, with the US government asserting control over every aspect of Indian education by the late nineteenth century and the Canadian and Venezuelan governments leaving the job to religious orders as late as the 1960s and 1970s. Schools in every region favored a gendered manual labor curriculum, where children would spend a portion of the day learning traditional subjects, such as math and reading, before receiving lessons in sewing, cooking, and cleaning for the girls, and trade skills such as carpentry and farming for the boys. Such schools usually completely suppressed indigenous languages as part of the "civilization" process. Over the course of the twentieth century, indigenous peoples slowly regained some control over their children's schooling, and most of the historiography points to the 1960s as a turning point in colonial education, with the founding of Native studies departments in the United States and Canada, the eradication of the Native Schools system in New Zealand, and the rise of indigenous movements in Latin America that pushed for bilingual, bicultural community schools to replace state-sponsored, Spanish-only schools that were designed to nationalize the indigenous population.

Canada's long history of colonial indigenous education begins with schools established by missionaries accompanying the first French settlers. These efforts often focused on providing day schools for First Nations peoples. The Indian Acts of 1876 and 1880 changed indigenous status, however, as they unilaterally abolished First Nations self-governance and placed social services, such as education, under government control through the newly established Department of Indian Affairs. In addition, the government commissioned a report in 1879 to evaluate the US policy of creating boarding schools for Indians that would remove children from the influence of their families and communities for the majority of their formative years. The Davin Report advocated for similar institutions in Canada with the recommendation that they would be run by missionaries. As in the United States, curriculum in these schools focused on practical training in order to prepare children for their future roles as farmers and housewives, and children attended for ten months of the year. In Canada, the results of this system were more complicated than the government anticipated. Often students returned to their reserves to become leaders, while others entered the labor market and competed with Euro-American workers. As one minister for Indian Affairs noted in 1897, "we are educating these Indians to compete industrially with our own peoples, which seems to me a very undesirable use of public money." The government, perceiving Indian education as too generous, reduced the services available to First Nations peoples beginning in 1910 and emphasized low cost schooling thereafter.[12]

Education for Indians was not mandatory in Canada until 1920, long after compulsory attendance laws were passed in the United States, although families frequently resisted sending their children to the residential schools. Many protested the lack of decent educational opportunities available, but the government took little action until after World War II, when European-Canadians first began to acknowledge discriminatory treatment toward

Indians. In 1951, the Indian Act was revised, permitting Indian children to attend public and private schools educating Euro-Canadians, with government financial support. By the early 1970s, following protests by the National Indian Brotherhood, the Canadian government recognized in principle that control over First Nations education should return to those nations, although in reality this process has been hindered by bureaucratic and legal issues. Some individual bands have taken full or partial control of many of the reserve schools, however, meaning that control over Indian education in Canada is returning to the First Nations.[13]

While there has been significant scholarly comparison of indigenous experiences in English colonial settler states, to date there has been little comparison across the Spanish-English colonial divide, one of the reasons we have pushed for a more hemispheric focus in this book. Nonetheless, a brief synopsis of historical events in New Zealand and Australia is in order, since the parallels are striking and, again, provide evidence of common racial and colonial scripts being enacted in multiple contexts. The points of divergence and local specificity also provide reason to pause and consider what other futures could have been possible in each place.

As an example of the surprising variety of experiences, colonial schools established for Maoris in New Zealand/Aotearoa ended up helping *preserve* Maori language and culture in some ways, despite their overall assimilationist effect. As in both the United States and Canada, Maori education began with a period of mission schools, established in 1816 and designed to assimilate children into British culture. In the 1830s, Maori learned through missionaries how to read and write their own language and eagerly embraced the new technology. A number of nineteenth century Maori language newspapers and manuscripts have survived, providing a valuable resource for contemporary Maori people. Mission schools lasted until the Land Wars of the 1860s forced their closure. In 1867, dissatisfied with the existing arrangement, the Crown passed the Native Schools Act, establishing the centrally controlled Native Schools system that existed for almost a century. The Act placed the responsibility for these schools on the Maori themselves. Communities had to write to request a school, gift a piece of land for the building, and help pay the cost of a teacher and schoolhouse. The geographical location of the schools often meant that Maori could and did undermine the Crown's assimilationist objectives, as they were isolated from bureaucratic centers. As such, Native Schools sometimes promoted Maori culture, despite their otherwise assimilationist curriculum, and the Native Schools system was finally dismantled in 1969.[14]

While Maori schools contributed to the survival of Maori language and communities in New Zealand, Aboriginal education in Australia has a far more troubled history. While mission schools existed, until the mid-twentieth century, educational opportunities were either nonexistent or restricted to lower elementary school levels taught in mismanaged and segregated schools. Through much of the twentieth century the Australian government forcibly removed many thousands of mixed-blood Aboriginal children from their homes to be educated in assimilationist schools. The aim and policy of these schools was to *never* send the children back to their families and communities, but rather to force them to marry whites and breed out their Aboriginal features over multiple generations.[15] During the Depression, efforts to control indigenous peoples intensified as Aboriginal people continued to be forcibly relocated to reserves on the basis that they needed to be "trained" for citizenship. This education, like that of other indigenous peoples, focused on manual labor and preparing children for futures in working-class trades.

In 1951, the Australian government introduced a new assimilation policy, designed to ensure Aboriginal people could join Australian society. During this period, Aboriginal children began to enter mainstream schools, but faced issues of racism and discrimination in the classroom as teachers were deeply influenced by dominant racial theories about them. Despite a policy shift toward self-determination in 1972 and self-management in 1975, educational issues continue, as racist attitudes persist and high dropout rates remain for Aboriginal youth.[16]

Shifting back to the Americas, we see similar ways of thinking about indigenous peoples and their education. In Mexico, history is again replete with examples of missionization in the early years to convert Native peoples into Christians who would speak a European language, adopt European practices, and reject indigenous lifeways. After Mexico won independence from Spain, missions were secularized and the treatment of Indians varied widely, with President Benito Juarez being remembered as a protector of Indians and the dictator Porfirio Diaz known as a scourge of Indians and campesinos. In the post-revolutionary period, indigenous education focused on rural schools, reflecting a distinct Mexican understanding of what it meant to be an *indio*. In particular, education debates centered on the roles Indians would play in society. Conservatives maintained that Indians needed separate communities, whereas liberals thought that Indians needed to be assimilated into a national culture. Both groups therefore considered Indians a problem, but debated over whether separation or inclusion would be the best solution. After the Mexican Revolution, from 1910 to 1920, the government focused on reorganizing the country through nationalism, incorporating indigenous peoples into a larger Mexican identity, in which Mexicans were the best of both indigenous and European races, with African heritage virtually absent from nationalist narratives. In doing so, they also appropriated Indians of the past as Mexican heroes, thereby laying claim to an indigenous heritage, but simultaneously placing that indigenous identity firmly in the past, a practice Philip Deloria has also noted in the United States.[17] As historian Alexander Dawson has phrased it: "Indians would contribute their artistic sensibilities and glorious past, but would be assimilated into a civilization defined by science, rationality, and modernity."[18]

The links between Mexican and United States' policies towards indigenous peoples were made more concrete in the 1930s, as John Collier traveled to Mexico to advise its president on Indian policy. Consequently, the Mexican government created Indian boarding schools, which were typically located close to Indian communities and did not force attendance. M. Bianet Castellanos points out in her essay in this volume that for Yucatec Mayan youth who were accustomed to early hard labor, boarding schools were sometimes viewed positively as an alternative to working in the fields at home.

As in other indigenous communities worldwide, the 1960s and 1970s were significant to education in Mexico, as Indians sought increasing control. In the state of Oaxaca, for example, Zapotec communities coordinated social movements often organized around taking control of local schools. Indigenous communities throughout the Americas have recognized the political and cultural stakes of language in education, and thus, language use was an important goal for Zapotecs, who published magazines in their indigenous language in order to teach it to their children.

In Peru, indigenous peoples have conducted a similar campaign for language rights. While some parents actively resisted sending their children to schools, others decided that schools offered valuable opportunities, particularly for learning Spanish. As María Elena García has noted, for example, some Quechua-speaking people in Cuzco believe that "climbing the Peruvian social ladder is possible only by learning Spanish" and so they have advocated for Spanish-language education in opposition to indigenous language activists.[19]

An important issue in indigenous education throughout Latin America lies in defining who is "indigenous." With a high proportion of the population having indigenous ancestry in some degree, indigeneity has typically been defined by resorting to measures of class, location, and culture more than blood quantum, the old standard in the United States. Often, indigenous identity has simply been associated with rural peasantry, which shapes indigenous educational endeavors in powerful ways. As Alexander Dawson has argued, it played an important role in the foundation of the Casa Del Estudiante Indígena in Mexico City in 1926. Hailed "as the centerpiece of the government's commitment to Indian education," the school was designed to take "a culturally diverse student population, speaking mutually unintelligible languages," and transform them into "models of the national culture."[20] In recruiting prospective students for the school, however, class issues seemed more important than race. While the students had to be "racially pure," this designation had little to do with a pupil's indigenous heritage. Rather, prospective students were considered to be "without culture," individuals "with little education, little knowledge of science or the implements of modern living, and a 'backwards' mental state."[21] Thus, cultural elements typically associated with class distinctions seemed more important to definitions of indigeneity in Mexico than genealogical factors. In Latin American countries and the Anglo settler states alike, the preoccupation of nationalist regimes has often been to erase cultural distinctions in a misguided effort to impose "equality" through forced homogeneity, and education has often been a central means of imposing such policies.

Public schools have dominated Native education in the United States, Canada, and New Zealand in the postwar years, though white and indigenous students shared a longer history of integrated school attendance. In some regions of the United States, nineteenth-century public schools were more diverse than in the early twentieth century. In Minnesota, American Indians living near the early city of Saint Paul attended public school in the territorial period, and segregation began somewhere after statehood and with the establishment of Indian boarding schools. In addition, until 1850, First Nations children in Canada were permitted to attend Euro-American schools, though policies after that time emphasized residential schools, and not until the late 1940s did public school integration again become a significant focus in Canada. Still, little is written about what this education policy shift has meant for Native students.

New Directions in Comparative Indigenous History

Indian Subjects seeks to open up the discussion of indigenous education in ways that challenge some of our deeply held beliefs, as contributors explore new scholarly directions and themes in indigenous education, including sexualities and gender assimilation in boarding school, the connections linking education to wage labor, indigenous educational rhetoric, healing and the law, bilingualism, and traditional systems of knowledge. One of the central tenets of *Indian Subjects* is that multinational, comparative research will reveal new understandings of the history of indigenous people. While there is some scholarly information gathered under the rubric of "the history of indigenous education" in Latin America, much discussion of assimilationist processes has fallen under a general history of colonialist practices. Combined with indigenous educational histories in the United States and Canada, such histories help us see the broad patterns of assimilationism and a global white supremacy firmly entrenched in histories there. Similarly, waves of resistance and *indigenismo* in Latin American countries complicate those narratives, revealing alternative possibilities for indigenous-settler relations elsewhere. We can see multiple dominating relationships in Hawaii and transpose those to understand other contexts. Indian segregation policies all over the United States force us to reconsider the role of race in Indian education and the role of colonial relationships in shaping racial segregation in other contexts. Even our fundamental beliefs about how we define indigeneity and easy assumptions about the indigenous-settler dichotomy need to be examined. Expanding indigenous educational histories beyond the walls of the federal boarding schools and outside the United States helps us see assimilationism happening in multiple ways in multiple places, perhaps leading us to feel less safe in our assumptions that the assimilationist period has ended. After all, is the curriculum of most public schools that indigenous students attend today really radically different from the curriculum of the boarding schools in the 1930s? In the United States, curriculum is still taught almost exclusively in English, it teaches students to participate in a capitalist, individualistic society, teaches Anglo values, still speaks of "our founding fathers," and for many Indians in reservation and urban communities, is still not on par with schools in middle-class, white communities. In prosperous cities of Canada and the United States, Indian schoolchildren still face a daunting achievement gap, with high school graduation a less likely outcome for them compared to white students.[22]

And so we struggle, as did indigenous people in the past, to decide what the purpose of contemporary indigenous education should be. Should we train students in colonial languages in order to give them the best chance to thrive in a capitalist economy? Or should we turn resolutely inward and perhaps backward (in a positive sense) to historical tribal values, less contaminated by colonial pollutants? In a fascinating essay in *Indian Subjects*, Canadian Ojibway legal scholar John Borrows reclaims indigenous traditions of knowledge and contends that even the most mainstream institutions—Canadian, US, and Latin American schools of law—might play an important role in developing innovative curriculums that include indigenous concepts of law, and in applying those ideas to historic and contemporary issues. How do we best twine the two systems of knowledge together, as Hopi chief Loololma suggested in 1890, creating a strong connection to both our indigenous communities and our nonindigenous neighbors?[23] The Ojibwe villagers at Ponemah understood that our own systems of knowledge must be defended, even as we allow for new schools to be built. The essayists in *Indian Subjects,* many of them Native scholars, follow the path of these ancestors, and it is our hope this book will broaden our collective understandings of indigenous education in the past, present, and future.

Notes

1. See Bureau of Indian Affairs, Correspondence of Interior Secretary Hitchcock, Leech Lake Agency, July 20, 1900. Record Group 75, National Archives.

2. The Johnson-O'Malley Act of 1934 authorized the secretary of the interior to enter into contracts and pay states for Indian education in public schools, whereas the former system required negotiation with individual school districts.

3. See Keith Basso, *Wisdom Sits in Places: Language and Landscape among the Western Apache*; Richard Erdoes and Alfonso Ortiz, *American Indian Trickster Tales*; Candace S. Greene and Russell Thornton, *The Year the Stars Fell: Lakota Winter Counts at the Smithsonian*; N. Scott Momaday, *The Names: A Memoir*; Anthony F. C. Wallace, *The Death and Rebirth of the Seneca*; Frank Salomon, *The Cord Keepers: Khipus and Cultural Life in a Peruvian Village*; Douglas Deur, "A Most Sacred Place: The Significance of Crater Lake among the Indians of Southern Oregon."

4. See David Beaulieu, "Native American Education Research and Policy Development in an Era of No Child Left Behind: Native Language and Culture during the Administrations of Presidents Clinton and Bush."

5. See María Elena García, "Indigenous Education in Peru."

6. See Alcida Rita Ramos, "Cutting Through State and Class: Sources and Strategies of Self-Representation in Latin America."

7. See Margaret D. Jacobs, "Maternal Colonialism: White Women and Indigenous Child Removal in the American West and Australia, 1880–1940."

8. See Piper v. Big Pine.

9. As quoted in *Piper*.

10. Lawrence R. Baca argues that American Indians in several states including California and Montana went to court for the establishment of public schools in their region or for integration, but it was a case involving Navajo students and families in a remote region of the Navajo Reservation in 1974, *Meyers v. Board of Education*, that was a decision most similar to *Brown v. Board of Education*. See Lawrence R. Baca, "*Meyers v. Board of Education*: The *Brown v. Board* of Indian Country."

11. Indigenous scholars have primarily written about boarding school history in the late nineteenth and early twentieth century. For examples, see W. Roger Buffalohead and Paulette Fairbanks Molin, "'A Nucleus of Civilization': American Indian families at Hampton Institute in the Late Nineteenth Century"; Brenda J. Child, *Boarding School Seasons: American Indian Families, 1900–1940*; K. Tsianina Lomawaima, *They Called It Prairie Light: The Story of Chilocco Indian School*; and Judith Simon and Linda Tuhiwai Smith, eds., *A Civilising Mission? Perceptions and Representations of the New Zealand Native Schools System*.

12. As Jean Barman, Yvonne Hebert, and Don McCaskill demonstrate in the preface to their edited collection, *Indian Education in Canada*.

13. See Jean Barman, Yvonne Hebert, and Don McCaskill, "The Legacy of the Past: An Overview"; also see Andrew Armitage, *Comparing the Policy of Aboriginal Assimilation: Australia, Canada, and New Zealand*, 103–113.

14. See John Barrington, *Separate but Equal? Maori Schools and the Crown, 1867–1969*; Judith Simon and Linda Tuhiwai Smith, eds., *A Civilising Mission? Perceptions and Representations of the*

New Zealand Native Schools System; Judith Simon, ed., *Nga Kura Maori: The Native Schools System, 1867–1969*.

15. See Jacobs, 458. This history is movingly dramatized in the acclaimed independent film *Rabbit-Proof Fence,* based on the account of Doris Pilkington, one of the children stolen from her family in the 1930s. See Doris Pilkington, *Follow the Rabbit-Proof Fence*.

16. See Anne-Katrin Eckermann, "Aboriginal Education in Rural Australia: A Case Study in Frustration and Hope"; Quentin Beresford, *Reform and Resistance in Aboriginal Education: The Australian Experience*; Ralph Folds, *Whitefella School: Education and Aboriginal Education*.

17. See Philip Deloria, *Playing Indian*.

18. See Alexander S. Dawson, "'Wild Indians,' 'Mexican Gentlemen,' and the Lessons Learned in the Casa Del Estudiante Indigena, 1926–1932," 331.

19. See María Elena García, "The Politics of Community: Education, Indigenous Rights, and Ethnic Mobilization in Peru," 72.

20. Dawson, 329.

21. Dawson, 335.

22. In the state of Minnesota, nationally regarded for progressive educational programming, "two out of five American Indian students graduate from high school in four years" (Minnesota Department of Education, 14). See Pilar Gonzalbo Aizpuru, *Historia de la educación en la época colonial: El mundo indígena*.

23. See Matthew Sakiestewa Gilbert, *Education Beyond the Mesas: Hopi Students at Sherman Institute, 1902–1929*.

2 Domesticating Hawaiians

Kamehameha Schools and the "Tender Violence" of Marriage

Noelani Goodyear-Kaʻōpua

In the nineteenth century, Kānaka Maoli (Native Hawaiians) faced the multifold threats of European and American imperialism, land alienation, and a dramatic population decline from introduced diseases.[1] In this context the *aliʻi* (chiefly leaders) found innovative ways to carry out their traditional obligations to care for the well-being of the people. One way they did so was to give their lands in perpetual charitable trusts to support new institutions of care: hospitals, schools, elderly care homes, and service programs for orphaned and destitute children and their communities.[2] The largest of these trusts established and maintains the Kamehameha Schools (KS), founded by Ke Aliʻi (the Chief) Bernice Pauahi Bishop.[3]

Pauahi was the great-granddaughter of Kamehameha, who united the islands under his rule in 1810 and thus laid the foundation for the modern Hawaiian Kingdom. By the time Pauahi was a young adult, her country had been recognized as an independent nation-state by the dominant Western powers of the world.[4] Within her lifetime (1831–1884), Kānaka Maoli lost roughly two-thirds of their population to foreign-introduced diseases. In this context, she willed over 375,000 acres, or approximately nine percent of the total lands in the archipelago, to be used for the creation of a group of schools named for her famous ancestor, Kamehameha. Pauahi's last will and testament designated her lands—the bulk of which had been inherited from her cousin, Ke Aliʻi Ruth Keʻelikōlani—for the creation of two schools (one for boys and one for girls) that would serve children of Hawaiian ancestry, particularly orphaned and indigent children.

The will establishing the Kamehameha Schools was written not long after Pauahi's husband, a *haole* (white foreigner) American settler named Charles Reed Bishop, had been pressured to leave his position as president of the Hawaiian Kingdom's Board of Education in 1883.[5] Pauahi named her husband as the executor of her will and president of the board of trustees for her estate, known as the Bishop Estate.[6] For the next fifty years, the trust and schools were run exclusively by white members of the business elite, many of whom were directly tied to, or at least politically aligned with, the overthrow of Hawaiian governance and the establishment of American imperial control. The Kamehameha School for Boys opened in 1887, six years before the illegal overthrow of the Hawaiian Kingdom government by a group of haole sugar businessmen and their associates, backed by the US military.[7] Since the national lands of the Hawaiian Kingdom were seized at the end of the nineteenth century and have not been used to benefit Kānaka Maoli in any meaningful way since, the KS trust remains the largest body of lands currently accessible for the direct benefit of Kānaka Maoli people.

Exploring the consequences of white male control over the Kamehameha Schools, particularly in the period from 1887 to 1900, I reveal that the leadership of the schools folded the Kamehameha Schools into a broader white supremacist project of subordinating and domesticating Kānaka within the new social and economic order they were building. Like earlier Protestant missionary projects, KS pedagogies worked to discipline Hawaiian sexuality and produce an industrial workforce according to gendered divisions of labor. These explicit goals became coupled with the implicit aim of obscuring Hawaiian national identity and producing consent to a new political regime—the white oligarchy— backed by the US military. Cultural processes of domestication, of making "good and industrious men and women"[8] at Kamehameha Schools, dovetailed with the political processes of establishing and maintaining US imperial control and military occupation.

In the first section of this chapter, I elaborate the ways I use the terms *domestication* and *marriage*. The second section provides an overview of the historical emergence of schooling in Hawai'i. Contrary to earlier historiography of schooling in Hawai'i, in which scholars have characterized schools as foreign impositions of essentially American design,[9] I argue that the achievements of literacy and the establishment of a public school system in the Hawaiian Kingdom resulted from a partnership between Kānaka and haole. The relationship between these actors could be described in the indigenous Hawaiian language as *hoa*, meaning companion, colleague, or peer, or as *hoa paio*, denoting opponents or antagonists in battle.[10] By examining this previously misinterpreted historical context we can more fully comprehend the consequences of exclusive haole control over the Kamehameha Schools, beginning in the 1880s and extending well past the mid-twentieth century. The third section addresses how a central technique of settler colonial rule was to reframe the hoa/hoa paio relationship as a *marriage*. I analyze the ways Kamehameha Schools' authorized stories about the marriage of Ke Aliʻi Pauahi to American capitalist Charles R. Bishop have worked to gloss over the ascendance of white businessmen to power over Kamehameha Schools and its lands and have legitimated US empire. A description of the establishment and the early curricula of Kamehameha Schools in the years leading up to the US occupation follows. Finally, I conclude with a meditation on the absence of Pauahi's voice as a result of her marriage.

Domestication and Marriage

My analysis of early Kamehameha Schools' efforts to domesticate Hawaiians draws on Anne McClintock's work on the emergence and solidification of British empire through popular pedagogies of domesticity and on Andrea Smith's theorizing of the connections between heteropatriarchy and the colonization of indigenous peoples under the United States. McClintock explains that "domesticate" and "dominate" share a similar etymology, linked to *dominus,* lord of the *domum,* or home. As such, domesticity denotes both spaces (like the Victorian home) and social relations of power (like the subordination of women and children within the Victorian home), ordered by hierarchical categories of race, gender, and class.[11] McClintock argues that the metaphor of the family was used to naturalize the categories, hierarchies, and divisions of labor undergirding British imperial power, arguing that the family metaphor sanctions both hierarchy and historical change as natural and progressive rather than revolutionary: "Projecting the family image onto national and imperial progress enabled what was often murderously violent change to be legitimized as the progressive unfolding of natural decree."[12]

Going further, recent scholarship at the intersection of Native and Queer studies calls us to look at the imbrication of white supremacy, heteropatriarchy, and colonialism and to understand this violence as not only historical, but endemic *and* on-going.[13] In both the past and present of settler colonial dominance, "Heteropatriarchy is the logic that makes social hierarchy seem natural."[14] In Hawaiʻi, Kamehameha's pedagogies of domesticity laid some of the groundwork for subordinating Kānaka to white oligarchic rule by teaching students how to be proper husbands and wives within a heteropatriarchal, Christian framework. By interrogating this educational site, I challenge the normative acceptance that it was natural and reasonable for the will, lands, and educational legacy of a Hawaiian chief to be controlled and interpreted by a group of white businessmen, and I underscore the ways heteropatriarchal marriage narratives have worked to occlude political struggles of the time.

Extending McClintock's discussion of colonial domestication dynamics, the processes of domestication I discuss in this article operate on at least three interconnected levels. First, domestication included training students in "industry" as part of an imperial civilizing process. Here, domestication suggests processes of taming Hawaiians and making them productive for the benefit of white power. Argued as a way to save a dying race, making "good and industrious" Hawaiians was both about cultivating certain habits of behavior based on introduced gender roles and marshalling Kānaka labor to support the haole sugar business elite's bottom line. Second, domestication was a feminizing project, aimed to mark Hawaiians by a beautiful but politically innocuous "culture." At Kamehameha certain aspects of Kānaka Maoli culture were forbidden, but a certain kind of Hawaiianness—shorn of political resistance and linked with new gendered and classed sensibilities—was encouraged. Third, domestication refers to the political processes of subsuming one state under another, in order to make the lands and peoples of an independent country part of the domestic or internal sphere of an imperial occupier. Kamehameha Schools' first trustees supported the overthrow of Native self-government. Under their direction the school's pedagogies cultivated acceptance of the new political order and institutionalized categories of difference that supported that order. Kānaka Maoli students were educated to see themselves as a race of people within the domestic sphere of the United States. These processes of domestication elide the historical existence of an aupuni Hawai'i (independent Hawaiian national government) and its systematic dismantling during the formative years of KS.

If earlier efforts to build schools and a public education system in the Hawaiian Kingdom can be described as a partnership between Hawaiian leaders and American missionaries, sometimes in struggle, the creation of Kamehameha Schools marks a shift toward framing this relationship in terms of a *marriage*. Stories about Kamehameha Schools frame the relationship between Kānaka and haole antecedents in these terms, largely because of Pauahi's marriage to American-born Charles R. Bishop, executor of Pauahi's legal will, which established the Kamehameha Schools. Beyond the Bishops' actual union, tropes of marriage and romantic love accomplished political and cultural work. Marriage naturalized white male control over this important landed resource of Kānaka Maoli, and the schools prepared young Hawaiians for Christian marriage, enforcing Euro-American gender roles. Moreover, stories about love made legitimate through marriage have served to cover the illegitimacy of American political rule over Hawai'i and Hawaiian people.

A feminist look at marriage underscores the elements of property, political rights, and social status embedded in this gendered relationship of subordination. Feminist scholars have shown that marriage has a dual nature: while constructed by religious and state authorities through laws, policies, and church doctrines, marriage is often represented as natural and pre-political.[15] Marriage is not simply about love and/or commitment: it structures social life, dispensing rights in an unequal manner. "Inegalitarian marriage has historically given women a status as different kinds of citizens than men."[16] In nineteenth century Britain and the US, marriage played a vital part in making upper- and middle-class women dependent on men. Once a woman married, her wealth and property were under her husband's control. According to the principle of *coverture*, wives were legally merged with their husbands, and therefore could not control their own property, file lawsuits, or execute contracts.

The patriarchal model of inegalitarian marriage was slow to insinuate itself into Hawaiian society, but laws enforced the institution throughout the 1800s, and schools took on the cultural work of training young Native Hawaiians how to become husbands and wives.[17] KS pedagogies built on these earlier efforts, not teaching Kānaka to be "good and industrious men and women," but specifically defining acceptable masculinity and femininity in terms of becoming husbands and wives. Like British and American laws, Hawaiian Kingdom law in the late nineteenth century imposed *civil death* (the status of being without civil rights) upon married women. Thus the institution of marriage fundamentally undercut the political *mana* (power) of Kānaka Maoli. As such, it supported white supremacist and imperialist efforts at usurping Native rule, even before the formal US takeover.

Schools of an Independent Kingdom

Kānaka Maoli are among the few aboriginal nations living under US empire who built a national school system under the laws of a Native-led government in the nineteenth century.[18] Until the end of the 1800s, 'Ōiwi Hawai'i also made up a majority of the teachers in the Kingdom. This history has been largely overlooked. Existing histories of schooling in Hawai'i have focused almost exclusively on the role of haole in teaching Kānaka Maoli and in developing the educational system. Dominant accounts claim public education in Hawai'i was made in the image of American public schooling, and they ignore the role of Kānaka leaders and teachers in establishing literacy and schooling. While Americans did influence the Hawaiian Kingdom's school system, schooling was not simply imported by missionaries and imposed upon Hawaiians.

Rather, the achievements of literacy and the establishment of a public school system resulted from a partnership between Kānaka and haole, often in struggle, as *hoa* (colleagues or peers) or *hoa paio* (competitors or opponents). Seeing this *hoa* or *hoa paio* relationship destabilizes and provides an alternative to the marriage model that became prominent as Americans sought to extinguish Native government.

In the wake of American missionary arrival in 1820, early schooling projects were closely tied to developing literacy among Kānaka so that they could be more easily converted to Christianity.[19] Kānaka were enamored with the technologies of the printed word. While American missionaries are largely credited with establishing a written form of the indigenous language and then teaching Hawaiians to read, it is clear that the achievements of printing and literacy were a result of the joint efforts of Native Hawaiians and foreigners. The first company of American missionaries who arrived in Hawai'i in 1820 were accompanied by four Kānaka Maoli who had made their way to the east coast of the United States years earlier. These men helped teach the missionaries elements of the Hawaiian language and translated for them upon arrival in the islands. Schutz notes that one of them, Thomas Hopu, was writing letters utilizing spelling that more closely mirrors the modern, standardized Hawaiian orthography well before the American Calvinist mission established its official orthography.[20]

Mission station schools became points of access to the new skills of reading and writing, and enrollments grew at an incredibly rapid pace with Kānaka quickly taking on the majority of the teaching roles. Wist writes that for Hawaiians, "'going to school' was a form of recreation."[21] He recounts that from the mid-1820s to the early 1830s, nearly the whole adult population went to schools to learn to read, but he downplays the role of Kānaka in this literacy boom. However, the numbers clearly indicate that it would have been impossible for missionaries alone to have taught the Kānaka students. Only 140 American Protestant missionaries came to Hawai'i between 1820 and 1848. At the height of school enrollments in 1832—when there were more than fifty-three thousand pupils in nine hundred schools—only four missionary companies had arrived in the islands, including just over fifty American men and women, plus eleven Native Hawaiians and Tahitians.[22] They could not have possibly overseen nine hundred schools or managed a ratio of one thousand Native students to each missionary.[23] The vast majority of teachers in these schools were 'Ōiwi.

Adult Kānaka came to schools for what they wanted—to learn to read and write—and then they left. Only five years after the high enrollment of 1832, the number of pupils was down to about two thousand.[24] However, Kānaka maintained their passion for reading, writing, and publishing in the following decades, when literacy was used not only as a tool for accessing or creating social capital, but also as an important tool of resistance.[25]

As the number of willing adult pupils in missionary schools waned through the 1830s, the focus shifted toward schooling children as proper national subjects for an evolving nation-state. The codification and institutionalization of public schooling in 1840 was adjunct to the creation of the first Hawaiian constitution under King Kamehameha III, Kauikeaouli, who declared, "He aupuni palapala koʻu; o ke kanaka pono ʻo ia koʻu kanaka."[26] Thus, King Kamehameha III established the Kingdom as a constitutional monarchy, transformed by the trappings of modern states including an emergent national public school system. Hawaiian leaders made schooling part of a self-modernizing project, in tension but sometimes articulating with the continuing missionary project of "civilizing" Kānaka. By 1842, elementary level education in reading, writing, geography and arithmetic was required for anyone to be married or hold high office.[27] Hawaiian was the predominant language of instruction in schools, and any attempts to teach English were within the context of a robust literacy within the indigenous language.

For the aliʻi class, King Kamehameha III passed an 1840 law establishing a school for chiefly children, in which they would learn English, history, geography, higher level math, and philosophy, among other things.[28] The government did not begin any broader allocation of funds to English-medium schooling until 1851. Throughout the second half of the nineteenth century, the struggle between Hawaiian and English language in government schools and in the law reflected the struggles for power in the Kingdom between ʻŌiwi statesmen and haole businessmen.[29]

ʻŌiwi leaders used compulsory schooling as an indispensable part of the production of modern Hawaiian national subjects. The two comprehensive historical accounts of public education in the Hawaiian Kingdom overlook those Kānaka who led the Kingdom's public education system, so it is worth summarizing their contributions here.[30] The Hawaiian Kingdom legislature appointed Hawaiian scholar, author, and ordained minister David Malo as the first luna (superintendent) of public instruction for the Kingdom—a post he held for four years. Under Malo, they also appointed five kahu kula (school agents or inspectors) who oversaw all government schools on each of the five major islands. All five appointees were Kānaka: John Iʻi for Oʻahu, Papohaku for Kauaʻi; Kanakaokai for Molokaʻi, David Malo for Maui, and Kanakaahuahu for Hawaiʻi.[31] They had power to grant teaching certificates and oversee teachers, to monitor the progress of students, to be the judges of the school law, and to provide for teachers' salaries.[32] Malo was a staunch advocate for Native teachers and their adequate compensation.

The educational leadership of Mataio Kekūanāoʻa, who led the Kingdom's public school system for eight years as president of the Board of Education from 1860 until his death in 1868, is similarly overlooked in existing histories.[33] Descended from high chiefs of Oʻahu and Hawaiʻi islands, Kekūanāoʻa was an experienced statesman who accompanied King Kamehameha II to London from 1823 to 1824 to strengthen diplomatic ties between Hawaiʻi and Britain, and he served as the governor of Oʻahu from 1839 to 1863. Kekūanāoʻaʻs predecessor as head of public education, the American Protestant Rev. Richard Armstrong, is often credited as bringing stability and developing the "public" character of the educational system—abolishing sectarian schools and introducing a tax-supported economic base.[34] However, reviewing the reports that heads of the Kingdomʻs Board of Education made to the legislature throughout the Kingdom era (1840–1893), it is apparent that Kekūanāoʻa was the leader who articulated the most explicit concern for distancing government schools from church powers and providing an adequate appropriation of public funds to support that separation. For example, in Kekūanāoʻaʻs report of 1866, he spent a significant amount of time talking about his concern for the lack of adequate school facilities resulting from insufficient funding. He advocated moving schools out of churches and mission stations, thus strengthening an inclusive national character:

> In many places the schools, for want of special buildings, are kept in the meeting houses or chapels of [the] Protestant or Catholic population residing on the land.... The result is that in almost all of these places, the public schools are merely tenants at the will of this or that religious denomination...another result of this absence of proprietary right on the part of Government is that these houses being looked upon as really and especially religious edifices, and not as national school houses, are avoided by parents and children of denominations different from that one which owns the building. It is necessary to provide as far as possible for all the people the advantage of a common school education...the common schools should come to be regarded as strictly neutral ground in religious matters.[35]

In addressing the problems of inadequate facilities, Kekūanāoʻa proposed that the national Board of Education match the funds of local districts in which parents wanted to build or thoroughly renovate a schoolhouse.[36] This enabled independence from mission and church. Although Kekūanāoʻa identified as Protestant, his arguments show he was able to keep his religious affiliation separate from his leadership of public education.

In the debates over language in the schools, Kekūanāoʻa firmly articulated the importance of the Hawaiian language in affirming Hawaiian national identity. While advocates for a predominantly English system of education and government pushed to reduce the status of the Hawaiian language,[37] Kekūanāoʻa asserted the importance of government support for Hawaiian-medium education:

> The theory of substituting the English language for the Hawaiian, in order to educate our people, is as dangerous to Hawaiian nationality, as it is useless in promoting the general education of the people. If we wish to preserve the Kingdom of Hawaii for Hawaiians, and to educate our people, we must insist that the Hawaiian language shall be the language of all our National Schools, and the English shall be taught whenever practicable, but only as an important branch of Hawaiian education.[38]

He urged the legislature to increase funding for schools taught in Hawaiian. It wasn't until after his administration that enrollment in English-medium schools grew significantly vis-à-vis the Hawaiian-medium schools.

Unlike Kekūanāoʻa, Charles R. Bishop, who served as president of the Board of Education throughout the 1870s and early 1880s, significantly increased funding for English-language schools while cutting from Hawaiian-language common schools.[39] By the end of Bishop's term in 1883, the select, English-medium schools were receiving more than seven times the funding of the common schools, even though they had far fewer students. Teachers' salaries at English schools—positions filled by non-Natives—were markedly higher, and the availability of teachers in Hawaiian language was curtailed when the courses of study at Lahainaluna Seminary and Hilo Boarding School, which trained many of the Native teachers, were changed from Hawaiian to English.[40] While some English advocates argued that rising enrollments demonstrated that Kānaka wanted to embrace English and move away from their own mother tongue, it is clear that this was no simple matter of abandoning one language for another. As Benham and Heck point out, the choices became unequal as the government increased funding support for English select schools over Hawaiian common schools, including more textbooks and professional development for English-medium schools.[41]

This brief history of public education in the Hawaiian Kingdom shows that schooling was not simply a colonial imposition. Kānaka and Haole together engaged in building popular literacy and a national school system. Aliʻi and foreigners both folded visions for schooling into competing projects of Hawaiian modernization and nation-building. Sometimes they worked in collaboration as hoa, partners and interlocutors embedded in complicated relations of power. At other times, they were clearly hoa paio, political opponents articulating and acting on very different visions of how education for Hawaiians should look.

By the mid-1880s, haole businessmen aimed to usurp governing power and use schools to build a hierarchical plantation society. After they conspired to overthrow Native rule in Hawai'i and took full control of the government school system, they cut *all* funding for Hawaiian-language education, leaving the vast majority of Kānaka teachers without teaching positions and keiki 'Ōiwi (Native children) without schooling in their ancestral language.[42] Their belief in the inherent superiority of white, Anglo-Saxon Protestants would structure the Kamehameha Schools. Yet, the historical context discussed above makes clear that Kamehameha could have been built and led differently.

The "Tender Violence" of Manual and Domestic Education

During the period in which the Kamehameha School for Boys (KSB), School for Girls (KSG), and Preparatory School (KPS) were built, the missionary–sugar industrialist faction ramped up their efforts to usurp power in the Kingdom government, then lobbied for American annexation.[43] Simultaneously, they used Kamehameha Schools as a vehicle for furthering their white supremacist vision of society, in which young Hawaiians would be integrated and subordinated, while Native self-government was snuffed out. Methods of using schools to realize racial hierarchies circulated between Hawai'i and the US, and KS became a key link in the trans-Pacific construction of educational approaches designed to promote imperial hierarchies under the guise of charity or "benevolent assimilation."[44] In the words of the founder of the Hampton Institute in Virginia, which served as a model for Kamehameha, it was an approach of domestication and "tender violence."[45]

"Tender" is an apt description of the kind of racialized and gendered violence committed against Kānaka Maoli at Kamehameha throughout the early years.[46] Kānaka Maoli were seen as a tender and vulnerable race, easily moldable by white educators through a program of manual and domestic training. Charles R. Bishop believed such an education would give Hawaiians the opportunity to make themselves "fit [for the] competition of the races," as he told students at the school's first Founder's Day ceremonies in 1888.[47] Yet the education provided was clearly not intended to train them to win any such imagined racial competition. Under Bishop's leadership (1887–1897) and into the first decades of the twentieth century, the school did not train students to take positions of power in government or business, as he himself held. Rather, like the rear car, or tender, that carries all the fuel and water necessary for powering a large steam locomotive, Hawaiians had to be permanently coupled as a productive force within the new white-led vision of society. Students provided the labor to maintain most aspects of the physical campuses of Kamehameha, a means of training them to become industrial and domestic laborers for a growing plantation capitalist economy in the islands.

As president of the Hawaiian Kingdom's Board of Education beginning in 1874, Bishop had supported industrial and moral education for the masses and elite English-standard education for the highest tier of society.[48] His administration marked a turn toward manual and industrial education, as well as increased funding for English-medium education.[49] Although there was already a history of educating Kānaka in higher branches of academic pursuit, Bishop argued against education that failed to produce an industrial agricultural workforce. He acknowledged that schooling tended to generate a "distaste" among students for labor on the plantations and in subsidiary industries in his arguments to the Hawaiian legislature: "But it is evident that a large portion of our community must depend upon such occupations for means of subsistence. And hence the instruction of our youth should have for its object, not only mental culture, but also the development of those faculties which most facilitate industrial effort."[50]

Bishop's ostensible concern for "our community" masked his own personal stakes in the industry and in training Hawaiian and Asian students to be laborers. Since he had spearheaded the efforts to bring Asian laborers to the islands specifically to work on the plantations, it is unlikely that he would have supported a system that would educate their children for opportunities beyond agricultural labor.[51] As a private school, Kamehameha School for Boys, or "the Manual," became an institution Bishop and other members of the white elite could control without serious accountability to Hawaiian government leaders, the Kānaka Maoli chiefly establishment, or a broader public electorate.

In the United States, the manual training movement gained popularity in the post–Civil War years.[52] Proponents of manual training pushed for the inclusion of "work with the hands" to supplement and enhance the "work of the mind" in schools. With its emphasis on training in the general use of hand tools, manual education did not just give students occupational skills for a changing economy independent of schooling. It actively worked to create these industrial plantation economies. The precursor to modern vocational training and industrial arts education, manual training was provided in high schools in over one hundred cities in the US by 1900. However, the integration of manual labor into school curricula was not universal in the United States nor in Hawai'i, and it was unevenly applied in the creation of an industrial and agricultural labor force shaped by race and class, as was the case for institutions like Kamehameha and Hampton.

Approaches to schooling black and brown children to produce racially ordered societies with whites on top developed through the exchange of techniques from Hawai'i to the US and back again. Samuel Chapman Armstrong, a Hawai'i-born missionary son, drew on his observations of the Hilo Boarding School, founded in 1836, and his father's efforts as head of the Hawaiian Kingdom's public education system from 1848 to 1860. Armstrong combined these experiences with his own military training as a retired general in the Union Army in designing the Hampton Institute, which emphasized moral reform of its African American and Indian students through a program of hard labor, Christian training, and military order.[53] He wrote, "There was worked out in the Hawaiian Islands the problem of emancipation, and civilization of the dark-skinned Polynesian people in many respects like the Negro race."[54] Armstrong was able to import the missionary and educational ideals of his heritage from Hawai'i to the Southern US, since in the eyes of white educational reformers like himself, blacks, Indians, and Hawaiians were similarly unfit to govern themselves or lead the broader society. While seen as "progressive" in the context of the post-slavery US South, Hampton's assimilationist approach still operated within a white supremacist frame, in which black and brown students could be educated to fit into their place within the social hierarchy. Moreover, in Hawai'i, such an educational approach was clearly *regressive* when compared with the heights that Hawaiian language based academic instruction had reached at schools such as Lahainaluna.[55] Hampton Institute served as a model for Kamehameha's educational program in manual and moral training.

This approach addressed the "problem" of black emancipation or Native survival and autonomy through an education aimed at domestication. In personal letters, Armstrong described the "Hampton method" as his invention that "only boosted darkies a bit, and so to speak, lassoed wild Indians all to be cleaned and tamed."[56] Like Hampton, Kamehameha's curriculum throughout its early decades served to prop a plantation economy with semi-skilled tradesmen who could be "civilized" and subordinated, thus protecting and increasing white capitalist investment and political power.[57]

Under C. R. Bishop's oversight, and with Armstrong's help in recruiting administrators and teachers, Kamehameha offered its Hawaiian pupils an industrial and agricultural curriculum. From 1887 to 1893, KSB enrolled Hawaiian boys over age twelve and engaged them in a three-year English-language program focusing on vocational training for semi-skilled trades, labor to maintain the school, and basic academic subjects. As part of the manual labor philosophy, the boys maintained the school buildings and grounds, built and repaired machinery, and sewed the uniforms, sheets, napkins, tablecloths, and mattresses that were used at the school. Students staffed the school's dairy and prepared meals. They even broke up rocks on the school's grounds to be used for ballast in ships coming in and out of

Honolulu. In addition to these responsibilities and Christian devotions, students spent half the day studying such subjects as arithmetic, algebra, and geometry; English and penmanship; business and bookkeeping; mechanical drawing; geography and health. The remainder of the day was devoted to vocational shops where forging, woodturning, carpentry, and pattern making were taught.[58]

Although the trustees and administration adopted a four-year curriculum after 1893, the primary thrust of the boys' program remained largely unchanged until well into the twentieth century. The aim of the boys' school in the early decades is aptly captured in this excerpt from a KSB report card, approved by the trustees in 1899:

> All the class-room work is elementary, but useful. We do not aim to make scholars. We aim to give the boys a working knowledge of English, and get them to reading good literature. In Arithmetic, we desire to make them quick and accurate in every day problems.... We do not teach any science as a Science.... We aim seven days in the week to hold the boys up to a high standard of moral and religious conduct, as was desired by the will of the founder of these schools.[59]

Interestingly, the report card template is not addressed to parents but "to patrons of the school." The report card is crafted to demonstrate that KS boys are desirable for hire by white businessmen and suggests that it would be therefore beneficial for such men to help sponsor the cost of educating students.

While KSB was preparing young Hawaiian men to become wage earners and bread-winners, as future husbands, Kamehameha School for Girls was preparing young Hawaiian women to be proper middle-class, Christian wives for those men. Unlike the Kingdom's coeducational public school system, Kamehameha was divided into separate schools for boys and girls, per the will of Ke Aliʻi Pauahi. Through this divided curriculum, teachers and administrators cultivated Euro-American gender norms and hierarchies. The feminized "domestic" sphere became associated with bourgeois, American Protestant notions of home and care of the nuclear family, while the masculinized "political" sphere became associated with military service and wage labor to support the family. Girls were taught elementary academic subjects and "domestic arts," as well as arts and athletics. Preparing students for marriage was not only about shaping the relationships between men and women but about prescribing particular notions of gender, of what it meant to *be* a man or a woman.[60] In this particular model, men were understood to be the dominant partner and economic provider, while women were expected to be dependent and subordinate.

The KSG, which opened in 1894, one year after the illegal overthrow of Queen Lili'uokalani, aimed to put Native women in their place—the home. Haole school leaders and teachers took great care in designing and implementing the academic courses, but like the boys' school, they were not aiming to produce scholars.[61] Rather, they aimed to produced "cultured" young ladies, who spoke proper English and knew how to run an American-styled home. Girls were trained to make introduced foods like breads, jellies, and jams.[62] Students again provided the bulk of the labor necessary for the school's functioning, and they were only given one day a month free from their duties.

The authors of *Legacy: A Portrait of Young Men and Women of Kamehameha Schools, 1887–1987* purport that the curriculum offered to KSG students simply mirrored the wider conventions of the time. They write, "At the turn of the century, proper education for a young woman meant training her for marriage and motherhood."[63] However, they overlook the fact that this curriculum was offered at the very time when KS trustees were involved in effacing Hawaiian sovereignty, led by a woman as head of state. Queen Lili'uokalani's own actions show that Kamehameha School for Girls did not need to educate its pupils in this manner. A highly educated Kānaka who was known for her fluency in multiple languages, her prolific musical compositions, her diplomacy, and her unswerving commitment to her people, Lili'u had advocated for a women's bank and a girls' college.

Drawing on extensive personal interviews with Lydia Aholo, the queen's hānai daughter and graduate of the first KSG class, Allen writes that Lili'u envisioned a school, like Mills Seminary-College for women, that would teach Hawaiian women to be scholars. "Liliuokalani knew only too well that many Hawaiian women had become domestic servants in the homes of the *haole*," and she saw a school of higher learning as a way to provide women with other opportunities.[64] In fact, before ascending the throne, Lili'uokalani visited Mills College in 1878, and her visit deepened her desire to create a similar school for girls in Hawai'i. When Pauahi, a hānai sister to Lili'u, was contemplating the creation of Kamehameha Schools, Lili'u spoke with her about providing the students more than vocational, domestic, and basic academic training. "Liliuokalani agreed a school was good, but the young Hawaiians needed to learn more than 'trades' and how to be good wives and mothers and 'domestics.'"[65] Perhaps embedded in Aholo's recounting of Lili'u's unrealized vision is her own implicit critique of Kamehameha School for Girls—her alma mater and later her employer.

Aholo became one of the figures who worked to change the fact that the indigenous Hawaiian language had been banned from KS since its founding.[66] While Pauahi's will does indicate that she saw "a good education in the common English branches" as a priority, there is nothing in the text of the will that would have excluded the Hawaiian language altogether from Kamehameha, as the trustees and administrators decided. Eyre suggests that her intent may have had to do with curriculum content, not with medium of instruction. It would have made sense for Pauahi to draw upon her own schooling experience, in which chiefs learned Western academic subjects but also developed higher levels of fluency in spoken and written Hawaiian. The English-only philosophy that governed KS was not mandated by Pauahi or her will but by haole administrators and teachers who, no matter what their intent, had bought into the white supremacist idea that English was best and that the indigenous language was not only irrelevant, but dangerous.

Through the first decades of Kamehameha's existence, administrators formulated racialized discourses characterizing Hawaiians as physically, morally, and spiritually endangered. In response to this endangerment, KS pedagogies during this period emphasized erasing indigenous cultural practice and inculcating gendered divisions of labor—training young Hawaiian men as part of a modern industrial and agricultural labor force and young Hawaiian women as wives who could care for their homes or earn supplemental income. Kamehameha was essentially in the business of producing a heteronormative middle class that would participate in an industrial, capitalist economy and consent to American political rule.[67]

Pauahi and Charles: Marriage as a Domesticating Pedagogy

Christian marriage has been the cornerstone of KS-authorized narratives about the school's origins and its founders. It seems logical to organize origin stories about Kamehameha Schools in this manner, since KS did come into being through the joint actions of Ke Ali'i Bernice Pauahi and her husband, Charles Reed Bishop. However, these romanticized stories have functioned to occlude the political struggles of Kānaka Maoli for land, sovereignty, and control of education futures, and they have worked to naturalize the kind of education described in the previous section, white male control of the lands and resources of Pauahi's estate, and US imperial rule over the islands.[68] Take, for instance, this excerpt from a KS-authorized biography of Pauahi, published in 1965:

> As the Kona storms of early spring gave way to halcyon days, the hearts of lovers also emerged from the clouds of dissent surrounding them and they basked in the light of their devotion.... It can be imagined that on one of these evenings, when the stars over Diamond Head seemed caught in a seine of clouds, they stood at the pump in the courtyard.... Charles drew a pail of cool water from the pump. He offered Bernice

Pauahi the dipper and before she could finish the drink, he took it from her and put it to his own lips.... Her face, as fresh and cool as the draught from the spring, came up to his and their embrace was sweet with the perfume of her hair. She lowered her head on his chest and thanked heaven for this blessing.[69]

Stories of the Bishops' union have naturalized American dominance over Hawai'i—to domesticate Hawai'i—by invoking assumptions about gender roles within a "proper" marriage. Accounts of the Bishops' courtship and marriage, authored *after* the American takeover of the islands, portray Pauahi as independent enough to disobey her family's expectation that she preserve the mana (spiritual and political power) of the royal family by marrying another ali'i, yet submissive enough to defer involvement in politics once married to her wealthy, white, American-born husband. Marriage narratives construct a teleological trajectory, wherein the joining of American and Hawaiian antecedents is made to seem both inevitable and fully consensual.

The texts discussed in this final section represent dominant KS narratives about Pauahi and Charles, printed in the twentieth century. I recall being told, as a student at Kamehameha from 1979 to 1992, similar stories about Pauahi's willingness to forego a position of political leadership in part to maintain domestic harmony within her marriage. What was emphasized was her grace as a "servant leader" and a good wife who never sought to overshadow her husband. Stories emphasizing romantic love between Pauahi and Charles close down critical questions about how a board wholly comprised of white businessmen and annexationists had the power to control the vast body of lands Pauahi inherited and the consequences of that control over the schools' design.[70] Within the foreign-introduced institution of marriage, male control of property is a given. This contrasts with Kānaka Maoli cultural practice, which affirmed both women and men as legitimate landholders.

The institution of Christian marriage introduced and enforced foreign notions of gender and sexuality, and the telling and re-telling of marriage narratives serve a pedagogical function, inscribing these introduced notions upon the Hawaiian psyche. As several scholars have argued, the disciplining of Hawaiian sexuality has been an essential part of the colonizing process.[71] Christian marriage, as advocated by missionaries and later enforced by Hawaiian Kingdom law, emphasized sanction by church and governmental authority, obedience, lifetime monogamy, female subordination, and the permanent binding of a couple.[72]

Traditional ethics and expressions of Hawaiian gender, sexuality, and intimate relations were very different, emphasizing the cultural values of generosity, minimizing jealousy, joyous and poetic appreciation for love and sex, and situating a relationship in terms of each person's genealogy rather than individualizing the couple. Drawing on Hawaiian language mo'olelo (stories) and mele (songs, poetry), Leilani Basham shows that the category of "marriage" as we think of it today—and as told within the KS narratives—did not fit within a Hawaiian cultural and linguistic frame and does considerable violence to the plurality, joy, and fluidity of Hawaiian practices of gender and sexuality.[73] She discusses multiple acceptable forms of intimate and loving relationships, including ho'āo (committed relationships that include cohabitation), punalua (polygamous relationships by either men or women), and aikāne (close same-sex relationships that often but not always included sex). While ho'āo is typically translated as "marriage," the term literally means "to make light" or "to stay until daylight." According to Basham, "This is an excellent description, because it was in the very simple act of staying together until it was daylight that a kāne and wahine were recognized as in a committed, public relationship."[74]

Unlike marriage, ho'āo or noho pū (to live together) relationships were typically established without ceremony, and they could be ended as easily as they were entered into, simply by ending the cohabitation.[75] Pukui and her co-authors note that, at times, both chiefs and commoners made binding betrothal agreements, and that the practice of breaking such agreements was so uncommon that there is not even a term to describe such a broken alliance. However, while the engagement was almost always honored, "the noho pū 'ana itself could be broken off. The man or woman could just say, 'I don't like you any more. I'm not going to live with you any longer.'"[76] These descriptions indicate that the consultation and honoring of agreements between families were more important than whether or not the couple continued their relationship indefinitely. They are also key to understanding Pauahi's family's displeasure with her marriage to Charles Bishop.

Kanahele begins his story of Pauahi's life like older Hawaiian oral traditions, with her genealogy, recounting her lineal connection to the highest-ranking chiefs and describing the auspicious events around her birth.[77] By rank and upbringing, Pauahi was expected to be a leader. She was raised in the practice of hānai by Kīna'u, a high-ranking female ali'i who served as kuhina nui (prime minister) of the Kingdom for eight years, and Kekūanāo'a, discussed in the previous section.[78] Thus, leadership and education were both in her genealogy. Kanahele focuses the biography, published by KS Press in anticipation of the school's one hundredth anniversary, around three major decisions the princess made that ultimately led to the establishment of the Kamehameha Schools. Each decision is celebrated as triumph: Pauahi's marriage to Charles Reed Bishop, her denial of Lot's offer of the throne, and her establishment of the charitable estate that funds KS.[79]

At age eighteen, Pauahi defied her family and the aliʻi establishment in marrying Bishop, and this episode is repeatedly narrated as the event that catapults her into womanhood. Forced to choose between her individual desires and her obligation to familial and ancestral tradition, Pauahi "follows her heart." Kanahele writes, "No other aspect of Pauahi's life was as important to her fulfillment as a woman—and as founder of the Kamehameha Schools—as her marriage to Charles Reed Bishop."[80] Her union with Charles is simplified and memorialized as a familiar narrative in which "love conquers all." The rhetoric of romantic love works to dismiss the substantive political objections Pauahi's elders had with C. R. Bishop, both before and throughout their marriage.

Instead, books like *Princess Pauahi Bishop and Her Legacy,* commissioned by KS for the seventy-fifth anniversary of its founding, celebrate the consummation of Pauahi and Charles' desire for one another, including chapters titled "Romance of a Princess" and "Happily Ever After."[81] More like a romance novel than a work of historical scholarship, the book is filled with frequent flourishes of fabricated detail. When Pauahi doubts, Charles assures her of the strength of their love, "gently letting his arm encircle her slim waist" as Pauahi "lowered her head on his chest and thanked heaven for this blessing."[82]

Both of these texts, however, signal the fact that Pauahi's and Charles' union was not just a matter of love. It was a matter of politics and the law. In Hawaiian society, the unions of aliʻi have always been political; strategic unions built alliances and potentially produced powerful progeny.[83] When Pauahi was a child, her hānai mother Kīnaʻu planned for her to unite with Lot Kapuāiwa—Kīnaʻu's son and future king—and it was widely known that the two were betrothed. As a young woman, Pauahi rejected this plan.[84] As a student at the Chiefs' Childrens' School, Pauahi was officially under the charge of the government, and governmental consent was necessary to proceed with the marriage.[85] Her parents and elder relatives, who attempted to block the marriage, seemed to have been peeved that both Charles Bishop and the Cookes—the missionary couple who ran the Chiefs' Childrens' School—were attempting to subvert their familial and chiefly authority by arranging the terms of the marriage without regard for customary practice.[86] Importantly, the struggles over Pauahi's marriage to Charles Bishop reflect the shift away from sexual unions of aliʻi being matters of familial and genealogical politics to their being matters sanctioned and regulated by the introduced legal apparatus that was now coming to define Hawaiian government.[87] Yet many Kānaka still understood chiefly unions as issues of broad political concern, evidenced by the numerous mele written in opposition to Pauahi's marriage to Charles Bishop.

The KS publication celebrating the one hundredth anniversary of the Kamehameha School for Girls in 1994 instead opens with one of the only nineteenth-century mele written in support of the Bishops' marriage, "I Haleakalā ka ʻolu."[88] The central image of this mele is Haleakala, the house that had been built for Pauahi's arranged marriage to Lot (who later became King Kamehameha V), and it is repeatedly invoked in KS narratives to emphasize familial and domestic harmony.[89] In the translator's interpretation of this mele, the house is a symbol of Pauahi's reconciliation with her family.[90] Yet, in emphasizing the interpersonal familial and emotional conflicts, the historical and political context by which the personal relationships became so highly contested is downplayed. For example, no mention is made of the thinning ranks of possible Kamehameha-lineage successors to the throne or the increasing concern about foreign influence and possible takeover of the Kingdom. The complexities of the historical, political conjuncture are covered over by the recuperation of the happy home.

In dominant KS narrations of the past, Haleakala comes to symbolize not only the love shared between Pauahi and Charles, but also the marriage of feminized Hawaiian royalty and masculinized white business and annexationist interests within a bourgeois, domestic sphere. KS-authorized biographies of Pauahi all describe her skill at homemaking and the admiration of key members of white society of the Bishops' residence at Haleakala.[91] For example, Black quotes Sanford Dole, who played a key role in the overthrow of the legitimate Hawaiian government and was later appointed by the US president as the first Territorial Governor of Hawaiʻi, in his praise of Pauahi's domestic skills, and Krout describes Pauahi's renown among the "officers of the American, British and German navies, men who, through the exigencies of their professions, become sticklers for etiquette, and rigid critics of all that pertains to the art of entertaining.[92] Kanahele interprets these abilities in "domestic management" as illustrating Hawaiian values, yet the descriptions he offers of her gardening, sewing, housekeeping, and managing her staff and retainers could just as easily be seen as epitomizing the ideals of Victorian ladyship or of the American "cult of true womanhood."

At forty-one, Pauahi refused Lot and her aliʻi lineage a second time when he tried, from his deathbed, to name her his successor to the throne. Kanahele's speculations about why Pauahi denied the throne suggest that the way to maintain a "happy marriage" between a Hawaiian and an American is to renounce Hawaiian political rulership. Pauahi didn't need the crown, he explains. In Kanahele's eyes, she already had all the land, money, status, and influence that she needed.

> Why would she want to give it up?... As Mrs. Bishop she could settle differences with Charles in the privacy of their home.... Charles already

represented some powerful economic and political interests, already at
variance with some of her own positions on preserving Hawai'i's po-
litical independence and cultural integrity. If Pauahi were the monarch,
these differences could easily be blown out of proportion and lead to
uncomfortable consequences between husband and wife. In short, her
partnership with Charles was the most precious and enduring relation-
ship she had and she was not about to jeopardize it in exchange for the
uncertainties of the crown.[93]

The narrative supports the construction of gendered spaces, in which the realm of politics and governance is marked masculine and white, while the realm of the home is marked feminine and Hawaiian. Furthermore, it is not based on any documentation of Pauahi's actual sentiment or reasoning.

Rather, in KS-authorized narratives, Pauahi is often portrayed as transcending the struggle or managing to deal with it quietly in the privacy of her own home—able to marry American but remain Hawaiian. If Pauahi is to be seen as a model for young Hawaiians, the entreaty is to leave behind the uncertainty of political independence and accept subordination to the white American. Here, Hawaiianness is not elided altogether, nor replaced by an American identity. As long as one makes his or her Hawaiianness subservient, conflict can be avoided. In fact, a certain amount of culture is seen as desirable and charming.[94]

By the time Pauahi had her will written in 1883, the Hawaiian Kingdom's Civil Code had firmly defined marriage in heteronormative terms as a contractual relationship between a man and a woman, and it clearly delineated the subordinate status of married female subjects. As in other countries at the time, male and female subjects of the Hawaiian Kingdom did not have equal political rights, and married women were subjected to civil death—the loss of civil rights—under the law. Marriage, as defined by the state, entrenched unequal status between women and men.[95] The enforcement of marriage in Hawai'i aimed to fit Hawaiian sexuality into Christian moral frameworks, and it also underwrote the same kinds of gendered economic and political relations of dependence at play in other Western countries.[96] Although Pauahi inherited enough land to be independently wealthy and self-sufficient, she was still bound by law to the authority of her husband.

Pauahi died of cancer in 1884, almost exactly one year after signing her will. The document gave little detail about how she envisioned the school, besides providing support for orphaned and indigent children, giving preference to aboriginal Hawaiians, and providing an education in the common English branches.[97] Thus, it was her husband, Charles Bishop, and the Estate's trustees who interpreted her will in the ensuing decades and who directed the educational program to prepare students for collective subordination in a new cultural and political order to be led by white Americans.

The persistence of the marriage trope within KS narratives about Charles and Pauahi, published throughout the twentieth century, helped occlude Hawaiian sovereignty and political struggle. These stories rehearse tidy narratives of progression in which Pauahi, Kamehameha students, and the Hawaiian social body as a whole grow from "childhood" to "adulthood," which becomes rhetorically associated with full participation as American citizens seasoned with some Hawaiian "culture" as an additive. Pauahi's "*blest type of womanhood*," memorialized as "*so true, so pure, so good*," thus functions as an acceptance of masculinized American imperial rule, cloaked in romantic love.[98] To preserve a counter-narrative that refuses to allow the submerged histories to be forgotten or covered, I conclude with a return to Haleakala.

Speaking Back to Marriage Narratives

Pauahi willed Haleakala, along with several other parcels, to her husband for his personal use. The quintessential capitalist, Mr. Bishop moved out of the house shortly after Pauahi's death and began using the property to generate income.[99] The home was used as a boarding house and hotel, known as "the Arlington." When Bishop's business associates and friends were plotting to overthrow Queen Lili'uokalani, the sister-in-law with whom he had resided in Haleakala, he described her as "deceitful and treacherous."[100] He allowed the US Marines to occupy Lili'u's childhood home as their headquarters and barracks when they landed to support the haole oligarchy's coup against her.[101] Disregarding the Hawaiian name, the Marines called the place "Camp Boston."[102] The upper floor of the main home became officers' quarters. A building formerly used by the retainers of the ali'i was used as an armory and hospital, as part of the Marines' complex.[103] When Charles Bishop left Hawai'i for good in 1894, returning to San Francisco to spend the rest of his years, he transferred Haleakala back to the Bishop Estate funding the Kamehameha Schools. Yet the story of his usage of Haleakala in supporting the overthrow of Hawaiian self-government is never recounted for Kamehameha students. Instead, the birth of the Kamehameha Schools is glorified as the gift made possible through the loss of Pauahi's life and Hawaiian independence. However, it was precisely the political sovereignty of the Hawaiian nation that was being undercut by the haole oligarchy, while they promoted individual "self-governance" among KS students.

Each time I look at photographs of Pauahi, I feel a burning desire to talk with her, to understand what she was thinking when she envisioned Kamehameha and named five white men, with deep connections to the sugar industry and annexationist movement, as board of trustees of her estate. Did she believe there were no qualified Kānaka who could steward her estate? Were her choices limited by the laws binding wives to their husbands? Was she behaving as she believed a proper, submissive, Christian wife should? Was she simply concerned to put successful businessmen at the helm, regardless of their politics and their condescending attitudes toward Hawaiians? I long to hear her voice, beyond the words written in her will or the few correspondences that remain, telling us about some of her travels but little about her opinions on education, politics, or the state of her country in tense times.

However, Pauahi's voice has been suppressed because of the circumstances of her marriage. Although we know that Pauahi loved to write and seemed to enjoy capturing the details of her experiences and feelings on paper, the vast majority of her writings have been lost. According to several sources, most of her letters and diaries were organized and sent to her husband, who had moved back to the United States after the overthrow. He reported that all of these papers were destroyed in the fires that resulted from the infamous 1906 San Francisco earthquake. One has to wonder, though, why Bishop wouldn't have left some of his wife's writings at the Bishop Museum, which he founded in her honor seventeen years prior to the earthquake? While her writings may have been of deep personal value to him, he must have known that the princess's writings would also be invaluable treasures to the Hawaiian people. Why he did not find some way to copy, preserve, or share these extensive writings in the twenty-two years between her death and the San Francisco earthquake is strange and, for me, suspicious, particularly since he demonstrated such acumen and attention to detail in so many other matters. Perhaps it is evidence of his view that in the context of marriage, it is only the man's voice that counts.

I am further convinced about the violence of the Bishops' marriage upon Pauahi's lands and people based on a final historical anecdote. When Pauahi was born, her parents had the placenta buried under a young tree, as is often practiced by Kānaka ʻŌiwi. In Hawaiian belief, a placenta that is carelessly disposed of can bring harm to the child and diminish the mana of that person in the years to come.[104] As Pauahi grew, so too did the tamarind tree to which she was linked. In her adult life, Ke aliʻi Pauahi was known to have sat under the tree on the grounds of her home at Haleakala, fulfilling her chiefly duty of listening to and counseling her people. Kānaka who came to her with troubles or conflicts took comfort in the shade of her tree, just as they took comfort in Pauahi's assistance. Following her death, Charles Bishop committed what would be considered a grave insult and injury within a Hawaiian cultural worldview when he had the tree cut down and sawed into lumber. The bulk of the wood was made into a table and sent to Bishop's relatives in America.[105]

These are the kinds of stories that have largely been left out of the dominant narratives about Kamehameha Schools and its founders. While such accounts may be uncomfortable and disconcerting for some, they call us to reckon with the fundamental ways in which romanticized marriage narratives mask the cultural and political struggles embedded in and played out through these relationships. Kānaka Maoli never consented to the taking of our government and national lands by the United States. Yet for the better part of a century Kamehameha's curriculum obscured the clear historical facts of the overthrow, in which its own trustees were implicated and from which they benefited, while school leaders claimed the school was strictly apolitical and told tales about the Bishops' love instead.

If education supporting white supremacist and settler colonial structures of power has relied upon the naturalization of the categories and legal regimes upon which the heteropatriarchal institution of Christian marriage is based, then a critical practice of liberatory Hawaiian education should work to actively question such discourses and to recover and defend a plurality of Hawaiian sexual and gender expression. Moreover, if the enforcement of heteronormative categories upon Hawaiian sexuality has been an essential part of the colonizing process in the past, it is necessary to continue critiquing the ways in which such pedagogies continue to support settler colonialism and racism in the present.

Acknowledgments

I am grateful to all those who helped with this paper. Participants in the short seminar sponsored by the School for Advanced Research provided valuable feedback: Brian Klopotek, Brenda Child, Tsianina Lomawaima, Alyssa Mt. Pleasant, Shari Huhndorf, and Laura Graham. *Mahalo nui* to readers Kāwika Eyre, James Slagel, Noenoe Silva, and Hokulani Aikau. Kamehameha Schools archivist Janet Zisk provided generous guidance through the KS archives.

Notes

1. I use a number of terms interchangeably to refer to the indigenous people of Hawai'i, people who are genealogically connected to Ka Pae 'Āina 'o Hawai'i (the Hawaiian archipelago) since time immemorial: Kānaka Maoli, Kānaka, Kānaka Hawai'i, 'Ōiwi, 'Ōiwi Hawai'i, Hawaiian, and Native Hawaiian. Kānaka Maoli is the singular form of the term and can refer to the whole group as a singular class. In my usage of these terms, I refer to all Kānaka Maoli, without any blood quantum restriction. I do not italicize Hawaiian terms in this essay. When terms are italicized, it is to emphasize their importance to my argument and analysis.

2. Queen Emma and King Kamehameha IV founded a hospital for their people in 1859. King Lunalilo designated all of his lands to be used for the creation of a care facility for the destitute and elderly. Concerned for the health and welfare of Hawaiian mothers and their babies, Queen Kapiāolani founded a maternity home in 1890, and in 1909 Queen Lili'uokalani established a trust to fund programs for orphaned and destitute children.

3. In 2010, over 120 years after its founding, the KS trust (also known as the Bishop Estate)

was valued at over $6 billion and remains the largest private landowner in Hawai'i. Through Pauahi's endowment, KS is able to defray about 90 percent of the cost to families for sending their children to Kamehameha.

4. In 1843, Hawai'i entered into international treaties, recognizing its status as a sovereign and independent state, with Belgium, the United States, France, and Britain. In the ensuing decades, the Hawaiian Kingdom government signed treaties with every other major European nation, as well as with Japan and Samoa. See Sai, "American Occupation of the Hawaiian State," and Sai, "The American Occupation of the Hawaiian Kingdom."

5. Bishop served again as president of the Kingdom's Board of Education from 1887 to 1893, after a shift in political power away from democratic rule and toward oligarchic control by haole sugar business interests due to an armed coup in 1887.

6. Given the laws about marriage at the time, could she have named anyone else? The civil codes defined wives as civilly dead and gave control of property to husbands, as indicated previously. More research needs to be done in this area to look at whether and how these laws applied differently to chiefly and commoner women.

7. The 1893 coup and invasion by the US military breached Hawaiian and US domestic laws as well as the international treaties in force between those two countries, and thus were a breach of international law. Following the 1893 actions, US President Grover Cleveland commissioned James Blount to complete a thorough investigation. Drawing on Blount's detailed report, President Cleveland addressed the US Congress on December 18, 1893, stating in part: "But for the lawless occupation of Honolulu under false pretexts by the United States forces, and but for Minister Stevens' recognition of the provisional government when the United States forces were its sole support and constituted its only military strength, the Queen and her Government would have never yielded to the provisional government.... By an act of war, committed with the participation of a diplomatic representative of the United States without the authority of Congress, the Government of a feeble but friendly and confiding people has been overthrown." As quoted in Blount, *Foreign Relations of the United States, 1894: Affairs in Hawai'i*, and in Trask, *From a Native Daughter: Colonialism and Sovereignty in Hawai'i*, 14–15.

8. The phrase "good and industrious" comes from Bernice Pauahi Bishop's will, in the one section in which she describes the schools' purpose and makes some very brief statements about curriculum. See Bernice Pauahi Bishop, "Last Will and Codicils of the Late Hon. Mrs. Bernice P. Bishop."

9. Maenette K. P. Benham and Ronald H. Heck, *Culture and Educational Policy in Hawai'i: The Silencing of Native Voices*; Alex L. Pickens and David Kemble, eds., *To Teach the Children: Historical Aspects of Education in Hawaii*; Benjamin Othello Wist, *A Century of Public Education in Hawaii, October 15, 1840–October 15, 1940*.

10. The noun *hoa* can be modified by various verbs to further specify the relationship. For example, *hoa hānau* (peers in birth) refers to cousins.

11. Anne McClintock, *Imperial Leather: Race, Gender, and Sexuality in the Colonial Contest*, 1st ed., 34.

12. For example, McClintock discusses the way a "Family Tree of Races" subsumed diverse peoples throughout the world within a single, purportedly organic, hierarchical grouping (45). My analysis focuses specifically on marriage rather than the family because marriage is the particular familial relationship repeatedly invoked in narratives about Kamehameha's origins, and it is the relationship that anchors the bourgeois heteropatriarchal construction of the nuclear family.

13. See Daniel Heath Justice, Mark Rifkin, and Bethany Schneider, "Introduction to Special Issue on Sexuality, Nationality, Indigeneity"; Scott Lauria Morgensen, "Settler Homonationalism:

Theorizing Settler Colonialism within Queer Modernities"; Qwo-Li Driskill et al., eds., *Queer Indigenous Studies: Critical Interventions in Theory, Politics, and Literature*; Andrea Smith, "Heteropatriarchy and the Three Pillars of White Supremacy: Rethinking Women of Color Organizing," 66–73, and "Queer Theory and Native Studies: The Heteronormativity of Settler Colonialism."

14. See Smith, "American Studies without America: Native Feminisms and the Nation-State."

15. Nancy F. Cott, *Public Vows: A History of Marriage and the Nation*; Jyl Josephson, "Citizenship, Same-Sex Marriage, and Feminist Critiques of Marriage"; Mary Lyndon Shanley, *Feminism, Marriage, and the Law in Victorian England, 1850–1895*.

16. Josephson, 275.

17. See Carl Kalani Beyer, "Female Seminaries in America and Hawaii during the 19th Century"; Sally Engle Merry, *Colonizing Hawai'i: The Cultural Power of Law*.

18. For example, the Cherokee National Council set up a national school system comprising eleven schools at roughly the same time as the Hawaiian national school system was being established. Similarly, the Choctaws set up a system of tribal schools in 1842. See Jon Allan Reyhner and Jeanne M. Oyawin Eder, *American Indian Education: A History*, 55–56. These Indian and Hawaiian national educational initiatives contrast the passage of school laws by the US Congress, which imposed schooling on Indian nations. See K. Tsianina Lomawaima and Teresa L. McCarty, *"To Remain an Indian": Lessons in Democracy from a Century of Native American Education*; and Lomawaima, "American Indian Education: By Indians versus for Indians," 422–440.

19. Schools were not the first educational institutions in the islands. Native educational institutions based on apprenticeship, mastery, and community predated and survived the advent of Western-styled schooling in Hawai'i. The ways those institutional and personal relationships transformed and were transformed by schooling is beyond the scope of this chapter.

20. Albert J. Schutz, *The Voices of Eden: A History of Hawaiian Language Studies*, 101.

21. Wist, *A Century of Public Education in Hawaii, October 15, 1840–October 15, 1940*, 22.

22. Additionally, some missionaries did not stay, so all fifty-two would not have been in the islands at the same time. See Hawaiian Mission Children's Society, *Missionary Album: Portraits and Biographical Sketches of the American Protestant Missionaries to the Hawaiian Islands*.

23. Kuykendall writes, "As soon as a bright pupil (and there were many such) had acquired a little facility in reading, he was sent out, or went out on his own initiative, to teach a school of his own." Ralph S. Kuykendall, *The Hawaiian Kingdom*, vol. 2, *Twenty Critical Years (1854–1874)*, 106.

24. Wist, 27.

25. Within the next two decades, the corpus of Hawaiian schoolbooks and literature amounted to over 80 million pages, as reported by the president of the Board of Education, Richard Armstrong, in 1852. See Hawaiian Kingdom, *Report of the Minister of Public Instruction Read Before the King to the Hawaiian Legislature. Report of Richard Armstrong on April 14, 1852*, 37. Chapin and Silva have documented the centrality of newspapers in struggles for political and cultural power in the islands. Silva argues that newspapers in fact became *the* primary battleground for competing political discourses and interests. See Helen Geracimos Chapin, *Shaping History: The Role of Newspapers in Hawai'i*; Noenoe K. Silva, *Aloha Betrayed: Native Hawaiian Resistance to American Colonialism*, 54.

26. This quote is included in the authoritative text on Hawaiian proverbs, *'Ōlelo No'eau: Hawaiian Proverbs & Poetical Sayings*. Pukui's translation is "Mine is the kingdom of education; the righteous man is my man." See Mary Kawena Pukui, *'Ōlelo No'eau: Hawaiian Proverbs & Poetical Sayings*, 64. An additional interpretation could also include that the king was indicating that his

government would be one based on documents (palapala) for which literacy was necessary. Both interpretations suggest that education and literacy were seen as critical elements of a modern Hawaiian nationhood and subjecthood.

27. Benham and Heck, 69.

28. There are conflicting interpretations of the intent and impact of the Chiefs' Children's School. Linda Menton's study emphasizes the colonizing and Americanizing aspects of the school. See Linda K. Menton, "Christian and 'Civilized' Education: The Hawaiian Chiefs' Children's School." On the other hand, Beamer argues that the intent of the school "was not to *Americanize* these keiki, it was to *Internationalize* them," preparing them as leaders for an increasingly internationally connected Hawai'i. See B. Kamanamaikalani Beamer, "Na wai ka mana? 'Ōiwi Agency and European Imperialism in the Hawaiian Kingdom," 208. Keahiolalo-Karasuda connects the education of ali'i at the Chiefs' Children's School with technologies of prosecuting and imprisoning Hawaiians in ways that have eroded political sovereignty. She argues that the school "largely resembled methods of disciplinary control and punishment often found in detentionlike settings." See RaeDeen Keahiolalo-Karasuda, "A Genealogy of Punishment in Hawai'i: The Public Hanging of Chief Kamanawa II," 154.

29. Beginning in 1846, the Kingdom government published laws in both Hawaiian and English, rather than in Hawaiian alone. When disputes arose and there were differences in the interpretation of the two versions, early courts recognized the Hawaiian language version as the prevailing and controlling law. Lucas argues that the shift in 1859 toward using the English version as the authoritative one signaled the rise of a growing "English-mainly" movement, led by certain missionaries and their descendants. See Paul Nahoa Lucas, "E ola mau kākou i ka 'ōlelo makuahine: Hawaiian Language Policy and the Courts," 3–4.

30. Benham and Heck; Wist.

31. John Papa 'Ī'ī also served as a teacher, trustee, and adviser of the Chiefs' Children's School, also called the Royal School. See Helena G. Allen, *The Betrayal of Liliuokalani: Last Queen of Hawaii, 1838–1917*. Allen notes that he was a teacher of the young Lili'u, future queen of the Hawaiian Kingdom, and that he instructed the young chiefs in reading, writing, English grammar, arithmetic, and spelling.

32. See Ralph S. Kuykendall, *The Hawaiian Kingdom*, vol. 1, *Foundation and Transformation*, 347–348.

33. By that time, the governance of public instruction had been restructured so that the presidency of the Board of Education was the highest post in the Kingdom. The president was also assisted by an inspector general starting in 1865.

34. It was under Armstrong's administration that the first government appropriation was made to support public education: $22,000. Benham and Heck, 91.

35. Hawaiian Kingdom, *Biennial Report of the President of the Board of Education to the Hawaiian Legislature of 1866. Report of Mataio Kekuanaoa*, 2.

36. Kekūanāo'a further expressed concern with the fact that the poll tax was not providing adequate funding for the common schools and called for increased funding of the schools serving the common people.

37. See Lucas.

38. Hawaiian Kingdom, *Biennial Report of the President of the Board of Education to the Hawaiian Legislature of 1864. Report of Mataio Kekuanaoa*, 1864. Also quoted in Kuykendall, *The Hawaiian Kingdom*, vol. 2, *Twenty Critical Years (1854–1874)*, 112.

39. In 1876, government funding for the select schools, some of which were also privately

supported, amounted to $38,000 for 2,678 pupils, while funding for the common schools was only $13,000 for 4,313 pupils (Hawaiian Kingdom 1878). The appropriations stayed about the same for the next biennium, and by 1883, just before Bishop's forced resignation, the difference in appropriation was $75,000 for the select schools and $10,000 for the common schools (Hawaiian Kingdom 1884).

40. In 1883, King Kalākaua and his Privy Council forced Bishop to resign from his position as head of the BOE. Four years later, a group of haole sugar businessmen known as the "Hawaiian League" forced the King to sign a constitution stripping him of crucial powers, allowing white foreigners to vote, instituting property and income requirements, and completely disenfranchising Asians. Subsequently, Bishop was reappointed to lead the Kingdom's Board of Education until 1893.

41. Benham and Heck, 93.

42. Schutz reports that the number of Hawaiian-language-medium schools took a dramatic decline, from 150 schools in 1880 to zero in 1902, whereas English-medium schools increased from 60 to 203 in the same period. See Schutz, 352. This was a direct result of the takeover by white businessmen backed by the US government. The suppression of education in the indigenous Hawaiian language and culture stifled the collective 'Ōiwi ability to define for themselves what it meant to be a lāhui—a nation or a people—particularly as the sugar oligarchy and the US federal government contested our ability to do so.

43. KSB opened in 1887. The Preparatory Department, for boys under age twelve, opened in 1888. The Girls' School opened in 1894, a year after the "Missionary Party's" coup against the legitimate Hawaiian government and Queen Lili'uokalani. On July 6, 1898, the United States Congress passed a joint resolution purporting to annex the Hawaiian Islands. A mere joint resolution of Congress, this domestic law has been rigorously criticized and protested by Kānaka Maoli who assert that no valid action, under Hawaiian, US, or international law, has ever been made extinguishing Hawaiian sovereignty. The year 1898 marks the beginning of US assertion of its control over Hawai'i as a colonial territory.

44. This term was used by US President William McKinley to describe the American colonial project in the Philippines.

45. See Talbot and Wexler.

46. In *Tender Violence: Domestic Visions in an Age of U.S. Imperialism*, Wexler shows that the sentimentality of photographic images from this period bound what was purported to be opposing approaches to colonial projects—domesticity and brutal violence. She argues that these were not opposites but two faces of US imperial projects. Andrea Smith has also argued that boarding schools were a form of sexual violence against Indians. In addition to the widespread instances of sexual assault that occurred within these schools, she sees them as part of colonizing projects that aimed to destroy Indians' sense of collective identity. (Smith, *Conquest: Sexual Violence and American Indian Genocide*.)

47. Bishop's address was reprinted in *Handicraft* (an early publication of the Kamehameha School for Boys) in January 1889. A section of this speech is also included in the Kamehameha Schools Strategic Plan of 2000.

48. Benham and Heck write that Charles Bishop supported a philosophy of "universal education geared to the masses and an elite cadre of boarding or independent schools for the chosen few" (96). Bishop was first appointed to the BOE presidency by King Lunalilo in 1874.

49. See Beyer, "Manual and Industrial Education during Hawaiian Sovereignty: Curriculum in the Transculturation of Hawai'i." Beyer, in "The Connection of Samuel Chapman Armstrong as Both Borrower and Architect of Education in Hawai'i," provides detailed examinations of the development of manual and industrial education in Hawai'i. Kanahele also notes the Kingdom

legislature's support for industrial and agricultural training in 1874 (155). Kanahele writes, "As a businessman he saw more clearly than most the value in [industrial and agricultural] training, which would help students become better fitted for jobs in the rapidly developing sugar and ancillary industries" (156). It certainly created value for Bishop and his business associates, who could then employ these young people of color in semi-skilled jobs.

50. See Hawaiian Kingdom, *Biennial Report of the President of the Board of Education to the Legislature of 1878. Report of Charles R. Bishop.*

51. Bishop personally benefited as a sugar investor and banker who had held a monopoly on banking since 1858. His interests in the banking and sugar industries made him one of the wealthiest men in the Kingdom. See Dougherty; Kent; and Kanahele. He was also one of the leading proponents of a proposal to cede Pearl Harbor to the US for use as a naval port in exchange for duty-free trade of Hawaiian sugar into American markets. We know from his own writings, as well as Queen Emma's, that Pauahi was opposed to the Reciprocity Treaty and to the cession of any Hawaiian territory to the US. See Kanahele, *Pauahi*, 120; Kent, *Charles Reed Bishop, Man of Hawaii*, 64.

52. Manual training in the US traces its origins to European educational reformers in Scandinavia and Russia, including Friedrich Froebel, Johann Pestalozzi, and Victor Della Vos. Calvin Woodward, who founded the Manual Training School for Boys in St. Louis, Missouri, in 1879, is often called the "father of manual training" in America. Interest in including manual arts in general public education across the country developed partly as a result of an acute shortage of skilled labor during the Civil War. Leaders of industry and statesmen turned to the schools to develop training programs to replace and supplement the apprenticeship system. See Westerink.

53. Booker T. Washington attended Hampton and drew on his experience there in founding the Tuskegee Institute.

54. Anderson, *The Education of Blacks in the South, 1860–1935*, as quoted in Benham and Heck, *Culture and Educational Policy in Hawai'i*, 95.

55. Beyer, "The Connection of Samuel Chapman Armstrong as Both Borrower and Architect of Education in Hawai'i."

56. Lindsey, 112.

57. In 1883, Kalākaua's privy council compelled Charles Bishop to resign from his position as president of the Board of Education. Pauahi's will establishing Kamehameha Schools was written that same year. He addressed the Hawaiian League—a segregated organization of white businessmen and missionary descendants—when they met on the eve of their action forcing Kalākaua to approve the illegitimate "Bayonet Constitution" of 1887. This faction re-appointed Bishop to the BOE presidency shortly after their grab for power. The Kamehameha School for Boys, also known as the "Manual Department," was designed and built during the four-year interim between Bishop's first and second stint as head of the BOE.

58. Chun-Lum and Agard, 7.

59. Unpublished document, courtesy of the Kamehameha Schools Archives, Kapalama, O'ahu.

60. Cott writes: "The whole system of attribution and meaning that we call gender relies on and to a great extent derives from the structuring provided by marriage. Turning men and women into husbands and wives, marriage has designated the ways both sexes act in the world and the reciprocal relation between them." Cott, *Public Vows*, 3.

61. The care and attention to detail among KSG administrators and faculty is evidenced by the extensive reports they prepared for the Board of Trustees each year. These unpublished reports are available in the Kamehameha Schools Archives.

62. Chun-Lum and Agard, 17.

63. Chun-Lum and Agard, 14.

64. Ke aliʻi Liliʻuokalani also met Susan Mills in the 1860s when Mills was teaching at Oahu College. See Allen, *The Betrayal of Liliuokalani*, 150–151, 160.

65. Allen, 178.

66. Eyre, "Suppression of Hawaiian Culture at Kamehameha Schools."

67. Beyer reports that up through the 1930s, critics pointed out that KS was training laborers, not leaders, even though there was a precedent for schools to serve that purpose for Kānaka Maoli. "Its curriculum was never intended to train its graduates to become ministers, lawyers, judges, or legislators, as Lahainaluna Seminary had done previously." See Beyer, "Manual and Industrial Education during Hawaiian Sovereignty," 39. Higher academic subjects and college preparation were not introduced until the mid-1930s and did not become a main focus at Kamehameha until the 1970s and 1980s. Even when college preparation became a more central goal for KS, questions of Hawaiian sovereignty and critical investigation of US imperialism have remained marginal, if present at all, in the curriculum.

68. The stories of Pauahi and her marriage to American Charles Bishop can be compared to stories about Pocahontas and John Smith. In her influential article on the image of Pocahontas within American national mythologies, Green explores the ways the figures of the Indian princess and the squaw, as symbols, are always constructed in relation to white male desire. The princess is represented as the "good Indian," a helper and comforter who is desired but remains sexually restrained and unavailable. On the other hand, representations of the squaw's overt, crude, and available sexuality create a negative counterpart. Green concludes that such caricatures make it difficult for Indian women to be seen as real and fully human, while US presence on Indian lands is normalized and legitimized. See Green, "The Pocahontas Perplex: The Image of Indian Women in American Culture," 698–714.

69. Black and Mellen, 62.

70. The first KS trustees included Charles R. Bishop, Samuel Damon, Charles Cooke, William O. Smith, and Charles Hyde. They were, for the most part, businessmen rather than educators, with ownership and control of corporations like Castle & Cooke, Lewers & Cooke, C. Brewer & Co., First Hawaiian Bank, Bank of Hawaiʻi, and the Damon estate. Of the five of them, three were sons of missionaries and one was a former reverend. They also held multiple influential government positions.

71. Hall, 273–280; Kauanui, 281–287; Merry, *Colonizing Hawaiʻi*; Trask, "Fighting the Battle of Double Colonization: The View of a Hawaiian Feminist."

72. Merry, *Colonizing Hawaiʻi*.

73. Basham argues that marking individuals by gender identity is less important in Hawaiian oral tradition. "This is reinforced by the lack of sex and gender identification within the language...neither the singular, third-person pronouns nor the possessives are gender-based...names are not gendered either, creating space in which gender and its performance can be chosen and altered." Basham, 3.

74. Basham, 10.

75. Pukui, Haertig, and Lee, *Nānā I Ke Kumu* (*Look to the Source*), vol. 2, 89–90.

76. Pukui, Haertig, and Lee, *Nānā I Ke Kumu* (*Look to the Source*), vol. 2, 90.

77. Kanahele, *Pauahi*.

78. Hānai is an important Hawaiian cultural practice of adopting or fostering children within the extended family system. It is distinct from, but can overlap with, legal adoption or temporary

caregiving. The practice is understood as *strengthening* familial bonds rather than distancing a child from their biological parents. A child's genealogy and identity within the larger family system is typically open, rather than concealed or secreted. Pukui, Haertig, and Lee, *Nānā I Ke Kumu* (*Look to the Source*), vol. 1, 49–51.

79. Kanahele's representation of the schools as the progeny of Pauahi and Charles is particularly salient since their marriage was childless. The metaphor of KS as the child of Pauahi and Charles is problematic because while Pauahi was present at the conception of the schools (the writing of the will), she was not present at the birth (the opening). Charles oversaw the writing of the first prospectus of the school, and he directed all matters in opening and implementing the schools. No metaphoric Kānaka midwives were present. Instead, the board of trustees were all white, male, missionaries, and businessmen, and all the school's principals were haole.

80. Kanahele, *Pauahi*, 55.

81. Black and Mellen, *Princess Pauahi Bishop and Her Legacy.* Similarly, the elementary-level biography on C. R. Bishop's life, *Heart of a Hero*, includes a chapter titled "Marriage Made in Heaven," which concludes: "Mr. and Mrs. Bishop were married for over thirty-four years. They loved each other deeply. No one can truly describe the depth of that love. 'Galuteria, *Heart of a Hero: Charles Reed Bishop*, 65.

82. Black and Mellen, 62.

83. Lilikalā Kameʻeleihiwa, *Native Land and Foreign Desires: Pehea La E Pono Ai?*; Samuel Manaiakalani Kamakau, *Ruling Chiefs of Hawaii*; Merry, *Colonizing Hawaiʻi.*

84. Kanahele interprets Pauahi's desire to marry Charles as a breakage with Hawaiian tradition because it challenged the familial authority of her biological and hānai parents. Kanahele, *Pauahi*, 67. While Kanahele asserts that racial prejudice was a likely, yet implicit, factor in her family's opposition to the marriage, there is no evidentiary basis to support such a claim. Instead what seems more plausible given the cultural and historical context is that Pauahi's ʻohana (extended family) was concerned that she, who bore a genealogical kuleana (responsibility) to possibly rule the Kingdom, would marry and have children with someone who had no chiefly rank or genealogical mana. In her review of Kanahele's book, Linda Menton critiques Kanahele for making statements and inferences about Pauahi's motivations, thoughts, and character that are "simply not supportable in a scholarly sense, even with the writer's knowledge of Hawaiian culture and its [nineteenth] century world view." Furthermore, she writes that while Kanahele's portrait of the princess is one who solidly maintained her Hawaiian roots and identity while moving in haole society without apparent conflict, we cannot be sure that she was as free from conflicts as she appeared. See Linda K. Menton, "Review of *Pauahi: The Kamehameha Legacy*," 177–179.

85. Pauahi's mākua (parents) used their influential positions in attempts to block the marriage, but these efforts were ultimately unsuccessful. Pākī asked Reverend Richard Armstrong to promise not to perform the ceremony, but he would not agree. Pākī and Konia appealed to Cabinet Minister Robert Wylie for intervention. Wylie called a meeting with Armstrong, Kekūanāoʻa, and Pākī. In his professional capacity as head of public instruction, Armstrong bore responsibility for students' well-being, including Pauahi. Later, when Charles Bishop went to apply for the marriage license, the clerk refused to grant it unless he had Pākī's consent. See Mary H. Krout, *The Memoirs of Hon. Bernice Pauahi Bishop*, 100; Black and Mellen, *Princess Pauahi Bishop and Her Legacy*, 60–63.

86. Bishop's inquiries and expressions of interest in courting and marrying Pauahi were made toward the Cookes rather than to Pauahi's parents and extended ʻohana. For example, early conversations and the written proposal of marriage were addressed to the Cookes, not to Pākī and Konia. (Kanahele, *Pauahi*, 65.) Understandably, any parent would be angered by this lack of

respect and courtesy. After Pauahi visited her father and he offered their home as venue for the marriage ceremony, there was some disagreement about the date and location of the ceremony. The home was still in construction, but C. R. Bishop pushed a particular date, at which point the home had not yet been completed. The wedding was then planned for the Cookes' place, and Mr. Cooke took it upon himself to "invite" Pauahi's parents. One can imagine a parent's ire at being denied the opportunity to host their child's wedding and then being invited by someone else. Amos Cooke writes that when Pākī came over to voice his displeasure and to find out why the Cookes had "helped their daughter against them," Cooke "drew up [his] artillery." (Cooke's May 30, 1850, correspondence, quoted in Kanahele, 72). At that point, Pākī and Konia communicated that they would not attend the wedding and that Pauahi would have to rely on the Cookes for all her pono (the necessities for survival).

87. Jonathan Kamakawiwo'ole Osorio, *Dismembering Lahui: A History of the Hawaiian Nation to 1887*; Merry, *Colonizing Hawai'i*.

88. Julie Kaomea-Thirugnanam, *Women of Kamehameha: A Collection of Oral Histories Commemorating the 100th Anniversary of the Founding of the Kamehameha School for Girls*.

89. The spelling and translation of the name of this home varies. Kanahele spells it *Hale'ākala*, translated as "pink house." DeSilva spells it as *Haleakalā*, "house of the sun." When I am not quoting a particular author's usage, I spell it as *Haleakala*, without diacritical markings, to allow for both possible interpretations.

90. Pauahi's father, Pākī, denied her the home when she decided to marry Bishop instead. Later, when Pauahi reconciled with her parents, Pākī left the home to her. Pauahi and Charles moved into Haleakala with Konia and Lili'uokalani, Pauahi's mother and hānai sister, shortly after Pākī's death.

91. It is worth noting that KS-authorized biographies of Pauahi are the only published biographies of Pauahi that exist: Kanahele, *Pauahi*; Black and Mellen, *Princess Pauahi Bishop and Her Legacy*; Krout, *The Memoirs of Hon. Bernice Pauahi Bishop*.

92. Black and Mellen, *Princess Pauahi Bishop and Her Legacy*, 65; Krout, *The Memoirs of Hon. Bernice Pauahi Bishop*, 115–116.

93. Kanahele, *Pauahi*, 117–118.

94. For example, in the memoirs Mr. Bishop commissioned to be written about his wife posthumously, Krout writes that Pauahi's maintenance of some of the "picturesque Hawaiian customs" added to "the charm and novelty of her entertainments," "in the eyes of the stranger." Krout, *The Memoirs of Hon. Bernice Pauahi Bishop*, 116.

95. Quoting from the Hawaiian Civil Code, Title 5, "Of Laws Affecting the Domestic Relations," Chapter XXVIII, Article LIII, Section 1287: "The wife, whether married in pursuance of this article or heretofore, or whether validly married in this Kingdom or in some other country, and residing in this, shall be deemed for all civil purposes, to be merged in her husband, and civilly dead. She shall not, without his consent, unless otherwise stipulated by anterior contract, have legal power to make contracts, or to alienate and dispose of property, except as hereinafter provided. She shall not be civilly responsible in any court of justice, without joining her husband in the suit, and she shall in no case be liable to imprisonment in a civil action. The husband shall be personally responsible in damages, for all the tortuous acts of his wife; for assaults, for slanders, for libels, and for consequential injuries done by her to any person or persons in this Kingdom." See Hawaiian Kingdom, "Civil Code of the Hawaiian Islands. Title 5, Of Laws Affecting the Domestic Relations."

96. In nineteenth-century Britain and America the institution of marriage made upper- and middle-class women, who might have been economically independent otherwise, dependent on men.

97. Bishop, "Last Will and Codicils of the Late Hon. Mrs. Bernice P. Bishop," 17.

98. The quoted phrases begin the song "Pauahi Ke Aliʻi," sung every year by the girls of Kamehameha at Founder's Day.

99. He relocated to the beautiful, recently built home of Ruth Keʻelikolani, called Keoua Hale and described as a "palace."

100. Allen, *The Betrayal of Liliuokalani*, 295.

101. Kent, *Charles Reed Bishop, Man of Hawaii*, 84.

102. Krout, *The Memoirs of Hon. Bernice Pauahi Bishop*, 102.

103. Kent, *Charles Reed Bishop, Man of Hawaii*, 35.

104. Pukui, Haertig, and Lee, *Nānā I Ke Kumu* (*Look to the Source*), vol. 2, 16.

105. At the time of Kent's 1965 biography of C. R. Bishop, the table was in California in the possession of Bishop's great grandniece.

3 Indian Education under Jim Crow

Brian Klopotek

In the United States South, Indian educational history has generally veered far from the familiar stories of federal boarding schools.[1] Particularly in the late nineteenth and early twentieth century, when many thousands of Indian children in the West and Midwest were attending federal boarding schools,[2] the central problems that most Indians in the South confronted were local racial segregation policies and federal neglect. The denial of federal services to Indians of officially unrecognized tribes when they sought education—and their simultaneous exclusion from local white schools for being Indian—frustrated tribal efforts and pressured groups to accept a strictly racial identity that would strip them of their political, legal, and cultural status as indigenous peoples. As a result of this problem and of the inferior economic and educational opportunities available to people classified as "colored," tribal political activities, racial identities, and ethnic identities in the Jim Crow South became tightly intertwined with asserting distance from blackness, most prominently through refusals to attend black schools and other demonstrations of anti-black racism.

Educational access issues served as a critical arena for the implementation of white supremacist policies on both the federal and local level, and educational policy therefore became, as it has been in so many times and places, a central venue for the assertion and contestation of Indian political and legal rights. Despite considerable variation in policy and practice, broad tendencies toward assimilationism, dispossession, and racial domination characterized both federal and Southern education for Indians, shifting our attention beyond the inconsistency of policy and toward the consistent ideology that informed these multiple practices. Viewing segregation policy and federal Indian policy together makes their shared ideological investment in white supremacy visible in new ways, and makes Southern Indian educational history a critical site for scholarly evaluation.

Two unique circumstances contribute to the distinct character of Indian educational history in the South during what came to be known as the boarding school era for Indians elsewhere. First, there were not supposed to be any more tribes in the South after the Removal Era of the 1830s and 1840s, when the federal government forced the remaining large Indian nations of the South (Cherokee, Choctaw, Chickasaw, Creek, and Seminole) to trade their homelands for land west of the Mississippi River.[3] Treaty language supposedly allowed for some nonremoved Indian individuals to remain in their homelands, but as regular US citizens without the protections of tribal sovereignty. Thousands of their descendants remain in the South today, many continuing to live tribally. Other tribes such as the Catawbas, Lumbees, Tunicas, Houmas, Chitimachas, Coushattas, Pamunkeys, and Mattaponis remained in the region despite government intentions to clear Indian tribes out of the South. The federal government either did not know or did not care that these tribes remained because they held too little land of value. With a few sporadic exceptions, the federal government did not extend the protections of tribal sovereignty to remaining Southern tribes. Only the Cherokees had consistent federal recognition throughout the boarding school era, having had their status as a tribe affirmed by the federal government in 1868 and continuously thereafter. The others have had to deal with federal nonrecognition at various points in their history, some into the present day.[4] Both Removal policy and the closely related federal nonrecognition of tribal sovereignty in the South are white supremacist practices that have heavily influenced the direction of Indian education in the region.

Second, racial segregation—though it existed in many ways both de facto and de jure throughout the United States—was notoriously rigidly enforced in the South. Its intent was not merely to separate blacks and whites, of course, but to enforce a system of racial privilege for whites and oppression for people classified as "colored." The South also had a much higher black population than the rest of the country, averaging 32 percent black in 1900, for example, when no other region of the country averaged more than 3 percent black.[5] Moreover, the black population of the South is far more rural than in any other area, so significant black populations live near most Southern Indian tribal communities, in contrast with most tribes in the West and Midwest in this era. While blacks have always been a part of the racial formation process[6] in the US even in areas with a low black population, black-white relations in the South unequivocally dominated the racial discourse in the Jim Crow era. That Indians were generally an afterthought by the twentieth century led to significant local variation in the application of segregation policy, though a core ideology of white supremacy was always present.

Indians in the United States have long had an ambiguous position in the racial hierarchy: in many times and places in the South, white officials classified Indians as "colored," especially, but not solely, when they had African ancestry of any amount in their community, while in other times and places, Indians were classified as "white," since "colored" came to be synonymous with "black." It is commonly said that Indians had a status somewhere "between" black and white, but—without undermining the *general* truth of this statement on a strictly *racial* basis—it would be more accurate to say that Indian status was *distinct* from black and white, because the colonial relationship (with attacks on tribal land, sovereignty, and culture) was always an additional factor in the equation for Indian tribes and it has not always been clear that Indian racial status was "above" that of blacks.[7] Nonetheless, the impact was that while whites often tried to categorize Indians as colored, with all the liabilities that went along with such a classification up to and including exclusion from white schools, Indians continually resisted such efforts.

To scholars of Southern Indian history in this time period, the central place of school segregation and racial negotiation in tribal histories is well known, but this history has not yet been woven into the broader narrative of indigenous educational history in the United States. The lack of attention to the issue outside of Southern Indian studies may derive from a casual assumption that segregation was "really" about blacks, or from the relegation of twentieth-century Southern Indian history to the periphery of Native American studies in general, but the history of tribes living under Jim Crow laws introduces the need and possibility for more rigorous scrutiny of Indian involvement in a racial system that always reaches beyond Indian-white or indigenous-colonizer dyads. Indeed it may force us to change how we think about indigenous educational histories altogether.

Contemporary racial theory in ethnic studies, American studies, and related fields has generally not accounted for the unique nature of indigeneity and the indigenous-colonizer relationship in the United States, contributing in some ways to the obfuscation of indigenous issues in the United States. In this light, it is understandable that scholars in Native American studies have struggled to find contemporary racial theory relevant to their own work. Unfortunately, however, as scholars in Native American studies have tried to focus attention on the distinctive features of indigenous status in comparison to other racialized groups, we have typically glossed over experiences shared—or at least bearing a family resemblance—with other racialized groups or the complicated issues of conflict among aggrieved groups. Moreover, we have missed opportunities to discuss the central role of colonialism in the development of historical racial formation processes and white supremacist ideology, knowledge that might lead to better inclusion of indigenous issues in contemporary racial analyses.

As a general prescriptive, simply adding indigenous status to the list of intersecting sociopolitical categories that must be accounted for in ethnic studies scholarship would go a long way toward developing common analytical ground.[8] Indeed, bringing the indigenous-colonizer relationship more consistently into ethnic/American studies also unsettles a frustrating tendency within those fields to see colonialism and/or imperialism as a relationship that the United States imposes only outside its present boundaries, rather than a process that created every square inch of its present boundaries and informs race relations for every other group.[9] But this simple adjustment is only a starting point.

In the US context (and indeed, in much of the world[10]), both racial domination and colonial domination have traditionally been centered in an ideology of white supremacy—an ideology in which white people and their ancestors are understood to be morally, intellectually, politically, and spiritually superior to nonwhites, and therefore entitled to various forms of privilege, power, and property.[11] The same patterns have been repeated in numerous contexts globally to such an extent that both racism and colonialism need to be envisioned as two sets of behaviors or practices resulting from the same basic—and these days often sublimated or unconscious [12]—belief in white superiority and entitlement. Once the connection between these two practices is established, it becomes easier to see the ways white supremacist ideology reverberates and reiterates itself through communities of color and indigenous groups, performing multiple tasks, diverting multiple resources away from oppressed groups and toward whites through multiple kinds of behavior.[13]

Jena Choctaws under Jim Crow and Outside the Federal Purview

The Jena Band of Choctaws are a small tribe, with about 250 members in 2010, and they have been federally acknowledged as a tribe since 1995, but they spent much of the twentieth century struggling to establish their rights as an Indian tribe, distinct from both blacks and whites. As such, they serve as a useful example of the intersecting strands of white supremacist ideology in federal Indian policy and Jim Crow segregation policy.

In the early twentieth century, the tribal population was small, typically hovering around thirty individuals in four families, comprised almost entirely of full bloods, most of whom spoke only Choctaw.[14] The community seems to have been established outside the town of Jena, Louisiana, shortly after the American Civil War.[15] They were somewhat isolated from other Choctaw communities in Mississippi and Oklahoma, but maintained social and political connections with Indians from several other central Louisiana Indian communities.

The tribe made their living in the early part of the twentieth century by performing wage labor, selling baskets, taking in laundry, tanning hides, and—increasingly—by sharecropping, since they possessed no land. When prices for cotton dropped dramatically in the mid-1930s, tenant farming became less viable as a means of support.[16] At that point, the Jena Choctaws entered into wage labor where it was available, working in the timber industry or moving to towns where jobs were slightly more plentiful. The local white power structure circumscribed the opportunities available to them, so their choices were quite limited through the first half of the twentieth century. A Jena Choctaw elder, recalling the ways local whites enforced the boundaries of white privilege in the 1930s, illustrates the denigrations tribal members endured. "They said to me, Indians don't need land. You don't need to buy land. They would not loan me the money. Then they said, Indians don't need education—they got work!"[17] This was not "unconscious" racism—local whites actively and forcefully prevented Jena Choctaw access to economic and educational resources available to white citizens.

Jena Choctaw racial status as nonwhites kept them locked economically and socially into the bottom rungs of the surrounding white supremacist society. They were not allowed to enroll in white schools locally, and they were barred from access to a variety of other economic opportunities. Jena Choctaw chief Bill Lewis was the first to actively pursue formal, Anglo-style education for his people in the late 1920s. He likely saw it as a way to open new opportunities for Choctaws, concerned about the limits that declining English language proficiency and illiteracy placed on them.[18] In 1929, he approached LaSalle Parish Superintendent E. E. Richardson about providing education for Choctaw children. Richardson hired the assistant principal of the Jena high school, Jay Pipes, to teach twenty-four lessons to Choctaw children at a local church, using money from the newly established literacy campaign in Louisiana.[19] Typically, state literacy funds were designated for the education of illiterate adults, but parish officials saw it as a reasonable solution to the problem of where to place the ten school-aged Choctaw children in a system designed for segregation only in black and white. After the initial twenty-four lessons, however, the white church where the classes were taught decided not to allow them to be held there anymore, leaving the Jena Choctaws without educational opportunities for the next several years.[20]

There was an effort underway to acquire federal funds for education of other Indians in Louisiana as early as 1931. Responding to an inquiry from US Representative René Louis DeRouen, the Office of Indian Affairs sent Special Commissioner Roy Nash to investigate the status of Indians in Louisiana. Nash's report began with a survey of the Coushatta tribe in DeRouen's district in southwest Louisiana, concluding that they should not receive aid because to do so would "brand as paupers one of the few groups of Indians who, unaided, have won full citizenship and equality."[21] The Coushattas, he noted, had a separate elementary school in their community, but attended high school with whites in Elton, where, "far from discriminating against them, the schools of Elton regard the Indians as favorites because of their athletic prowess."[22] Moreover, he said, the Coushattas were no poorer than their white and "colored" neighbors, and their situation certainly compared favorably to the state's three thousand Houma Indians, "whose plight is infinitely more pathetic."[23] Local whites in Terrebonne Parish had barred the Houmas from attending white schools because some of the tribe had African ancestry, and the Houmas, like every other Indian group in the state, would not attend black schools. Nash thought the Terrebonne Parish school board seemed amenable to opening a school strictly for Houmas the following year, a contrivance that prompted him to comment, "One can only pity a state where three sets of public schools are required to educate American citizens."[24] In fact, Terrebonne Parish refused to establish separate schools for Indians, but neighboring LaFourche Parish treated Indians as whites, and operated two elementary schools serving Indian children living in Terrebonne Parish, indicating the ambiguous and even fickle nature of racial classification of Indians in Louisiana.[25]

Nash concluded from his brief visit with the Coushattas and Houmas that the Indian communities of Louisiana were "too scattered" to make it feasible for the federal government to provide school facilities for them. He was aware that there were "a few Tunica Indians about Marksville," and listed some other parishes with Indian populations, but he was entirely unaware of the Choctaw community near Jena or any other group north of Cajun country. Moreover, he never suggested the possibility of federal contracts with Louisiana school districts to pay for separate Indian education. The federal government set the matter aside.[26]

State Superintendent of Education T. H. Harris, who had met with

Nash in 1931, pressed further for funding for Louisiana Indian education in February 1932. He was rebuffed by Secretary of Interior Ray Lyman Wilbur, an avowed assimilationist who argued that bringing Louisiana Indians into federal programs would run counter to the federal government's goal of eventually forcing Indians to survive in American society without federal protections.[27] The idea of separate Indian education implied by federal policy in other places meshed well with Southern ideas about white supremacy and educational segregation, but the federal government sought to establish and maintain white power over tribes in a different way—through coercive assimilation and the erasure of tribal polities within its borders rather than the kinds of segregation typically associated with Jim Crow laws. Federal officials considered political erasure an accomplished fact for Louisiana Indians, so federal involvement seemed gratuitous by 1931. Nonetheless communication between the Louisiana Department of Education and the Office of Indian Affairs would continue throughout the decade with more success for tribes in later years.

Mattie Penick, a white school teacher who had been forced to resign her position under Louisiana law after she was married, was likely behind Harris's inquiries in 1932.[28] She became interested in educating Jena Choctaw children, she said, after seeing two of them that summer, "look[ing] mournfully at the white people in the swimming pool."[29] She learned that they spoke no English and were not allowed to enroll in white schools, and, according to a 1938 newspaper article, "she thought suddenly she could help them and help herself by going back to teaching—there were no bars against a married woman teaching Indians."[30] She contacted Senator Huey Long to find out whether the Jena Choctaws might be eligible for a government-funded day school. Long contacted Indian Affairs Commissioner C. J. Rhoads, who replied that only groups with a previous relationship with the federal government were eligible for such schools, not "scattered groups of Indians who have never been under the jurisdiction of the federal government" such as the Jena Choctaws.[31] Their status as nonfederal Indians meant not only that they suffered the effects of segregation because they were Indians, but also they were doubly excluded, ironically being denied educational opportunities available to other Indians because they were not federally recognized as a tribe in 1932.

While efforts to secure federal funds failed that year, Penick found other resources to provide education to the Jena Choctaws. She convinced a local lumber company to pay for supplies to build a one-room school house for the Jena Choctaws and enlisted LaSalle Parish Schools Superintendent E. E. Richardson in her cause. Richardson found money still available from the state literacy campaign to pay for supplies and a salary for Penick.[32]

Students from ages five to eighteen were enrolled in the school the first year, and all of them worked with the same reading materials. A representative of the State Department of Education who visited the school in 1933 suggested that "only two or three knew any of the English language" when they began in the fall, but that they had now completed a primer and were all working on first grade English reading materials.[33] Unfortunately, the literacy program funds upon which the school relied for this anemic curriculum derived from the state malt tax, which evaporated following the end of prohibition in 1933.[34] With its principal source of support gone, the school closed, and Penick and Superintendent Richardson resumed requests for support from the federal government.

Richardson's initial efforts for federal funding were as unsuccessful as those of Penick and State Superintendent T. H. Harris. In May 1932, Richardson wrote US Senator John Overton requesting federal educational funds for the Jena Choctaws. "There are about fifteen full-blood Choctaw Indian children in this Parish growing up almost totally illiterate," he wrote. "They will not, and should not, attend our negro schools, and they are too far behind in their studies (most of them cannot even read) to attend the white schools, *embarrassment alone preventing....* Anything you might get done for these Indians will be highly valued by the citizens of the Parish."[35]

Setting aside for a moment the issue of federal support for the Jena Choctaws, several issues jump out from the superintendent's letter. One of the most obvious deductions from the letter is that blacks and Indians were categorically distinct. Indians in Louisiana, while certainly not treated as the equals of whites, were far enough from black that the white superintendent was willing to advocate for funds to be disbursed on their behalf and suggested that it would be inappropriate for them to attend black schools. In Jim Crow Louisiana in the 1930s, even full-blooded, non-English-speaking Indians were becoming nearly "white" enough to attend white schools. Indians began attending white schools in Jena by the end of World War II, long before most LaSalle Parish whites would educate their children alongside black children, indicating again the prevalence of the graded distinction between the social, economic, and political positions of the races. In fact, in areas only a slight distance from clustered Indian populations, individual Indian children were often allowed to enroll in white schools, as was the case for one Jena Choctaw student in this era who was half white.[36]

While the Choctaws themselves clearly remember being barred from white schools in Jena at this time and other documentary evidence supports their memory, the superintendent's letter implies that they stayed away from white schools by choice, that it was only their embarrassment over lack of adequate preparation and English language proficiency that kept them away from white schools.[37] Richardson lied about the school board's willingness to enroll Choctaw students in white schools. That Richardson expended any effort on behalf of the Choctaws indicates that there was some interest in obtaining educational facilities for the Choctaws, but this interest stemmed from a belief that a white education might make the Choctaws less of a "liability in the community," as Richardson's successor would characterize them, rather than from a belief in racial equality between Choctaws and whites.[38] Parish officials and newspapers displayed similar enthusiasm for rudimentary education for blacks under segregation, but just as such sentiment could hardly be interpreted as belief in racial equality between blacks and whites, so we should be careful about what meaning we make of white efforts to educate Jena Choctaws.[39] Richardson's closing statement that "anything you might get done for these Indians will be highly valued by the citizens of the Parish" suggests he and the white LaSalle Parish citizens considered the Choctaws a bewildering public burden, since they did not neatly fit into the system of racial oppression that provided facilities for only two races.[40] Richardson hoped that federal funds could be used to "uplift" Jena Choctaws, since local whites would not approve of expenditures on behalf of such a project.[41] He probably concealed local discrimination against the Choctaws to make the request for separate school funding more palatable to federal officials. By appearing to have made every effort to induce the Choctaws to attend available local schools, he could give the impression that Choctaw reticence—rather than the segregated school system—was to blame for their situation. Thus the parish could preserve white privilege under segregation and at the same time relieve themselves of the obligation to pay for the education of Indian citizens.

Because of the continued segregation of Choctaw students from white students, efforts to find federal funding were underway even before the school closed in 1933. Funding was discussed again at a March 1933 meeting in Baton Rouge between the Office of Indian Affairs (OIA) and Louisiana state education officials. Samuel H. Thompson, supervisor of Indian education in charge of public school relations for the Office of Indian Affairs, misidentified the Choctaw school run by Penick as "the Cherokee Indian School" in his report on this meeting, and seemed skeptical that the school would merit federal Indian education funds. Since the Louisiana State Department of Education had no firsthand information on the school, Assistant State Supervisor of Elementary Education Helene Sliffe was sent to investigate its status. While Sliffe's report on the school's activities glowed, no funding was forthcoming at that time.[42]

In the early 1930s, the OIA had begun trying to shift away from the off-reservation boarding school model and toward a progressive education model, in which schools reflected and supported the needs of the communities they served.[43] This policy shift had contradictory effects for Jena Choctaws. While it made it more likely that the OIA would eventually fund a local school for them, it made it less likely that the boarding school option would ever be available to them. Of course, it is foolish to suggest that boarding school education set students up for success on any terms, but Brenda Child has documented the ways some Indian families viewed boarding schools as a resource to be used in hard times to prevent greater hardships,[44] and Tsianina Lomawaima has observed that experiences at boarding schools could foster pan-Indian and even tribal identity in students.[45] For better or worse, the option was never available to the Jena Choctaws. At least federal nonrecognition allowed the Jena Choctaws to avoid the more easily identifiable physical, emotional, and cultural assault typically associated with education in a federal boarding school. When coupled with other internal and external mechanisms identified by Marilyn Watt as contributing to their enclavement, it is likely that ineligibility for boarding school enrollment left them more socially and culturally intact than they might have been if they had been sent to federal boarding schools.[46] Though their culture and language were protected for another generation, they had to sacrifice the broader economic opportunities that might have accompanied education, even in a federal boarding school. Still, the assimilative impact of the federal educational apparatus in the early twentieth century should not be overlooked, making federal nonrecognition somewhat of a blessing in disguise.

Of course, local schools would certainly not provide a curriculum that honored Choctaw culture and history either, but arguments about the values and culture reflected in the curriculum were moot for the Jena Choctaws in the 1930s. Looking back from the twenty-first century, they would have certainly chosen an education that reflected Choctaw history, language, and culture, but at the time they simply sought a form of education that might help them move out from under the thumb of the Whatleys and other whites in the area. They could learn Choctaw culture and values at home. What they felt they needed most desperately was an opportunity to learn to read and write in English. In that regard, a federally funded Indian community day school represented the best opportunity for them, given their circumstances.

The Penick Indian School, as it came to be called, had closed for the 1933–34 school year, but the passage of the Johnson-O'Malley Act removed funding obstacles that had impeded federal assistance previously.[47] The school planned to reopen in the fall of 1934 after Louisiana official M. S. Robertson interceded and convinced Carson Ryan to fund the school.[48] A. C. Hector, superintendent of the Choctaw Indian Agency in Mississippi, was not pleased with the arrangement agreed to by Ryan. Hector suggested that rather than funding a school for them, they "be offered an opportunity to remove to some of our Mississippi schools, otherwise, I do not believe I would be justified in recommending much in the way of assistance for such a small group who have for years been separated from any other Indians."[49] He later comments that "if we start taking care of other little groups in the State I am afraid the Department will be called on to keep it up indefinitely."[50]

At the time, the Bureau and Hector had never had any direct contact with the Jena Band, and Hector in particular wanted to make sure they were not mixed with blacks, as some of the other Indians in the state were rumored to be.[51] Hector's attitude toward tribes with African ancestry indicates a critical way in which anti-black racism among tribes was encouraged at the federal level: mixing with blacks would virtually guarantee federal nonrecognition, and thus, lack of federal services and protections. Moreover, since part of what tribes sought in this context was distinction from blacks, federal definitional authority mattered a great deal, as well. Nonetheless, based on the reports of those in contact with the Jena Band, Hector believed that they were a distinct group of nearly full-blooded Choctaws, since he proposed that they might be moved to Mississippi to take advantage of resources available to other Choctaws there.[52]

By 1935, the Penick Indian School began receiving federal funds for Indian students, and funding was renewed every year thereafter until 1938.[53] Funding provided for facilities, materials, the teacher's salary, transportation, and free lunch for the students. Academic curriculum at the Penick Indian School seemed to consist largely of learning to read and write in English, though progress in this area received mixed reviews from federal officials. Though there does not seem to be any evidence that Penick had been informed about federal Indian school curriculum or new recommendations for Indian education, she followed the federal pattern of making the students responsible for a large part of the upkeep of the tiny school, using it as a "model living environment." Students not only constructed some of the school's furniture, but they also cooked the lunch for the other students and chopped the wood for the stove.[54] Penick devoted a considerable amount of class time to making crafts, such as baskets and beadwork items, and to what might be called practical skills, such as sewing and woodworking.[55]

The school was closed in 1938 when the OIA deemed it a waste of money based on low attendance and minimal accomplishments of the pupils under Penick's guidance.[56] Willard W. Beatty, Director of Indian Education by that time, visited the school that year and it was at his suggestion that funding was cut off. He endorsed A. C. Hector's earlier suggestion that the group be moved to Mississippi to attend school there, and said that the several Jena families with whom he had talked about the matter were "entirely willing to make the move."[57] But L. W. Page, A. C. Hector's successor as superintendent of the Choctaw Indian Agency in Mississippi, responded with clear frustration to the suggestion that the Jena Choctaws be given housing in Mississippi, stating that "to date we have taken no action looking toward the transfer of these families for the reason that we have not, as stated in my former communication, sufficient homes to accommodate Indians already living in the Mississippi area who have made application for places."[58] He notes that he had hoped accommodations could be made with the Jena public schools for the education of the Choctaw children, but failing that, he saw it as no great misfortune if the Jena Choctaws went without any schooling at all that year. A replacement teacher could have been found if the federal government wanted to maintain recognition of the Jena Choctaws, but decisions were being made at the federal level that would prevent any further educational funding for the tribe.

In 1940, M. S. Robertson continued his earlier efforts to secure federal funding for the education of the Jena Choctaws, who had been without a school for a year and a half. He located two new teachers for the Penick School and hoped the federal government would pay their salaries. The new superintendent of the Choctaw Indian Agency, Harvey Meyer, recommended that funding be renewed, but he was rebuffed by Paul Fickinger, Associate Director of Education for the OIA. "We have given considerable study to this entire matter and...we had a conference about the whole Louisiana group. With the possible exception of the Chittimanchi and Coushatta Indians [who each had land in federal trust status] it is the general feeling that there is little responsibility accruing to the Federal government for these groups.... It seems to us that our responsibility in the matter lies more in the line of insisting that the state assume its obligation for the education of these children, than for us to step in and finance such a program. These groups of people are to all intents and purposes in the same status as whites, negroes, and other groups in Louisiana, and the justification for paying tuition for them does not exist. After all, they own no land which is outside of tax paying status."[59] Marilyn Watt notes that Jena Choctaws were not "in the same status as white, negroes, and other groups in Louisiana" in that whites and blacks "at least... had schools to attend."[60] While Choctaw refusal to attend black schools contributed to their lack of options, they also seemed to sense that not only their racially inflected self-worth but also their unique political and cultural status as Choctaws would be threatened if they gave an inch on white efforts to classify them racially as "colored."[61] Thus, after a brief interlude, the Jena Band was again left with no resources for their education.

When the Bureau disavowed its responsibility to the Jena Choctaws in 1940, Choctaw Agency Superintendent Harvey Meyer protested. He had recently met with Superintendent Russell of LaSalle Parish schools, who informed him that he had no intention whatsoever of providing a separate school for the Choctaws, and that they would not be allowed into white schools. The Parish was too poor to begin with, Russell argued, and he saw no way that he could "overcome local prejudice" and convince the school board to spend money on Indians at any rate. The sixteen dollars per pupil that the state had already allocated to the parish for the education of the Choctaw children based solely on their status as "educable" citizens of the state had already been granted to the white and black school budgets. Superintendent Russell justified his position, stating that "local merchants claim the Choctaws of the community steal smaller articles from the stores and that it is generally believed the Indians are a liability in the community and that schooling would not benefit them.... Doubt was expressed about any interest being shown in school work except on account of the lunch being provided."[62] Ironically, local segregationists were jeopardizing federal assimilationist goals drawn from the same ideological well of white supremacy.

Meyer concluded from his visit that "if the Choctaw pupils at Jena are to have any school training, it must be provided from the payment of tuition from Federal funds."[63] Knowing that his decision meant that the Choctaws would go without even an elementary education, Fickinger held firmly to the committee decision that the federal government had no obligation to educate them.[64] There is some merit in the Bureau's insistence that the state take responsibility for the education of its Indian citizens, but it was a feeble sort of logic that left the Jena Choctaws with no education, allowing local whites to continue funneling resources away from them and their children.

Local school boards may have allowed Indians into black schools if they would go, but the Choctaws themselves strictly maintained boundaries between themselves and blacks in an effort to maintain their distinct identity and a simultaneous attempt to access the privileges of the white side of the color line. In some sense, Jena Choctaws simply longed to be treated as people worthy of equality and respect. The experience of being treated otherwise and the misery of ongoing oppression left Southern Indians desperate to move up the racial hierarchy, and, as has happened many times in United States history, people responded to their own subjugation by jockeying for position over other oppressed groups rather than forging alliances.[65] There was never any censure of this sentiment among the Bureau's files, and no suggestion that Choctaw enrollment in black schools was even an option.

Jena Choctaws maintained a strong prejudice against blacks in these years as a result of their own precarious racial situation in a white supremacist state and nation, and educational segregation was only part of the picture. When Jena Choctaws began marrying out extensively in the 1950s because of the lack of unrelated potential Choctaw spouses in the area and the increasing acceptance of Choctaws by local whites, they only married whites. Marriage of Indians with blacks was, in fact, made illegal under state law in 1920, while marriage of Indians with whites was legal.[66] Their ambiguous racial status also meant that Jena Choctaws were segregated for many years but integrated into white schools more than twenty years before blacks. That Jena Choctaws also maintained strict self-segregation from blacks helped them integrate with whites sooner; where there was any hint of African ancestry, whites were more reluctant to accept Indians into their schools or to intermarry. Like other Indian groups in the South whose children were refused entry into white schools, Jena Choctaws pursued separate schools for Indian children.[67] In these actions, Southern tribes were complicit in the segregation and subjugation of blacks, even if on some level they were simply pushing for respect and opportunity for themselves under the same racial regime. But while it helped them avoid some of the indignities whites in Louisiana heaped on African Americans and perhaps added some thin psychological comfort, it also meant that Choctaws were participating in and benefitting from the oppression of African Americans, even if it was in a different way than their white neighbors. Their prejudice against blacks cost them in some ways, because for many years it meant that they went without education while blacks had their own schools, terribly funded as they were. Still, Jena Choctaws affirmed the racial logic of white supremacy when they refused to attend school with blacks, supporting the idea of a color line in general, as long as they were on the right side of it.

What has not been obvious in histories of Indians refusing to attend black schools is that in their embrace of anti-black stereotypes, they also unknowingly assumed positive stereotypes about whites, since every negative stereotype about people of color and indigenous groups contains a corresponding positive stereotype about whites—what might be called a shadow stereotype. For example, negative stereotypes that constructed blacks as inherently suited to labor, immoral, and unworthy of full protection before the law contained a shadow stereotype that whites, as the unspoken norm, must be inherently intellectual, moral, and entitled to full protection before the law. The idea behind *Indian* anti-black racism was that it would extend the positive shadow stereotypes to Indians, making them entitled to the same privileges as whites had, but the implied affirmation of racial thinking more clearly endorsed positive stereotypes about whites. If we start thinking of race as centered around the shadow stereotype—the myth of white people's inherent superiority—rather than around the various supposed shortcomings of people of color and indigenous groups, it becomes a much simpler system to understand. The seemingly "unique" racializations of various racial groups cease to be perplexing as negative stereotypes become permutations of the same basic idea of white supremacy. In that light, it is easier to see that Indians could never attain the positive shadow stereotype. To do so would require them to abandon their racial, cultural, and political identities as Indians in a paradoxically self-defeating act of racism. Moreover, even if they wanted to "become white," as dark-skinned, culturally and linguistically distinct Indians, they could never benefit from racial privilege in the same way that Anglo-Americans could.

Choctaw racism against blacks is fading and shifting as the racial formation process continues to evolve in Louisiana. Overt racism is being replaced, as Jena Choctaws officially support and receive support from local black community leaders in recognition of the commonalities of their distinct struggles as peoples of color in a racist nation. Prejudices now are more subtle and publicly disavowed by Jena Choctaws, remaining in part as a scar and a legacy of more brutally racist days for Indians and African Americans alike. In the 1930s, white supremacist ideology was enacted through multiple means, but Jim Crow policy and federal Indian policy were among the most powerful. Each was structured in such a way as to encourage a fear among Indians of being associated with blacks. Being classified as "colored" threatened to erase the moral, political, cultural, and legal claims of indigenous peoples. Perhaps more powerfully, it undermined people's sense of themselves as worthy human beings. Consciously or not, anti-black racism became a critical component of tribal senses of self. The ambiguity of Indian racial status made small amounts of racial privilege available to the tribe, like a carrot on a stick leading toward further anti-black sentiment. Without recognizing white supremacist ideology as the source of both the experiences of racism Indians shared with blacks and the colonialism that dispossessed tribes of their land and sovereignty, it would be easy to disconnect Indian fate from that of blacks; after all, race is an idea so powerful it can make people disown their own children, so it would hardly be surprising that it would relieve people of a sense of responsibility to an unrelated group. White supremacy twisted Choctaw longing for respect, self-esteem, and opportunity into something oppressive of others and even self-defeating.

Similarly, Jena Choctaw educational history reveals the ubiquity of white supremacist ideology in both federal and local racial projects directed toward Indians.[68] Though not operated by the federal government, the Penick School nonetheless followed many of the same racial and colonial impulses as federal schools, evidence of a common ideology behind each. Penick drew on this ideology as a child, when she "often said to herself, 'When I grow up I'd like to go to Alaska and teach the Eskimos.'"[69] She knew the script from an early age; the racial, cultural, and national superiority of whites was assumed and enacted. The predominantly racial narrative of segregation and the predominantly colonial narrative of assimiliationist education for indigenous people shared the same roots. The white supremacist foundation of the Penick Indian school emerges not just from the racial exclusion of Choctaws from local white schools, but also from the colonial impulse to "uplift" them, and even display them through a series of visits from busloads of "Little Indian Clubs" around the state that Penick had formed.[70] Despite the desire of Jena Choctaws to have access to the opportunities formal education might provide, racial and colonial baggage continually impeded the process. That baggage is difficult to miss in comments made in 1938 by Louisiana education official M. S. Robertson. Though he was one of the most effective advocates for Jena Choctaw education, he nonetheless commented to a reporter that the tribe was "probably living on as low a scale as people ever get to. Shiftless, lazy, without direction or intention. They are interbred, too, I think. They seem to have forgotten all their ancestors ever knew."[71] His statement reveals not just racial derision, but also a particularly colonial mindset as he hints at "scales" of evolution, and a people who simply "forgot" anything beyond where the next meal might come from. Such thinking is slightly distinct from anti-black racism, but again, bears a close familial resemblance. Simultaneously colonially and racially charged, education for Southern Indians was thoroughly soaked in white supremacy, the common denominator in federally operated and locally administered segregated schools.

Though the precise date and reasons for Choctaw integration into local white schools, which had seemed impossible prior to the war, remain elusive, integration during World War II likely resulted from a combination of earlier Choctaw efforts, Choctaw military participation in white units in the war, a compulsory education movement in 1944, and the election of "friendly" whites to the school board in 1945.[72] Whatever the cause, the result was that by 1965, the tribe had its first high school graduates. Elsewhere in Louisiana, Indian integration happened haphazardly. Coushattas had always been integrated into local white schools, as had Choctaw-Apaches. Houmas were integrated with whites in Lafourche Parish since the 1930s, but not in neighboring Terrebonne Parish until the 1960s. Clifton-Choctaws built their own primary school in their community, which was designated as white and provided with white teachers by Rapides Parish, but they were not allowed to attend the white high schools in the parish until 1970. Tunica-Biloxis without black ancestry were integrated into white schools in Avoyelles Parish shortly after World War II, but those with black ancestry went to black schools until blacks were integrated as a whole. Chitimachas sent some students to Carlisle in 1906, had a federally funded elementary school on their reservation as of 1934, and sent some students to Catholic schools off the reservation, but they were not allowed to attend white schools near the reservation until the late

1950s. Beyond Louisiana, there were further variations, with some districts in North Carolina and Virginia having separate schools systems for Indians, whites, and blacks.[73] Every Southern tribe negotiated its identity in relation to both whiteness and blackness within the context of a white supremacist society, and in this process, tribes and individual Indians all too often became complicit in the subjugation of blacks. Local and national racial and colonial projects overlapped and at times conflicted in the South, but never failed to impose the simple idea that whites were superior and therefore entitled to privilege, power, and property.

It is no accident, then, that the Jim Crow era and the boarding school era overlapped. They were both generated by the same ideology, even if one seemed to encourage racial segregation while the other favored racial assimilation. If we look beyond the policies to see the simple idea of white supremacy at the center, we see that the fates of indigenous peoples and racialized minority groups are interconnected in profound ways at many levels, and that supporting any aspect of that ideology undermines tribal well-being. Paying attention to the root ideology as much as the policies used to implement it reminds us that the struggle for tribal well-being has to include battles against all forms of racism, or else the ideology that generates colonialism and racism alike will continue to thrive. Likewise, anti-racist activism must include support for indigenous rights and tribal sovereignty, or again, the root ideology of white supremacy survives. Seeing ideology is difficult by definition, since part of its power lies in the ways it not only attaches to, but generates people's deepest senses of self, making particular kinds of fear, longing, and comfort seem natural, as "common sense." But ideology remains the most powerful weapon deployed against colonized and racialized peoples, because it convinces people to subjugate each other, and even to subjugate themselves.[74]

Looking at Indian racial histories with an eye toward white supremacist ideology offers new conclusions about how race and colonialism have worked in the US context and around the world. When we start to think of indigenous educational histories as part of the story of racial segregation in US education, whether in Alaska (Huhndorf and Huhndorf, this volume), California (Bauer, this volume), or Louisiana, or start thinking of indigenous education as being shaped by global forces as much as by nation-states or local authorities (Goodyear-Ka'ōpua, García, Graham and Palmar Barroso, Castellanos, this volume), we might envision different kinds of alliances, different senses of belonging, different histories, and different futures.[75] If it is the ideology and not solely the policy that is shaping indigenous education, then comfortable assumptions that assimilationist education and its racial projects are safely contained in "the boarding school era" might start becoming less comfortable, and indigenous education may require different kinds of interventions than we have previously imagined.

Notes

1. Portions of this chapter appear in Brian Klopotek, *Recognition Odysseys: Indigeneity, Race, and Federal Tribal Recognition Policy in Three Louisiana Indian Communities* (Durham, NC: Duke University Press, 2011). All rights reserved. Reprinted by permission of the publisher.

2. For a distribution chart of Indian student attendance, see David Wallace Adams, *Education for Extinction: American Indians and the Boarding School Experience, 1875–1928,* 320.

3. Tsianina Lomawaima has argued that Removal policy was Andrew Jackson's attempt to protect the United States against secession of the South thirty years before the Civil War, and that the same racially charged battles over states' rights and federalism that led to the Civil War led Jackson to support this other form of white racial privilege in the South in an earlier era. After the invention of the cotton gin, Southern whites sought new land for the expansion of cotton agriculture and access to tribal land became a more urgent matter. The kinds of thinking that characterized whiteness, Indianness, and blackness in the twentieth century were already tightly intertwined by this time, then, and heavily reliant on notions of civilization and savagery that both Indians and Africans represented to colonial whites. (Lomawaima, personal communication, October 29, 2009.)

4. For a useful overview, see Walter L. Williams, ed., *Southeastern Indians Since the Removal Era.*

5. Campbell Gibson and Kay Jung, "Historical Census Statistics on Population Totals by Race, 1790 to 1990, and by Hispanic Origin, 1970 to 1990, for the United States, Regions, Divisions, and States."

6. Following Omi and Winant's definition of racial formation as "the sociohistorical process by which racial categories are created, inhabited, transformed, and destroyed," and a racial project as "simultaneously an interpretation, representation, or explanation of racial dynamics, and an effort to reorganize and redistribute resources along particular racial lines." See Michael Omi and Howard Winant, *Racial Formation in the United States from the 1960s to the 1990s,* 55–56.

7. In Louisiana, for example, the Chitimacha tribe was given a condemned black school-house to bring to their reservation and use for their school in 1934. See Sara Sue Goldsmith, Risa Mueller, *Nations Within: The Four Sovereign Tribes of Louisiana,* 10–11. At the Hampton Institute, a school founded for black freedmen that had an extensive Indian education program for several decades, there was considerable debate over the relative position of the two groups. See Donal F. Lindsey, *Indians at Hampton Institute, 1877–1923,* esp. 32, 96. Moreover, I generally find little value in "more oppressed than thou" arguments, which tend to undermine legitimate complaints and create resentment instead of sympathy, division instead of unity.

8. Haunani-Kay Trask has been a leader in explicating this relationship. See Haunani-Kay Trask, "Settlers of Color and 'Immigrant' Hegemony: 'Locals' in Hawaii."

9. Ned Blackhawk compellingly argues that violence against Indians cannot be separated from the process of the creation of the United States, from Jamestown forward. "The indigenous body in pain" has to be accounted for as a constant and intentional product of its creation, and therefore of US national character. See Ned Blackhawk, *Violence over the Land: Indians and Empires in the Early American West.* Reginald Horsman has similarly argued that white racial thinking took on its virulent mid-nineteenth-century form as a result of white needs for justification of this violent process through the first half of the 1800s. See Reginald Horsman, *Race and Manifest Destiny: The Origins of American Racial Anglo-Saxonism.*

10. Francis Jennings and James Brooks, among others, have convincingly demonstrated that racial thinking has long roots in the conquest of darker-skinned Others dating to the Crusades, when the logics of Christian-infidel relations and rights of conquest, with closely related ideas about civilization and savagery, justified violent European conquest of the Americas. As Jennings wrote, "When racism later emerged as the dominant principle of European conquest, it grew naturally by easy stages out of feudal religiosity. The overwhelming importance of this fact can be seen in a single glance at the behavior and rationalizations of the Crusaders. Their enemies were also the enemies of the Crusader's god and therefore outside the protection of moral law applicable to that god's devotees. No slaughter was impermissible, no lie dishonorable, no breach of trust shameful, if it advantaged the champions of true religion. In the gradual transition from religious conceptions to racial conceptions, the gulf between persons calling themselves Christian and the other persons, whom they called heathen, translated smoothly into a chasm between whites and coloreds. The law of moral obligation sanctioned behavior on only one side of that chasm." See Francis Jennings, *The Invasion of America: Indians, Colonialism, and the Cant of Conquest*, 5–6. See also James Brooks, *Captives and Cousins: Slavery, Kinship, and Community in the Southwest Borderlands*. In any historical rendering, the colonial encounter of what would become Europeans with what would become Native Americans (North and South), Africans, Pacific Islanders, Australians, and Asians spurred a long process of the global production of white racial identity formation and white supremacist ideology. The United States had its own unique contours that resulted from its internal processes of racial oppression and external processes of territorial conquest, but the ideology of white supremacy thrived far beyond its borders.

11. While typically the term "white supremacy" conjures images of Klan robes and Neo-Nazi skinheads, the term as it is used in contemporary ethnic studies also refers to the everyday ideology of white racial superiority and domination carried even by people who do not consider themselves racist, carried even by people of color. For a general discussion of white racial ideology and material advantages in the United States, see Paula S. Rothenberg, ed., *White Privilege: Essential Readings on the Other Side of Racism*; and George Lipsitz, *The Possessive Investment in Whiteness: How White People Profit from Identity Politics*.

12. On unconscious racism, see Charles R. Lawrence III, "The Id, the Ego, and Equal Protection: Reckoning with Unconscious Racism."

13. On this line of thinking, I closely follow Phil Deloria's thinking and language as he discusses the ways "the stereotype of Indian savagery...worked in a number of different contexts—the 'kill or be killed' hatred of the frontiersman, the scientific racism of the intellectual, the evangelical demand of the missionary, the sympathetic disdain of the reformer, the justified expediency of the politician. The idea of savagery undoubtedly enabled white Americans to exercise multiple kinds of power over multiple kinds of Indians." See Philip J. Deloria, *Indians in Unexpected Places*, 8–9. The stereotype of white superiority does similar work on the opposite end of the racial relationship.

14. I use the term "full blood" here not to endorse blood-quantum politics, but, paired with their language use, to make clear the kinds of racial politics the group might expect to encounter as indigenous nonwhites and nonblacks.

15. Mary Jackson Jones claimed that her mother's family, whose last name was Batise/Baptiste, had been in Louisiana for much longer than other families, but the tribe accepts that most of its ancestors had been in Mississippi prior to the 1870s. See Brian Klopotek, *Recognition Odysseys: Indigeneity, Race, and Federal Tribal Recognition Policy in Three Louisiana Indian Communities*.

16. See Marilyn Watt, "Federal Indian Policy and Tribal Development in Louisiana: The Jena Band of Choctaw," 130–131. Watt also notes that the Jena Choctaws would not likely have

sharecropped if they had been in an area where blacks were the predominant sharecroppers or tenant farmers. LaSalle Parish sharecroppers and tenant farmers were predominantly white, so the Jena Choctaws could enter that line of work without risking identification of themselves with blacks. Watt, 122.

17. See Hiram F. Gregory, "The Jena Band of Louisiana Choctaw," 6.

18. Some of the older group members who had likely come from Mississippi in the 1870s spoke English, while their Louisiana-born children and grandchildren could not. See Office of Federal Acknowledgment, Historical Technical Report, Jena Band of Choctaw Indians, 26.

19. See J. P. Wade, "First School for State Indians Held in LaSalle Parish; History of Tribe Near Jena Is Related." The literacy campaign included blacks and whites throughout the state. See "From School Board Office," *The Weekly News* (Marksville, LA), vol. 26, no. 7, February 16, 1929, 4; "Negroes of Avoyelles Eager to Attend School," *The Weekly News* (Marksville, LA), vol. 26, no. 10, May 16, 1929, 1; "Night School Being Established," *The Weekly News* (Marksville, LA), vol. 26, no. 13, May 10, 1929, 1. In LaSalle Parish, "school officials established schools for both whites and negroes in various parts of the parish. About the time the schools had accomplished their purpose—to a great extent at least, Supt. E. E. Richardson of the LaSalle parish schools found that near Eden several families of Indians resided, none of whom could read nor write. Steps were immediately taken to educate the Indian children insofar as 24 lessons (the number furnished from state funds) would do so." Wade, "First School...."

20. Gregory suggests that the "school" was not permitted to reopen because the all-white church in which the classes were held opposed education of the Choctaws in general, since education might free Choctaws from their subservient status. See Gregory, 6. Mary "Pick" Pipes, the 103-year-old widow of J. L. Pipes, confirmed that whites were opposed to holding Indian school in the white Baptist church, and recalled that whites finally stopped the classes from being held in the Methodist church, too.

21. Roy Nash, "Indians of Louisiana," June 12, 1931, BIA Central Correspondence File 25436–31–150, General Services, Record Group 75, National Archives, 9.

22. Nash, 7.

23. Nash, 9.

24. Nash, 12.

25. See Ann Fischer, "History and Current Status of the Houma Indians," 222.

26. Assistant to the Commissioner of Indian Affairs Fred Daiker accepted Nash's conclusions in August of 1931, when he penned his inspection of the report. "No action is recommended," he stated, "altho[ugh] the Indians are poor, etc. Apparently except to inform ourselves and others who may inquire, there is nothing to do on this report." Handwritten note on "Inspection Report," signed Daiker. See Daiker, "Inspection Report 5–358."

27. See Ray Lyman Wilbur, Secretary of the Interior, Response to T. H. Harris, Louisiana State Superintendent of Education, March 3, 1932, File 68776–1931–800, Part I, Record Group 75, National Archives.

28. Several sources reference the law prohibiting married women from teaching (for example, "Jena Indians Learn What Their Ancestors Forgot," *The Times-Picayune* (New Orleans, LA), vol. 102, no. 69, April 3, 1938, Section 2, 5), but other articles in the *Jena Times* contain reference to married women teaching in public schools by the 1940s, so I am not clear when, how, or where the rule barring married women from teaching was enforced. Mrs. C. W. Flowers, for example, is noted as a schoolteacher in the 1946 article: "Lasall Parish Teachers Seek $400 Pay Raise; Refuse $250," *The Jena Times*, vol. 42, no. 9, August 22, 1946, 1.

29. "Jena Indians Learn...."

30. "Jena Indians Learn...."

31. See C. J. Rhoads to Senator Huey Long, March 3, 1932, File 68776–1931–800, Part I, Record Group 75, National Archives.

32. Mrs. Charles S. Penick to W. Carson Ryan, June 1, 1934, Bureau of Indian Affairs, Central Correspondence File 25436–31–150, General Services, Record Group 75, National Archives. E. E. Richardson, Superintendent, LaSalle Parish School Board, to Senator John Overton, May 10, 1932, File 68776–1931–800, Part I, Record Group 75, National Archives. Watt, 142.

33. Helene Sliffe to T. H. Harris, April 13, 1933, Bureau of Indian Affairs, Central Correspondence File 25436–31–150, General Services, Record Group 75, National Archives. Sliffe also reports that older students found the reading material "too juvenile," and that efforts were underway to find more age-appropriate reading materials. Margaret Connell Szasz notes that this was a common enough problem in Indian education because of the large number of "overage" Indian students who had had no access to education as younger children. Szasz, 1999, *Education and the American Indian: The Road to Self-Determination Since 1928*, 117.

34. Gregory, 7; Watt, 136. Malt tax was levied on malt syrup, a legal substance widely used to make home-brewed beer during prohibition. See Rex Halfpenny, "Michigan Home Brewing During Prohibition."

35. Emphasis mine. E. E. Richardson, Superintendent, LaSalle Parish School Board, to Senator John Overton, May 10, 1932, File 68776–1931–800, Part I, Record Group 75, National Archives.

36. M. S. Robertson reports that a "half-breed Indian girl completed the seventh grade in 1928 in the public schools of Columbia, Louisiana, where she was living at the time." Columbia is thirty-four miles from Jena. See M. S. Robertson, Assistant State Supervisor of Elementary Schools, to W. Carson Ryan, March 28, 1934. Earlier correspondence indicates that a similar situation occurred for a Chitimacha boy, who was allowed to attend the white school in nearby Franklin, Louisiana, but whose tribal status prevented him from attending white schools in Charenton, only ten miles away. A. C. Hector to C. J. Rhoads, December 15, 1932, File 68776–1931–800, Part I, Record Group 75, National Archives. Tunica oral histories indicate that Tunica children who could pass for white were enrolled as whites in east Texas schools. See Klopotek, *Recognition Odysseys*. Houma children similarly enrolled as whites in schools outside of Terrebonne Parish. See Fischer, "History and Current Status of the Houma Indians."

37. State education official M. S. Robertson stated in a New Orleans *Times-Picayune* article in 1938 that "Nobody wanted the Indians when we put up a school for them. The La Salle parish school board refused to let them go to the white schools. They themselves would not go to the negro schools." "Jena Indians Learn What Their Ancestors Forgot," *The Times-Picayune* (New Orleans, LA), vol. 102, no. 69, April 3, 1938, Section 2, 5. Oral corroboration came from multiple personal discussions, as well as the statement, "Indians don't need education—they got work!" in Gregory, 6, discussed in the text of this essay. Watt also cites the case of a Jena Choctaw who left the community in 1927, returning for the first time in 1985. The tribal member cited the exclusion from schools in Jena as the primary reason he left. Watt, 132.

38. J. D. Russell, as reported by Harvey K. Meyer, Superintendent, Choctaw Indian Agency, to Commissioner of Indian Affairs, February 19, 1940, February 23, 1940, File 68776–1931–800, Part I, Record Group 75, National Archives.

39. See, for example, "Briefs from the School Board Office," *The Jena Times*, vol. 43, no. 12, September 11, 1947, 1, which, after citing enrollment numbers for blacks and whites (but not Indians), says, "An intensive drive is being planned to get all children of school age in school."

Similar efforts among both white and black (but not Indian) illiterates are noted in Marksville during the years of the state's illiteracy campaign. See "From School Board Office," *The Weekly News* (Marksville, LA), vol. 26, no. 7, February 16, 1929, 4.

40. E. E. Richardson, Superintendent, LaSalle Parish School Board, to Senator John Overton, May 10, 1932, File 68776–1931–800, Part I, Record Group 75, National Archives.

41. Harvey K. Meyer, Superintendent, Choctaw Indian Agency, to Commissioner of Indian Affairs, February 19, 1940, February 23, 1940, File 68776–1931–800, Part I, Record Group 75, National Archives.

42. Samuel H. Thompson to W. Carson Ryan, Jr., March 27, 1933; Helene Sliffe to T. H. Harris, Louisiana Superintendent of State Education, April 13, 1933, File 25436-31-150. Record Group 75, National Archives. Available in Gregory, 12. The Bureau of Indian Affairs was known as the Office of Indian Affairs prior to 1947.

43. Szasz notes that this shift was at least partially inspired by Mexican rural education models, in which the head of the OIA John Collier asserted in 1932 that the school "exists only incidentally as a school; it is rather the promotion center for a multitude of community activities." See Szasz, 1999 34.

44. Brenda Child, *Boarding School Seasons: American Indian Families, 1900–1940.*

45. Lomawaima, *They Called It Prairie Light,* 129–167.

46. Watt, 233–251. Federal recognition, of course, was no guarantee that any educational opportunities of value would be available to a tribe. The Chitimachas of south Louisiana had been "federally recognized" since 1916 by virtue of having taken 261 acres of land donated to them by a local benefactor taken into trust by the federal government. Nonetheless, the Office of Indian Affairs seems to have forgotten about this relationship over the years, and continuously tried to evade trust responsibilities. See Goldsmith, *Nations Within: The Four Sovereign Tribes of Louisiana.*

47. Samuel H. Thompson to W. Carson Ryan, Jr., March 27, 1933, File 25436-31-150. Record Group 75, National Archives; Fred Daiker, handwritten note on "Inspection Report 5–358," Roy Nash's report on Louisiana Indians (June 12, 1931), August 7, 1931. BIA Central Correspondence File 25436–31–150, General Services, Record Group 75, National Archives.

48. M. S. Robertson, Assistant State Supervisor of Elementary Education, to W. Carson Ryan, Jr., Director of Indian Education, March 28, 1934. W. Carson Ryan, memorandum to Higgins, April 5, 1934, File 68776–1931–800, Part I, Record Group 75, National Archives.

49. A. C. Hector, Superintendent of Choctaw Indian Agency in Mississippi, to John Collier, Commissioner of Indian Affairs, August 10, 1934, File 68776–1931–800, Part I, Record Group 75, National Archives. A. C. Hector to John Collier, July 17, 1935, File 68776–1931–800, Part I, Record Group 75, National Archives.

50. A. C. Hector to W. Carson Ryan, Jr., September 12, 1934, File 68776–1931–800, Part I, Record Group 75, National Archives.

51. A. C. Hector to W. Carson Ryan, Jr., September 12, 1934, File 68776–1931–800, Part I, Record Group 75, National Archives.

52. A. C. Hector to John Collier, July 17, 1935, File 68776–1931–800, Part I, Record Group 75, National Archives.

53. The Office of Indian Affairs indicated that funding would be forthcoming for the school in 1934–1935, but it is not clear whether this funding was ever disbursed. As the Office of Federal Acknowledgment notes in its historical report, although Carson Ryan agreed to fund the school through the Louisiana Department of Education, correspondence with M. S. Robertson and Penick and funding allotment records for the state suggests that funding was never received. Watt (141)

suggests that funding had been disbursed, probably based on the earlier correspondence between Ryan and Robertson, though she cites the correspondence files generally, rather than naming a specific document to support the statement. There is some evidence that federal funding may have been disbursed in some other way, however. The Office of Federal Acknowledgment (OFA) cites a letter written by Penick and dated March 3, 1935, to the Commissioner of Indian Affairs, with the file annotation in its bibliography reading "File ?" The letter notes that a building in the town of Jena was being rented that spring to use for the school. It is not clear what became of the earlier schoolhouse in nearby Searcy. M. S. Robertson wrote to A. C. Hector later that spring with the comment that "it is necessary for us to rent a little building in Jena," phrasing that suggests the building was already being rented. Since the *only* agency that suggested in 1935 that it would fund the school was the BIA, rather than the state or parish boards of education, it seems likely that funds were allocated to the school for this purpose. See Office of Federal Acknowledgment Historical Report, 31, "Source Materials," 18. See also M. S. Robertson to A. C. Hector, May 23, 1935, Central Correspondence File 68776–1931–800, Part 1, Record Group 75, National Archives.

54. Watt, 142–147, citing various newspaper clippings from the papers of Mattie Penick.

55. In fact, students in later years recalled that they spent more time making crafts than doing schoolwork.

56. Willard W. Beatty, Director of Education, Bureau of Indian Affairs, memorandum to William Zimmerman, Assistant Commissioner of Indian Affairs, May 16, 1938, File 68776–1931–800, Part I, Record Group 75, National Archives.

57. Willard W. Beatty, Director of Education, Bureau of Indian Affairs, memorandum to William Zimmerman, Assistant Commissioner of Indian Affairs, May 16, 1938, File 68776–1931–800, Part I, Record Group 75, National Archives.

58. L. W. Page, Superintendent, Choctaw Indian Agency, to John Collier, Commissioner of Indian Affairs, September 8, 1938, File 68776–1931–800, Part I, Record Group 75, National Archives.

59. Paul L. Fickinger, Associate Director of Education, BIA, to Harvey K. Meyer, Superintendent, Choctaw Indian Agency, February 17, 1940, Harvey K. Meyer to Commissioner of Indian Affairs, January 25, 1940, M. S. Robertson, in his new capacity as Director of Education for the Works Progress Administration, to Harvey K. Meyer, January 23, 1940, File 68776–1931–800, Part I, Record Group 75, National Archives. The "we" referred to in Fickinger's statement included Fickinger, William Zimmerman, Joe Jennings, Ruth Underhill, and Willard Beatty. See "Memorandum for the Record," Paul L. Fickinger, March 5, 1940, same file.

60. Watt, 154.

61. For a discussion of a case where tribal members were racially reclassified as "Negro," see Ruth Wallis Herndon and Ella Wilcox Sekatau, "The Right to a Name: The Narragansett People and Rhode Island Officials in the Revolutionary Era," 433–462.

62. Harvey K. Meyer, Superintendent, Choctaw Indian Agency, to Commissioner of Indian Affairs, February 19, 1940, February 23, 1940, File 68776–1931–800, Part I, Record Group 75, National Archives.

63. Harvey K. Meyer, Superintendent, Choctaw Indian Agency, to Commissioner of Indian Affairs, February 19, 1940, February 23, 1940, File 68776–1931–800, Part I, Record Group 75, National Archives.

64. Paul L. Fickinger to Harvey Meyer, April 22, 1940, File 68776–1931–800, Part I, Record Group 75, National Archives. Note the two-month lapse in reply, indicating the priority Jena Choctaws were given at the time.

65. This is consistent with other studies of the nature of racial thinking among lower class whites and others who positioned themselves in opposition to blacks, especially on labor issues, when other modes of alliance-making would have had more material benefits. See, for example, Neil Foley, *The White Scourge: Mexicans, Blacks, and Poor Whites in Texas Cotton Culture*; and David Roediger, *The Wages of Whiteness: Race and the Making of the American Working Class*. Neil Foley draws heavily on Toni Morrison's ideas about southern European immigrants becoming white in the US by demonstrating their hatred of blacks as he grapples with similar racial formation issues in Mexican-American integration activism in Texas in the 1930s. Neil Foley, "Becoming Hispanic: Mexican Americans and Whiteness," 49–59. Eric K. Yamamoto deals with these issues broadly in *Interracial Justice: Conflict and Reconciliation in Post–Civil Rights America*. In other times and places, immigrant communities have been placed in conflict with racialized minorities in the US, and gender, sexuality, and class continue to provide similar fault lines in US sociopolitical relations.

66. Act 220 of 1920, "An act prohibiting marriage between persons of the Indian race and persons of the colored or black race...." In 1932, the Louisiana Attorney General issued an opinion stating that marriage between Indians and whites was not prohibited under the state's anti-miscegenation laws, confirming that Indians could be classified with whites for many purposes. *Opinions Attorney General* (1932–1934), 587.

67. In Louisiana, the Tunica-Biloxis, Clifton-Choctaws, Chitimachas, and Houmas also refused to be placed in black schools. The Clifton-Choctaws developed their own school K-8 school, but it was designated as a white school, though they were not allowed to attend white high schools in their home parish. Lumbees developed an extensive Indian school system in Robeson County, North Carolina. See Gerald Sider, *Lumbee Indian Histories: Race, Ethnicity, and Indian Identity in the Southern United States*. See also Walter L. Williams, "Patterns in the History of the Remaining Southeastern Indians, 1840–1975," 193–210.

68. Following Omi and Winant's definition of racial formation as "the sociohistorical process by which racial categories are created, inhabited, transformed, and destroyed," and a racial project as "simultaneously an interpretation, representation, or explanation of racial dynamics, and an effort to reorganize and redistribute resources along particular racial lines." See Michael Omi and Howard Winant, *Racial Formation in the United States from the 1960s to the 1990s*, 55–56.

69. "Jena Indians Learn...."

70. Penick wrote to Willard Beatty regarding the possibility of placing Choctaw children in a boarding situation at Louisiana State Normal College in Natchitoches, and described the Little Indian Club to him. "During their last year of school," she wrote, "the many letters requesting information concerning the Indians, prompted me to organize a State-wide Indian Club. School bus loads of club members from various points in the State came to spend the day with the Indian boys and girls and a beautiful relationship was born among them. The Indian children were in the spotlight and felt that they were 'wanted,' for the first time in their lives. Continuation of this club under the sponsorship of the La. State Normal College will help the children in the training school to accept them and at the same time offer a history of the Louisiana Indians to the children of our state." Penick to Willard Beatty, November 8, 1940, File 68776–1931–800, Part I, Record Group 75, National Archives. Despite the likelihood that it did make Choctaw students feel "wanted" in some way, the element of racial display and colonial curiosity is reminiscent of anthropological displays of living people at world's fairs.

71. "Jena Indians Learn...."

72. The Office of Federal Acknowledgment suggests that the date of integration was 1943, based on oral testimony given in 1990 that Choctaw children were enrolled when Choctaw men enlisted to fight in World War II. OFA, Historical Technical Report, 39, citing "Governor's

Commission, 1990," which matches no document listed in the bibliography. Tribal elder Mary Jackson Jones corroborated this date and the reason for integration in a 2004 interview with the author. OFA also suggests that the Whatley family told Will Jackson to send his kids to school because they were making a nuisance of themselves, lending credence to the idea that white townspeople wanted to use the school as a form of paternalistic social control asserted over Choctaws. Marilyn Watt's research, based on oral testimony as well, vaguely notes that "for some reason, the attitude of the LaSalle Parish School Board changed after World War II, and by 1945 the [Jena] Choctaws were enrolled in the white public schools." She reports that one of the first Jena Choctaws to enroll in white Jena schools remembers only that the decision to enroll Choctaw children was "sudden," so the Choctaws do not seem to have been directly involved in creating this change of heart on the school board. Watt, 154. Sarah Sue Goldsmith gives 1946 as the date of integration, presumably based on interview sources. See Sarah Sue Goldsmith, "The Jena Band: Choctaw Traditions Keep Tribe Together."

73. On Coushatta, Tunica, Clifton-Choctaw, and Chitimacha education generally, see Klopotek, *Recognition Odysseys*. Information on Choctaw-Apache educational history provided by Choctaw-Apache tribal members during a July 2009 visit. Information on Houma education from Ann Fischer, "History and Current Status of the Houma Indians," 222. Detail on Chitimacha education in Sarah Sue Goldsmith, with Risa Mueller, *Nations Within: The Four Sovereign Tribes of Louisiana,* 10–11. On Lumbee and Virginia Indians, see Walter L. Williams, "Patterns in the History of the Remaining Southeastern Indians, 1840–1975," who notes that some Virginia Indians were sent to the Cherokee Indian school in North Carolina.

74. Here I follow a line of postcolonial thinkers too long to cite, but certainly it will be evident that my thinking is heavily influenced by the work of Ngugi Wa Thiong'o, Frantz Fanon, and Antonio Gramsci.

75. Jonathan Warren has noted that in the Brazilian context, indigenous perspectives have often been dismissed as irrelevant to contemporary racial politics, but it is precisely in the perspectives of people reclaiming indigenous identities that he sees the most resistance to white supremacy in Brazil. The idea that "race" belongs to blackness, however, has prevented scholars from seeing this possibility. As we continue to interrogate Indian racial histories in the United States context, perhaps new visions for the future of race will emerge, as well. See Jonathan Warren, *Racial Revolutions: Antiracism and Indian Resurgence in Brazil.*

4 Creating Wage Workers

Indigenous Boarding Schools in Rural Yucatán, Mexico

M. Bianet Castellanos

Jesús May Pat does not know how to make *milpa*, the indigenous practice of cultivating corn through swidden agriculture.[1, 2] He left Kuchmil (a pseudonym for a rural Maya village in Mexico's Yucatán Peninsula) at ten years of age to attend a *casa escuela* (boarding school) in the town of Maxcanú, located at least a full day's travel from Kuchmil. Initially, his parents, don Jorge and doña Berta, refused Jesús's request to attend this school because as the eldest son, his labor was needed in the milpa. Jesús asked his uncle, who planned to send his two eldest sons to the casa escuela, to convince his parents to let him go. A scholarship from the Ministry of Education paid for boarding school expenses, but Jesús's parents were responsible for his transportation to Maxcanú. As a subsistence farmer, his father did not earn a wage, which meant that Jesús could not return home too often. At first, Jesús missed home, but his cousins' presence helped him to adjust until he learned to enjoy boarding school life. The students raised animals, grew vegetables, and tailored their own clothes. Since Jesús was a good student, his teachers encouraged him to continue with his education. With their support, Jesús was awarded a scholarship to attend a *secundaria técnica* (a three-year vocational agriculture school) in the town of Tekax.

Given that he did not know how to make—nor did he much like working in—the milpa, Jesús did not plan to return to Kuchmil after he completed the secundaria. During his final year in Tekax, he volunteered to work as a rural teacher with the *Consejo Nacional de Fomento Educativo* (National Council of Education Promotion, or CONAFE), which assigned him to teach fifth and sixth grade in a small rural community near Tekax. One year of service with CONAFE guaranteed Jesús a three-year scholarship to study the *bachillerato* (three-year college preparatory or vocational degree program) at a *Colegio de Bachilleres del Estado de Yucatán* (Preparatory College of the State of Yucatán, or COBAY). His parents agreed to provide him with a modest sum of money for his daily expenses and arranged for Jesús to live with his cousins, who had moved to Felipe Carrillo Puerto, Quintana Roo, a town with a population large enough to support a COBAY. After earning his vocational degree as an electrician in 1990, Jesús found work in a hotel in Cancún, where he lives to this day. Jesús's decision to become a wage worker instead of a farmer had long-term consequences for his family and for his community. This essay focuses on these outcomes.

During the 1970s and early 1980s, it was quite common for rural Maya families to send their adolescent sons to study at *internados* (boarding schools) scattered throughout the peninsula. Twenty-eight students from Kuchmil attended boarding schools. Although these schools were co-educational, only four girls from Kuchmil were enrolled. These youth studied in places as far west as Maxcanú, near the Campeche state border, and as far east as Bacalar in the state of Quintana Roo, near the national border with Belize. This youthful mobility marked a new turning point for the future of Kuchmil. The first migrants from Kuchmil to settle in the tourist city of Cancún were alumni of boarding schools.

Indigenous boarding schools in Mexico, like Indian boarding schools in the United States, were considered key institutions through which the state could transform indigenous people into modern citizens.[3] By establishing rural boarding schools, the Mexican government aimed to incorporate indigenous populations into national life through a process of assimilation and de-racialization. As a result, boarding schools recruited children as young as five years of age with the objective of training them to become leaders of rural communities. These schools taught children how to become good citizens of the nation-state, but they failed to produce rural leaders because they did not teach agriculture skills that increased milpa yields. In contrast to the state's efforts at assimilation, Kuchmil families did not send their children to boarding schools to become less Maya, nor to become the future leaders of Kuchmil. By improving and expanding their children's educational opportunities, Maya parents positioned their children as wage laborers, rather than as subsistence farmers. Through these efforts, Kuchmil families improved their future access to a cash economy via the wage labor of their children. However, this transformation came with a heavy price tag. Boarding schools absolved the state from investing in the development of infrastructure, like schools, in rural communities. And over time, this separation disrupted Maya family life and threatened the survival of indigenous cultural practices as adolescent migration drained rural populations.

Internados

In 1921, the *Secretaría de Educación Pública* (Ministry of Education, or SEP) was established to provide a public education to Mexico's peasantry. Education was considered to be the best way to unify, civilize, and modernize the nation.[4] The dearth of bilingual teachers willing to teach in rural communities, however, made it difficult to educate rural and indigenous populations. In 1926, the SEP created boarding schools in urban centers to fill this void. The main objective of these schools was to transform pupils into rural leaders who would educate and modernize their communities of origin.[5] These schools, however, failed due to lack of funding and because students once removed from their rural communities preferred to remain in the city. In 1964, to consolidate funding and outreach, the SEP joined forces with the *Instituto Nacional Indigenista* (National Indigenous Institute, or INI) to provide an elementary and junior high school education to children from isolated rural and indigenous communities. The INI was created in 1940 to acculturate indigenous communities. Like the SEP, the INI established boarding schools to educate isolated indigenous populations with limited access to schools.

Merging INI schools with SEP schools substantially increased the presence of bilingual teachers and bilingual books in rural classrooms.[6] The SEP trained the teachers who staffed these schools.[7] Although the SEP and INI shared resources and ideological goals, they continued to administer their schools independently. Therefore, internados took different shapes depending on their location and source of funding. The SEP created the casa escuela, a program that solely provided housing while students attended local elementary schools, and the secundaria técnica, a junior high school that housed students on school grounds who lived too far to commute, whereas the INI established *albergues escolares*, which were boarding schools that recruited elementary school age students from towns located within a fifteen kilometer radius and housed all students on school grounds.[8] Albergues escolares were supervised by the *Centros Coordinadores Indigenistas* (Coordinating Indigenous Centers, or CCI), regional administrative centers funded by the INI that coordinated programs and resources directed toward indigenous communities.[9] By providing meals, housing, and medical care, boarding schools improved student attendance in rural regions.[10]

Boarding schools formed part of a large complex system intended to assimilate indigenous peoples—both adults and children—by transforming rural life through the inculcation of new agricultural techniques and domestic practices, civic pride, and personal hygiene. Not surprisingly, curriculum and instruction at the INI and SEP boarding schools was similar. The internados in the Yucatán Peninsula helped transition indigenous children into mainstream society by teaching them Spanish, personal hygiene, vocational skills, and citizenship. Hence their purpose was similar to Indian boarding schools in the United States, which isolated Indian children to make them "forget their barbarous practices and acquire the knowledge and benefits of civilization."[11] Labor formed an important component of indigenous boarding schools. Students were expected to wash their own clothes, clean the facilities, and maintain the grounds. Chores were assigned before and after school.[12] Students were also taught vocational skills, such as tailoring, horticulture, agronomy, and animal husbandry, that students applied on-site, but unlike indigenous schools in early twentieth century Mexico and Indian boarding schools in the United States, these schools did not send students to labor off-site.[13]

To recruit students, radio announcements extolled the benefits of this type of education, as did teachers from the internados who traveled to rural villages. Between 1964 and 1973, twenty-nine internados were established throughout the Mexican countryside to provide a continuing co-education (fourth to sixth grade) to indigenous students who completed the third grade.[14] By 1976, the SEP administered 591 albergues escolares in Mexico. In response to the teacher absenteeism that plagued Kuchmil's one-room elementary schoolhouse, twenty-eight children from Kuchmil attended internados in the late 1960s and throughout the 1970s. At this time, Maya parents typically sent their eldest son to school. They kept their daughters at home rather than expose them to potential physical and sexual abuse from male teachers.[15] Parents also believed that the dormitories placed their daughters' sexual innocence at risk because although the children slept in same-sex dormitories, adult supervision was not provided at night. This trend resulted in an educational gender imbalance that was not corrected for decades, leaving the young women of Kuchmil with few options but to marry upon reaching adulthood.

Of the twenty-eight students who attended elementary boarding schools, fifteen pursued a secondary education at internados located throughout the peninsula. Where they continued their secondary education was determined by costs.[16] Four went to the internado in Nohbec in Quintana Roo, whose tuition was gratuitous to children who scored a "B" average in elementary school. Two of these young men, Nicolas Can Tun and Enrique May Kauil, did not complete their studies due to economic hardship. Since they were not awarded a scholarship to cover room and board, their families attempted to cover these expenses, but fell short most months. After facing near starvation, Nícolas and Enrique dropped out. Another boy attended an internado in Balantún, near Valladolid, on scholarship. Three boys earned full scholarships (tuition, room, and board) to study in the *secundaria agrícola*, which was also an internado, located in the town of Tekax. One of these young men was Jesús May Pat. The families of the remaining seven students (five boys, all of whom were brothers, and two girls) paid for their children to attend a public secundaria in Tihosuco. One of these girls (who was the older sister of Celia, a girl that discusses her school experiences later in this chapter) did not finish the secundaria because she eloped. The youngest boy of the five brothers transferred to the Balantún internado after he was awarded a scholarship.

Of these fifteen children, nine (eight boys and one girl) went on to study their bachillerato. To pay for this degree, three joined CONAFE and completed their degree with the scholarship CONAFE gives in exchange for one to two years of service. The girl became a teacher, but this was possible because her parents moved with her to Carrillo Puerto where she studied this profession. Another student became a *promotor* (community advocate) for INI with the help of his uncle, but he moved to Cancún before completing his training. Four of the boys decided to end their studies early and try their luck in the new international tourist center of Cancún.

The Hardships of Schooling

Like Native American families who used boarding schools to resolve economic problems,[17] Maya families also turned to internados to ease their poverty and to improve their children's physical and nutritional well-being. Hunger and sickness constantly plague rural families. In 1991 during my first visit to Kuchmil, the majority of the infants in Kuchmil were malnourished and underweight.[18] Children followed me, begging for food and snacks. At this time, over 60 percent of the indigenous children who attended albergues escolares in Yucatán suffered from chronic malnutrition.[19] In the 1960s, the hunger may have been worse. The internados, proclaimed the radio commercials and recruiters, provided access not only to better schools, but also to food and clothing. According to Enrique May Kauil, a student at the albergue escolar in Ke'eldzonot, the internados relieved parental stress.

> *The government sent food. They built a large house, like a dormitory. They gave us a hammock once, a blanket. Everyone has their little locker with their key. [The school] helps with all of your expenses, with the food. It behooves the parents [to send their children to boarding schools] because sometimes at home with difficulty [their children] eat. They don't even drink milk. During that time period, they get a small scholarship, a bit of money. It helps.*

Kuchmil parents improved their children's nutritional intake by sending them to boarding schools.

Agrarian crises were at the root of the hunger facing these families. As the economic sustainability of the ejido diminished and mass produced goods flooded markets in the 1960s, Maya families turned to wage labor to supplement or replace farm work and gain access to cash. Wage work, however, was more difficult to obtain. Due to their poor educational backgrounds, adult males seeking wage labor faced limited options. They could only find work in construction.[20] As a result of these experiences with the labor market, parents did not want their children to be restricted to manual labor or farm work. Roberto Can Kauil explained his own parents' frustration with farm work and manual labor.

> [He did not want me to] follow the same path he took, that of being a campesino, because he doesn't want me to work in the campo. My mother agreed.... We heard from others that a school was going to be built, that food would be given. No one would have to pay anything, not one cent. My father told me that I had to go. I didn't want to go. "Too bad," replied my father. "We have to get ahead." According to him, his father had a bit [of money] so they could go to school but they never sent him. My father was happy that I agreed to study there. His idea was for me not to return to the pueblo. During that time period, the milpa did produce but not 100 percent. How are you going to produce 100 percent when there is always a loss?... [Parents] knew that when their sons go there [the internado], they will learn more and maybe will acquire a better job so that they won't have to work in the milpa. That was how each father thought.

As one father put it, "one cannot get ahead by working in the milpa." This economic vulnerability made Maya families more susceptible to state interventions in family life and to assimilationist projects disguised as educational programs. Encouraged by the teachers sent to recruit students, Kuchmil parents turned toward education as one solution to agricultural crises. Given the structural inequalities facing rural communities, few options existed. Thus, Maya communities were forced to adopt colonial languages (in this case Spanish) and break up their families in order to gain access to new economies.

Maya families knew that enrolling their children in boarding schools would transform their lives and might sever their children's ties to rural Maya culture. Doña Berta, Jesús's mother, acknowledged that an education would alter her son's life course. "I think that he isn't going to return to make his milpa. I know that he will live there [far away] always, to work with a profession." Ironically, even as internados trained pupils to be rural leaders, they curbed children's exposure to village life and agricultural production techniques used in the village. The boys and girls who attended internados located far from home spent only two months of the year in residence in Kuchmil. Their absence prevented them from learning or practicing the skills necessary to effectively run and support an agrarian household: to plant and harvest corn; to prepare the *nixtamal* (tortilla dough) and make tortillas; to cook; to develop the endurance to pull and carry water from the wells; to learn the names and uses of healing herbs and plants; to hunt; and to perform rituals, such as the *ch'a chaac* (rain ceremony), to the necessary gods. Instead, they were taught to speak Spanish fluently; to read and write; to design and construct engineering and art projects; to plant fruits and vegetables not grown at home; and to develop their leadership, teaching, and oratory skills. These students became accustomed to life in busy commercial towns or cities and were trained to be small commercial farmers or for a vocation in such a setting. Their parents also expected them to migrate to a city where they could use their skills and education and earn an income. Both students and parents pointed out that Kuchmil youth could not find a job for which they were trained in Kuchmil because its size and isolation inhibited the growth of industry and commerce. If they wished to use their education and help their parents financially, they had to migrate, regardless of the sacrifices this move entailed.

Although boarding schools were subsidized by the state, few families dependent on subsistence farming could afford to pay the additional expenses incurred by a boarding school education (e.g. transportation, money for personal expenses, and clothes). Although in some cases, like that of Jesús, rural youth received scholarships to attend internados, these scholarships did not cover all expenses. Jesús' mother explained, "The school supplies, clothes, shoes, and food were given there [in the internado]. He [their son Jesús] hardly asked for money. He worked for his own *gastada* (allowance). We only provided additional school supplies [supplies required, but not provided, by the school]. We sold pigs, we sold chickens [to pay for these]." Yet, not all students excelled in the required exams. In these cases, parents paid for school expenses from personal funds or requested financial help from a relative. Few families in Kuchmil could afford to continue their children's education without financial and social support from relatives. Extended kin networks provided housing, food, or money for tuition and school supplies. In order for children to continue their education beyond the sixth grade, they had to leave their community to do so. This move entailed paying for housing, meals, transportation, tuition, and school supplies. When Rubén Can Kauil's uncle offered to pay for his education, his father sent Rubén to Valladolid, where he completed elementary and junior high school. Rubén remained in Valladolid until the age of sixteen when he migrated to Cancún in search of work. However, not all families took advantage of their kin networks because they could not repay such a debt. Nicólas Can Tun provides such an example. "There wasn't a way for me to keep studying [beyond the secundaria]. We were too poor in those days. What little we had was to maintain us [the household]. Until one day, don Jerónimo Kauil Balam offered to take on the expense so that I could continue, but since he wasn't my father, I didn't accept."

By sending their children to internados, Kuchmil parents sacrificed their children's household labor and future involvement in reproducing rural Maya cultural practices and knowledge to the next generation. When the eldest son was sent away to school, campesino households lost the additional farm labor provided by the eldest and strongest son. The absent child's chores were divided among the parents or the remaining children, increasing the workload for each individual. For those families who educated more than one child, maintaining and reproducing a rural household economy was difficult. In addition to the loss of labor, boarding schools extracted emotional costs from Maya families and their children and in the process altered local conceptions of childhood and transformed village life.

Rethinking Childhood

Given that childhood is a social construction and that modern childhood is culturally and historically specific,[21] it is not surprising that Maya conceptions of childhood did not align with the pedagogy of boarding schools. The state's modern conceptualization of childhood is based on a Western ideal, in which children's innocence must be protected.[22] For the state, boarding schools disciplined Mexico's future workforce and transformed indigenous children into modern Spanish-speaking Mexican citizens. But children also played games and watched movies. Therefore, play, along with labor and discipline, formed an integral part of a boarding school education.

In contrast, in the 1960s, Maya parents did not consider education to be central to a child's development. Given their limited experience in schools, these parents perceived schools to be institutions for Spanish language acquisition and literacy. They considered discipline to be their domain, not the schools, and did not consider play to be an integral part of formal education. Rather, in their early years, children were allowed to play and were given few responsibilities. In many ways, this stage corresponds with the contemporary Western concept of "childhood" as a separate life stage requiring care and nurturance in order to develop the physical, emotional, and social needs of the child.[24] During these years, children were introduced into social and religious life through baptism and the *hetzmek*, the straddle-hip ceremony conducted during the early months of life with the purpose of developing the intellectual, physical, and social capacities of the child. Maya children were given few responsibilities because they were not yet mature and strong enough to handle them. By the age of three, parents typically began to teach their children how to do small chores, but children were not expected to obey parental demands until around age six, at which point they were entrusted with errands. Among certain families who needed the labor, children were expected to participate fully in the household at this early age, which significantly reduced the early years of play.

By the age of ten, children contributed significant labor to their household.[25] Although children were recognized as individuals early on, usually after six months of age, they did not become involved in the household decision-making process until they contributed to its upkeep.[26] As sentient beings with individual personalities, young children were expected to perform acts of mischievousness and disobedience. These antics entertained adults. As one family member amusingly noted when a young toddler threw a tantrum on the tile floor of her grandfather's store, "she has a *chan mal genio* [bad temperament]." However, by the age of ten, children were expected to have learned how to properly respond to adult authority and complete their chores, but without losing their sense of self. As children mature, their opinions are held in higher esteem within the household. For most students, attending school gave them the opportunity to extend their early childhood years of play and no chores.

Similar to Native Americans whose boarding school experience was traumatic for some and enjoyable for others,[26] Maya students recalled their internado experiences with mixed feelings. Some children, like Alberto Can Uc, dreaded the idea of leaving home, while others were anxious to attend school away from home. Alberto emphasized that he was not given a choice. Jesús also claimed that he left because his parents made him attend the internado, but doña Berta recalled, "[Jesús] cried to leave because he liked school. He wanted to go. He wouldn't eat, wouldn't do anything that I told him to do. He was upset all day. That's why we let him go." Only two of the boys left the boarding school in Maxcanú before finishing their first year. Like Native American students who relied on flight to escape a boarding school education,[27] one boy escaped late at night. The other never returned after coming home for Christmas vacation. Sebastián, one of those two boys, explained, "I didn't like to study much." Enrique, who studied at the secundaria near Chetumal, suffered emotionally and physically while away at school.

> I began the secundaria but I went too far away to study it. It was harder because I couldn't come home every week [like before when he studied in Ke'eldzonot]. It was too far which is why I couldn't stick it out.... Also the food, they gave so little: two

tortillas with a soda, fried beans. One can't stand the hunger pangs. Four months I stayed.... I wanted to study, but I couldn't handle it. I returned, began to work in the milpa. I was fifteen years old.

Enrique did not wish to experience another year of the financial hardship involved in studying away from home. Unfortunately, Enrique could not study closer to home because his family did not have any social networks in Valladolid and Felipe Carrillo Puerto. These children had a difficult time adjusting to the rigid schedule and extended separations from their families. Their increasing discomfort was compounded by their nostalgia for their home environment.

In contrast, Abel Kauil Tun suggested that attendance "was our choice." Children who attended the albergue in Ke'eldzonot experienced less homesickness because they could go home every weekend due to the school's proximity to Kuchmil. Some students, such as Enrique, were even allowed to go home during the week. "The school was close to my home. There was a path behind my house. At first they told us that those who attend, enter on Monday and leave on Friday. But they gave us breakfast [and before the first session of classes began in the morning], we could go home if we liked." However, not all children lived as close as Enrique. In many cases, the children's acquiescence to attend school was spurred by the threat of milpa work and by their parents' desire to relieve them from the harsh physical labor involved in subsistence agriculture. According to Abel, "During that time, it was said by parents, 'You don't want to go to school? Then grab your machete and head out to the milpa.' I'd rather go to school than go to the milpa. I never liked it because it was extremely hard. We worked hard. It's better to say 'school' because I know that I won't be working in the *campo* [fields]." Similarly, Gustavo Kauil Tun stressed the difficulty of making milpa.

I don't like working in the campo.... It's far more difficult. You spend the entire day in the sun, you have to carry water with you, you have to carry your food with you...and you have to walk through the forest.... It's matado [loosely translated as "wears you out"], they say, because you cannot not work in order to have something.

During the early years of settlement, even the girls were sent to work in the milpa. "We worked like men," complained Carla Be' Can, who eagerly accepted work as a domestic servant for a local schoolteacher in order to avoid being "treated like a man."

Although these young men and women considered boarding school attendance to be an active choice, this "choice" was predetermined; structural inequalities and the economic constraints of rural life limited their options and thus forced Maya families to give up their children. At a young age, these young men and women were asked to dedicate themselves to manual labor or boarding school life. Each option came with a price tag. Their parents opted for the latter, in spite of the pain of a long separation and the risk of cultural loss. It was a difficult choice to make for all involved.

Kuchmil parents described their children's departures with a sense of pragmatism rooted in the local conception of childhood, in which children were considered capable of bearing responsibility by the age of ten (at which point they contribute a significant amount of labor to the household).[28] When I asked doña Andrea if she had had any qualms about sending her young daughter to boarding school, she explained, "She wasn't little, she was ten years old, she washed her own clothes." Being capable of washing clothes, an arduous task, demonstrated to doña Andrea that her daughter was not only responsible, but also mature enough to live away from home. Visiting the casa escuela also alleviated parents' fears, as is evident by doña Andrea's remarks. "We couldn't afford her books, which is why we sent her to Maxcanú. I never cried for her because the girl was fine where she studied. I saw it [the school]. There was a bed, there was a hammock." Doña Berta also spoke pragmatically about her son's departure, but she recalled the pain of letting him go as well. "When one thinks of him not returning to live with us…when I would sleep every night, *lo estoy soñando* [I would dream of him]." Dreaming about someone in Maya culture is associated with nostalgia, yearning, and grief. According to Allan Burns,[29] dreams also serve as a way to communicate these feelings to others. Doña Berta's melancholy was exacerbated by her fears of what might happen to Jesús in a city that "is full of bad men."

In spite of these fears, boarding schools became places where indigenous children felt taken care of. Thus, once at school, the majority of the children truly enjoyed their boarding school experience because it offered a respite from work and an opportunity to partake in activities difficult to come by in their isolated community.[30] The boys recalled meeting boys from all over the state. Abel, who attended the internado in Ke'eldzonot, pointed out the attractive proposition the schools presented for poor rural schoolboys. "We liked [the internados] because of the scholarship. Since we lived close to home, we didn't spend the money, except on soda pop. They gave you three meals per day." With a wide smile and a far-off look, Celia reminisced over the activities she enjoyed in the internado in Maxcanú.

I really liked it. There we ate. They gave us everything.… We had physical education, carpentry, sewing, and even dance classes. Saturdays and Sundays they showed movies in one of the classrooms, of the old kind like Cinderella. *Vendors would sell cookies. Every fifteen days they gave us an allowance, fifteen pesos.… I liked it. Sometimes you think about your mother and your father, like during the time of the new corn [in the month of October].*

After the casa escuela shut down in Maxcanú, Celia returned to Kuchmil to complete the sixth grade. "I didn't like it [the single schoolhouse in Kuchmil] because I wasn't used to being there." After school, Celia's parents now expected her to perform arduous chores like pulling water from the well, washing clothes, cooking over an open fire, and working in the milpa. The pleasures of boarding school life, such as the dance classes, movies, and a small allowance, were not provided by her family or the local school. Historically boarding schools have served as places of containment, but they have also provided a space where many indigenous children felt protected from the physical demands and economic privations of rural life. As Maya parents became more exposed to rural education through the presence of bilingual teachers and as education became more accessible, school attendance increasingly became part of the stages of growth for children and adolescents.

Living Contradictions

For Kuchmil farmers, wage work offers a tempting proposition because it gives workers access to a steady income, which can be used to generate and accumulate social and economic capital. Kuchmil families, then, consider wage work a vehicle for social mobility, which is conceptualized as the ability to move from the position of powerlessness and poverty (the position in which many Maya find themselves) to one of being an educated and knowledgeable person with financial stability. Yet, Kuchmil migrants who worked in service positions realized that this work was not all they and their parents had dreamed about. As short-term contract employees, they lacked job security. Entry-level positions as bus boys, stewards, and assistant bartenders did not provide a living wage. These jobs failed to provide the freedom and respect they were seeking. More importantly, wage work also required Maya children to leave their communities and learn new ways of being—practices that placed indigenous customs and rituals at risk of being forgotten. To illustrate the work experience and social mobility of migrant workers and how they sustained indigenous practices in spite of the distance, I narrate Jesús May Pat's experiences after he moved to Cancún.

After obtaining certification as an electrician in the late 1980s, Jesús's job search led him to Cancún. His friends and neighbors informed him that this city offered the best employment opportunities and the highest wages in the peninsula. Jesús was fortunate that his aunt and uncle, who were his hosts while he studied in Carrillo Puerto, also owned a home in Cancún. They offered to house him during his job search. As a skilled laborer, Jesús quickly found work in the maintenance department of an international hotel.

A model worker, Jesús steadily moved up the labor hierarchy within the hotel industry. However, this work ethic required that he spend most of his time working, thereby limiting the amount of time he could spend in Kuchmil and with other Maya migrants in Cancún.

Even as Jesús acquired new titles, moving from an "electrician's assistant" to "maintenance supervisor," increasing his wages accordingly, he still struggled to earn the respect of the managerial staff, and eventually hit the wage ceiling for his trade.[31] Jesús describes this growing disenchantment by relating his experiences working as maintenance supervisor in a chain of five-star hotels.

> *Well, I was sent over there [to another hotel] and I knew that it wouldn't be worth my while. He [the boss] didn't pay attention to me; he put me in charge of the rooms and then would disappear.... And since there were a ton of problems, [the job] was no longer the same. His support wasn't the same. Even though the rest [of the employees] sat down, he didn't say anything to them. And I observed and said no. I went directly to [the person in charge of] maintenance [for the entire hotel] and told him, "Here you have my radio. Here you have everything. I am leaving." I turned in everything and about two days later, I began working as a bellboy at the Horizon.*

In other words, his occupational mobility did not translate into a shift in class status, from a subordinate position to a position of *confianza* (trust) in which employees have more control of their labor and are treated with respect.[32]

Jesús's occupational shift from an electrician, which requires a bachillerato and certification, to a bellboy, which in the 1990s typically required at least the completion of the secundaria, may appear to be a case of downward social and economic mobility.[33] As a bellboy, however, Jesús increased his wages via his monthly tips, which exceeded his wages as an electrician. More importantly, he had more control of his wages because he could augment his salary with what he earned in tips. By acquiring a job that required public demonstrations of congeniality, respect, and a willingness to help, Jesús felt that his ability to offer these qualities in abundance earned him more respect and esteem from his colleagues, the administration, and the tourists.[34] These are the qualities, after all, that garner an employee big tips. By making his labor visible to the clients of the tourist industry, Jesús reaped more rewards than through his previous highly skilled but "invisible" position.

Jesús was able to make the transition from electrician to bellboy because he spoke fluent English, the *lingua franca* of the leisure industry in Mexico. In Cancún's tourist industry, fluency in English is a requirement for most professional and upper-level service positions. To work as a waiter, bellboy, and bartender, positions that depend on customer-client interaction, hotels require up to 80 percent English fluency.[35] Recognizing the importance and necessity of this language in the service industry, and that his mobility within the hotel industry depended on his language skills, Jesús studied English at a language school for three years. When I asked Jesús why he studied English, he responded, "Well, practically speaking, you could remain [in your job], but if you want to improve yourself, you have to look for other options." Jesús spent ten years working as an electrician before he switched careers. In the meantime, he prepared himself for this transition by learning English, talking to other service employees about their employment experiences, and experiencing the corporate culture of different hotel chains. Like his parents, who associated education with class mobility, Jesús identified the study of the English language as his ticket to a higher salary.

Although his parents' investment in his education helped Jesús acquire a skilled job, these skills and background failed to significantly improve Jesús's class status. In spite of his skills and his position as a supervisor, Jesús worked in a blue-collar job with minimal job security. Electricians earned a maximum salary of five hundred dollars a month, excluding the food and transportation subsidies provided to hotel employees. Jesús reached this ceiling a few years before he became a bellboy. Job stability did not come with the bellboy position, but as Jesús explained, "There is more money than where I was [as an electrician], the wages are higher.... That is enough." But Jesús acknowledged that earning high wages was not enough because he lacked the power to influence his work environment. As a bellboy, although he earned more, Jesús encountered similar power struggles between the management and the staff, and between tourists and service employees. Yet, now he was more dependent on fostering smoother working relations than in his previous career because bellboys were easily replaced.

As a result of his disillusionment, Jesús and a partner prepared a business plan. A few months into his new job, Jesús and his partner opened up a corner grocery store in a developing region. What began as a few cartons of Coke turned into a thriving business within a few months. Jesús quit working for others to work full-time for himself. Although he continues earning much of his income as a bellboy, this employment is seasonal. The rest of his time is spent as a small business owner, a position that allows Jesús to control his labor and to be treated respectfully by his employees and neighbors. In many ways, this position is similar to that of his parents who as subsistence farmers control their time and are respected by their neighbors, with the exception that Jesús does not perform manual labor and earns a profit from his business. More importantly, this position allows him to make frequent visits to Kuchmil and partake in ritual practices and renew acquaintances that had been ignored during the years he dedicated to moving up the hotel hierarchy.

Childhood in a Global Era

Although more than 50 percent of working children in Mexico are concentrated in rural areas, particularly in export agriculture,[36] a significant number of children and juveniles work in the informal sector in urban areas, a sector characterized by a lack of job security, health insurance, regulated working conditions, or a living wage. As a result, we cannot ignore the plight of working children in Latin America. Doing so, Ernest Bartell suggests,[37] will produce a generation of exploited individuals who lack knowledge of their rights and of alternative models for economic development in a global economy. Given that many of these children come from indigenous families, indigenous peoples bear the brunt of these changes.

The case of Kuchmil demonstrates how modernization projects and a global economy transform social constructions of childhood by reinforcing structural inequalities. Prior to the declining prices for agricultural products, rural communities were somewhat self-sufficient.[38] Maya children were valued for the warmth and joy they brought as infants, and the work they performed during adolescence. However, campesinos' increasing dependence on global markets, along with expanded telecommunications and transportation networks, shifted children's roles in the countryside. Children accrued another role, that of potential wageworker. To accomplish this transformation, Maya children were enrolled in boarding schools, postponing their work contributions to the household. By becoming wageworkers during their adolescent years, Kuchmil's youths experienced an early departure from their nurturing households and became important economic contributors to their natal families, earning a central decision-making role in the household. In spite of these economic benefits, this shift came at the expense of Maya family life and cultural practices for the sake of Mexican nationalism and modernization projects like tourism.

Even as Maya families consider education to be one solution to their marginalization within a market-driven economy, the experiences of their educated sons and daughters demonstrate the limitations of this approach. On the one hand, the education their children receive is not sufficient to meet the demands of a technologically oriented and increasingly English-dominated economy. On the other hand, the abundance of jobs made available as a result of NAFTA and free-market economics are low-skilled, low-wage jobs that lack job security, as is evident by Jesús's experiences in Cancún's labor market. Kuchmil parents fail to recognize that providing their children with an education will not immediately translate into job security, a living wage, and middle-class status. Regardless of their educational background, whether they earned vocational degrees or not, Kuchmil migrants must enter the labor market at the bottom of the labor hierarchy. The lack of alternatives and the declining productivity rates and market value of milpa cultivation force the majority of Kuchmil migrants to ignore the downward mobility of the urban labor market in an effort to work diligently towards improving their future prospects.

As such, migration jeopardizes the continued engagement with Maya cultural practices rooted in rural life. The boarding school experience taught young men and women to farm, but these practices differed from traditional swidden agriculture. And as young men and women migrate to urban centers, farming and the knowledge necessary to sustain a rural household are at risk of disappearing. In the case of Kuchmil, this threat is mitigated by the young men and women who remain at home. In spite of the sub-subsistence nature of farm work, and with the advent of an improved public school system in and near Kuchmil, many young men and women prefer rural life to tourist work. They point out that farm work offers greater stability than tourist work, which is dependent on tourist flows, and provides a more meaningful existence because it constitutes an integral part of Maya cultural practices. Since tourist work cannot absorb everyone and not everyone desires to work in urban centers, the residents who remain in Kuchmil serve as the guardians of Maya customs and rituals, thus ensuring their preservation in the face of encroaching global consumer and market practices.

Notes

1. To protect the privacy of my informants, I use pseudonyms for the people and places I mention here, with the exception of large towns like Cancún.

2. This chapter is a condensed and updated version of Bianet Castellanos, "Indigenous Education, Adolescent Migration, and Wage Labor" (chapter 3) in *A Return to Servitude: Maya Migration and the Tourist Trade in Cancún* (University of Minnesota Press, 2010). Reprinted courtesy of the publisher. This chapter was much improved by the thoughtful feedback provided by the editors, Brian Klopotek and Brenda Child, the contributors of the volume, and the audience who attended the NAISA panel in Minneapolis where I presented this work.

3. See Alexander S. Dawson, *Indian and Nation in Revolutionary Mexico*; Paul K. Eiss, "Deconstructing Indians, Reconstructing Patria: Indigenous Education in Yucatan from the *Porfiriato* to the Mexican Revolution"; Ben Fallaw, "Rethinking Mayan Resistance: Changing Relations between Federal Teachers and Mayan Communities in Eastern Yucatan, 1929–1935"; Mary Kay Vaughan, *Cultural Politics in Revolution: Teachers, Peasants, and Schools in Mexico, 1930–1940*.

4. This approach, of education as an act of containment and of "retraining" of indigenous subjects, was adopted throughout the Americas. See García (chapter 9, this volume) for a discussion of how contemporary teacher training programs, like the PROEIB-Andes, struggle with this legacy of colonialism.

5. See Engracia Loyo Bravo, "Los centros de educación indígena y su papel en el medio rural (1930–1940)."

6. See Anthony Robert Berkley, "Remembrance and Revitalization: The Archive of Pure Maya"; Nancy Modiano, *Indian Education in the Chiapas Highlands*.

7. See Cecilia L.Greaves, "Entre la teoría educativa y la práctica indigenista: La experiencia en Chiapas y la Tarahumara (1940–1970)."

8. Contemporary albergues escolares do not offer academic instruction on-site; children reside at the albergue during the week while they attend the local elementary school. The students visit their families during the weekend. (See Mario Alberto Baas Lara, Pedro Antonio Sánchez Escobedo, and Francisco Rafael Mena Chiu, "Papel de los albergues escolares en el desempeño escolar del niño de la zona rural de Yucatán.")

9. See Instituto Nacional Indigenista (INI), *Instituto Nacional Indigenista, 1989–1994*.

10. See Instituto Nacional Indigenista (INI).

11. See Ronald Niezen, *Spirit Wars: Native North American Religions in the Age of Nation Building*, 47; K. Tsianina Lomawaima, *They Called It Prairie Light: The Story of Chilocco Indian School*.

12. See Baas Lara, Sánchez Escobedo, and Mena Chiu.

13. See, for example, Brenda Child, *Boarding School Seasons: American Indian Families, 1900–1940*; Eiss; Fallaw.

14. See Héctor Aguilar Padilla, *La educación rural en México*.

15. Fear of sexual abuse arose from a history of abuse by male teachers dating to the early twentieth century. See Fallaw.

16. This experience was typical of rural indigenous communities in the Americas. Bolivian educator and activist Flor Ángela Palmar Barroso also had to leave her community in order to advance her education beyond the sixth grade. See Laura R. Graham and Flor Ángela Palmar Barroso (chapter 11, this volume).

17. See Child, *Boarding School Seasons: American Indian Families, 1900–1940*; Lomawaima, *They Called It Prairie Light: The Story of Chilocco Indian School*.

18. As more commerce came through on the newly built road, a wider variety of foods became available, for example, fresh fruits, meat, and canned fruits and vegetables. After purified drinking water became available, the gastrointestinal diseases that commonly afflicted the residents diminished. Households with access to remittances had more money to spend on these products, whereas households without access to remittances continued to participate in temporary migration and participated in multiple state subsidy programs through which they improved their access to cash. By 1999, children were stronger and healthier because they ate more frequently. However, now they face new health concerns. The new influx of cash makes it possible for children to consume more candy and junk food, which places them at greater risk for diabetes, obesity, and other related illnesses.

19 See Ricardo Hernández Murrillo and Marjorie Thacker, *Diagnóstico de salud y nutrición en albergues escolares para niños indígenas*.

20. Male adults educated in Kuchmil prior to the 1960s were functionally literate, but few had the skills and educational background required for many service jobs in the tourism industry today.

21. See Sharon Stephens, "Introduction: Children and the Politics of Culture in 'Late Capitalism.'"

22. See Philippe Ariès, *Centuries of Childhood*.

23. Based on time allocation studies of Maya children's labor, biological anthropologist Karen L. Kramer shows similar expectations and practices among Maya households in southwestern

Yucatán. According to Kramer, Maya children begin helping their parents with household chores at three years of age. Between seven to eleven years of age, their work contributions double. Between the ages of eleven to fifteen, this time allocation doubles again.

24. Compare to Ariès.

25. Around the age of six months, parents consider babies capable of stating their tastes through body language, even if these tastes are limited to food, music, and television programs. After the child's first birthday, parents begin to accommodate these tastes. As evidence of her son's growing individuality, Fátima Can Tun informed me that her ten-month-old son cried for hours if she failed to take him for a stroll in the park or to the store every day.

26. See Lomawaima, *They Called It Prairie Light: The Story of Chilocco Indian School*.

27. See Child, *Boarding School Seasons: American Indian Families, 1900–1940*.

28. Up until the early 1980s, children spent much of their time working: pulling water, cutting firewood, clearing fields, and performing other menial tasks. After the mid-1980s, some of these responsibilities were reduced as a result of the introduction of new technologies (for example, potable water systems, stoves, and washing machines), the growing emphasis on school attendance, and the presence of migrant remittances that allowed households to hire workers to clear fields.

29. See Allan Burns, *An Epoch of Miracles: Oral Literature of the Yucatec Maya*.

30. Compare to Child, *Boarding School Seasons: American Indian Families, 1900–1940*.

31. Jesús had reached the wage ceiling for his official qualifications as a licensed electrician. In spite of his knowledge and skill, an increase in salary or a promotion required a university degree or recruitment by the hotel manager.

32. Compare to Richard Sennet and Jonathan Cobb, *The Hidden Injuries of Class*.

33. As Cancún has grown, labor shortages have decreased. As a result, hotels have changed the educational requirements for employees. Today it is common to find university graduates working as bellboys and security guards.

34. In "Producing the Superior Self: Strategic Comparison and Symbolic Boundaries among Luxury Hotel Workers," Rachel Sherman shows that luxury hotel employees also adopt this congenial demeanor as a form of protection against their subordinate position and as a way to mark themselves as superior to the people they serve.

35. These requirements were provided by Luis Escada Roman (personal communication, 2001), a hotel supervisor of a four-star hotel in Cancún.

36. See Francisco Cos-Montiel, "Sirviendo a las mesas del mundo: Las niñas y niños jornaleros agrícolas en México."

37. See Ernest J. Bartell, "Opportunities and Challenges for the Well-being of Children in the Development of Latin America: An Overview."

38. See George Collier, *Basta!: Land and the Zapatista Rebellion in Chiapas*; Arturo Warman, *Y venimos a contradecir*.

5 The Economy of Indian Education in California, 1902–1945

William J. Bauer Jr.

In the late nineteenth century, reformers and government officials vowed to transform Indian Country's economy. These so-called "friends of the Indian" argued that treaty-negotiated rations made American Indians dependent on federal handouts, a communal land base failed to promote individualism, and isolation prevented American Indians from learning job skills necessary for upward mobility. Building on long-standing beliefs about liberty, anticollectivism, centralized power, and the importance of the market, reformers intervened in the inner workings of Indian economies.[1] First, they instituted the policy of allotment, whereby the federal government divided communal reservations into individual plots of land and distributed them to Indian heads of household. Once Native men had their own property, the "friends" believed Indians would learn the important traits of self-reliance, individualism, and, as Massachusetts Senator Henry Dawes famously said, "selfishness."[2] Off-reservation boarding schools were the second policy intended to transform Indian Country's economy. By taking Native children away from what reformers considered the harmful social and economic environment of the reservation, boarding school teachers could train Native children in skills that might enable them to advance in American society. The schools used vocational training and "outing," the famous program inaugurated by the founder of Carlisle Indian Industrial School Richard Henry Pratt that placed Native children at work on farms and businesses near the school, to inculcate the Protestant work ethic and possessive individualism as well as to provide students with new skills. Both policies were disastrous. Between the beginning of allotment in 1887 and 1934, when the policy ended, Native peoples lost title to seventy percent of their land base. Allotment was truly an economic catastrophe and contributed to Indian Country's underdevelopment in the twentieth century. Yet, we lack the same kind of appreciation for the long-term consequences of education on Indian Country's economic standing. How did the federal off-reservation boarding school program affect the immediate and long-term economic conditions of Indian Country?[3]

In the early twentieth century, the federal off-reservation boarding school program contributed to the underdevelopment of northern California's Round Valley Indian Reservation. By "underdevelopment," I mean the process by which a core or metropolis undermines the economy and culture of a peripheral region, which results in the periphery becoming impoverished and dependent on the core/metropolis. Scholars interested in underdevelopment, such as Paul Baran, Andre Gunder Frank, Immanuel Wallerstein, and Joseph Jorgenson, examined the processes and outcome of colonialism across the globe. They hold that "metropolis" or "core" nations exploit the "satellite" or the "periphery" nations, thereby making the "satellite/periphery" underdeveloped and dependent on the "metropolis/core." Sociologist Jacqueline Goodman-Draper writes, "Underdevelopment...specifically refers to the subversion of Indian values and subsistence and the creation of Native dependence on non-Native society."[4] Scholars have identified several factors that contributed to the underdevelopment of American Indian economies in the nineteenth and twentieth centuries, many of which are rooted in the history of the off-reservation boarding school. First, the federal government created a policy of assimilating indigenous peoples. Reservation officials wanted Round Valley Indian children to attend boarding schools in order to learn skills that would enable students to escape the economic conditions that existed on the reservation. Consequently, this produced an idea that the reservation was an economic dead end, not a homeland that could and needed to be developed. Second, once at the school, Round Valley students learned skills and gained knowledge that, in the early twentieth century, was either anachronistic or nearly useless. The gendered instruction—work out of doors for boys and indoors for girls—often prepared Native students for an economy in which they already participated or provided skills that were inadequate in promoting economic development. If anything, Native child labor aided in the growth of southern California's "metropolis." Finally, by simply taking away children, the schools drained important sources of work from the reservation and undermined preexisting family labor arrangements.

Although the boarding schools harmed Round Valley's economy, we would be remiss if we only focused on what the schools did *to* Round Valley Indians. Building on the work of Brian Hosmer, Colleen O'Neill, and others, this essay explores the efforts of Round Valley Indian students and parents to shape boarding school education for the purposes of cultural and economic development. Hosmer, for instance, argues that top-down or deterministic histories of economic underdevelopment ignore narratives of Native agency and the ways in which Natives constructively negotiated the meanings of economic change and Indian policy.[5] The boarding school system provided students with skills and experiences with which they could eventually revitalize Native political economies. Some Round Valley Indian families used northern California's economy to resist the boarding school system. While some Round Valley students internalized the schools' message and left the reservation permanently to work and live, others returned to Round Valley and found ways to use their knowledge and experience to take advantage of new opportunities presented to Native people in the mid-twentieth century. The Indian Reorganization Act of 1934 (IRA) and the Indian New Deal ushered in a new era in American Indian economic development. Although still paternalistic, the IRA presaged an era when Native people organized their own tribal governments and developed their reservation economies. At boarding schools, Round Valley Indians gained knowledge, skills, and experiences that have enabled them to make significant contributions to tribal governments in the years after 1934, despite the federal government's intent to undermine reservation communities and their economies.

This essay complements and reframes the analysis of the boarding schools and American Indian economic development. Historians David Wallace Adams and Clyde Ellis, for instance, ask scholars to provide full portraits of the boarding school experience, to balance the oppression students experienced at the schools with stories of the innovative ways Native peoples forced schools to adhere to their expectations.[6] The issue of economic underdevelopment complements Ellis and Adams's suggestions and builds upon the previous work on the boarding schools and Indian economies. Anthropologist Alice Littlefield argues, "'Proletarianization' better characterizes the efforts of the federal Indian schools than assimilation." Between 1880 and 1930, the goals of Indian education changed from assimilating American Indian students to creating a docile agricultural workforce to meet fluctuating labor demands and economic conditions in the United States.[7] Largely, "proletarianization" equipped Native students with nearly worthless knowledge and skills because, as historian Peter Iverson writes, "the Indian schools, like many other education institutions, appeared determined to prepare their students for the previous century rather than the current one; they kept churning out tinsmiths rather than teachers."[8] Furthermore, Indian education benefited settler economies, rather than Native communities.[9] Historian Robert Trennert found that businesses near the Phoenix Indian School took advantage of the cheap labor offered by the school and students found very limited employment opportunities in Phoenix.[10] Yet, Native people found ways to use boarding schools to their economic advantage. Historian Brenda Child illuminates the intertwined nature of reservation economies and boarding school education. Reservation families viewed boarding schools as a way to escape reservation poverty, whether because of the lack of rations at home or by learning a new skill at the school.[11] This study pays attention to the effects of the off-reservation boarding schools on reservations and to their impact on students. It seeks to place greater emphasis on the short- and long-term implications of the boarding school system. A significant effect, of course, is the off-reservation boarding school system's contribution to the underdevelopment of Indian Country.

The Round Valley Reservation is located in northern California's Mendocino County, approximately 180 miles north of San Francisco. From the beginning of the reservation system in California, federal officials hoped to use cheap Indian labor to fund federal policy. State and federal officials removed California Indians from mining and agricultural areas to isolated reservations and farms, where Indian labor would grow the food necessary to provide for the government wards on the farm and in other parts of the state. In 1856, federal officials created the Nome Cult Farm to supply the reservations that dotted California. Federal officials placed members of perhaps fourteen different tribal groups on the farm, including the current constituents of the federally recognized Round Valley Tribes of the Covelo Indian Community: Yukis, Wailackis, Nomlackis, Concows, and Pomos. By the 1860s, the renamed Round Valley Reservation was one of the few reservations in California, as the federal government closed others because of government malfeasance and to reduce federal costs.[12]

In the late nineteenth century, reservation agents began to persuade Round Valley Indian students to attend off-reservation boarding schools. At first, reservation agents sent Round Valley students to the Chemawa Indian Boarding School in Salem, Oregon, and the Phoenix Indian School in Arizona. In the twentieth century, students attended the Stewart Indian School in Carson City, Nevada, and the Sherman Institute in Riverside, California in greater numbers.[13] Reservation officials had many reasons to send Round Valley children to off-reservation boarding schools, but one of the most prominent was their desire to save Indian children from what they perceived to be the miseries of reservation poverty. By 1900, Round Valley Indians' economic situation was precarious. During the previous decade, federal officials had allotted the reservation. Agents hoped that allotment would transform Round Valley Indians from migrant farmworkers into sedentary farmers. Round Valley Indians understood allotment differently. Instead of farming their own allotments, Round

Valley Indians preferred to lease their lands and earn cash from picking hops and other crops in northern California. Reservation officials criticized these economic decisions. They lamented the fact that Round Valley Indians had wasted their opportunity to be self-supporting and often argued that Round Valley Indians were racially inferior to their white neighbors. Rather than perceived racial deficiencies or laziness, however, a flawed federal policy contributed to reservation impoverishment. Agents and school officials conveniently ignored the fact that Round Valley Indians received allotments of 5 and 10 acres (hardly enough land to sustain a market farm) and the reservation was isolated from centers of economic activity. Instead of relying on one economic activity, such as farming, Round Valley Indians cobbled together a multisource economy of wage labor, hunting, small-plot gardens, and leasing lands. Despite the effective economic strategies of Indian families, white reservation officials still did not believe that Native children had a bright economic future on the reservation.[14]

Government officials suggested that an off-reservation education offered hope to Round Valley Indian children through vocational training. In 1914, Concow Horace Anderson was one of three Round Valley Indian children accused of burning down the reservation's boarding school. Instead of seeking criminal charges, the school's superintendent shipped Horace to Sherman and the other boys to Chemawa.[15] After three years at Sherman, Round Valley superintendent Walter McConihe recommended that Horace remain. "This boy has put in one term at Riverside, and it is deemed in his best interests that he remain there and finish his education and get a trade."[16] Of course, McConihe likely suggested that Anderson remain at Sherman because he did not want an arsonist to return to the reservation. However, economic calculations played a role in McConihe's recommendation that Anderson stay at the school. He viewed a "trade" as a potential opportunity for Anderson to escape what McConihe viewed as the economic deprivation of reservation life. If Anderson honed the skills necessary to become a blacksmith, for instance, he would not have to return to the reservation.

Round Valley Indians agreed with federal officials that Sherman might offer an opportunity for upward mobility in a region with limited economic opportunities. In 1925, Sacramento Area Office Education Field Agent Edward Swengel reported that Concow-Wailacki Mervin Goodwin wanted to attend Sherman because he "wishes to obtain vocational training."[17] It is possible that Swengel presumed Goodwin's desire to attend Sherman, but Mervin apparently told Sherman officials that his sister Mary suggested he become an auto mechanic. If Mervin learned this skill, he might escape a difficult economic situation and migrant wage work.[18] Female students, too, expressed interest in new work skills. Concow Erla Neafus aspired to be a nurse in nearby Ukiah, California, when she completed her schooling. Erla's desire to be a nurse probably stemmed from her mother, Ellen Dorman, who earned money by working as a nurse and dressmaker and, in 1931 when Erla enrolled at Sherman, was under doctor's care for an undisclosed illness. Erla no doubt hoped to use her education to earn a good living and assist her ill mother in the future.[19]

The assimilationist and racialist rhetoric that federal officials used to convince Round Valley students to attend and stay at boarding schools stultified Round Valley's economy. Federal officials attempted to detribalize Native peoples by giving Indian parents individual allotments and sending children to faraway boarding schools. From the outset, assimilationist Indian policies deterred tribal nations from creating economic enterprises that would benefit the entire Indian nation. More than that, assimilationist policies directed Native children to apply their knowledge, education, and skills at places other than their homelands. Federal officials informed Indian parents and children that the reservation was an economic dead end; that the future for Indian children was off reservations, not on them. The only way to escape a bleak future was to learn a trade or skill that students could apply at off-reservation places. Agents erected these assimilationist ideas on a foundation of racialist beliefs, which held that people of color were only fit for menial labor. These ideas came to dominate federal Indian policy in the early twentieth century as many officials lost hope in the ability of American Indians to assimilate. Some Indian children, such as Mervin Goodwin and Erla Neafus, internalized these messages as they desired to learn specialized training at Sherman that they could apply in off-reservation settings.

Federal assimilation policy had a couple of implications for the present and future of Round Valley's economic development. For one, assimilationist policies initiated a brain drain, where a generation or two of bright Native students left the reservation, convinced or told that their homelands were economically unproductive. Additionally, these policies had negative implications for those students who returned to the reservation. Rather than working with those students, who might have been able to use their education to promote economic development on the reservation, federal officials disdained returned students and viewed them as failures.[20] Of course, not all students agreed with the federal mentality. Although Ellen and Mervin wanted new skills and training, ties to kin and place remained strong. Erla desired to learn skills that could help her ill mother. Moreover, Ukiah, where Erla worked, is a little more than sixty miles from Round Valley, so Erla could have maintained ties with the reservation, if she chose. Too, her father, Ben, periodically worked in the area, allowing her to maintain contact with her divorced parents. Still, federal officials' efforts to send Native children to off-reservation boarding schools fostered a mentality that the reservation was an economic dead end and Indian children should look elsewhere for personal economic development.

The instruction that Round Valley students received at the boarding schools separated Native students from their home economies and perpetuated underdevelopment. When students arrived at Sherman, they entered into three-, four-, or even five-year terms. Those students who initially joined the school on a three-year stint could apply for another three years, like the aforementioned Horace Anderson. Most Round Valley students had attended a day or boarding school on the reservation for grades one through three and entered Sherman in the fourth grade. As historian Thomas Andrews points out in his study of residential schools in South Dakota, beginning in 1894, the Office of Indian Affairs created a three-tier education system for Native children. Students would first attend local day schools, then reservation boarding schools, and finally, usually around the age of sixteen, advance to the off-reservation boarding school, where they finished their education. Although not all students followed this path, many Round Valley students spent at least some time in each of these educational facilities.[21]

Instruction at the boarding schools provided both educational and vocational training. Wailacki June Britton remembered, "We had math, history, English, science, we had the major classes. We went to school half the day and worked half the day. It was a self-supporting boarding school…. Oh, and we had home ec, I guess. That was kind of a subject, too. We learned to cook and sew and make gardens and stuff like that."[22] The boarding schools provided instruction that enforced what scholar Katrina Paxton calls "gender assimilation." Boys and girls received an education based on the gender roles that school officials thought they should play in US society. Paxton notes, "Male vocations were to lead to wage work in the public sphere—outside the home—whereas the female training, also to lead to wage work, remained within the private sphere—inside the home of white employers or in their homes as mother."[23] The separate economic spheres taught at the boarding schools did not mesh with Native economies of the late nineteenth and early twentieth century. School instructors expected Native women, like June, to work indoors. However, June remembered that her siblings and her mother worked as migrant workers while her father worked on a ranch.[24] What is more, the emphasis on wage work ensured that Indian students contributed to northern and southern California's settler economies as an agricultural and domestic working class.

Grade sheets and progress reports available in student case files reveal how "gender assimilation" functioned in the Sherman classroom and contributed to reservation underdevelopment. In 1916, Wailacki-Nomlacki

Clarence Willburn enrolled at Sherman for a five-year stint, where he entered the vocational division. This course of study trained students in a variety of agricultural jobs. In order to pass each unit, Clarence had to complete a series of tasks within a prescribed period of time, and, when completed, he received a rating for his progress. On September 11, 1916, Clarence entered the farm blacksmithing program and finished November 18, 1916. Beginning November 20, 1916, he took farm masonry and finished a couple of days before Christmas. After that, he took classes in farming, farm engineering, and farm carpentry. Farming was the most extensive program at Sherman, where students devoted forty weeks to instruction. School officials expected students, like Clarence, to finish the instruction during the course of their enrollment. On February 6, 1917, Clarence began fifteen weeks of instruction in farming, and would presumably finish learning how to farm in subsequent years. To receive a passing grade in farming, Clarence had to demonstrate a proficiency in stock raising, plant production, road maintenance, care for implements, and landscaping. Clarence was evidently a solid student, consistently earning marks of "good" or "excellent." Instructors also left glib comments, indicating that Clarence was "attentive," "doing fine," or "did good work."[25]

Meanwhile, Round Valley Indian girls took classes that placed them indoors. On September 11, 1916, Concow-Wailacki Amy Goodwin enrolled in Sherman's sewing program. As with boys and farming, school officials required girls to take sewing for four years. In year one, Amy had to know the origin, manufacture, cost, testing, and use of cotton, linen, wool, and silk; use paper patterns; draft patterns; renovate, alter, and repair garments and household furnishings; and use dyes. Like Clarence, Amy was a good student, earning marks of "good" and "excellent."[26] At any rate, students like Clarence and Amy did not learn skills that would help them foster and promote a reservation economy. If anything, students learned skills that they already knew from growing up in a rural and farming region or that they could only apply in the labor and service sectors of off-reservation agricultural or urban economies.

In the mid 1920s, boarding school officials expanded the educational offerings available to Native students. During this time, critics of the off-reservation boarding school system outlined the inadequacies of the boarding school curriculum and the limited opportunities available to graduates.[27] As a response to this criticism, off-reservation boarding schools offered new courses to Native students. In 1926, Nomlacki Maxine Pina enrolled at Sherman at the age of ten and matriculated from the fifth grade to the ninth. Her coursework included five years of arithmetic and English, four years of general exercise, three years of geography, American history, and physiological hygiene, and one year of civics and agriculture. Maxine's vocational training consisted of one year each of cooking, housekeeping, food, clothing, and sewing, not altogether novel subjects. In September 1928, Maxine enrolled in the cooking program and finished in November. She had to make muffins, biscuits, three kinds of steak, baked potatoes, shortcake, and creamed vegetables in order to pass. After that, Maxine had to prepare a breakfast of five articles and demonstrate good table service. Other girls took vocational courses in domestic art, domestic science, home training, home management, laundering, nursing, and poultry, all of which reinforced Sherman's attempt at "gender assimilation."[28]

For boys, the new curriculum included blacksmithing, dairying, mill and cabinet making, painting, printing, and shoe repair. In the 1920s, vocational education emphasized specialization and skill, instead of learning a diversity of farm chores. Under the new system, students followed the trajectory of an artisan as they advanced from helper to apprentice.[29] In 1926, Nomlacki Eugene Jamison entered the printing program at Sherman. School officials had high hopes for Jamison. "Gene is a very capable operator," one of his instructors wrote, "and with his present experience both school and commercial [he] could go into a commercial shop and do well." Eugene trained to be a linotype operator, which required him to study the keyboard, practice on both a dummy and live machine, and set newspaper headlines.[30] School officials, of course, had no intention of Gene returning to Round Valley with his printing knowledge. Rather, they hoped that he would find a job in southern California, or in other parts of the state, thus depriving Round Valley of his education and skills.

Sherman offered students several opportunities to use their skills outside of the classroom. As with many other schools, Sherman relied on its student population as a workforce. Wailacki-Nomlacki John Willburn critically recalled, "At Sherman you went to school half the time; you worked half the time. Different things: mowing lawns, scrubbing floors. It was all a headache."[31] Work at Sherman conformed to the "gender assimilation" of the school's curriculum. Girls worked in jobs that kept them indoors or in care of other people. As part of Concow Bertha Whipple's industrial grade, she worked in the school's dining room and hospital. Meanwhile, Concow Blanche Feliz cleaned the superintendent's office. Boys worked in the school's garden, fed cattle, and built fences. Concow Horace Anderson worked as a mail boy at the superintendent's office.[32] Work outside of the classroom fulfilled a dual purpose. It served as another opportunity for students to learn and apply work skills. Additionally, many off-reservation schools relied on Native student labor to stay afloat and reduce operating costs. As with the foundation of the reservation system in California, boarding schools used

Indian labor to subsidize federal programs. Federal officials directed Indian labor away from their communities and nations and toward an entity that fostered Indian wardship.

Students also found jobs in southern California through the outing program, which only reinforced the "gender assimilation" that existed in school instruction. Boys worked on farms and ranches in southern California, while girls performed domestic chores in nearby towns and cities. Before the 1920s, Round Valley boys went to work in southern California's growing agricultural economy. In 1918, Wailacki-Nomlacki Clarence Willburn picked oranges for the A&H Fruit Company. Wailacki Robert Hanover worked as a teamster for W. C. Weaver, and Wailacki Sidney Pete bailed hay at the Castle Brothers Ranch.[33] Native girls worked inside southern California houses and businesses. Concow Minnie Graves spent the summer of 1913 working as a maid at the Glenwood Hotel. She and other girls also worked as domestic servants in private homes, washing clothes, preparing meals, and caring for children.[34] It could not have been lost on Native students that these jobs closely resembled the economic activities of their parents in northern California. Round Valley Indian families migrated to pick crops, Round Valley Indian men worked as teamsters for the reservation, and Round Valley Indian women worked as domestic servants in Mendocino County. Rather than broadening the economic experiences for Round Valley Indians, the outing program replicated the multisource economy of Round Valley Indian families. However, Round Valley Indian families did not benefit from the work of their children. Instead, the growing agricultural economy of southern California benefitted from cheap Indian labor.

In the 1920s and 1930s, Sherman officials expanded the outing opportunities to match the changing vocational education provided at the school. Concow Doran Lincoln worked on a construction site in southern California for three summers, and Nomlacki Eugene Jamison spent an equal time working at J. B. Smith's printing office in Arlington, California.[35] Aside from learning blue-collar work skills, Native boys contributed to the growth of southern California's urbanizing economy.

From top to bottom, the off-reservation boarding school curriculum and outing program harkened to long-held ideas about "civilizing" Indians. Since the early nineteenth century, so-called "friends of the Indian" linked agriculture and domestic industry to the effort to assimilate Indians. The emphasis on farm labor at Sherman exemplified the ideal of the yeoman farmer, whereas the shift in the 1920s reflected ideas about skill, specialized labor, and artisanal work.[36] Both programs, however, ignored the realities of reservation life and economic change in the United States. It was extremely difficult for white Californians, let alone Indians, to farm small plots of land.

Large agribusinesses and the legacy of the latifundia system of land owner-ship dominated the California landscape and allowed little room for small farming enterprises.[37] Sherman's vocational training and the outing programs restricted, rather than expanded, the post–boarding school opportunities for Native children. The outing system and classroom instruction reinforced the gendered division of labor that reformers attempted to inculcate among American Indians. Girls learned how to be housewives, teachers, or nurses. Boys gained knowledge of the tasks and techniques of agricultural labor. These programs trained Indian boys and girls for the lives they would lead when they *returned* to the reservation (agricultural or domestic workers), even though their intended goal was to induce Natives to *leave* the reservation. Few of these skills were necessary for Indians to develop Round Valley's econ-omy. Indeed, these skills usually benefited the settler economy of California.

If boarding schools failed to prepare Indian children to improve or develop Round Valley's economy, they also had an immediate impact on Round Valley's economy. Boarding schools drained important sources of labor from the reservation. In January 1918, Wailacki-Nomlacki Clarence Willburn wanted to leave Sherman and enlist in the Navy. His mother Minnie refused to give school officials permission to let Clarence leave school because "a person joining the navy ought to have an education, and another thing, his father is under the doctor's care and may have to call on him to do the farming."[38] When boarding schools took Native children from their families, it often left those families a hand short on the farms or in the fields. For the Willburns, the necessity of having Clarence come home became more press-ing as the months edged toward summer. In March, Minnie repeated that Aaron, Clarence's father, "isn't able to work very much and times are pretty hard with us, and we are not able to hire help."[39] Sherman superintendent Frank Conser did not believe Minnie and thought that the Willburns wanted to prevent Clarence from enlisting in the Navy. He informed the Willburns that Clarence desired to remain at Sherman and work in the outing program for the summer.[40] Minnie, however, persisted, and wrote a pleading letter to her son. She first noted "there is lots of work up here. Ben wanted you to work with him, said that you both could make a hundred dollars a piece a month." Minnie then described how the Willburns had planted a garden, the quality of the family's horses (fatted during the winter), and that a neighbor had taken Clarence's coyote-hunting dog, named Buck, for a debt Clarence apparently owed. Minnie ended her letter with her hopes for Clarence's future, "[Your father Aaron] wants you to come and take up a homestead, the land here will be throwed open to settlement the 20th of June. You know we haven't but little range to run our stock on." If Clarence acquired some land, Minnie suggested, the family could enlarge their economic endeavors.[41]

Minnie's letter apparently did the trick. That summer, Clarence returned to Round Valley and never went back to Sherman. By August 1918, he married Irene Campbell and began to establish his own farm.[42]

Perhaps in particulars, Clarence's story was unique. He wanted to join the Navy, but instead returned to Round Valley, got married, and forgot about Sherman. However, many of the issues that prompted his mother to request Clarence's return affected many other Round Valley families. Round Valley Indians relied on the combined labor power of all family members. When a parent or sibling became sick, it was especially dangerous to have a child at Sherman because there was no one to pick up the slack. In many cases, Indian families, like the Willburns, could not afford the loss of labor when a child went to school. These labor demands only increased during the summer, when gardens needed to be tended and harvested, horses and cows required attention, and crops needed to be picked.

Boarding school education certainly assisted in the underdevelopment of Round Valley's economy. Government officials convinced students that they need to leave the reservation to escape reservation poverty, and the education that students received directed them toward settler, off-reservation, and metropolitan economies. Yet, students and families found ways to shape the boarding school system. Some students had positive memories of the instruction and outing program. Wailacki Arvella Freeman recalled, "I learned how to run a sewing machine, how to work in a laundry, I worked in the building, and I worked in the dining room, [as a] dining room inspector. Then I worked in the cottages."[43] The outing program also offered Round Valley Indian students an opportunity to earn their own wages, although boarding school officials exercised considerable control over them. On the reservation, families pooled the wages they earned picking hops and performing other migrant agricultural jobs and used the money to purchase clothes for children and food during the winter. At Sherman, students, such as Arvella, Grace, and Maxine, earned money for themselves and became consumers. They spent their wages on items that they considered important. That feeling of consumerism, limited as it was, was liberating for some Native girls. Freeman remembered, "I didn't get much. They'd pay me five dollars a month, and as soon as I got my money I'd go to that little store they had and buy snails [danishes] and you know, something nice. Treat all of my friends and I would be broke."[44] Freeman not only purchased tasty treats for herself, but used her money to purchase items for her friends.

Students and their families had high expectations for the curriculum offered at off-reservation boarding schools. As Mervin Goodwin and Erla Neafus's applications to Sherman indicated, students expected to learn important skills. When boarding school education failed to meet those anticipated results, students vented their frustration at federal officials. In 1908, Yukis Myrtle Duncan and Amanda Heath and Concow Eveline Ackerman enrolled at Sherman. In 1910, the girls received information about the vocational training at the Carlisle Indian Industrial School in Pennsylvania, and the trio wanted to attend that school. They wrote to Round Valley superintendent Thomas Wilson, "We cannot learn anything we desire that is along house-keeping, cooking, or in the dress-making department [at Sherman]." The girls explained that Sherman officials designated those important jobs for "large" girls, and since they were "middle size girls only sixteen of age" they had few opportunities for these tasks.[45] Upon hearing the girls' request, Sherman superintendent Frank Conser explained that many students had received promotional literature from Carlisle, "I have already written to the superin-tendent of the Carlisle school that I think it unwise to request pupils of one school to go to another." Conser believed that students needed to develop a "loyalty" to their boarding school and advised against changing schools in the middle of a term.[46] All three girls stayed at Sherman that year.[47] Since fed-eral officials, Native students, and their families expected them to learn new skills that would assist in their personal economic growth, students, like Myrtle, Amanda, and Evaline, were disappointed when school instruction failed to live up to the propaganda.

Students and their employers also expressed varying levels of satisfaction with the outing program. In the summer of 1913, school officials found a job for Yuki Myrtle Duncan with Nora Turner, the wife of a teacher at Anaheim Union High School. Turner was quite pleased with Myrtle's work.[48] The fol-lowing year, however, Myrtle worked for Mrs. H. A. deWit of Los Angeles. In June 1914, Myrtle requested permission to quit her job. Mrs. deWit explained that she had been sick the previous week, which caused Myrtle's workload to be "heavier." Myrtle had to wash the Mrs. deWit's baby's clothes, table linen, and stockings as well as take care of the breakfast dishes. With these jobs completed, Myrtle had time off until 2:30, when the baby woke up and Myrtle had to take the baby for a walk. At 5:30, Mrs. deWit expected Myrtle to assist with dinner. "She had no housework *whatever* to do. I did it all," Mrs. deWit insisted. Mrs. deWit identified the genesis of Myrtle's request to quit not in an increased workload but in a confrontation that occurred between herself and Myrtle. One day, Mrs. deWit asked Myrtle to take her jaundiced baby outside and give the child some sunlight. Instead, Myrtle went next door and "sat out in the shade with two colored maids." Mrs. deWit asked the trio to take the baby to the front yard and in the sunlight. Although the domestic workers agreed to this request, Mrs. deWit shortly found her baby in the shade once again. After Mrs. deWit reprimanded her, Myrtle refused to talk to Mrs. deWit and asked Sherman officials for a new job.

Mrs. deWit thought she knew the source of Myrtle's changed behavior: "There is a colored cook next door that is known throughout the neighborhood as a trouble maker." Mrs. deWit alleged that Duncan spent her afternoons with the cook. "She tells the girls that are working around here that they should not do this or do that." Since Myrtle requested the change, deWit returned Myrtle to Sherman.[49] Despite deWit's insistence that Myrtle's workload was not "heavier" than normal, Myrtle clearly believed that the working conditions in deWit's house were unsuitable. Add to this the racial dynamics of Indian education and the reason for Myrtle's request to leave deWit's employment is clear. Myrtle found common cause with African American domestic workers and they no doubt spent many of their afternoons together complaining about their employers. Mrs. deWit's public chastisement of Myrtle likely distanced employer and employee.

Wages were another vexing issue for students, employers, and school administrators. Students at Sherman earned less per month than other employees in Riverside, thus non-Indians in southern California sought out Indian children as fruit pickers or domestic servants. Employers often docked student pay for the cost of transportation to and from Riverside. Finally, employers paid the school, not the student, most of a student's salary.[50] This last issue irritated Native students. In 1913, F. M. Snider, who employed Victoria Duncan as a domestic servant, mailed a check for eight dollars, two-thirds of Victoria's salary, to Sherman superintendent Frank Conser.[51]

Students, and some of their employers, recognized the inequity in such a system. In the summer of 1915, Concow Grace Wright worked for the family of W. T. Dinsmore of Riverside. On June 17, 1915, Mrs. Dinsmore contacted Orrington Jewett, Sherman's outing agent, and asked to advance Grace four dollars for new clothes, including a hat and shoes. Dinsmore noted, "Grace is a capable, willing, and pleasant little girl and I feel very much pleased with her."[52] Yet, school officials balked at advancing students their pay because they believed that students would profligately spend their money. Similarly, in 1932, Nomlacki Maxine Pina was working for a Los Angeles family when she wrote to Sherman superintendent Donald Biery requesting her full month's wages in order to buy a coat, shoes, and "other necessities." Pina suggested that it was both economical and practical to receive her full wages: "I think that I can get a better buy here in Los Angeles than in Riverside, and what's the difference of getting them now or later?"[53] Sherman's outing agent Olive Ellis paternalistically rejected Maxine's request. Ellis informed Maxine that students received one-third of their salary and school officials deposited the remaining two-thirds into an account. "You will have need next winter for all that you have earned, Maxine," Ellis wrote, "and we can advise you much better concerning your expenditures."[54] Although Maxine appeared to be a shrewd shopper, Ellis distrusted her judgment with money and withheld wages until the appointed time.

Resistance took place on the Round Valley Reservation as well as off of it. Since the boarding school often robbed families of essential labor, families utilized economic means to resist the boarding school. In 1917, Fred Long, who worked at the Round Valley Reservation, wrote to Sherman superintendent Frank Conser, informing him that Concow Blanche Feliz and Yuki Blanche Moore would not be returning to Sherman because they were working in the Sacramento Valley. During World War I, agricultural wages were quite good in California, prompting many Round Valley families to look beyond Mendocino County for work. Since the families pooled their wages, the Feliz and Moore families could use the extra hands in the fields. Yet, Long added, the girls had grievances about the school: "[Reservation superintendent] Mr. McConihe said that they had complaints, and he did not believe them but he did not know about them. There [are] very few children here, most all out of the valley working."[55] The children's criticism of Sherman and the possibility of earning good wages in the Sacramento Valley convinced these families to keep their children at home and at work in northern California. Such a strategy persisted during the next decade. Although agricultural wages and prices slid from their war-time heights, families continued to use migrant wage labor as a way to avoid sending their children to boarding schools. In 1924, Peter Clark, an Indian who worked as the reservation's farmer, reported, "Several of the children who have signed up for Sherman Institute have left for the Hop fields and the Bean fields.... I did not get to see any of the parents before they left. As they left Sunday morning bright & early on trucks. There are only a few children staid [sic] here."[56] Round Valley Indian families learned one lesson of boarding schools quite well: the schools could not take the children who did not remain on the reservation. And what better way for a family to keep their children than to take them to the fields with them?

Students could also use local job opportunities to avoid attending a boarding school. In 1914, Yuki/Wailacki Stella McKay attended Chemawa. In 1915, she returned to the reservation, and took the time to write a brief letter to her friend, Pomo/Huchnom Veltha Frazier, who remained at the Salem-based school. McKay informed Frazier that she felt uncomfortable on the reservation. Her former friends ran around without any parental supervision and threatened to "bring her down," people dressed cheaply, and her ex-boyfriend ignored her. Stella could not identify what had changed in Round Valley, but she longed to leave the reservation. However, she was certain that she was not returning to Oregon. Instead, McKay wrote, "I want to go to Ukiah this summer, so I can get work there. And perhaps I may stay there awhile. I don't know whether I'll get back to school or not. But I wish to travel, that's all." The prospect of a job enabled McKay to avoid returning to the Chemawa School and federal education efforts.[57]

For those students who finished off-reservation boarding schools, life after school brought mixed results. For some, a boarding school education opened the door for a job in the Indian Service. Concow Benjamin Neafus had a peripatetic existence after Sherman. In 1911, Neafus worked as a stableman and farmer at South Dakota's Crow Creek Reservation. In 1914, Neafus served as the Round Valley Indian boarding school's disciplinarian, the same year that Concow Horace Anderson and three other boys burned down the school. His daughter, Erla Neafus, attended Sherman in the 1930s.[58] In 1930, Mabel Pina found a job in the Commercial Department at Haskell Institute in Lawrence, Kansas. Afterwards, she worked at the Cheyenne and Arapaho Agency in Oklahoma. In 1936, Pina moved again and was a clerk at the Navajo Agency.[59] Mabel certainly benefited from the John Collier's efforts to hire Native people in Indian administration in the 1930s. As government officials intended, Neafus and Pina found opportunities for off-reservation upward mobility after attending a boarding school.

Many Round Valley boarding school students were like Clarence Willburn; they returned to the reservation after short stints at boarding schools. Concow Randolph Lincoln remembered, "I went to Sherman…went there for about a year…came home for vacation and I'm still here."[60] Once on the reservation, returned boarding school students inserted themselves in the local economy. In 1902, Round Valley superintendent Harry Liston reported, "Several pupils have returned home after an absence a few years at Chemawa, Oregon and Phoeniz [sic], A. T. and their future is a matter of deep interest to me. They all seem to have been greatly benefitted [sic] and anxious to continue their improvement. Of the two who returned last year one has returned to Chemawa, Oregon, the other is farming his allotment and teaming."[61] Students had several opportunities to use the skills they learned at boarding schools on the reservation. In 1903, Round Valley Superintendent Horace Johnson needed to hire someone to paint buildings at the Round Valley Reservation boarding school. "In support of this request I would most respectfully state that I have employed Walter Card, a returned student from Chemawa, at One dollar and twenty-five cents ($1.25) per day. He is doing good work, though not so much as a first class, experienced workman would do, and cannot complete the labor in twenty days, the time authorized."[62] Still, farming, working as a teamster, or even painting government buildings were temporary and seasonal occupations that Round Valley Indians performed before attending schools. The job skills Native boarding school students possessed did little to improve the depressed economic conditions of the post-allotment reservation. If anything, it appears that most boarding school students at Round Valley were mired in low-paying, seasonal work.

During the Great Depression, students struggled to utilize the new skills they learned at off-reservation boarding schools. In 1932, Nomlacki Eugene Jamison finished his schooling at Sherman, where he spent six years in the printing program and worked in printing companies in the outing program. However, there was little demand for his skills in Depression-era California. "I had no home to speak of," Jamison recalled. "No life at home to speak of, and nothing to earn a living from." He attempted to find work in Healdsburg, Ukiah, and Covelo, but the only response he received was "No Money." After describing the severity of the crisis in which he found himself, Eugene asked school officials if he could return to Sherman and study more printing. School officials rebuffed his efforts, and suggested that he find work with the Civilian Conservation Corps, saying, "Our advice right now would be to work in one of these camps for several months—save your money," after which they would help find a place for him at the Frank Wiggins Trade School in Los Angeles. Although Jamison's job prospects improved after the Great Depression, when he obtained a job at a newspaper in Mendocino County, it is clear that his Sherman education neither prepared him for the Great Depression nor to pursue economic development programs on the reservation. Instead, he returned to the reservation and worked on his grandfather's dairy farm—a job he performed before going to Sherman.[63]

It was not until the 1930s that Round Valley Indians found ways to use off-reservation boarding schools to escape underdevelopment. In 1936, Round Valley Indians accepted the Indian Reorganization Act (IRA). The Act enabled Round Valley Indians to vote on accepting an IRA constitution and a corporate charter to create tribal economic ventures. One former boarding school student, for instance, flourished in the new environment. Wailacki Robert Hanover was born on April 29, 1899, the son of Wailacki Dora Goodwin and a non-Indian man named Frank Hanover. In 1914, Robert attended Sherman because he thought he could find "better advantages." Robert's school record, unfortunately, is rather sparse, a contrast to the voluminous record he left behind once he returned to the reservation. Between 1945 and his death in 1964, Robert worked on the Round Valley Tribal Council, including a couple of terms as tribal president. One of the pressing issues that the tribal council addressed during these two decades involved land. Hanover and other tribal council members consistently worked to utilize the reservation's land base for the benefit of the entire Round Valley Indian community and to protect Round Valley Indian land from the interloping of non-Indian neighbors. In 1964, when Robert passed away, the Round Valley Tribal Council authorized a modest amount of money to purchase a floral wreath in tribute to Hanover's service to the reservation.[64] In this instance, Hanover was not alone. Wailacki-Concow Doran Lincoln attended Sherman in the 1930s. He worked in construction with the outing program, but found few job prospects when his time at Sherman ended. During World War II, Doran enlisted in the Navy. When the war ended, he returned to Round Valley. In the 1960s, Doran entered tribal government and participated in anti-alcohol programs on the reservation made possible by the development of the policy of self-determination.[65] Not all boarding school students returned to the reservation and joined the tribal council or worked in tribal programs. Yet, those who did relied on their boarding school educations to attempt to create a better economic and social future for the Round Valley Reservation.

As with many aspects of the history and long-term implications of the off-reservation boarding school program, assessing its effect on Indian Country's economy is both complex and lacks a concrete conclusion. Native children, their parents, and reservation officials wanted children to learn a "trade" at off-reservation boarding schools. Such a perspective initiated a "brain drain," whereby many Round Valley Indians left the reservation to live, taking their skills and knowledge with them. It is quite likely that the Round Valley agency or, later, the tribal government could have used the talents of someone like Mamie Pina, who preferred to work in Oklahoma and Arizona rather than on the reservation. Additionally, when students left for Sherman, it deprived families of the children's work power. Since Round Valley Indian families relied quite extensively on child labor, whether on allotments or in the hop fields, the loss of just one set of hands could have negative implications for the family's economy. By siphoning workers' skills, wages, and abilities away from the reservation, Sherman and other boarding schools contributed to the underdevelopment of Round Valley's economy in the early twentieth century.

Boarding school education failed to improve the economic outlook of Round Valley students or the reservation. Before the Meriam Report, most students took vocational classes in farming or domestic industries. These were precisely the types of jobs that they and their parents performed before the students went to boarding schools. Furthermore, in the aftermath of allotment, farming was a low-profit, nearly unviable enterprise. Allotments were simply too small to maintain in the sense that reservation agents desired. Even the changes initiated in the 1920s failed to immediately offer Round Valley Indian students better economic prospects, because they coincided with the Great Depression. Many students had the same experience as the aforementioned Nomlacki Eugene Jamison: there was simply no work available. What is more, neither the farming-oriented curriculum nor the later artisanal program equipped Native children with skills that could immediately sustain economic development projects on reservations. Instead, the boarding schools were bent on eradicating Native culture (thus eliminating the option of a culturally appropriate political economy) and developing individualism, not community-directed economic growth.

Yet, when Jamison and many of the post–Meriam Report generation returned to Round Valley they used their education in unintended ways. The development of the Indian Reorganization Act in 1934 and Round Valley's decision to accept the Act in 1936 offered boarding school students an opportunity to apply what they had learned. Boarding school students, like Hanover and Lincoln, figured prominently in the new tribal government and the ways in which it matured in the late twentieth century. Recently, Eugene Jamison, Jr., the son of Eugene Jamison, the printer, served as the tribal president. One of the most recent economic developments on the reservation is the creation of a small casino, with revenues being directed back to the reservation. Although the off-reservation boarding school contributed to the underdevelopment of the reservation and harmed family economies, Natives succeeded despite these federal policies because of their own desire and vision for the future of the Round Valley Reservation.

Notes

1. Odd Arne Westad, *The Global Cold War: Third World Interventions and the Making of Our Times*, 8–38, esp. 9–13.

2. See *Proceedings of the Third Annual Meeting of the Lake Mohonk Conference of the Friends of the Indian, Held October 7 to 9, 1885*, 43.

3. For an overview of this era in American Indian history see Frederick Hoxie, *A Final Promise: The Campaign to Assimilate the Indians, 1880–1920*. For studies of allotment and dispossession see Melissa Meyer, *The White Earth Tragedy: Ethnicity and Dispossession at a Minnesota Anishinaabe Reservation, 1889–1920*; Emily Greenwald, *Reconfiguring the Reservation: The Nez Perces, Jicarilla Apaches, and the Dawes Act*; David Rich Lewis, *Neither Wolf nor Dog: American Indians, Environment, and Agrarian Change*; Alexandra Harmon, "American Indians and Land Monopolies in the Gilded Age."

4. Jacqueline Goodman-Draper, "The Development of Underdevelopment at Akwesasne: Cultural and Economic Subversion," 42. For underdevelopment see Gary C. Anders, "Theories of Underdevelopment and the American Indian"; C. Matthew Snipp, "The Changing Political and Economic Status of the American Indians: From Captive Nations to Internal Colonies"; Edward Valandra, "Rethinking Indigenous Underdevelopment in the United States." Historians Richard White and Daniel Boxberger have written effective books using dependency theory. See White's *The Roots of Dependency: Subsistence, Environment, and Social Change among the Choctaws, Pawnees, and Navajos*, and Boxberger's *To Fish in Common: The Ethnohistory of Lummi Indian Salmon Fishing*.

5. See Brian Hosmer, *American Indians in the Marketplace: Persistence and Innovation among the Menominees and Metlakatlans, 1870–1920*, esp. 9–12; Colleen O'Neill, *Working the Navajo Way: Labor and Culture in the Twentieth Century*; Brian Hosmer and Colleen O'Neill, eds., *Native Pathways: American Indian Culture and Economic Development in the Twentieth Century*. Jacqueline Goodman-Draper points out, "The process of 'underdeveloping' a people is never straightforward. There is resistance, partial acceptance and residual ties based on traditional values and family." "The Development of Underdevelopment at Akwesasne," 48.

6. See David Wallace Adams, "Beyond Bleakness: The Brighter Side of Indian Boarding Schools, 1870–1940," 35–64, and Clyde Ellis, "'We Had a Lot of Fun, but of Course, That Wasn't the School Part': Life at the Rainy Mountain Boarding School, 1893–1920," 65–89, both in *Boarding School Blues: Revisiting American Indian Educational Experiences,* Clifford E. Trafzer, Jean A. Keller, and Lorene Sisquoc, eds.

7. Alice Littlefield, "Learning to Labor: Native American Education in the United States, 1880–1930," 43–59, quote p. 43; Alice Littlefield, "Indian Education and the World of Work in Michigan, 1893–1933," 100–121; Littlefield, "Native American Labor and Public Policy in the United States," 219–231, esp. 220–223. For a similar argument see K. Tsianina Lomawaima, *They Called It Prairie Light: The Story of Chilocco Indian School,* 65–99.

8. Peter Iverson, *Diné: A History of the Navajos,* 118.

9. By "settler," I mean, borrowing from Adam Barker: "Settler people in this context include most peoples who occupy lands previously stolen or in the process of being taken from their Indigenous inhabitants or who are otherwise members of the 'Settler society,' which is founded on the co-opted lands and resources." "The Contemporary Realism of Canadian Imperialism: Settler Colonialism and the Hybrid Colonial State," 328.

10. Trennert, "From Carlisle to Phoenix: The Rise and Fall of the Indian Outing System, 1878–1930," 267–291.

11. Brenda Child, *Boarding School Seasons: American Indian Families, 1900–1940.*

12. For the history of the Round Valley Reservation and Mendocino County Indians see the recent works: William Bauer, *"We Were All Like Migrant Workers Here": Labor, Community, and Survival on California's Round Valley Reservation, 1850–1941*; Jason Charles Newman, "'There Will Come a Day When White Men Will Not Rule Us': The Round Valley Indian Tribe and Federal Indian Policy, 1856–1934"; Khal Schneider, "Citizen Lives: California Indian Country, 1855–1940"; Lynwood Carranco and Estle Beard, *Genocide and Vendetta: The Round Valley Wars of Northern California*; Todd Benson, "The Consequences of Reservation Life: Native Californians on the Round Valley Reservation, 1871–1884."

13. For an introduction to the federal off-reservation boarding school system see David Wallace Adams, *Education for Extinction: American Indians and the Boarding School Experience, 1875–1928*. For Phoenix see Robert Trennert, *The Phoenix Indian School: Forced Assimilation in Arizona, 1891–1935*. For Sherman see Jean Keller, *Empty Beds: Indian Student Health at Sherman Institute, 1902–1922* and Matthew Sakiestewa Gilbert, *Education Beyond the Mesas: Hopi Students at Sherman Institute, 1902–1929.*

14. Bauer, *"We Were All Like Migrant Workers Here,"* 130–155.

15. For the burning of the reservation boarding school see Wendy Wall, "Gender and the 'Citizen Indian,'" 219. For sending Horace Anderson to Sherman see F. G. Collett to Ben Neafus, April 9, 1914, National Archives and Records Administration, Archives I, Record Group 75, Central Classified Files, 1907–1939, Round Valley Agency (hereafter CCF), Box 3: 13087–1917 [2 of 2]; E. B. Merritt to T. B. Wilson, National Archives and Records Administration–Pacific Region (Laguna Niguel), Record Group 75, Records of the Sherman Institute, Student Case Files (hereafter SCF), Box 9, Folder: Anderson, Horace.

16. Application of Lawson Anderson for the Enrollment of Horace Anderson in the Indian School at Riverside, CA, December 20, 1917, SCF, Box 9, Folder: Anderson, Horace.

17. Medical Certificate for Mervin Goodwin, August 16, 1935, SCF, Box 130, Folder: Goodwin, Mervin. The dash ("-") signifies that Goodwin was bi-tribal: one parent was Concow and another, Wailacki.

18. Vocational Information Record for Mervin Goodwin, SCF, Box 130, Folder: Goodwin, Mervin.

19. Application for Admission to Non-Reservation School and Test of Eligibility for Erla Neafus, August 1, 1931, and Home Record for Erla Neafus, January 15, 1932, both in SCF, Box 261, Folder: Neafus, Erla.

20. In this way, boarding schools resembled the stance federal officials took on urbanization and relocation in the 1950s. As American Indian Studies scholar Myla Carpio points out, federal officials criticized those Native men and women who returned to the reservation from the cities, considering them "failures" and "bad" Indians. See Myla Carpio, "Countering Colonization: Albuquerque Laguna Colony."

21. Thomas Andrews, "Turning the Tables on Assimilation: Oglala Lakotas and the Pine Ridge Day Schools, 1889–1920s." See also Adams, *Education for Extinction,* 28–60.

22. June Britton, interview by William Bauer, March 19, 2002, Covelo, CA (tape and transcript in author's possession).

23. Katrina Paxton, "Learning Gender: Female Students at the Sherman Institute, 1907–1925," in *Boarding School Blues: Revisiting American Indian Educational Experiences,* 179.

24. June Britton, interview by William Bauer, March 19, 2002, Covelo, CA (tape and transcript in author's possession).

25. See SCF, Box 388, Folder: Willburn, Clarence.

26. Record Card, Vocational Division, Sewing, for Amy Goodwin, September 11, 1916, SCF, Box 129, Folder: Goodwin, Amy.

27. Margaret Connell Szasz, *Education and the American Indian: The Road to Self-Determination since 1928,* 24.

28. Vocational Record Card of Maxine Pina, September 1928 to November 1928, SCF, Box 288, Folder: Pina, Maxine.

29. Felix Pina's Blacksmithing and Welding Attendance Record and Mill & Cabinet Attendance Record both in SCF, Box 288, Folder: Pina, Felix.

30. Printing Department, Gene Pina, September, 1931, SCF, Box 288, Folder: Pina, Eugene.

31. John Willburn in *Voices and Dreams: A Mendocino County Oral History*, Sally Russell and Bruce Levene, 316.

32. Record of Pupil in School, SCF, Box 384, Folder: Whipple, Bertha; F. M. Conser to Frank Feliz, April 30, 1917, SCF, Box 111, Folder: Feliz, Blanche; F. M. Conser to Mary Eagder, July 9, 1917, SCF, Box 285, Folder: Pete, Sidney; F. M. Conser to T. B. Wilson, August 6, 1914, Student Case Files, Box 9, Folder: Anderson, Horace.

33. Pay records of Clarence Willburn, National Archives and Records Administration–Pacific Region (Laguna Niguel), Record Group 75, Records of the Sherman Indian Institute, Record of Student Outings (hereafter RSO), Time/Pay Worksheets, 1917–1929, Box 1, Folder: 1918–1919; pay record of Robert Hanover, RSO, Boys Outings, 1914–1916, Box 1, Letterbook: 2; pay record of Sidney Pete, RSO, Time/Pay Worksheets, 1917–1929, Box 1, Folder: 1918–1919.

34. Pay Receipts for Minnie Graves, 1912, SCF, Box 132, Folder: Graves, Minnie.

35. Doran Lincoln interview by Acklan Willits, April 25, 1990, Round Valley Oral History Project, Round Valley Public Library, Covelo, CA (hereafter RVOHP); Ralph Johnson to F. M. Conser, June 20, 1929, SCF, Box 288, Folder: Pina, Eugene.

36. For the roots of farming and domestic industry in Indian policy see Francis Paul Prucha, *The Great Father: The United States Government and the American Indians*, 51–53.

37. See Donald Pisani, *From Family Farm to Agribusiness: The Irrigation Crusade in California and the West, 1850–1931*.

38. Minnie Willburn to Walter McConihe, February 10, 1918, SCF, Box 388, Folder: Willburn, Clarence.

39. Minnie Willburn to Frank Conser, March 5, 1918, SCF, Box 388, Folder: Willburn, Clarence.

40. Frank Conser to W. W. McConihe, April 30, 1918, SCF, Box 388, Folder: Willburn, Clarence.

41. Minnie Willburn to Clarence Willburn, May 22, 1918, SCF, Box 388, Folder: Willburn, Clarence.

42. Minnie Willburn to Frank Conser, August 29, 1918, SCF, Box 388, Folder: Willburn, Clarence.

43. Marian (Arvella) Freeman interview by William Bauer, June 20, 2002, Covelo, CA (tape and transcript in author's possession).

44. Marian (Arvella) Freeman interview by William Bauer, June 20, 2002, Covelo, CA (tape and transcript in author's possession).

45. Amanda Heath, Eveline Ackerman, and Myrtle Duncan to Superintendent Wilson, August 25, 1910, SCF, Box 102, Folder: Duncan, Myrtle.

46. Frank Conser to T. B. Wilson, September 13, 1910, SCF, Box 102, Folder: Duncan, Myrtle.

47. Frank Conser to T. B. Wilson, June 3, 1911, SCF, Box 102, Folder: Duncan, Myrtle. Amanda Heath later came down with tubercular symptoms and went home.

48. Nora Turner to F. M. Conser, June 21, 1913, SCF, Box 102, Folder: Duncan, Myrtle.

49. H. A. deWit to F. M. Conser, June 18, 1914, SCF, Box 102, Folder: Duncan, Myrtle.

50. Paxton, "Learning Gender," 182.

51. F. M. Snider to F. M. Conser, June 25, 1913, SCF, Box 102, Folder: Duncan, Victoria.

52. Mrs. Dinsmore to Orrington Jewett, June 17, 1915, SCF, Box 398, Folder: Wright, Grace.

53. Maxine Pina to D. H. Biery, n.d., SCF, Box 288, Folder: Pina, Maxine.

54. Olive Ellis to D. H. Biery, n.d., SCF, Box 288, Folder: Pina, Maxine.

55. Fred Long to F. M. Conser, October 26, 1917, SCF, Box 111, Folder: Feliz, Blanche. Similarly, Walter McConihe informed Harwood Hall, the superintendent at Chemawa, that everyone had left the reservation and that Native families were reluctant to send their children to the boarding school. W. W. McConihe to Harwood Hall, August 31, 1917, National Archives and Records Administration–Pacific Region (San Francisco), Record Group 75, Records of the Round Valley Agency, Administrative Files, 1908–1924 (hereafter AF), Box 39, Folder: Chemawa Indian School.

56. Peter Clark to L. A. Dorrington, August 19, 1924, National Archives and Records Administration–Pacific Region (San Francisco), Record Group 75, Sacramento Area Office, Coded Records, 1910–1958, Box 34, Folder: Round Valley Sub-Agency, Mr. Peter Clark [No. 3].

57. Stella McKay to Veltha Frazer, July 13, 1915, AF, Box 39, Folder: Chemawa Indian School [1914–1916]. I note the tribal ethnicities of Stella and Veltha with a "/" because their ethnicity is unclear. McKay is listed on a census that listed Yukis and Wailackis together. The same stands for Veltha.

58. Bauer, *"We Were All Like Migrant Workers Here,"* 140–144.

59. Mabel Pina Curley to D. H. Biery, June 4, 1936, Box 288, SCF, Folder: Pina, Mabel.

60. Randolph Lincoln interview by Les Lincoln, April 9, 1990, RVOHP.

61. Harry Liston to the Commissioner of Indian Affairs, August 20, 1902, National Archives and Records Administration–Pacific Region (San Francisco), Record Group 75, Records of the Round Valley Agency, 1859–1930, Correspondence of Agent/Superintendent to the Commissioner of Indian Affairs, 1873–1914 (hereafter CACIA), Box 2, Letterbook 2C: 78.

62. Horace Johnson to the Commissioner of Indian Affairs, October 27, 1903, CACIA, Box 2, Letterbook 2C: 300.

63. See Victoria Patterson, DeAnna Barney, Skip Willits, and Les Lincoln, eds., *The Singing Feather: Tribal Remembrances from Round Valley*, 35; Eugene Jamison to K. A. Marmon, September 12, 1933, and K. A. Marmon to Gene (Pina) Jamison, September 20, 1933, SCF, Box 288, Folder: Pina (Jamison), Eugene. The Wiggins school was a vocational training school in downtown Los Angeles. See *Life*, 59–60, and *Report of the Commissioner of Industrial and Vocational Education for the Year Ending June 30, 1914*, 51.

64. Round Valley Tribal Council Meeting Minutes, April 11, 1964, National Archives and Research Administration, San Bruno, CA, Record Group 75, Sacramento Area Office, Tribal Group Files, 1915–1975, Box 94: Round Valley—Minutes, 1960–1964.

65. Follow Up Record for Doran Lincoln, June 28, 1940, SCF, Folder: Lincoln, Doran; D. Lincoln interview.

6 *Guiding Principles*

Guswenta and the Debate over Formal Schooling at Buffalo Creek, 1800–1811

Alyssa Mt. Pleasant

On a mid-October day in 1800 Nicholas Cusick set off from the Tuscarora village near the falls at Niagara. His task was to conduct Reverend Elkanah Holmes to the reservation at Buffalo Creek, approximately thirty miles from the Tuscarora Nation's territory. Riding horseback, the two men made good time, and soon Cusick and his companion dismounted at one of the Seneca villages along Buffalo Creek. Holmes was interested in speaking with the leading figures at the reservation. He carried a commission from the New-York Missionary Society charging him with a preliminary mission to establish relationships with the Tuscaroras and Senecas in western New York State. It did not take long to find Farmer's Brother, one of the leading Seneca men, and make introductions. Farmer's Brother listened politely while Cusick, a Tuscarora who became familiar with Americans during his Revolutionary War service, translated Holmes's words. Commenting that he had heard the missionary was in the area, the Seneca leader noted that he would have to consult with other community members regarding Holmes's request for an audience. Satisfied with this initial interaction, Holmes promised to wait nearby for word of their decision. He parted ways with Cusick, climbing back on his mount and following the narrow path along the creek that led five miles back to the shore of Lake Erie. There the missionary found lodging in a modest neighborhood of cabins that several American families maintained at the mouth of Buffalo Creek.[1]

This vignette, which draws on Holmes's account of his travels, provides a glimpse of one of the early interactions between missionaries and Indians at Buffalo Creek. Over the course of the first decade of the nineteenth century, representatives of several missionary organizations traveled to the reservation seeking to establish an American-style school. In this essay I argue that Buffalo Creek residents, in crafting responses to missionaries who extolled the virtues of Christianity and pleaded for the opportunity to construct a school, drew on principles embedded in the *Guswenta* wampum belt. The belt, also known as the Two Row wampum, consists of two rows of purple beads (described metaphorically as a canoe and a sailboat) separated by three rows of white beads, which hold the respective meanings of peace, friendship, and forever. As Haudenosaunee traditionalists explain, like vessels traveling along parallel courses on the same body of water, the canoe and sailboat remain perpetually separated. Guswenta conveys the understanding that peace and friendship can be maintained in a colonial context when both parties (represented by the purple rows) embrace policies of noninterference in the other's government, religion, or way of life.[2] The principles symbolized by and strengthened through Guswenta served as a touchstone in diplomatic relations throughout the colonial period and, in the aftermath of the Revolutionary War, Haudenosaunee people drew on this philosophy of mutual respect as they struggled to educate Americans about appropriate nation-to-nation relations. Although the belt itself is never mentioned in discussions of formal schooling, careful reading of the recorded speeches of Haudenosaunee orators reveals unmistakable references to the foundational principles embedded in Guswenta. This essay shows that as formal schooling became a crucial site where Haudenosaunee people negotiated their relationship with the United States' emerging settler colonial regime, they articulated their opposition to Americans' efforts to assert rights of conquest and impose colonial state structures and social forms on American Indians through the language of Guswenta.[3]

The rich documentary record of speeches by Haudenosaunee orators (preserved in reports, letters, and memoirs created by missionaries and government officials) illuminates the ways Buffalo Creek residents brought indigenous philosophies of intercultural diplomacy to bear on their interactions with missionaries, modeled appropriate protocols for receiving visitors and engaging with them, and articulated elements of their spiritual belief system. These speeches also provide a glimpse of the meticulous deliberations of a community unsure if formal schooling would have a positive or negative impact on its survival. Because this early phase of American policy has received scant attention from scholars of American Indian education, the voices of American Indian people and the strategies they utilized in interactions with missionary-educators serving as the vanguard of United States set-tler colonialism are poorly understood.[4] The history of Buffalo Creek pro-vides insight into these interactions, and careful attention to the voices of Haudenosaunee people reveals their determination and pragmatism as they navigated the rapidly shifting political and demographic landscape of the early American republic. In the pages that follow I situate the Buffalo Creek reservation and introduce elements of Haudenosaunee diplomatic practice, then move on to an extended examination of the ways the reservation resi-dents, whose actions were guided by the principles of Guswenta, gradually and selectively implemented the United States' emerging Indian education policy in ways that met their needs while subverting American policy mak-ers' intentions.

Confronting the "Missionary Problem"

The village where Reverend Holmes first met Farmer's Brother was one of several settlements on the Buffalo Creek reservation in western New York State. Senecas and other Haudenosaunee people (members of the six nations who subscribed to the prophetic teachings of the peacemaker Dekanawida) settled there in the midst of the Revolutionary War, forming the largest Haudenosaunee community south of the Great Lakes.[5] In the years follow-ing the war this reservation, located on the far western edge of the Seneca homelands abutting Lake Erie, served as their political center. Because of its political and social prominence (and despite its relative geographic isola-tion), many visitors made their way to Buffalo Creek. American and British officials, traders, land speculators, and missionaries visited frequently, as did members of American Indian nations near and far.[6] Haudenosaunee people received these visitors, whether they were motivated by commercial or diplo-matic interests, kinship obligations, or spiritual concerns, according to long-established protocols for intercultural interactions.[7] When Holmes returned to Buffalo Creek he was introduced to these formalities.

Standing before a capacity crowd, the Seneca orator Red Jacket addressed one hundred and fifty people who gathered at the council house to meet the visiting missionary. The captivating speaker, whose rhetorical skills were admired by Indians and Americans alike, employed some of the ritualized language of Haudenosaunee diplomacy as he welcomed Holmes.[8] Expressing thanks to the Great Spirit, who smoothed Holmes's travel, protected him on "rugged paths," and kept "briars or thorns" from pricking his feet, Red Jacket acknowledged both the practical difficulties of travel and the potential imped-iments to intercultural interactions.[9] This metaphorical language was part of the protocol Haudenosaunee people employed to set the tone for productive conversations. Providing a welcome that acknowledged and soothed any pain or suffering a visitor may be experiencing is one of the initial rituals of the condolence ceremony that is integral to Haudenosaunee social, political, and spiritual life. This practice was introduced by the peacemaker when he sought to unify five warring nations whose territory stretches across today's New York State.[10] The "welcome at woods edge" was first recorded by a French missionary in the mid-seventeenth century.[11] Subsequent generations of colonial actors noted the practice in their records of diplomatic exchanges and, in the period following the Revolutionary War, Americans, like their predecessors, slowly developed facility with the forms of Haudenosaunee diplomacy.[12]

When Red Jacket formally welcomed Holmes using diplomatic protocols, he signaled that Haudenosaunee people understood the missionary was a political actor who not only represented his Baptist faith and his employer, the New-York Missionary Society, but also played a larger role in the relationship between the United States and Haudenosaunee people. Holmes espoused the virtues of Christianity and urged Buffalo Creek residents to embrace formal schooling. Like other itinerant missionaries working for evangelical societies established in the midst of the Second Great Awakening, he enjoyed the support of an organization that embraced a transformational "civilization" program rooted in economic individualism, republicanism, and individual liberty along with instruction in literacy, numeracy, and Christianity.[13] These vigorous efforts coincided with federal policies articulated in the Trade and Intercourse Acts, where Congress authorized the Secretary of War to oversee a substantial fund supporting "civilization" efforts.[14] As the historian Francis Paul Prucha has noted, "missionary groups were indispensable" to the implementation of the civilization program at a time when the federal bureaucracy for Indian affairs was just emerging.[15] With the full support of the federal government and backing from numerous private individuals, missionaries like Holmes intended to establish schools where Indians would acquire skills and practices that were familiar to Americans.[16]

When Holmes finally addressed the crowd at Buffalo Creek, he conveyed the New-York Missionary Society's sincere interest in their well-being and shared brief messages from the Tuscaroras, Oneidas, and Mahicans he had visited on his way to the reservation.[17] Holmes received assistance conveying his message from Nicholas Cusick, the Tuscarora man who initially brought him to Buffalo Creek, and William Johnston, an American trader married to a Cayuga woman.[18] They translated the missionary's brief remarks and drafted the transcription Holmes included in his report. The missionary approached his audience in a deferential manner, perhaps due to coaching from Cusick or Johnston, and he was careful to save his request to speak further about the Great Spirit and Jesus Christ for the end of his speech. This approach brought positive results; after consulting for half an hour, those assembled at the council house agreed to let Holmes speak about Christianity the following day. Encouraged, the missionary returned to lodge at the small American settlement near the lake shore and prepare his upcoming sermon. Reporting on his experiences at Buffalo Creek, Holmes expressed appreciation for the opportunity to deliver an address regarding "modes of Christian worship" and commented on the "good attention" and "solemn impressions" he observed on faces in the audience, prompting him to consider the talks a success.[19]

Haudenosaunee people's responses to the missionary belie Holmes's rosy interpretation of his audiences at Buffalo Creek. The community had a strong critique of the formal sermon the missionary delivered. Their objections emerged in a speech Red Jacket delivered during Holmes's third visit to the reservation, following a period of consultation with the audience after Holmes concluded his remarks. Such consultations, part of a practice of formulating collective responses to formal speeches, were a typical feature of Haudenosaunee diplomacy. In this case Red Jacket's speech revealed that while Holmes was received cordially, the assembled Indians had grave concerns about the American's apparent misapprehension of their spiritual beliefs. Perceptive and well-informed, they also recognized the pitfalls of formal schooling that frequently operated as a technology of settler colonialism linked with dispossession.

Relaying these reactions, Red Jacket first addressed spirituality. He reminded the missionary of Indians' belief in a "Great Being above, who has made Heaven and earth and all things that are therein," then noted their understanding that "there is something great after death."[20] The orator, who was known for his biting commentaries, went on to express "astonish[ment] at you whites," chastising those who "when Jesus Christ was among you, and went about doing good…did not pay attention to him, and believe him, and that you put him to death" rather than embrace his teachings.[21] Indians, he observed, were not involved in the betrayal of Christ: they had their own distinct spiritual traditions. Elaborating on these remarks, Red Jacket suggested that "the Great Spirit has given to you white people the ways you follow to serve him, and to get your living…he has given to us Indians the customs that we follow to serve him."[22] These comments invoke the principles of Guswenta, acknowledging that Christian beliefs, like those of Haudenosaunee people, originated with a higher power and were equally worthy of respect.

Turning to the topic of education, Red Jacket continued his critique with a broad overview of Indians' experiences with schooling. Perhaps gesturing toward the early experiments of missionary-educators in New England, he noted that "when learning was first introduced among Indians, they became small, and two or three nations have become extinct." Similarly, Red Jacket remarked that when schooling "was also introduced to our eldest brothers the Mohawks, we immediately observed that their seats [land base] began to be small; which was likewise the case with our brothers the Oneidas."[23] Given this interpretation, that extinction and dispossession (becoming "small" or possessing steadily shrinking "seats") were the inevitable consequences of embracing formal schooling, it is unsurprising that most people at Buffalo Creek rejected Holmes's offer of instruction. As the orator explained, many feared it "might be the means of our fairing the same misfortunes of our brothers [the Mohawks and the Oneidas]." Lamenting that "our seat is but small now," Red Jacket alluded to the flurry of land speculation in the late eighteenth century that resulted in massive land cessions.[24] Further emphasizing Americans' perpetual hunger for Indian lands, he reminded the missionary that Buffalo Creek residents feared the dire consequences of dispossession, noting that "if we were to leave this place, we would not know where to find another."[25] Because they recognized clear linkages between formal schooling, dispossession, and threats to their political autonomy, Red Jacket concluded that "we here cannot see that learning would be of any service to us."[26]

Reservation residents were determined to preserve their land base and economic, social, and political structures. Buffalo Creek was a place where over 1,400 people found refuge following a devastating scorched-earth campaign where Continental Army regulars and militia members laid waste to their homeland in 1779.[27] In 1797 it was one of eleven substantial parcels Haudenosaunee people reserved for themselves at the Treaty of Big Tree.[28] Named for the watershed it surrounded, the Buffalo Creek reservation covered an area of over 83,000 acres organized in a rectangular tract just over seven miles wide and extending nearly nineteen miles east from the shore of Lake Erie. In selecting these boundaries for their reservation, the people retained control of rich alluvial soils along the low-lying creeks, as well as rolling hillsides at higher elevations to the east. Here they farmed in a micro-climate that was particularly well-suited to three-sisters agriculture, the complex of corn, beans, and squash that had sustained American Indian communities in the eastern woodlands for many generations.[29] They also enjoyed hunting, gathering, and fishing within their expansive reservation. Buffalo Creek residents traveled freely to other reserved lands along the Genesee River, the Allegheny River, Cattaraugus Creek, and Tonawanda Creek. In each of these places villages, fields, waterways, and sacred sites were protected. Outside of their reservation boundaries Haudenosaunee people retained the right to hunt, fish, and gather as they had before.

Although land company surveys undertaken in 1798, and the maps that followed, purported to constrain Indians within reservations in western New

York, in practice the region remained a Haudenosaunee place well into the nineteenth century.[30] The Holland Land Company retained title to several million acres west of the Genesee River; however, the United States census of 1800 listed only 764 non-Indians residing in the region.[31] A small portion of this population, no more than fifty people (including traders, blacksmiths, tavern keepers, and their families), lived in close proximity to Buffalo Creek.[32] The largest American populations were found at Fort Niagara, the military installation located along Lake Ontario at the mouth of the Niagara River, and the town of Canandaigua, some eighty miles east of Buffalo Creek. Both Fort Niagara and Canandaigua were regular stopping points for visitors. Those new to the region frequently relied on American officials in both places to broker introductions and suggest guides. At Fort Niagara the commander, Major John Rivardi, proved to be a welcoming host, offering hospitality and facilitating introductions for Reverend Holmes when he first arrived in the region.[33] Another missionary found Israel Chapin, the federal agent to the Haudenosaunee who was posted at Canandaigua, most helpful when he traveled through western New York in September 1800.[34] For newcomers, knowledgeable local residents proved to be indispensable guides who helped them make their way from one settlement to the next.[35]

While visiting missionaries had a great deal to learn about the landscape west of the Genesee River (to say nothing of Haudenosaunee people, their beliefs, and their way of life), Buffalo Creek residents were quite familiar with American ways. Some of this knowledge was gained through diplomacy and trade, as well as kin relations with adopted captives and sexual liaisons or marriages.[36] Before Holmes departed from Buffalo Creek, Farmer's Brother reminded him that the community also had prior experience with missionary-educators.[37] Addressing the missionary in a meeting at a local tavern, the Seneca leader noted that one of his grandsons began drinking, gambling, and frequenting brothels while under the care of the Quakers. Echoing Red Jacket's sentiments, Farmer's Brother worried that "if we should send more of our boys, and they should learn such bad ways as he had, that our land would be cut into small pieces, and our nation dispersed and ruined."[38] Yet despite these grave concerns he was willing to give the Christians another chance. Explaining that Holmes's "good words" and the "good talk" of the missionary society inspired him, Farmer's Brother shared his hope that education would be "of great use to us Indians."[39] To that end, he asked the missionary to take responsibility for educating another one of his grandsons.[40] This decision, which departed from the initial position taken in the public council, signaled that some people at Buffalo Creek believed knowledge of "the good customs of the white people" could benefit the community.[41] Cautious optimism regarding the promise of literacy and numeracy, and possibly even biculturalism, seemed to outweigh the fears about the impact of formal schooling.

Changing Conditions Prompt "Cool Consideration" of Formal Schooling

In the years following Holmes's initial visit, the grandson (whose identity is unclear) experienced remarkable success in his educational endeavors.[42] The same cannot be said for the people of Buffalo Creek. Intercultural interactions in the region were increasingly strained. Reservation residents sought reparations for thefts committed by Americans, and in 1802–1803 a dramatic murder prosecution focused attention on issues of sovereignty and criminal jurisdiction.[43] Diplomatic exchanges in Washington and Albany reinforced Haudenosaunee people's keen awareness of federal and state efforts to erode customary practices that were grounded in the nation-to-nation relationship.[44] In the wake of several assaults on their sovereignty, Buffalo Creek residents received another visit from Elkanah Holmes. The missionary returned to the area in September 1803 to propose construction of a house for school and public worship on the reservation. Following an initial meeting, a council debated the merits of Holmes's proposal for over ten days.[45] When they reconvened with Holmes, Red Jacket acknowledged the missionary's advice and indicated that their lengthy deliberation had allowed the community to take his proposal "coolly into consideration, so that all our people may understand it."[46] Reminding the missionary that "your customs are different from ours," Red Jacket went on to say, "We agree to yours; but are not content to forget some of our own customs, which have been handed down to us by our forefathers."[47]

Explaining the community's reasoning in accepting instruction from the missionaries, Red Jacket cited examples from the region: "from want of education and a knowledge of your customs" Delawares, Tuscaroras, and others became victims of deception and fraud who were reduced to the status of menial laborers.[48] The orator concluded by remarking that "if [these nations] had followed the customs of their forefathers, they would have known better."[49] These statements suggest competing notions that facility with American ways was useful and necessary to Haudenosaunee people in the early nineteenth century, as well as concern that acquiring this knowledge might lead to abandonment of time-honored indigenous traditions, beliefs, and practices.[50] They also emphasize Buffalo Creek residents' insistence on maintaining their way of life. After careful consideration, the people decided to "gradually comply with what the Missionary Society has recommended to us, that we may not be deceived and taken advantage of."[51] Literacy and numeracy held potential advantages for people anxious to avoid deception at the hands of land speculators and unscrupulous traders. Nonetheless, formal schooling also posed a potential threat, and community members considered that it should be embraced cautiously. The decision to build a school and church reflected a compromise worked out through lengthy deliberation. Wary of deception and threats to their beliefs, yet hopeful at the prospect that formal education would increase literacy and enable better understanding of written documents such as leases and treaties, the community was willing to entertain the idea of hosting a missionary-educator.

At the same time, reservation residents reiterated their commitment to maintaining customary religious beliefs and practices. Explaining the community's thinking, Red Jacket noted that the assembled Indians believed their forebears had resisted "allaying hold of the gospel" because they considered themselves geographically isolated and independent of their white neighbors. Recognizing that such isolation no longer existed, Buffalo Creek residents acknowledged that increasing familiarity with American customs and practices was necessary for their continued survival and prosperity. They sought a carefully negotiated agreement with Holmes and the New-York Missionary Society that balanced the imperatives of Guswenta with the exigencies of the early nineteenth century. Further emphasizing the limited nature of this agreement, Red Jacket worked to diminish expectations by explaining, "We, the chiefs of the Seneca, Onondaga, and Cayuga nations, have agreed to listen to what has been recommended to us:—not that we say all will listen; but that the greater part have agreed to hearken to what our fathers, the Missionaries, have said to us."[52]

While members of these Haudenosaunee nations at Buffalo Creek would tolerate the presence of missionaries, it was clear that no one would be compelled to embrace the society's suggestions. Illuminating pockets of resistance to the missionaries' project, Red Jacket directed Holmes to "look around the room, and you will see a number of us with the appearance of old age upon our countenances, who have no idea of leaving off some of our ancient customs."[53] Here he illuminated an on-going debate within the larger Haudenosaunee society regarding innovation within the spiritual realm. For several years, Handsome Lake, a prominent Seneca man residing at the Allegany Reservation, had been sharing a message he received through a series of prophetic visions. While Handsome Lake's teachings have been described by some scholars as the foundational elements of a revitalization movement, he re-envisioned a number of important Haudenosaunee spiritual practices in ways that aligned with some elements of Christianity.[54] In the early decades of the nineteenth century these prophetic teachings were controversial, as was the presence of Quaker missionaries at the Allegany Reservation. No stranger to heated debates regarding spirituality, Red Jacket shared a moderate response with Holmes, suggesting that younger members of the community may "judge for themselves" about the missionaries and their project, while insisting that Haudenosaunee people would continue to observe their "customary worship" during annual Mid-winter and Green Corn celebrations.[55]

Despite reservation residents' apparent willingness to erect a mission house, construction did not begin. The lengthy deliberations during Holmes's 1803 visit, as well as the content of Red Jacket's remarks, suggest the decision to permit formal schooling was a contentious one. Unsurprisingly, the compromise did not hold. Although it is impossible to pinpoint when this shift occurred, by the time the Reverend Jacob Cram of the Massachusetts Missionary Society arrived at Buffalo Creek in November 1805, the community was strongly opposed to missionary presence on their reservation.[56] Responding to Cram's brief speech, Red Jacket unleashed a scathing critique of colonialism. He described Haudenosaunee experiences of loss and destruction following the arrival of Europeans, dwelling on the discomfort and misery resulting from missionaries' efforts to instruct young people. According to Red Jacket, instruction in "incompatible," "ill adapted," and "useless" skills created individuals who were "despised by the Indians, neglected by the whites, and without value to either."[57] These emphatic remarks (which bear some resemblance to observations Farmer's Brother made years earlier regarding Quaker education) preceded the orator's rejection of further instruction, a rejection couched in the belief that "the great Spirit made the whites & the Indians but for different purposes."[58] Reflecting on the Great Spirit's intentions, he argued that those who followed the practices of their ancestors were blessed with abundance, contentment, and strength, experiences that contrasted starkly with those of individuals who received education at the hands of Christian missionaries.[59] Innovation, especially the acquisition of alien skills and practices shared by adherents of another religion, was deeply threatening. "Why," Red Jacket asked, "may we not conclude that [the Great Spirit] has given us a different religion according to our understanding?"[60] Reflecting on principles recorded in Guswenta, Red Jacket suggested that tolerance based on acceptance and understanding of difference was the most promising way to approach the question of religion. Peace was attainable when intercultural relations were grounded in respect and people refrained from interfering in others' ways of life. Haudenosaunee people, he noted, "do not wish to destroy your religion, or take it from you. We only want to enjoy our own."[61]

Shifting gears, Red Jacket offered a pointed critique of the Americans whose settlement neighbored Buffalo Creek. Noting that Cram had been preaching in nearby Buffalo, he suggested, "If we find that it does them good, makes them honest and less disposed to cheat Indians; we will then consider again of what you have said."[62] The orator hoped that Christian teachings would "make the whites generally less inclined to make Indians drunk & to take from them their lands."[63] These comments speak to the increasing difficulty of coexistence. Within a few weeks of Cram's visit, Julian Ursyn Niemcewicz, a Polish poet, traveled through the Niagara frontier and spent some time at Buffalo. The poet was impressed by the elaborate dress of Indians who filled the streets of Buffalo.[64] He also noted drunkards and beggars among the throngs of Indians in the village streets, and expressed surprise when a few prominent Haudenosaunee people were refused service by a tavern keeper.[65] Niemcewicz's account illuminates some conditions Buffalo Creek residents confronted at the time of Cram's visit; the material benefits of living in close proximity to a growing American village and an English fort just across the Niagara River, where lively trade provided silver jewelry and other lavish adornments, could not overshadow instances of alcohol abuse, destitution, and discrimination. In his closing remarks to Cram, Red Jacket's suggestion that the missionary focus his efforts on Americans in the region expressed Buffalo Creek residents' frustration with this situation, as well as their resolution that the best way to manage their relationship with Americans and missionaries was by adhering to the principles of Guswenta.

Cram, entirely offended by Red Jacket's remarks, refused to shake hands with his hosts and departed abruptly. This indecorous departure marked the end of the community's initial flirtation with formal schooling and renewed their commitment to steadfast resistance to Christian missionaries and the educational programs they offered. After five years of carefully considering the risks and benefits of accepting the ministrations of Christian missionaries, reservation residents lacked confidence that missionaries would make a positive contribution to their community. Rather, as Red Jacket remarked, the message Cram relayed to the council represented the latest attack against the Indians: "You have got our country, but are not satisfied; you want to force your religion upon us."[66] Determined to resist this onslaught, the people of Buffalo Creek renewed their commitment to the principle of peace and friendship based on noninterference, a commitment which would keep missionaries at bay into the second decade of the nineteenth century.

New Imperatives for Literacy and Numeracy

In the years that followed, Red Jacket's complaints about troublesome Americans continued to resonate within the community. Grievances regarding stolen livestock and the ready availability of alcohol, as well as concern about encroachment, increased as the village of Buffalo expanded. Anxious to maintain peace and order in their territory, Haudenosaunee people pursued several management strategies. In an effort to control liquor sale, they petitioned the New York State legislature to enact a law prohibiting state residents from selling alcohol to Native people.[67] Following protocol established in treaties with the United States, they addressed their concerns about livestock theft to their agent and the Secretary of War.[68] Potentially volatile situations were defused by Haudenosaunee people who navigated the American bureaucracy at the local, state, and federal level. In doing so they relied frequently on terms negotiated in 1794 at the Treaty of Canandaigua, an agreement that affirmed the nation-to-nation relationship between Haudenosaunee people and the United States and translated some of the principles embedded in Guswenta into a written document that remains in force to this day.[69]

When representatives of the New-York Missionary Society returned to Buffalo Creek in 1811, they did so at a time when Buffalo Creek residents faced accelerating threats on a number of fronts. In addition to the challenges mentioned above, concerns about land cessions figured prominently in people's lives and shaped interactions with missionaries. Although some Buffalo Creek residents believed that instruction in literacy and numeracy would provide a safeguard against deception in the negotiation of treaties and leases, they remained concerned that missionary-educators who established schools in their midst would make unwelcome claims to reservation land. As a result, reservation residents initially refused to receive the emissaries from New York. When they finally granted Reverend John Alexander an audience, suspicions that the missionary society was "endeavoring to gain possession of their lands" prompted the Indians to refuse Alexander's request to establish a mission church.[70] Undeterred by this indictment and the accompanying refusal to embrace Christianity, Alexander and his associate Jabez Hyde remained in the region, proselytizing among the American community at Buffalo. Their persistence eventually paid off. Seven months after the initial appeal, perhaps encouraged by the positive effect the missionaries had upon their American neighbors, Buffalo Creek residents permitted Hyde to open a school at the reservation.

By 1811 there was a new imperative for improved facility in literacy and numeracy. Land sales in Buffalo had grown steadily since the Holland Land Company completed its survey of the village in 1804, and new American residents were rapidly transforming the settlement from a hamlet composed of ramshackle houses to a prosperous village.[71] In 1808 Niagara County was organized and Buffalo designated as the county seat. By 1810 the Holland Land Company completed construction of the county courthouse and jail.

That same year, on his tour through western New York, the governor estimated there were between thirty and forty houses in the village, as well as several stores and taverns.[72] Although the village had no church or school, it did boast five lawyers, and in 1811 Smith and Hezekiah Salisbury began publishing the settlement's first newspaper, the *Buffalo Gazette*. The village was beginning to show commercial promise as a transshipment center, as people and goods moved through Buffalo on their way from the east coast to western territories, and property values ranging from $100 to $250 per half acre lot reflected the village's growing economic strength.[73] For residents of Buffalo Creek, their decision to reconsider formal schooling represented one of several strategies the community employed for dealing with the demographic and political changes associated with the growing American village nearby.

It would be a mistake, however, to assume that the new educational program was quickly embraced or that it represented a radical departure from earlier opposition to formal schooling that was grounded in the language of Guswenta. Over the course of a decade Haudenosaunee people at Buffalo Creek consistently reiterated their suspicion of formal schooling and the missionary-educators who offered their services. Throughout this period a segment of the community also displayed cautious interest in literacy and numeracy. When reservation residents finally agreed to construct a building where Jabez Hyde could offer lessons, they balanced long-standing principles with their interest in literacy and numeracy. In striking an agreement with the New-York Missionary Society, reservation residents demanded that Hyde and his colleagues eschew religious instruction and accept voluntary attendance. These limitations indicate that advocates of a cautious approach to innovation prevailed in their efforts to allow individuals and families to make their own decisions about formal schooling, and that they did so by insisting that missionary-educators adhere to distinctions outlined in Guswenta, particularly those related to spirituality. The 1811 agreement is best seen as a pragmatic compromise worked out by Haudenosaunee people determined to confront settler colonialism on their own terms.

This principled response to the shifting demographic and political landscape of western New York allowed a small number of Haudenosaunee children to seek instruction at the missionary-run school. Because our understanding of the early years of the school's existence, like the decade of debate surrounding the place of formal schooling at Buffalo Creek, is filtered through the lens of missionary-educators who documented their work at the school, it is difficult to understand children's experiences of the school during the early years of its existence. Jabez Hyde, the catechist who spent six years teaching at Buffalo Creek, reported initial successes with a "goodly number" of students during his first year as an instructor. In later years attendance was sporadic, and Hyde gained little satisfaction from his work. His students did not achieve the proficiency he hoped for them and he was deeply frustrated by the community's prohibition of religious instruction.[74] These challenges are evidence of reservation residents' selective engagement with formal schooling, as well as their commitment to maintaining customary educational practices within their community. Indeed Hyde briefly described these practices, noting the importance of orality and experiential learning among Haudenosaunee people, as well as their emphasis on careful deliberation and preference for "mild and quiet" family governance.[75]

Despite his difficulties, the young missionary-educator persisted, and by the time Reverend Timothy Alden visited Buffalo Creek in the summer of 1817 there were thirty students attending the school.[76] In the years that followed, Hyde's successors continued to offer girls and boys instruction in "English studies," music, spinning, and sewing in the classroom on the second floor of the mission's two-story log structure.[77] Records from the later period indicate that while some people remained deeply skeptical about the goals of missionary-educators, the majority of reservation residents had come to appreciate the possibility of formal schooling.[78] After painstakingly negotiating a respectful agreement grounded in the principles of Guswenta, they gradually incorporated a school into the landscape at Buffalo Creek.

Notes

1. This vignette draws on Holmes's descriptions recorded in Elkanah Holmes, "Mr. Holmes' Letter," 64; Elkanah Holmes, "Letters of Rev. Elkanah Holmes from Fort Niagara in 1800," 194. For biographical information on Cusick, see Rufus Wilmot Griswold, The Biographical Annual: Containing Memoirs of Eminent Persons, Recently Deceased. A brief biographical sketch about Elkanah Holmes can be found here: J. W. Grant, "Elkanah Holmes (1744–1832)," in Dictionary of Canadian Biography (1821–1835).

2. See Chief Irving Powless, "Treaty Making."

3. For a concise discussion of the features of colonialism, see Jurgen Osterhammel, Colonialism: A Theoretical Overview. Hoxie has argued that colonialism and settler colonialism are important (and under-utilized) frames of analysis for those working in American Indian history; see Frederick E. Hoxie, "Retrieving the Red Continent: Settler Colonialism and the History of American Indians in the U.S."

4. Studies of American Indian education place a heavy emphasis on the boarding school period, covering institutional histories and policy developments, as well as the experiences of students and their families, beginning in the mid-nineteenth century. For a thorough overview of this scholarship, see K. Tsianina Lomawaima, "American Indian Education: By Indians Versus for Indians." Attention to earlier periods can be found within biographies of prominent individuals, several policy histories, and some studies of tribal nations. There is one survey of education initiatives in the colonial period, Margaret Szasz, Indian Education in the American Colonies, 1607–1783.

5. The oral tradition regarding the establishment of the Great Law of Peace has been

recorded numerous times since the early nineteenth century. Versions recorded by Haudenosaunee people can be found in David Cusick, "David Cusick's Sketches of Ancient History of the Six Nations (1828)"; Elias Johnson, *Legends, Traditions, and Laws of the Iroquois*; Carl F. Klinck and James J. Talman, eds., *The Journal of Major John Norton, 1816*; Jacob E. Thomas et al., *Great Law Workshop, January—February 1992*. Fenton's treatment of the Great Law provides an extended scholarly discussion as well as an exhaustive bibliography of scholarly work published through the early 1990s. See William N. Fenton, *The Great Law and the Longhouse: A Political History of the Iroquois Confederacy*.

6. Alyssa Mt. Pleasant, "After the Whirlwind: Maintaining a Haudenosaunee Place at Buffalo Creek, 1780–1825."

7. While the historiography of Haudenosaunee (Iroquois) diplomacy is expansive and cannot be adequately summarized in this footnote, a good overview of practices and protocols associated with the Great Law of Peace can be found in Fenton's substantial tome, *The Great Law and the Longhouse: A Political History of the Iroquois Confederacy*.

8. Red Jacket's oratory, which was recorded in government documents, published in newspapers, and circulated in pamphlets during his lifetime, has been collected in Granville Ganter, ed., *The Collected Speeches of Sagoyewatha, or Red Jacket*. The most recent biography of Red Jacket is Christopher Densmore's *Red Jacket: Iroquois Diplomat and Orator*.

9. Holmes, "Letters of Rev. Elkanah Holmes from Fort Niagara in 1800," 197–198. An explanation of these phrases can be found in "Glossary of Figures of Speech in Iroquois Political Rhetoric," in *The History and Culture of Iroquois Diplomacy: An Interdisciplinary Guide to the Treaties of the Six Nations and Their League*, ed. Francis Jennings et al., 121.

10. This initial protocol of Haudenosaunee diplomacy is discussed in William N. Fenton, "Structure, Continuity, and Change in the Process of Iroquois Treaty Making." An overview of the condolence ceremony can be found in Elisabeth Tooker, "The League of the Iroquois: Its History, Politics, and Ritual."

11. The interaction between a Mohawk delegation led by Kiotseaeton and French people at Trois Rivières is discussed in Francis Jennings et al., eds., *The History and Culture of Iroquois Diplomacy: An Interdisciplinary Guide to the Treaties of the Six Nations and Their League*, chapters 1, 7. See also Matthew Dennis, *Cultivating a Landscape of Peace: Iroquois-European Encounters in Seventeenth-Century America*, 76–82.

12. An example of Americans' developing cultural literacy is seen in Timothy Pickering, who benefited from tutoring in the nuances of Haudenosaunee diplomacy, and the treaties and agreements he negotiated during the 1790s reflect these efforts; see Gerald H. Clarfield, *Timothy Pickering and the American Republic*. On the other hand, Thomas Proctor's account of his 1791 mission to solicit Haudenosaunee support in the Ohio Country illustrates the difficulties faced by envoys who lacked language skills and familiarity with diplomatic protocols; see Mt. Pleasant, 95–98; Thomas Proctor, "Narrative of the Journey of Col. Thomas Proctor to the Indians of the North-West."

13. See Robert F. Berkhofer, Jr., *Salvation and the Savage: An Analysis of Protestant Missions and American Indian Response, 1787–1862*, chapter 1. For discussion of the intellectual underpinnings of Americans' belief that Indians could and should be subjected to such transformative, assimilative programs, see Roy Harvey Pearce, *The Savages of America: A Study of the Indian and the Idea of Civilization*; Bernard W. Sheehan, *Seeds of Extinction: Jeffersonian Philanthropy and the American Indian*.

14. See Reginald Horsman, *Expansion and American Indian Policy, 1783–1812*, 62; Francis Paul Prucha, *American Indian Policy in the Formative Years: The Indian Trade and Intercourse Acts, 1780–1834*, chapter 9.

15. See Francis Paul Prucha, *American Indian Policy in the Formative Years: The Indian Trade and Intercourse Acts, 1780–1834*, 219.

16. In a chapter discussing US civilization and removal policies, Prucha notes that early federal record-keeping practices make it impossible to determine how the War Department allocated funds at the turn of the century, however later records indicate that the government's civilization fund and treaty provisions accounted for 12 to 15 percent of missionary schools' annual funding, with the remainder of their funding coming from private donations. See Prucha, 217, 223.

17. Holmes, "Letters of Rev. Elkanah Holmes from Fort Niagara in 1800," 195.

18. Holmes, 201.

19. Holmes, 201.

20. Holmes, 198.

21. Holmes, 198.

22. Holmes, 199.

23. Holmes, 200. For discussion of missionaries' efforts to establish schools among the Mohawks and Oneidas during the second half of the eighteenth century, see Szasz, 233–257. Oneida history in the Revolutionary and early Republic periods is examined in Karim Michel Tiro, "The People of the Standing Stone: The Oneida Indian Nation from Revolution through Removal, 1765–1840." Kelsay's biography of Joseph Brant attends to Mohawk history during a similar period. See Isabel Kelsay, *Joseph Brant, 1743–1807: Man of Two Worlds.*

24. Here I refer to the Treaty of Big Tree as well as the flurry of speculative activity in New York State during the late eighteenth and early nineteenth centuries. See Laurence M. Hauptman, *Conspiracy of Interests: Iroquois Dispossession and the Rise of New York State.*

25. Holmes, "Letters of Rev. Elkanah Holmes from Fort Niagara in 1800," 200.

26. Holmes.

27. Barbara Graymont, *The Iroquois in the American Revolution,* chapter 8. For population statistics derived from the Haldimand Papers, see Mt. Pleasant, 34–35.

28. See Norman B. Wilkinson, "Robert Morris and the Treaty of Big Tree."

29. Mt. Pleasant, 45–47. See Jane Mt. Pleasant, "The Iroquois Sustainers: Practices of a Longterm Agriculture in the Northeast."

30. William Chazanof, *Joseph Ellicott and the Holland Land Company: The Opening of Western New York*; Joseph Ellicott, "Map of Morris's Purchase or West Geneseo in the State of New York: Exhibiting Part of the Lakes Erie and Ontario, the Straights of Niagara, Chautauque Lake, and All the Principal Waters, the Boundary Lines of the Several Tracts of Land Purchased by the Holland Land Company, William and John Willink, and Others, Boundary Lines of Townships, Boundary Lines of New York and Indian Reservations, Laid Down from Actual Survey, Also a Sketch of Part of Upper Canada, 1804," Map Division, New York Public Library, New York City.

31. Records associated with Northampton Township, Ontario County, enumerate the American population living west of the Genesee River. See "Second Census of the United States, 1800."

32. Antiquarian historians provide detailed references to many of the men who initially inhabited the region near Buffalo Creek. By comparing their names with households enumerated on the census, it is possible to estimate the number of Americans living in the region at the beginning of the nineteenth century. Such histories of Buffalo include Henry W. Hill, ed., *Municipality of Buffalo, New York: A History*; William Ketchum, *An Authentic and Comprehensive History of Buffalo*; Wilma Laux, "The Village of Buffalo, 1800–1832"; Orsamus H. Marshall, *The Niagara Frontier: Embracing Sketches of Its Early History, and Indian, French and English Local Names.*

33. Holmes, "Letters of Rev. Elkanah Holmes from Fort Niagara in 1800," 194.

34. David Bacon, "Rev. David Bacon's Visits to Buffalo, in 1800 and 1801," 184.

35. It would be several years before the Holland Land Company published its first map in 1804, and while the map's scale provided a useful overview of the region for potential investors, those who planned to conduct visits required more specific information from knowledgeable local residents.

36. Mary Jemison is the most well-known captive adopted into Seneca families. Other captives with long-standing relationships with Haudenosaunee people at Buffalo Creek include Jasper Parrish and Horatio Jones. See G. H. Harris, "The Life of Horatio Jones"; Jasper Parrish, "The Story of Captain Jasper Parrish"; James E. Seaver, *A Narrative of the Life of Mrs. Mary Jemison*.

37. Seneca people's earliest recorded interactions with missionaries took place in the mid-seventeenth century when Jesuits established three short-lived missions. During the second half of the eighteenth century Presbyterian missionary Samuel Kirkland made a number of trips into the Seneca homelands, combining sacred and secular concerns with limited success. Sixty miles from Buffalo Creek at the Allegany Reservation, Senecas were well-acquainted with Quakers who established a presence there at the close of the eighteenth century. David Swatzler, *A Friend among the Senecas: The Quaker Mission to Cornplanter's People*; Anthony F. C. Wallace, *The Death and Rebirth of the Seneca*.

38. Holmes, "Letters of Rev. Elkanah Holmes from Fort Niagara in 1800," 202.

39. Holmes.

40. It is possible that this young man was not a direct lineal descendant of Farmer's Brother, but rather the son of his niece. William Johnston, a former British officer who served in the Indian Department at Fort Niagara, married a niece of Farmer's Brother, with whom he had a son named John Johnston. According to Ketchum, there were "much pains taken" with John Johnston's education, which he may have received at Yale College. See William Ketchum, *An Authentic and Comprehensive History of Buffalo*, 60–61, 141–142. A reference is made to a young Seneca chief named John Johnston in the 1802 annual report of the New York Missionary Society. This man traveled to New York with Rev. Elkanah Holmes in April 1802, and is described as "entrusted to the Society for his education." In all likelihood, the grandson described by Farmer's Brother is this same person. See: New-York Missionary Society, *A Sermon Delivered before the New York Missionary Society, to Which Are Added the Annual Report of the Board of Directors and Other Papers Relating to American Missions*, 65.

41. Holmes, "Letters of Rev. Elkanah Holmes from Fort Niagara in 1800," 202.

42. New-York Missionary Society, 65.

43. Mt. Pleasant, "After the Whirlwind," 111–120.

44. For example, in pursuing appropriate resolution of the murder case against Stiff-Armed George in 1802–1803, Haudenosaunee people learned of provisions in the 1796 Trade and Intercourse Act that authorized prosecution within the United States legal system. Mt. Pleasant, 117–120.

45. Lemuel Covell, "Visit of Rev. Lemuel Covell to Western New York and Canada," 216, footnote; J. W. Sanborn, ed. *A Long-Lost Speech of Red Jacket*. For Covell's full account of his travels, see Deidamia Covell Brown, *Memoir of the Late Rev. Lemuel Covell, Missionary to the Tuscarora Indians and the Province of Upper Canada Comprising a History of the Origin and Progress of Missionary Operations in the Shaftsbury Baptist Association, Up to the Time of Mr. Covell's Decease in 1806.*

46. Sanborn, ed.

47. Sanborn, ed.

48. Brown, 99–100.

49. Brown, 100.

50. Wallace, in his analysis of Handsome Lake's "social gospel," argues that during the same period the Seneca prophet based at the Allegany Reservation attempted to strike a similar balance between maintenance of time-honored practices and adoption of Euroamerican practices. Wallace, chapter 9.

51. Brown, 100.

52. Sanborn, ed.

53. Sanborn, ed.

54. Handsome Lake's life and teachings are treated in great detail by Anthony F. C. Wallace, who notes that the prophet's teachings (known as *Gaiwiio*) were finally codified in 1845. See Wallace, Introduction.

55. Sanborn, ed.

56. Christopher Densmore, in his biography of Red Jacket, is critical of the authenticity of this speech. Christopher Densmore, 67–68. According to both Densmore and Harry Robie (Harry Robie, "Red Jacket's Reply: Problems in the Verification of a Native American Speech Text," 100) this is the orator's most anthologized speech, and the person who originally transcribed and submitted it for publication is unknown. My research has revealed that Reverend Henry Channing, a resident of Canandaigua when the speech was first published, may have submitted the document to James D. Bemis, the original publisher. Documents in Erastus Granger's papers at the Penfield Library, State University of New York at Oswego, indicate that in 1809 Channing was involved with the publication of a speech by Red Jacket. Robie's essay explores the publication history of the speech, ultimately concluding that it is authentic. Densmore is more circumspect, noting significant differences between the first publication of the speech and a manuscript copy of the speech. However, he finally concludes that the speech contains elements similar to those found in other speeches by Red Jacket.

57. Dr. [Cyrenius] Chapin, Red Jacket to Cram a Missionary, 1805, pp. 2–3, B00–2, Box 1, Folder 1, Buffalo and Erie County Historical Society, Buffalo, NY.

58. Chapin, 4.

59. Chapin, 5–6.

60. Farmer's Brother and Red Jacket, *Indian Speeches; Delivered by Farmer's Brother and Red Jacket, Two Seneca Chiefs*, 9.

61. Brother and Jacket.

62. Brother and Jacket.

63. Chapin, 13.

64. Metchie J. E. Budka, 104.

65. Budka, 104–105.

66. Brother and Jacket, 8.

67. "Petition of Sachems, Chiefs and Warriors of the Seneca, Onondaga, Cayuga and Tuscarora Nations for Prohibition of Sale of Ardent Spirits, January 20, 1808."

68. Red Jacket, "Speech to Secretary of War on Behalf of the Six Nations, February 15, 1810," letters received by the Secretary of War relating to Indian Affairs, 1800–1823, M271, Roll 1, National Archives and Records Administration, Washington, DC.

69. Jack Campisi and William A. Starna, "On the Road to Canandaigua: The Treaty of 1794"; G. Peter Jemison and Anna M. Schein, eds., *Treaty of Canandaigua, 1794: 200 Years of Treaty Relations between the Iroquois Confederacy and the United States*.

70. New-York Missionary Society, *Report of the Directors of the New-York Missionary Society, Presented at the Annual Meeting, Held on Tuesday, April 7, 1812,* 3.

71. Ketchum, 154–155, 177–178, 183–184.

72. Dewitt Clinton, "Private Canal Journal, 1810," August 5 entry.

73. Dewitt Clinton, "Private Canal Journal, 1810," August 5 entry.

74. Jabez Backus Hyde, "A Teacher among the Senecas: Narrative of Rev. Jabez Backus Hyde, 1811–1820," 252.

75. Hyde, 241–242.

76. Timothy Alden, *An Account of Sundry Missions Performed among the Senecas and Munsees; in a Series of Letters,* 39.

77. The mission building is described in Esther Rutgers Low, "Narrative of Esther Rutgers Low, 1819–1820," 278. The Tuscarora artist Dennis Cusick painted watercolors depicting the school's exterior and interior (including images of girls and boys engaged in literacy instruction and girls at work spinning and sewing) during the late 1810s; see William C. Sturtevant, "David and Dennis Cusick: Early Iroquois Realist Artists."

78. A number of these debates centered on the actions of Thompson S. Harris, the missionary who succeeded Jabez Hyde. Thompson S. Harris, "Journals of Rev. Thompson S. Harris, Missionary to the Senecas, 1821–1828." For an extended discussion of these debates see Alyssa Mt. Pleasant, "Debating Missionary Presence at Buffalo Creek: Haudenosaunee Perspectives on Land Cessions, Government Relations, and Christianity," in *Ethnographies and Exchanges: Native Americans, Moravians, and Catholics in Early North America.* It is important to note that a similar heated debate about schooling took place at the Allegany Reservation between 1816 and1822; see M. A. Nicholas, "A Little School, a Reservation Divided: Quaker Education and Allegany Seneca Leadership in the Early American Republic."

7 Worlds Apart

A History of Native Education in Alaska

Roy M. Huhndorf and Shari M. Huhndorf

The history of indigenous education in Alaska has been largely overlooked in studies of Native American education, in part because of its uniqueness.[1] Alaska Native education stands apart from policies governing American Indians because of the distinct history of colonization in Alaska and attendant ambiguities surrounding the legal and political status of its Native peoples. While colonization in the lower forty-eight states entailed military conquest, the appropriation of land, treaty agreements, and forced removal to reservations, the sheer enormity of Alaska, much of it rugged and remote, initially diminished pressures on Natives to surrender their land. Consequently, colonization unfolded through gradual encroachment rather than outright warfare,[2] and many communities, especially Athabascans in the interior regions, avoided direct contact with whites until the twentieth century. (Indeed, only a few years ago, a ninety-year-old Athabascan elder from the Copper River area remarked to the Alaska Federation of Natives convention that he had "seen his first white man" around the turn of the century, when he was a teenager.) Ironically, the relative autonomy of Native communities and the absence of overt instruments of conquest (large-scale military force, treaties, reservations) have undermined rather than supported tribal status and powers in Alaska.[3] A primary tool of dispossession, treaties have also established a legal basis for the status of Indian communities as "nations within" the United States with claims to political sovereignty as they obligated the federal government, for better or worse, to provide education and other services.[4] In Alaska, by contrast, there are no treaties to document sovereignty or to formalize federal obligations to Natives, and Congress and the courts have ruled inconsistently on whether Indian Country exists in Alaska.[5]

The vexed political status of Alaska Natives has created a paradoxical history of Native education that is shaped, on one hand, by the assimilationist objectives of turn-of-the-century federal Indian policy[6] and, on the other, by racism and segregation akin to the experiences of African Americans. Our title invokes the various social divisions—those brought by colonization and segregation as well as the differences between American Indian and Alaska Native experiences—that have shaped educational policies in Alaska. In this chapter, we trace the little-known history of education in the broader context of Alaska Native history and politics, sometimes through our own family's experiences, as they fill out the sketchy written history and reflect those of other Alaska Natives. Our recounting of this story is a collaborative effort born of different experiences and perspectives: Roy Huhndorf brings the perspective of a longtime Alaska Native leader with personal experience of many of the policies we describe (along with other parts of the essay, all of the personal experiences recounted, unless otherwise indicated, are his), and his daughter Shari Huhndorf writes as an academic with interests in cultural politics and the relationship of Alaska Natives to other indigenous and racialized peoples.

Ambiguities surrounding the political status of Alaska Natives emerged shortly after Alaska became part of the United States,[7] and they ultimately accorded education the central role in the US colonization of Alaska Natives. While western Europeans were the primary colonial powers in what became the continental United States, the Russians first colonized Alaska. In 1867, the United States purchased Alaska from Russia, although Russia was not its rightful owner and Alaska Natives never consented to rule by either colonial power. At the time of the purchase, about sixty thousand Natives resided in Alaska, and they became the first non-Indian indigenous population in the United States. In the years that followed, their differences from American Indians generated conflicting opinions about their racial type and thus which office should exercise jurisdiction over them. Frances Walker, then Commissioner of Indian Affairs, opined that Alaska Natives were not Indians but instead were likely of "Asiatic origin," concluding that federal Indian law should not be "extended unnecessarily to races of a questionable ethnical type, and occupying a position practically distinct and apart from the range of the undoubted Indian tribes of the continent."[8] After the Office of Indian Affairs thus declined responsibility for Alaska Natives, Congress placed them under the Bureau of Education, which became the sole federal agency charged with Alaska Native services.[9] This remained true until 1931, when responsibility for Alaska Native education and other services was transferred to the Office of Indian Affairs (soon to become the Bureau of Indian Affairs).

But the transfer did not resolve questions about the status of Alaska Natives and their relationship to American Indians: although Alaska Natives have fallen under all subsequent legislation affecting Indian education,[10] the statehood act of 1959 charged Alaska, rather than a federal agency, with responsibility for Native education. This is a significant distinction in Indian Country because tribal nations, at least in theory, hold a status that is higher than and apart from individual states.[11] The history of education we trace thus embodies contradictions surrounding the legal status of Alaska Natives that make sovereignty a pressing but highly contested issue in Alaska. As this history embeds education in the broader terrain of Alaska Native politics, it reveals the special role of Native education in Alaska as the sole instrument of the US "civilizing" mission for several decades, and it also shows the stories of Alaska Natives as interwoven with, yet still distinct from, those of American Indians.

* * *

The Russians established the first schools in Alaska—perhaps as many as fifty in all, primarily in the coastal regions—under the auspices of the Russian Orthodox Church and the Russian-American Company.[12] The school system they created set the stage for the creation in the nineteenth and twentieth centuries of mission and boarding schools, institutions that were heavily influenced by educational policies designed for American Indians. When Russian explorers arrived in Alaskan waters in the early 1740s, their primary interest was claiming the vast territory and its natural resource wealth, particularly the fur of its marine and land animals. Slavery became common as the Russians conscripted Natives, most of them Aleut and Yupiit, to supply the burgeoning fur trade. Czar Paul formally declared Alaska as Russia's possession in 1799. The Russians' second interest was proselytizing the indigenous populations. Russian Orthodox priests and other religious workers accompanied many expeditions to the so-called New World. The principal impact of the Russian presence was on Alaska's south coast, an area extending from the Aleutian Islands to the southeast Alaska coastline. Missions were established near Kodiak and Sitka where young Native men were trained as priests and lay workers. Russian Orthodox churches were built in most communities of the region. Many of these still survive; some remain operational, and others are historical landmarks. Russian cultural influence endures to this day, and many Native families (including our own, the Demientieffs) bear Russian names, while others speak Russian and practice the Russian Orthodox faith inflected by Native traditions.

The Russian schools aimed to advance the twin goals of resource exploitation and missionization, but little is remembered about them. Some likely served Native and Russian children alike, and others were dedicated to Natives. The Russian Orthodox Church established the first mission school in Nushagak, a Yup'ik village in southwest Alaska, in 1843.[13] Although Russian schools emphasized Christianity and language education, there is some evidence that they accommodated Native languages and cultural practices to a greater degree than the assimilationist programs later implemented by American missionaries and the US federal government.[14] By some accounts, they offered education beyond religious training, in part because many schools served the children of Russian colonialists along with Alaska Natives. When the United States purchased Alaska in 1867, Russia's principal legacies were the moderately successful effort at converting indigenous peoples to the Russian Orthodox faith, partly through the schools, and a severely depleted fur-bearing sea mammal population. Russian influence, however, remained largely confined to coastal regions in the southern part of the territory. Despite numerous attempts, the Russians were never able to establish a lasting foothold on either the west or north coasts or in the vast interior where significant numbers of Native peoples lived.[15] But the new colonial government would soon bring an end to the isolation of these communities. For the first century after the Alaska purchase, the United States, along with Christian missions, would exert influence on Native communities primarily through educational programs.

Most of the Russian schools closed in the years after the purchase as the US Bureau of Education, the territorial government, and the missions collaborated to create new educational programs for Alaska Natives. In 1867, the Northwest Council of Churches met in Seattle to establish missionary enclaves in Alaska, and the Evangelical, Moravian, Presbyterian, Episcopalian, Congregational, and Roman Catholic churches numbered among the dozen or so denominations that subsequently established schools throughout Alaska.[16] They divided the territory into districts that were exclusively assigned to each participating group. For example, the Covenant Church claimed the Nome/ Bering Sea coast, while the Catholic Mission took the central Yukon River district and the Episcopal Church received the Fairbanks/Upper Yukon area. For nearly two decades following the purchase, the missions assumed sole responsibility for Native education, establishing day schools and boarding schools throughout Alaska, but this changed after the 1884 passage of the Alaska Organic Act. The Act established the first US territorial government in Alaska, and along with it, the first formal school system. The next year, the Secretary of the Interior appointed Sheldon Jackson, a Presbyterian missionary, as its General Agent of Education. Within two decades, Jackson had overseen the establishment of day schools throughout the territory, including in most Native villages.

Sheldon Jackson's philosophy evinces the influence of late-nineteenth-century Indian reform, which was closely allied with Christian missionary societies.[17] The schools established under his leadership emphasized acculturation, including the elimination of Native languages, along with literacy, industrial training, and moral instruction.[18] "The training of the schools should be extended to the heart as well as the mind and hand," he wrote, and "the teacher who would be true to his mission and accomplish the most good, must give prominence to moral as well as intellectual instruction."[19] Following the model of Indian reform in the lower forty-eight states, Jackson viewed Christianity as essential to civilizing endeavors, and he contracted with religious groups to operate schools, some of them already established by the missions, in Native villages. (Federal subsidies to mission schools continued until 1894, though many mission schools remained open long after.) But Jackson departed from Indian reformers by opposing the removal of Native children from their home communities. Alaska Natives were economically self-sufficient in their villages, and this was one reason for their initial placement under the Bureau of Education rather than the Office of Indian Affairs. Because their autonomy, Jackson insisted, depended upon Native children remaining in their villages, Jackson eschewed the boarding school system in favor of day schools. Along with the day school policy, this cultivation of self-sufficiency and autonomy distinguishes Alaska Native education from the nineteenth-century policies governing Indians, which facilitated federal power through forced dependence.

But Jackson implemented his policies during a tumultuous period in Alaskan history. Beginning in the 1890s, the gold rush radically transformed Alaskan life, and with it the educational system, in ways he could not have foreseen. In the late nineteenth century, as the pace of settlement of the western United States began to wane, Alaska quickly became the new frontier. Whaling in the Bering Sea and the Arctic Ocean greatly accelerated. The commercial fishing industry for salmon and herring also expanded, along with fur harvesting in the interior. These activities, together with a series of gold discoveries in the 1890s that spurred the Klondike gold rush, significantly expanded traffic on the sea trading routes. By 1900, more than forty thousand trappers, miners, merchants, and others had entered the territory, exploring even the remotest corners in search of quick wealth. Largely unnoticed at first was the enormous impact this large influx of newcomers had on indigenous peoples. The new settlers initiated land conflicts largely unknown in the Russian period, the consequences of which endure to this day. An even more deadly threat arose in the form of disease. The devastating losses experienced by Native communities, along with the racist attitudes of the new settlers, transformed Native education for the next century.

Beginning with the arrival of the Russians, disease radically altered the course of history in Alaska as it did throughout the Americas. Yup'ik people still remember a tragedy in the 1850s, when Yupiit throughout western Alaska joined forces to oust the Russians, whose population never numbered more than a few hundred traders and administrators. They amassed at a location on the Upper Kuskokwim River, but their encampment was struck with a deadly virus that wiped out hundreds of young people in one fell swoop and with them the resistance effort. Today the site is dubbed the "field of bones."[20] The "great deaths" brought by gold seekers began a few decades later, in the 1890s. Natives of the interior, who had largely avoided contact with Europeans and exposure to the diseases they brought, died in unprecedented numbers. Common diseases of the time, such as influenza, measles, and other childhood diseases, became killers. Epidemics of more virulent diseases such as smallpox, diphtheria, tuberculosis, and pneumonia regularly swept through communities with devastating effects, sometimes wiping out entire villages. Especially hard hit were young adults, who often left behind orphaned children. Ivan Demientieff, Roy Huhndorf's grandfather and a riverboat captain on the Yukon, recalled accompanying the priests to villages in the wake of the epidemics in the 1910s. Often only barking dogs met them on the riverbank, as the villagers all lay dead or dying. Ivan and his wife Elizabeth responded as many Native families did: in the Yup'ik village of Holy Cross on the Yukon River, they raised nineteen orphans along with their own seven children. For their part, the missions reacted to the crisis by establishing boarding schools for the orphans. Offering food, clothing, shelter, and medical care to the children, the mission boarding schools also provided academic and vocational training as they pressed for religious conversion and conformity to European social norms.

The mission boarding schools became the precursors of federally sponsored Native boarding schools in Alaska. First established in the late nineteenth century, the mission boarding school system significantly expanded in 1917–1919. These years also saw the opening of first federal boarding school in the Inupiat village of White Mountain, and it became one of about a dozen such institutions in Alaska, the best-known of which is Mount Edgecumbe High School, founded by the BIA in 1947 in southeast Alaska. In 1926, White Mountain school was renamed White Mountain Industrial School, and in this incarnation it inaugurated a policy of industrial training for boarding school students. The boarding school system—which consisted of mission, vocational, and federal (first Bureau of Education, then Bureau of Indian Affairs) schools—continued in Alaska until the mid-1970s, decades after the end of the boarding school program for American Indians.

Education in mission and boarding schools was the norm for most Alaska Native students until the latter part of the twentieth century, with mixed consequences. The academic program extended through the eighth grade, after which Alaska Natives, unlike their American Indian counterparts, were encouraged to re-enter their home communities. For many, the education and training they received prepared them to confront their rapidly changing social world, and many prominent Native leaders—those associated with the Alaska Native Brotherhood and Alaska Native Sisterhood early in the century, and those involved with the formation of the Alaska Federation of Natives and the land claims efforts in the 1960s and 1970s—emerged from the mission and boarding school systems. Indeed, as was the case for American Indians in the early twentieth century, this sense of common political cause emerged in part from the social mixing that occurred in the schools.

Yet, at the same time, the assimilationist programs of the schools were undeniably destructive. Together with a rapidly changing society, the schools immersed students into ways irreconcilable with their own traditions, creating cultural confusion, self-doubt, and even self-destructive behavior. Of his own experiences at the mission school in Kotzebue, Inupiat leader Willie Hensley writes that Native parents accepted the "wrenching changes" brought by the school system in hopes that their children "might have a better life if they just allowed Uncle Sam to provide the tools we needed."[21] But these tools came at a high price:

> Children never forgot the message that our language was inferior, that it was inadequate to our future. Year after year, day in, day out, the children of Alaska Natives were told that who they were was not good enough, that they should leave behind the world of their parents and grandparents and become something different.[22, 23]

This damage is still evident today as Alaska Natives continue to struggle with the transition from the traditional socioeconomy of shared land and resources to one of individualism and self-interest that characterizes the western capitalist system.

Roy Huhndorf attended Catholic mission school in his birthplace of Nulato, a small Athabascan village located on the Yukon River in central Alaska.[24] Several nuns and a Jesuit priest provided primary education in a day school affiliated with the larger Catholic mission located downriver in the Yup'ik village of Holy Cross, where his mother and grandmother received their education. The Nulato mission school had just two rooms, each accommodating about thirty-five students, one for grades one to five and the other for grades six to eight. The school was taught by nuns who had little tolerance for rebellious behavior. They prohibited Native languages and other cultural practices. Students caught breaking the rules were subjected to public scolding or corporal punishment. The nuns saw their mission as delivering quality education, a solid grounding in religion through catechism, and "proper" social behavior through obedience, hard work, and self-discipline, and this involved the eradication of traditional knowledge and social practices.

Three of the older Huhndorf children went on to attend the BIA-operated Mount Edgecumbe High School in southeast Alaska, hundreds of miles from home. But the separation proved immensely difficult, as it did for many other Native students. Loneliness was intensified by the separation from family and the familiarity of village life, and this led to self-doubt and cultural anxieties. In boarding schools such as Mount Edgecumbe, the immense gap between the village subsistence lifestyle and the highly westernized environment of a school far from home proved a bridge too large to cross. As a result, the Huhndorf children, like many other Native students, returned home before completing their first year. When the time came for the younger children to attend high school, the Huhndorfs left the village, relocating to Anchorage to stay together and to make it more likely that the younger children would complete high school. (In this way, educational policies contributed to broader population shifts as Native people moved from villages to urban areas because of assimilationist pressures and in search of educational and employment opportunities.) The move to Anchorage and a large public high school, where Natives were a minority, proved a difficult transition as well, and the young Huhndorfs spent their first years away longing for their small home community and life on the land, the patterns of subsistence that gave their lives pattern and meaning. In the end, they did achieve high school degrees, but their diplomas came at a high personal and social cost.

Others weathered the turbulence of change, often because they had no options. Jake Lestenkof, an Alaska Native of Aleut descent, tells a story of his own education that, like many others, is marked by painful losses and removals. Born in the Pribilof Islands in the Bering Sea at the village of St. George, Lestenkof attended a government school run by the Bureau of Fisheries, the federal agency that had assumed responsibility for fur seal harvests on the Aleutian Islands. The Bureau of Fisheries was responsible for all aspects of island life. It controlled the economy, employing Native people to process harvested seals. It supplied a small wage plus food and housing for the workers. It also provided an elementary school, where Lestenkof began his education.

In 1943, the seven-year-old Lestenkof, along with other Aleuts, was evacuated by the US Army and interned in an old cannery site in southeast Alaska. (This is yet another little-known Alaska Native story, one that runs parallel to that of Japanese Americans who were similarly interned during World War II, and Lestenkof has made a remarkable film, *Aleut Story*, about this history.) He remained in the internment camp until the end of World War II. During that period, his mother died along with many other Aleuts, perhaps as many as one in ten, in part because conditions in the camps were shockingly poor.

(Nazi soldiers in a nearby prisoner-of-war camp in Alaska fared far better.) Lestenkof's schooling was interrupted because, as he recounts, the Bureau of Fisheries teachers who had accompanied the evacuees could not bear the harsh conditions, and they left within the first two months of the internment. At the end of the war, Lestenkof, by then an orphan, was placed with a family in Juneau, where he completed his primary education and went on to school at the Wrangell Institute, later finishing his high school education at Mount Edgecumbe. He remembers his loneliness, especially during holidays, but other than his grandfather, there was no family to return to at St. George. Lestenkof went on to have a successful military career in the National Guard, from which he retired as a general officer, subsequently pursuing a career with the Bureau of Indian Affairs. As the Alaska supervisor for the BIA, in 1982 he concluded the negotiation to transfer the thirty-seven remaining BIA village schools to the state of Alaska, completing the phase-out of BIA school administration in Alaska.

* * *

While the Russians, missions, and federal agencies created an educational system for Alaska Natives that bore key similarities to the one for American Indians, the development of public education in Alaska recalls the history of racial segregation in the US South.[25] An official system of public education emerged in Alaska around the turn of the twentieth century as the burgeoning population brought by the gold rush forced the territorial government to expand and formalize its operations. Following the 1884 Organic Act, a few schools had been created on a more or less ad hoc basis in incorporated townships, but in 1905, the Nelson Act required the territory to create a system of public education. Responding to pressures from white settlers, the legislation mandated a dual, or segregated, system for Native children (who remained under the control of the Bureau of Education) and white children (whose schools were managed by the territory) that had begun to develop under Sheldon Jackson's administration. In the words of the Act:

> The schools specified and provided for in this Act shall be devoted to the education of white children and children of mixed blood who lead a civilized life. The education of the Eskimos and Indians in the district of Alaska shall remain under the direction and control of the Secretary of the Interior, and...the Eskimo and Indian children of Alaska shall have the same right to be admitted to any Indian boarding school as the Indian children in the States or Territories of the United States.[26]

Despite the exception granted for "civilized mixed bloods," the Nelson Act seems to have been motivated by "a concern for racial and ethnic integrity" that made "civilized" a nearly impossible criterion for Native children to meet.[27]

Shortly after its passage, six students from prominent families in Sitka sued for admission to the public schools as "civilized mixed-bloods," but the court rejected their claims. The suit prompted the court to define what constituted a "civilized life" in impossibly ambiguous terms. Even living in a frame house, working for wages, and renouncing Native languages, food, and religious practices[28] were insufficient:

> Whether or not the persons in question have turned aside from old associations, former habits of life, and easier modes of existence; in other words have exchanged the old barbaric, uncivilized environment for one changed, new, and so different as to indicate an advanced and improved condition of mind, which desires and reaches out for something altogether distinct from and unlike the old life—Civilization—includes—more than a prosperous business, a trade, a house, white man's clothes and membership in a church.[29]

Needless to say, few Natives gained admission to public schools on this basis, and some school boards adopted resolutions to exclude all Native children, including those of mixed race.[30]

Segregated education was part of a broader Jim Crow–like system in Alaska.[31] Although Natives were the majority population until the late 1930s, theaters, restaurants, other businesses, and even churches either barred Natives from entry or created "whites only" sections. Signs warning "No Natives or dogs allowed" remained commonplace even after the 1945 passage of the antidiscrimination bill, and whites systematically refused Natives the right to vote.[32] Exclusive hiring procedures, wage disparities, and other formal mechanisms of discrimination were the norm. Until at least the second half of the twentieth century, the situation of Alaska Natives, as one World War II correspondent aptly observed, was "equivalent to that of the Negro in Georgia or Mississippi."[33] Education became a key battleground in Native resistance to segregation,[34] a fight that was waged primarily in the court system. Later in the twentieth century, the public school system's overt racism and institutionalized segregation, along with diminished access to education for Native students, provided the legal foundation for massive education reform.

A turning point came in 1929 in *Jones vs. Ellis*, a legal decision that struck down the resolution of the Ketchikan school district to exclude all Native children (even so-called "civilized mixed-bloods," ostensibly the exception to the Nelson Act). Over the next two decades, legal decisions and Congressional acts phased out institutionalized segregation, though it endured (and arguably still does) as a de facto system. Access to secondary education remained an urgent problem. A key difference between Native and white schools—and one that would be decisive in a later legal battle against segregation—was that most Native schools provided instruction only through eighth grade, while white schools continued through high school. Alaska provided the smallest white communities with local high schools, but high schools even in large Native villages were rare, forcing students to leave their homes to pursue education beyond the eighth grade. These students had few alternatives. Many attended boarding schools. Because space in mission schools was limited, for many the only in-state public option was the BIA-supported Mount Edgecumbe High School. Demands for admission quickly exceeded Mount Edgecumbe's capacity, so many Alaska Natives were sent to boarding schools in the lower forty-eight states, usually Chemawa in Oregon or Chilocco in Oklahoma. In 1966, the state established the boarding home program that placed Native students with individual families in urban areas. Ours was among the homes open to students from villages, but most host families were white, and students commonly reported that social alienation augmented their homesickness and difficulties adjusting to city life, problems that together contributed to low graduation rates. (One frequent complaint about host families, for example, was that they prohibited Native foods.) Also in 1966, the state initiated a regional boarding school system explicitly designed to destroy village communities through forced location to larger community centers. The program failed badly. In addition to high failure and dropout rates (in one school, as high as 96 percent), officials reported urgent social problems, including chain suicides, and the program was short-lived.[35] Finally, students could complete high school through a correspondence system.

Many Native students were forced to leave their villages to attend high school until after the 1976 settlement of the class action lawsuit *Tobeluk vs. Lind,* better known as the "Molly Hootch case." The largest legal settlement in the history of US education, the case was also a watershed in Alaska Native history: it officially ended nearly a century of segregated education and diminished access to secondary education for Native students. In 1972, Molly Hootch headed the list of plaintiffs who sued for the establishment of high schools in 126 Native villages. The lawsuit, writes Stephen E. Cotton, an attorney involved with the case, ultimately succeeded on a claim akin to the basis of *Brown vs. Board of Education of Topeka,* the landmark 1954 case that desegregated schools in the lower forty-eight states. In *Tobeluk,* the plaintiffs argued that "the state's failure to provide local high schools in native villages constituted a pattern and practice of racial discrimination against natives in violation of the United States Constitution, federal nondiscrimination laws, and the Alaska Constitution." While the state provided high schools to the tiniest white communities, some with fewer than five children of high-school age, it did not support schools in many large Native communities so that 95 percent of children coming from villages to attend high school were Natives. Moreover, the state had even provided separate schools to whites who simply wished not to attend nearby biracial schools with Natives.[36] In 1976, more than two decades after the *Brown* decision, the state settled the *Tobeluk* case with an agreement to establish high schools in all villages that requested them. Within a decade after the settlement, most of the villages represented in the suit had high schools.

Even now the effects of the Molly Hootch decision prove difficult to assess. With the availability of village schools, dropout rates are down and graduation rates up,[37] but these problems persist and achievement test scores remain quite low.[38] Many of these schools are tiny, enrolling in some cases fewer than a dozen students, and curricular offerings often compare poorly to those of larger institutions. Attracting competent teachers presents a serious challenge. Also, employment opportunities remain scarce in villages, a problem that emerges from the ongoing exploitation of Native lands and resources. As a result, even those young people who earn high school degrees in their home communities are frequently forced to relocate to urban centers to secure employment. Additionally, few Alaska Natives attain graduate degrees, and Native teachers remain underrepresented at all levels in the school system.

Responding to these problems, in 1985 the state government reopened Mount Edgecumbe High School—which had closed in 1983, subsequent to the *Tobeluk* decision—for rural secondary students, most of them Native. In contrast with its early mission as a BIA institution, the school now promotes Native cultural identity, features an academically rigorous curriculum, and places a remarkable 90 percent of its graduates in colleges and universities. Applications far exceed capacity, prompting interest in more boarding schools, and plans are now underway for a Native-run boarding school in Anchorage that will recruit Native students statewide who are falling through the cracks of the public education system. But the risks remain high: not only would the re-establishment of a boarding school system further weaken rural schools, it could replicate the problems of the mission and BIA boarding schools by eroding village life and cultural continuity. In addition, many Native students, particularly adolescents, fare poorly away from home, and this could reverse increases in graduation rates achieved through the establishment of local schools.

Other initiatives are underway for addressing the needs of Alaska Native students. In recent decades, Native education in Alaska has followed the course of American Indian education by emphasizing local control of educational programs, an endeavor fundamentally connected to endeavors to achieve political autonomy.[39] These programs—many of them authorized by the 1972 Indian Education Act and the 1975 Indian Self-Determination and Education Assistance Act—develop culturally appropriate programs targeted to specific communities. In the absence of federally recognized tribal governments in Alaska, these programs are administered by nonprofit organizations affiliated with regional and village corporations established under the 1971 Alaska Native Claims Settlement Act (ANCSA). These organizations function effectively as tribes for a range of purposes. On another front, several institutions, including public schools, are experimenting with interactive distance learning to allow students in remote locations virtual access to large classrooms in the cities. A promising development in postsecondary education comes in the form of the Alaska Native Science and Engineering Program (ANSEP), developed by Herb Schroeder at the University of Alaska Anchorage. By cultivating Native cultural values, community support, and student mentoring, the program has had astonishing success at recruiting Native students and retaining them through graduation, and it has inspired a number of pilot programs elsewhere in the United States. What remains true in all of these cases is that education, as it did in the past, connects to the broader political and social challenges that Alaska Natives confront—in particular, the often conflicting imperatives of supporting cultural continuity and social cohesion while also empowering communities to negotiate the Western capitalist system and thus to achieve some measure of self-determination.

Acknowledgments

We owe special thanks to General Jake Lestenkof for telling his own story and for contributing in other ways to our understanding of Alaska Native education, a history he knows well. Conversations with the other contributors to this volume during a seminar at the School for Advanced Research also greatly improved this essay.

Notes

1. Among the challenges presented by the immense diversity of Alaska Native peoples is that of finding appropriate terminology. Alaska has five major cultural groups with twenty distinct Native languages, and Native peoples reside in urban centers and more than two hundred villages. Reflecting conventional usage among Alaska Native peoples, we use the terms *Eskimo, Indian,* and *Aleut* as broad categories for these diverse groups, *Alaska Native* to refer to them all, and tribal and/ or villages names to designate individual communities. The term *American Indian* refers to Native peoples in the lower forty-eight states.

2. This is not to say, however, that conquest in Alaska was nonviolent. Among the best-known acts of violence were the institution of slavery under the Russians and the 1882 US military bombardment of Angoon in southeast Alaska. Individual violence against Native peoples, likely driven by racism, was common throughout the colonial period and remains endemic.

3. See Thomas A. Morehouse, "The Dual Political Status of Alaska Natives under US Policy."

4. See Vine Deloria and Clifford M. Lytle, *The Nations Within: The Past and Future of American Indian Sovereignty.*

5. This is reflected in contradictory court rulings over the last two decades: in *Native Village of Steven v. Alaska* (1988), the courts held that Alaska tribes possess no inherent sovereignty, but an appellate court ruled in the *Tyonek* decision (1992) that Alaskan tribes may have inherent governmental powers. Most recently, the US Supreme Court declared in *Alaska v. Native Village of Venetie Tribal Government* (1998) that Indian Country does not exist in Alaska. For detailed discussions of the legal and political status of Alaska Natives, see Morehouse, "The Dual Political Status of Alaska Natives under US Policy," and David S. Case and David A. Voluck, *Alaska Natives and American Laws.*

6. See David Wallace Adams, *Education for Extinction: American Indians and the Boarding School Experience, 1875–1928.*

7. See Case and Voluck.

8. Frances Walker, in *Annual Report of the Secretary of the Interior,* 134.

9. See Stephen W. Haycox, "'Races of a Questionable Ethnical Type': Origins of the Jurisdiction of the US Bureau of Education in Alaska, 1867–1885."

10. These include the 1934 Johnson-O'Malley Act, which was extended in 1936 to include Alaska Natives, as well as the 1972 Indian Education Act and the 1975 Indian Self-Determination and Education Assistance Act.

11. See Deloria and Lytle.

12. See David H. Getches, "Law and Alaska Native Education: The Influence of Federal and State Legislation upon Education of Rural Alaska Natives."

13. See, among other sources, Alaska Native Knowledge Network's timeline of Alaska Native history: http://www.alaskool.org/cgi-bin/java/interactive/timelineframe.html. For other key events in Alaska Native history, see Haycox et al., *Alaska Scrapbook.*

14. See Richard Dauenhauer, "Two Missions to Alaska."

15. This is not to say that these areas had been entirely spared the impacts of Western culture. Beginning in the mid-nineteenth century, whaling ships had begun to harvest the whales of the Bering Sea, and the occasional prospector or trapper began to appear with greater frequency along the Yukon River in the interior of the territory. But these incursions, especially in central Alaska, were uncommon until the 1890s gold rush.

16. See National Resource Center, "'Voices of Our Elders': Boarding School and Historical Trauma," (http://elders.uaa.alaska.edu/powerpoints/boarding-school_historical-trauma_3–08.pdf) and the Alaska Native Knowledge Network timeline (cited above).

17. Haycox, "Sheldon Jackson in Historical Perspective: Alaska Native Schools and Mission Contracts, 1885–1894," 19.

18. A stark example of the impracticality of many missionary endeavors comes from the Bristol Bay region of southwest Alaska, a region assigned to the Seventh-day Adventist Church. Seventh-day Adventists advocate a vegetarian diet and tried to convince their charges—who depended on a subsistence diet consisting mostly of fish and meat and whose community supported no farms or stores—to renounce the consumption of meat. What they were supposed to eat remains unclear.

19. Cited in Haycox, "Sheldon Jackson," 22.

20. Reported to Roy Huhndorf by Chief Eddie Hoffman (now deceased) and Matthew Nicolai, current president of Calista Corporation, one of the regional corporations established under the 1971 Alaska Native Claims Settlement Act.

21. William L. Iggiagruk Hensley, *Fifty Miles from Tomorrow: A Memoir of Alaska and the Real People,* 74.

22. Hensley, 78.

23. Among the most critical contributions to studies of indigenous education have been analyses of Native students' accounts of their own experiences; see, most prominently, Brenda Child, *Boarding School Seasons: American Indian Families, 1900–1940,* and K. Tsianina Lomawaima, *They Called It Prairie Light: The Story of Chilocco Indian School.*

24. Roy Huhndorf has written about his educational experience in more detail in "Preparation through Education" in *Reflections on the Alaska Native Experience: Selected Articles and Speeches by Roy M. Huhndorf.*

25. For an analysis of racial segregation in indigenous education in the US South, see Klopotek (chapter 3, this volume).

26. Nelson Act of 1905, Section 7.

27. See Getches, n.p.

28. See Terrence M. Cole, "Jim Crow in Alaska: The Passage of the Alaska Equal Rights Act of 1945," 317.

29. Cited in Getches, n.p.

30. See Cole, 319.

31. This system and Native opposition to it is the subject of a new documentary, *For the Rights of All: Ending Jim Crow in Alaska.*

32. See Cole.

33. Joseph Driscoll, cited in Cole, 315.

34. See, for example, the work of the Alaska Native Brotherhood and Alaska Native Sisterhood, the first major Alaska Native political organizations.

35. See Stephen E. Cotton, "Alaska's 'Molly Hootch Case': High Schools and the Village Voice."

36. See Cotton.

37. See Cotton.

38. See Judith Kleinfeld, "Alaska Native Education: Issues in the Nineties," 7, 11.

39. For an illuminating discussion of the significance of Native control of educational programs, see Lomawaima, "American Indian Education: *By* Indians versus *for* Indians."

8 "All Our People Are Building Houses"

The Civilization of Architecture and Space in Federal Indian Boarding Schools

K. Tsianina Lomawaima

In his wonderfully titled book *Everything You Know about Indians Is Wrong,* cultural critic Paul Chaat Smith[1] poses two guiding questions for indigenous intellectual engagement. He challenges us to ask: Who were we? What *happened* to us? He directs us always to begin by "look[ing] to the ground beneath our feet." To understand some of the great transformations wrought in Indian Country in the last century, this chapter looks to the ground beneath our feet, to the spaces we inhabit, to the walls around us, and to the shelters over our heads.[2] Architecture, both domestic and public, is a key domain of human life. Architectural forms and the bounded spaces of domestic and public life have long been ascribed powers to transform and uplift. In the assimilation program of the nineteenth and twentieth centuries, Native American homes and peoples were targeted as sites of cultural and moral uplift, to be accomplished through the transformation of Native domestic homes and spaces, and through the influences of the grand institutional architecture and highly organized spaces of boarding schools.

Domains of Transformation in the Assimilation Program

In the late nineteenth and early twentieth centuries many American citizens were intrigued by "the Indian problem": what to do about the nation's indigenous "primitives"? Concern ranged from mild curiosity to active engagement in "the Indian work," and opinions varied widely. Christian missionaries of competing denominations; federal legislators; Indian Office (OIA) policy makers and employees; schoolteachers; physicians; Indian traders; progressive reformers; and a range of citizens debated the question. Extinction or assimilation? Assimilation as equals or segregation as a subordinate working class? Constrained tribal life on reservations or individualization through allotment? Some advocated a totalizing "erase and replace" strategy that would scrub indigenous cultural expressions from the face of the earth; others proposed a domestication process of quarantining selected traits deemed "safe" enough to tolerate for "practical" reasons of economy or education; a few even argued for the inherent worth of Native lifestyles.[3]

Despite this cacophony of opinion, many in the Indian work agreed on key *domains* as pivotal markers of civilization. The human body;[4] clothing;[5] health;[6] foods;[7] economy;[8] architecture and the built environment: these domains operated as compelling *symbols* and *tools* of the "civilizing" process of American Indians.[9] Each domain mapped out a salient and charged arena of human life upon which colonizers focused their gaze, their attention, and their powers. The work of "civilizing" Native Americans operated across these linked domains in a multidimensional process. Images repeated in thousands of photographs, key terms reoccurring in reams of written documents, and violence repeatedly mobilized to discipline and control Native peoples: taken together, these map each domain of human life as a key battleground in the attempted transformation of American Indians. Over time, each domain has generated evocative metaphors of "savagery vs. civilization."[10]

Architecture constituted one prominent domain, including public and domestic buildings, and the segmentation, organization, and furnishing of spaces within, among, and outside buildings. The domain of architecture and space includes settlement planning, land use, building materials, design principles, construction techniques, finishing and furnishing, and the character and quality of housekeeping. As *symbols* certain Western architectural forms stood for the attainments and accomplishments of civilized, technologically and socially "progressive" society. These same architectural forms— as well as clearly identified furnishings of interior and exterior spaces—were also believed at the time to tangibly uplift "primitive" societies and individuals. Contemporary ideology imbued architectural forms and spatial arrangements as *tools* with powerful physical, moral, and spiritual effects on human beings. In this chapter, the federal assault on traditional architectural forms is described, as Native domestic and public architecture was suppressed or destroyed as part of the "Americanization" process. Western institutional architectural forms were consciously designed to act in the service of acculturation and colonialism. Federal Indian boarding schools segmented and organized space inside and outside of buildings, as design, construction, and furnishings were consciously formulated to maximize their inherent powers to uplift Native pupils. Finally, connections to architectural transformation beyond the institutional confines of boarding school campuses are examined through the remarkable 1920s surveillance tools, the federal Industrial Surveys that set out to photograph and document every single Indian home on every single reservation in the country. Federal activities targeting the architectural domain can thus be traced from Indian homes, to the schools, and back again. Surveys and correspondence from the Havasupai reservation in northern Arizona show us that a canny Native leader could ingeniously and successfully circumvent federal control, while evidence from the Omaha reservation in Nebraska shows how stubbornly the federal bureaucracy clung to its powers over Indian people. Both agency's records document the never-ending power struggles between Native and federal sovereigns. Turning our attention to the battleground of architecture reveals part of the story of "what *happened* to us?"

Indigenous Architecture

In all human societies, architecture is functional and symbolic, domestic as well as public. For those dedicated to transforming Indian peoples, an all-out assault on indigenous architectural forms made perfect sense because of architecture's symbolic and functional significance. Native homes and public buildings necessarily housed and protected—from a federal viewpoint and by federal definitions—inappropriate family structures; immoral reproductive units or sexual alliances; sexual disease and moral degradation; unproductive, inefficient (or worse yet, competitive) economies; filth and vermin; strange and unappetizing foods; and heathen religious practices linked with "injurious" health practices (such as sweats).

A defining case of the federal assault on Native architecture was the officially ordered arson of D'Suq'Wub, known in English as Old Man House, on Agate Pass, across Puget Sound from present-day Seattle in western Washington. D'Suq'Wub, meaning "clear salt water," was an important village home for the Suquamish people, who translate their name as "people of the clear salt water."[11] Old Man House exemplified the Pacific Northwest architectural form known as a shed-roof house. Suttles[12] describes shed-roof houses as flexible spaces for multifamily Coast Salish households who shared food and cooperated in economic, social, and ritual activities. Divided into family sections, conceptually at least, by the weight-supporting vertical posts, the house design was well-suited to variable or fluid occupancy. Portable house parts—the beams, and roof and wall planks—could be transported

Figure 8.1. Group at Old Man House village on Agate Pass, circa 1875. Photo courtesy of the Suquamish Tribal Archives.

to and reconstructed at summer food camps. The houses provided physical spaces for food processing, such as air drying and smoke drying; food storage; workshop use, especially in the rainy fall and winter months; and recreational pursuits, including gambling games. Powerful spirit helpers were often represented on house posts, and houses were the sites for spiritual life, including winter dances. Northwest coast houses are living entities, bearing prestigious inherited names.[13] Big houses such as D'Suq'Wub were honored as "potlatch" houses, sites for economic redistribution, the legal functions of legitimating inheritance, and centers for nurturing and invigorating the emotional ties of Native social life and kinship.[14]

D'Suq'Wub is said to have been built around 1815 by the brother of the chief for whom the city of Seattle is named. In 1855 the framework of this house was measured and found to be "520 feet long, 60 feet wide, 15 feet high in front and 10 in the rear."[15] The year 1855 marked important changes for Native societies whose homelands were now claimed by the United States. In that year, territorial governor and railroad surveyor Isaac Stevens negotiated treaties with the Washington tribes; the treaties were ratified by the US Senate four years later. A plan of "Americanization" was implemented on the reservations, and traditional religious ceremonies were outlawed. Old Man House, described by Suquamish historian Leonard Forsman as "the physical and spiritual heart of the Suquamish community," was destroyed by arson in the 1870s, by order of the acting federal agent at Port Madison, Washington.[16] The remnants of D'Suq'Wub can be seen in figure 8.1, in a photograph taken a few years after the arson.[17]

The power of Old Man House was visible to federal agents, and so it was destroyed. What was not visible—or perhaps was simply willfully ignored—were the ways in which Old Man House (like other Native structures) embodied many of the traits deemed to be characteristic of "civilized" architecture. Impressively large, even by American standards of the day, D'Suq'Wub was clearly more than a "home"; it functioned as public architecture, embodying "the heart" of the Suquamish community. Internal space was segmented and organized, differentiated by function and the status of resident families and users. Political, religious, family, and economic activities unfolded in interior and exterior spaces defined by D'Suq'Wub's presence, identity, and spiritual power. Colonizing power could not tolerate such a tangible expression of indigenous power, however, and the erasure of D'Suq'Wub required two linked processes: first, that it be classified as "primitive" (with all that allegedly entailed: nonstandard building materials, unsophisticated building technologies, dirty, unsanitary, unhealthy, cramped) and, second, that it be burned.

Federal policies and agents promoting "civilization" targeted Native architectural forms, convinced that domestic architecture was a potent symbol of the savagery/civilization dichotomy. Visitors to reservations, rancherias, and Indian communities across the country commented on how "primitive" architectural forms keep "nonprogressive" Indians in their thrall. Hampton Institute founder Samuel Chapman Armstrong, traveling in the Southwest in 1884, found Navajos living in "miserable huts" while the Apaches "live in a filthy way," "all…in 'wick-i-ups,' made of brush, with more or less mud covering…and raise, on an average, but one-tenth of their support."[18] Architectural backwardness encoded economic inefficiencies as well as cultural inadequacies. In 1923, the federal agent at Havasupai sent the photograph seen in figure 8.2 to the OIA central office in Washington, DC, commenting: "The rude construction of the place has a tendency to show how far these Havasupai people [are] from what may be called a home. This risembles [sic] more a huge crows nest than it risembles the home of a human being."[19] There was some recognition of diversity among Native groups and house types, and some Indians were given more credit than others for resemblances to the American domestic architectural ideal.

Pueblo architecture of the American Southwest, for example, appeared to satisfy several criteria of "civilized" architecture. Large, square, multifamily room blocks were favorably compared to apartment buildings, and some reformers felt that the Pueblos needed only education and Christian teaching to achieve civilized status.[20] Others objected to Pueblo architecture because of its "primitive" shortcomings: ladders and roof-top entries rather than ground floor doors, small rooms that housed entire families, spatial arrangement

Figure 8.2. "This [structure] risembles [sic]...a huge crows nest" (Havasupai Indian School *Industrial Survey* 1923:2). National Archives.

around communal outdoor work spaces and ceremonial plazas, and, of course, the always alleged "vermin" and "filth."[21]

The Christian Civilized Home: The Powers of Architecture

Architecture, understood broadly as "built environments,"[22] includes public institutional structures such as government buildings and libraries; an assortment of early twentieth century public structures were understood as broadly educational in function, including public or common schools, asylums, reformatories, Indian boarding schools, even prisons. Domestic structures including "houses," "homes," "cabins," and outbuildings (particularly in the late nineteenth and early twentieth centuries, structures such as outhouses, barns, sheds, summer kitchens, ramadas, and root cellars), and the organization and furnishings of internally segmented spaces within domestic architecture are further components of the "built environment." The sense used here of a "built environment" also includes the planned and organized spaces around, between, and among buildings—thoroughly "domesticated" spaces such as yards, fences, sidewalks, home gardens, and orchards. In this sense, architecture creates boundaries that organize space as well as families, activities, and economies.[23]

Federal policy makers of the nineteenth and early twentieth centuries assumed that exposing Indians to new forms of architecture would automatically generate new "civilized" forms of behavior. They would have agreed wholeheartedly with the statement that:

as one moves from preliterate environments through traditional vernacular to the present there is an almost evolutionary development in the number of specialized settings, i.e., those set aside for specific situations and activities, and their differentiation one from the other.[24]

Removing the word "almost" precisely sums up federal assumptions about the signs of civilized housing, and their evolutionary implications for marking the relative development of human races. Progress was both measured by and motivated by an increasing number of rooms, number of stories, and differentiation of function among rooms.[25] Interior spaces were differentiated by name, location, walls or other enclosure, furnishings, and furniture arrangement. Add to this list appropriate materials (mass-produced brick, not mud or hand-made adobe bricks; milled lumber and siding, not hand-hewn planks; manufactured shingles, not grass, no matter the technical sophistication of the thatching) and an obsessive concern about cleanliness, and you have all the components of the federal definition of a *nice, pretty, decent,* and *happy* home.

> *[There is a] settlement of Indians located in a pretty valley in the Indian country, which they have come to call the Happy Valley.... We thought it a great achievement, when one chief was at last persuaded to break away from one of those large mischief-brewing camps and lead his little band off to this chosen valley...and there begin putting up log houses and planting corn, pumpkins and potatoes.*[26]

Bishop Hare's description of the Indians' "Happy Valley" reminds us that select words were wielded as hammers in the assimilation campaign, carrying a common-sense English meaning as well as a freight load of assumptions, connotations, and metaphorical baggage about the savagery/civilization battleground. "Happy," "pretty," "nice," and "decent" litter the documentary record of the organized assault on Native lives, cultures, and architectures at the turn of the twentieth century.[27]

The markers of civilized versus primitive architectures and lives permeate federal and mission policy documents from the era, and the visual images mustered to encode some Indians as "backward and traditional" and others as "forward and progressive." In 1805, the Society of Friends of Pennsylvania and New Jersey reported on the progress of civilizing the Seneca:

> *...near one hundred new houses have been built since they were last visited by a committee; most of these are well put up, of hewn logs very perpendicular at the corners, and nicely fitted together, many of them two stories high, and covered with shingles, some have paneled doors, and a great many have glass windows, and are kept much cleaner than formerly. Their farms are enclosed with good fences, from seven to ten rails high.*[28]

The Friends pointed out another positive sign, the habit of settling houses up rivers, rather than the Senecas' former habit of "crowding together in villages."[29] Given the entrenched ideology of the time that "civilized" folk lived in urbanized, nucleated centers, while "wild" Indians "roamed" across the landscape, the Friends' observation might sound odd. They spoke to a powerful theme, however, that endured to the turn of the next century (and well beyond), that Indians living in *tribal* villages were shackled by the communal tribal bond, while those in disaggregated homesteads lived as free individuals. Political power and sovereignty were the key threats that resided in *tribal* (as opposed to *civilized*) villages.

Homes that housed acceptable economic and social arrangements garnered praise. Samuel Chapman Armstrong, on the same trip that took him to Navajo and Apache territory, lauded the so-called Five Civilized Tribes then residing in Indian Territory (later the state of Oklahoma): "There is not a blanket or a wild Indian among them; they have been humanized; they are clothed, right-minded, intelligent, live in good, decently furnished houses, and are self-supporting."[30]

Boarding Schools and the Civilization of Space

The schoolhouse is an infallible index of the educational status of the community in which it is located. From the forbidding shanty on the country crossroads in the backwoods to the palatial edifice in the most enlightened city, this building tells a story in letters so plain and so unmistakable that "he who runs may read." The schoolhouse teaches not only a lesson in architecture, but also lessons in sanitation, in engineering, in aesthetics, and in pedagogics.[31]

Indian boarding schools organized the built environment to mark the boundaries of civilization and to construct a civilized method of living among Native students. In this setting we can see linked metaphors of perceived emptiness: the Indian child as an empty vessel to be filled, and the Indian home as an empty space to be filled. The arson of Old Man House and the suppression of students' Indian identities were thus linked; if something can be destroyed, it leaves an empty place to fill.[32] Figure 8.3 illustrates the organization and regimentation imposed on students' bodies; here, the marching band at Chilocco Indian Agricultural School. Schools regulated student posture, physical activities, and the ways in which they were required to move through the spaces of the school environment: marching in double file, in military companies, and in government-issue (GI) uniforms.[33] The image of St. Joseph's Mission School, Williams Lake, British Columbia, in figure 8.4 illustrates the organization and regimentation imposed on space that was common to the residential school campuses: yards distinguished

Figure 8.3. Marching band, circa 1904, at the Chilocco Indian Agricultural School, Newkirk, Oklahoma. Photograph courtesy of K. Tsianina Lomawaima.

Figure 8.4. St. Joseph's Mission School, circa 1900. Image E-05558 courtesy of Royal British Columbia Museum, British Columbia Archives.

Figure 8.5. Entry arch leading into Chilocco Indian Agricultural School campus, 1938. Chilocco *Yearbook*, courtesy of K. Tsianina Lomawaima.

from fields by plantings and by fences, straight roads, neat sidewalks that led only from one side of the yard to the other, and cleared areas that set the large, stately building to good advantage to be viewed by—and to suitably impress—Native and non-Native onlookers.

Boarding schools aggressively separated Indian children from Indian homes, and civilized spaces from uncivilized wilderness. Two of the flagship US off-reservation boarding schools, Chilocco and Haskell, were established in 1884.[34] By the 1930s, both utilized the ancient European architectural tradition of the arch to demarcate entrance into civilized space. The 1938 Chilocco *Yearbook* portrayed the arch at the entry to the mile-long "avenue" that led west to the campus (figure 8.5). In the early 1930s, my father, Curtis Thorpe Carr, had been part of the student work gang that planted the Chinese elms along the driveway, intended to recreate the shady living arch of trees familiar along less arid European boulevards. In 1984, when my father and I revisited the closed campus, the Chinese elms revealed the ravages of a half-century of Oklahoma's extreme weather: shattered, straggly hedgerows instead of a majestic and formal living arch (figure 8.6).

One of the first institutions to play a central role in the education of Indian people was Hampton Normal and Agricultural Institute, located in tidewater Virginia. Hampton was founded by General Samuel Chapman Armstrong,

Figure 8.6. Chilocco entry arch and avenue in 1984. Photograph by K. Tsianina Lomawaima.

who was raised on the islands of Hawai'i where his missionary father advised King Kamehameha and founded the Hilo Manual Labor School for Native Hawaiians. After the Civil War, General Armstrong settled in Virginia where he faced the "cabins and tents" of ten thousand "refugee 'contrabands' [of war]," the freedmen and women whose livelihoods now lay in federal hands.[35] General Armstrong was tasked to make the "crowds of Negroes" around Fort Monroe self-supporting. A three-part plan was devised: first, send hundreds north to work or place them in domestic service; "second, he endeavored to provide houses for them, for he realized that there could be no morality as long as fathers, mothers, children, dogs, and strangers huddled together in the one-room cabins;" and, third, provide schools and churches for practical and moral education.[36]

According to the biography written by his daughter, Armstrong persuaded the American Missionary Association to buy farm land for a "permanent and great educational work."[37] Ground was broken in 1867, and the "first temporary buildings" were "cheap wooden structures."[38]

> General Armstrong...said: "That's just the place for an academic building; don't take too much pains with these barracks; three years will demonstrate whether we can make teachers out of these colored people; then we shall make some substantial, lasting buildings."[39]

Armstrong designed Hampton as a normal school stressing manual labor and the education of newly emancipated black Americans as teachers, teachers of a dogma of white racial superiority and black acceptance of manual labor. Soon convinced of the viability of his plan to produce a moral and subservient black working class, by 1869 Armstrong had determined to build an "expensive and elaborate brick building" in which to hold classes. Richard Morris Hunt was hired as the architect, and Armstrong later called the construction of this building "the most responsible and conspicuous and fateful single executive act of my life."[40]

The imposing "eclectic High Victorian" buildings erected at Hampton were "symbols and tools" of Armstrong's plan for freedmen and Indians and central to his "primary goal of building character."[41] Armstrong believed that "surroundings had a greater influence on an individual than did heredity."[42] New students at Hampton were suitably impressed: Robert Russa Moton, who succeeded Booker T. Washington as president of Tuskegee in 1915, wrote of his arrival at Hampton:

> *It was to me the most beautiful place I had ever seen.... Looking upon the well-kept grounds of the Institute, the water front, the neat and imposing buildings and farm lands, I felt almost as if I were in another world.*[43]

Architecture at Hampton carried heavy symbolic and functional freight, and studied contrasts between the rustic homes of freedmen and the grandeur of Hampton were laden with cultural import. The "other world" from which Moton came was characterized in Hampton correspondence and publications as "the cabin," a loaded term that condensed assumptions and stereotypes about black American lives. The carefully constructed contrast between "cabin" and "home" was captured in photographic images by renowned American photographer Frances Johnston, who displayed 159 stunning platinum prints, taken at and near Hampton, at the Paris Exposition of 1900.[44] In a foreword to the republication of Johnston's work in 1966, photo historian Leonard Kirstein resurrected both the language and ideology of the times that produced these striking "before and after" images:

> *There must have been plenty of rude and primitive log cabins nearby then (as, indeed, now); without any contrivance or editing she could have observed scenes of Southern domestic life.... But with what relish does she turn her page to show the triumphant advance of progress, this new dispensation of freedmen, in their decent, neat, immaculately hygienic homes, frozen as in habitat groups, almost, but not quite entirely—believable.... Without overt irony, we have the helpless yet not hopeless discrepancy in concept of the white Victorian ideal as criterion towards which all darker tribes and nations must perforce aspire.*[45]

Order, cleanliness, family structure, civilized economies of mass production versus handcraft, segmentation of interior space, aesthetic markers of "higher

Figure 8.7. "The Old Folks at Home." Photograph by Frances B. Johnston, courtesy of Hampton University Archives.

taste": all are on display and highlighted by the contrast between figure 8.7, "The Old Folks at Home" and figure 8.8, "A Hampton Graduate at Home."

A jumble of handmade furniture confronts the neat dining room set, as darkness confronts light; the "old folks" face the nuclear, male-led family; vernacular materials appear shabby next to mass-produced lumber, millwork, moldings, bricks, and windows. In the one room cabin, we see the dining table in the central living space, where the multipurpose kitchen hearth provides warmth and cooking fire. It looks cramped, not cozy, compared to the function-restricted dining room of the Hampton graduate's home. Here we see the importantly visible staircase, a link to multiple floors and "sleeping," "sitting," and "living" rooms; handmade crockery is replaced by a uniform china set, with framed artwork and a piano close at hand. The stairs are important visual clues. They not only lead to the implied second story and other function-demarcated rooms, but at Hampton they also posed literal stumbling blocks to the less-civilized, and by implication, less physically coordinated Indian race.

Figure 8.8. "A Hampton Graduate at Home." Photograph by Frances B. Johnston, courtesy of Hampton University Archives.

Booker T. Washington was house father to the Indian boys quartered in the Hampton dormitory called the Wigwam, and he carefully described Indian difficulty with stairs: "The untutored Indian is anything but a graceful walker. Take off his moccasins and put shoes on him, and he does not know how to use his feet. When the boys and girls are first brought here it is curious to see in what a bungling way they go up and down stairs, throwing their feet in all sorts of directions as if they had no control over them."[46] It is no accident that stairs were the culprit in tripping up untutored Indians: they are a key technology in the segmentation of civilized space. A column in the Hampton publication *Talks & Thoughts* made the same point as it described a Saturday evening entertainment at the Wigwam:

> The last part of the entertainment was unique, and the source of much amusement to Indians and guests. "An Indian Boy Coming down Stairs to Breakfast" was announced, and everyone looked expectantly toward the stage curtain. An unmistakable sound of heavy boots, hurriedly pounding across the hall above, and stumbling and jumping and sliding down the long staircase in the noisiest way possible

"All Our People Are Building Houses" 161

Figure 8.9. "The Old Well." Photograph by Frances B. Johnston, courtesy of Hampton University Archives.

was all of that scene; but it was sufficiently realistic to be recognized, and with great applause.[47]

The pair of photographs showing the "Old Well" and the "Improved Well" (figures 8.9 and 8.10) focus attention on the hygienic advancements of *nice, decent* homes: a covered well instead of the open-to-contamination descent of a rough bucket; children in clean, starched, and crisply pressed clothes; even the juxtaposition of split rail and picket fences remind the viewer of technological, industrial progress. Here we see the "redundancy of clues"[48] that defines environments in complex societies from primitive ones: bare dirt versus a lawn with sidewalk, rickety sticks versus a whitewashed picket fence, a few straggly trees versus lush "landscaping" where the (fruit?) trees show every sign of heavy pruning throughout their lives. Even the landscaping of civilization is well disciplined.

Kirstein's perception of the "discrepancy in concept of the white Victorian ideal as criterion" for other races is a crucial perception, one that has to be examined to understand federal policies and practices in the architectural

Figure 8.10. "The Improved Well (Three Hampton Grandchildren)." Photograph by Frances B. Johnston, courtesy of Hampton University Archives.

arena. On the one hand, the grandiose institutional architecture of the schools was designed to inspire the lesser races, to uplift them by direct example and influence. It also served as a visible statement addressed to America and to the world, symbolizing the moral right and grandeur of the Indian Service's "civilizing program." On the other hand, the schools also set out to fit the lesser races for their proper place in the world: as servants, domestic workers, and manual laborers—surely, not people who should become *too* accustomed to large, grandiose, artfully furnished homes *as their own*. In this light, the architecture of Hampton and the large Indian boarding schools might be seen as quite inappropriate to the schools' expressed goal of fitting black or Indian people for a modest place in the world. The schools functioned architecturally as *extreme* statements of principles that were fundamental to the "civilizing" process. They existed at one end of a gradient of expression of uplifting architectural values: at one extreme, imposing institutional architecture in the schools would transform the tastes and habits of Indian students, who were expected to implement more modest expressions of their new tastes and habits in *nice, decent* reservation homes suitable for Indian people. The tension of the discrepancy was felt at Hampton, where, although the buildings were designed to be imposing, "The girls' rooms were intended to be simple as Armstrong believed that 'costly buildings stimulate self-respect; but beds, furniture and clothing are good but simple, no better than what they can, by their own industry, get at home.'"[49] When Richard Henry Pratt escorted the first American Indian students to Hampton in 1878, Armstrong had pledged to build two large new buildings to house them.[50] Winona Lodge was the dormitory for girls, and the Wigwam housed the boys.[51] Hampton staff recognized the dual roles of the buildings as *symbols* and *tools* of uplift:

> Winona Lodge not only functioned as a place where adjustments were made under the supervision of a maternal matron to life off the reservation, but also served as a vehicle for increasing the self-respect and self-help of its residents. To accomplish the latter, the girls were encouraged to feel that the whole residence belonged to them and were given responsibilities for its daily maintenance, such as scrubbing the floors.[52]

Hampton staff imbued Winona and the Wigwam with mystical civilizing powers. A teacher described the first evening in Winona, where teachers led a prayer:

> Darkness and silence fell upon the building, clouds of mist and rain shut it in, but angel wardens seemed to guard it and make it light and musical.... Years of instruction could not do for the Indian girls what a building of their own had accomplished immediately.[53]

Given the power ascribed to the form and furnishings of the girls' rooms in Winona, it is no surprise the care and detail with which they were described to the world in the school's public-relations newsletters.

> It is a double bed room with hard finished white walls, trimmed with yellow pine, and has one window. The floor is bare, but well scrubbed. The window, well washed, is partly screened by a white drop curtain; the walls are adorned with pictures, not by Rubens or after Raphael, but cut from pictorial news-papers or magazines.... The pictures are all around the walls, not in confusion, there is a kind of order which gives a very pretty effect. Think of it! the tops of two Chinese parasols as pictures for this room; the girls say they are pretty and so do I. Two pine chairs stand in such positions as prove that the occupants must have had a little gossip before dinner; in the middle of the floor is a small oval shaped toilet table made of pine, in the corner stands a large wardrobe.... On one side of the room is a pine bureau with a mirror attached; nicely arranged around the edge of the glass are little motto cards; there are two small iron bedsteads in the room, the beds on which are well made and covered with white spreads.[54]

The forms of building and furnishings were inextricably linked with cultur- ally loaded notions about gender roles (women gossip), economy and clean- liness (bare but well-scrubbed), appropriate tastes (pictures not by Rubens or Raphael), with individual property owners who are defined through and by their material possessions, and with the striking symbols of lightness and brightness—white curtains at the window and white spreads on the beds.[55]

What about the world outside the large boarding schools such as Hampton? Several avenues of information illuminate activities on the reser- vations: reports on "returned students" compiled by Hampton and Carlisle staff; letters from families to students, and from students and alumni back to the schools; and the reports of federal Indian agents, missionaries, and others. All of these documentary sources repeat the themes of civilized hous- ing. Roger Buffalohead and Paulette Molin[56] have detailed the story of the Hampton "model family"/"model home" project. Inspired by anthropologist Alice Fletcher, the Women's National Indian Association (WNIA) established a permanent Home Building and Loan Committee in 1895 to assist school graduates to achieve "American-style housing."[57] "Various chapters of this group lent interest-free money to young reservation couples to construct modest but 'modern' homes as well as to purchase items such as livestock, farm equipment, sewing machines, and looms."[58]

By the early 1900s, the Indian Home Building Fund petered out; a series of droughts in the Midwest, family illnesses, and the high mortality among Indian populations (including school graduates) all undermined the pro- gram. It would be a mistake, however, to call the WNIA "cottage" building project a failure. It was part of a multipronged attack on Native architec- ture and domestic arrangements, an attack that was making inroads on res- ervations. Some of the changes that came to Indian homes were brought by returning students, and some were instigated by parents, eager to please their children and to help them build what all hoped would be "a better life." Parents sent letters to children at school, expressing their sincere wishes to stay in touch, and to assure their children they were not alone. Parents seemed intent on reassuring their children that just as they had traveled far for an education, their families back home were also working hard to adapt to the new world around them, and to prepare a place that would be familiarly civilized when students returned home. Brave Bull wrote to his daughter: "My Dear Daughter—Ever since you left me I have worked hard, and put up a good house and am trying to be civilized like the whites!... I have dropped all the Indian ways, and am getting like a white man, and don't do anything but what the agent tells me."[59]

Life on many reservations was changing rapidly and radically under fed- eral pressures at the turn of the nineteenth to the twentieth century, but Native parents and school alumni also found ways to resist federal agendas, adapt according to their own wishes and goals, preserve "traditional" architectural forms, and integrate "civilized" ones into new patterns of living. Glimpses of this complex process of architectural transformation outside the schools can be found in the Industrial Surveys mandated by the commissioner of Indian Affairs in the 1920s.

The Industrial Surveys

Cloud Shield, Lakota, wrote to his son at Carlisle Indian School in Pennsylvania: "All our people are building houses and opening up little farms all over the reservation. You may expect to see a big change when you get back."[60] Big changes, indeed, were sweeping Indian country. A remarkable archive of images and commentary on American Indian homes across the country was amassed in the 1920s, as far as I can tell, for federal bureaucratic consumption only.[61] With a few exceptions, most of these images were not reproduced or disseminated as part of the government's public relations campaign promoting its assimilation programs. Photographs were taken through the 1920s to document living conditions of Indian households; the photos, mounted on boilerplate forms recording data such as names, ages, health, and level of schooling of all residents, as well as signs of economic progress, were compiled in Grip Files called "Industrial Surveys." Each superintendent was instructed to plan individual five-year programs of improvement, to itemize the objectives to be achieved for each family, and to attach a picture "to include surroundings and some members of the family. Such pictures furnish the means of visualizing home conditions better than pages of description."[62]

Comparison of the Industrial Surveys at two sites—Havasupai in northern Arizona in the Grand Canyon, and Omaha in Nebraska, the site twenty to thirty years earlier of the WNIA-funded "cottages" built for Hampton alumni—charts the trajectory of the enduring federal focus on the home as primary domain of the civilization process. Evidence from Havasupai shows how even the extraordinary powers wielded by federal agents could be circumvented by Native ingenuity. Evidence from Omaha reveals how the defining markers of civilized living were continually redefined. The ante kept going up, and Native peoples' "progress" proved eternally incapable of keeping pace with the need for federal surveillance, control, and power over Native lives.

In the federal view of the world, a wonderful thing happened in the Havasupai canyon in 1910: there came a great flood. Floods were nothing new, of course, in this tributary to the Grand Canyon. The Havasupai had learned to cope long ago, and their architectural choices were shaped by the

Figure 8.11. A post–1910 flood home at Havasupai Agency (Havasupai Indian School *Industrial Survey*, 1923). National Archives.

predictability of reoccurring floods. But as any simple survey of American suburban development or patterns of insurance claims will teach you, many Americans interpret the words "flood plain" to mean "build here," and the agent at Havasupai was no exception to that rule. After the 1910 flood, the government imported "civilized" building materials to the canyon floor, at considerable expense: the milled lumber, millwork, windows, and doors all had to be packed down on mules from the canyon rim.[63]

The home in the foreground of figure 8.11 is one of the federally built post-flood homes, and the agent described the home, and its family, in glowing terms in the 1923 Industrial Survey:

> *The building is a frame structure, the house consisting of two rooms. It possesses a good floor with ample provision made for light and ventilation.... In the line of cleanliness, the...family unquestionably keep a tidy neat home similar to the more enlightened and progressive Indians of other tribes.*[64]

Not all Havasupai were amenable to this determined imposition of new architectural forms. "Captain Jim," pictured to the right of the "modern" home in figure 8.11, rebuilt a traditional Havasupai dwelling adjacent to his son's new frame home, and the agent was not impressed:

> *The home just in the rear of the frame building is the home that Captain Jim permanently occupies now. This is crude of construction without a floor nor windows. The roof consists of sand. No fire place and when the food is cooked in this dwelling, the wood smoke affects the eyes to a considerable extent. A breeder of trachoma.*[65]

We need to go back to the Industrial Status Reports that were being written as early as 1912 in order to understand how Indians were being judged; why agents felt threatened by the pressure to produce Industrial Surveys; and how Indians as well as agents responded to the call for surveys: "The efficiency rating of [government] farmers as well as superintendents in the future will depend largely upon the increase of lands farmed by Indians, the character of the farming, and the nature of the improvements [made]."[66] In other words, an agent's job was on the line. He had to produce Industrial Surveys whether he wanted to or not, and, more to the point, whether "his" Indians were cooperative or not. Indians tended to be acutely aware of such points of leverage in their dealings with "their" agents. The Havasupai agent's response to Circular #1774 was determinedly realistic. In letter after letter, he reminded the Washington office that each year a percentage of the Havasupai fields were "overflown," that is, flooded, so increasing acreage every year was not practical. He could not completely overcome cultural tradition, either; "his" Indians would not work land inherited from the deceased for three years (an effective fallowing system).

While the agent was attempting to talk sense, from his perspective, to clueless bureaucrats in DC, the Havasupai were making their case as well. Although Captain Jim could not speak or write English, a few years before the Industrial Survey he employed an interpreter to write letters to the commissioner of Indian Affairs. The superintendent forwarded Jim's letter, with an introductory note as patronizing to Jim as it was complimentary to the commissioner. He cited Captain Jim's belief that the commissioner took a personal interest in every individual Indian, and that Jim had advised other Indians to do as he instructed: "a beautiful compliment to the personal element" that the commissioner had "injected" into the office. The superintendent closed by saying, "I sincerely trust that you may find time and strength to answer Jim's letter as it will encourage him, and incidently [sic], help a number of Indians over whom Capt. Jim exercises considerable and wholesome influence."[67] In this conclusion, Superintendent West edged closer to the truth. Captain Jim was a leader in this community, the community was leveraging a voice for itself, and the superintendent really needed the commissioner to respond.

Captain Jim's letters bear careful reading. He opened with a chatty, personal tone ("well, I like to tell you what I am been doing here to Supai Canyon"), news from the canyon (he was recovering from a broken arm; he was "very happy" about the school opening; he was talking to the Indians whenever there was trouble and telling them to behave), and praise for the agent ("my superintendent is a good agent to Supai Canyon...the agent he was help to us to what I was doing on the farmes [sic].")[68] The commissioner responded promptly, praising Jim and urging him to continue his loyal support of his agent. A few months later, Captain Jim resumed the correspondence, once again praising the agent, but making his point in the second paragraph:

> Some of the Indians have big alfalfa. We want to sell our hay to the agent, but he has not bought much hay. He has not got enough money to buy some hay. I think that I shall keep my hay and sell it to the tourists who come down to Supai. I think that is the best way. Your friend, Capt. Jim.[69]

Catering to tourists was not on the government's agenda as appropriate or civilized economic development. Reservation agents relied on the captive labor force of "their Indians" in order to accomplish the objectives set by the central office, and they were actively discouraging tourism economies at Havasupai and elsewhere. By September, a new superintendent, Fred S. Lovenskiold, discovered that most young Havasupai men were working as wage laborers for white ranchers, the Forest Service, or the Park Service, and he simply could not muster an adequate labor force to accomplish reservation "advancement." The traditional leaders, such as Captain Jim, had won this round; Captain Jim's stance in the 1923 Industrial Survey photo, his refusal to live in the new housing, and his successful circumvention of federal attempts to control the local economy and damage Havasupai income all speak to the complicated realities playing out in reservation arenas that could not be as strictly regulated as boarding school environments.[70]

The Industrial Surveys from the Omaha reservation tell a slightly different story, of federal intransigence to surrendering any powers over Indian lives. These surveys make clear that the government's assimilation programs had built into them sliding scales of success, ever-shifting standards that

Figure 8.12. Sample home picture from the Omaha Industrial Survey, 1922. National Archives.

Figure 8.13. Sample home picture from the Omaha Industrial Survey, 1922. National Archives.

Indian people were never going to meet, if true success meant the end of federal bureaucratic control over Indian people.

These images appear to represent the neat, tidy, decent homes of federal policy makers' and schoolmasters' dreams. They appear to be "picture perfect" after-images in the famous "before and after" genre of photography of Indians, making the point that assimilation programs were working and

Indian people were being transformed. Correspondence between the Omaha agent and the commissioner of Indian Affairs complicates the story told by these after-images, and reveals how critical it was that the federal government continue to justify their surveillance of, and powers over, Indian lives.

In May of 1922 Omaha Superintendent Lohmiller sent his Industrial Surveys to Washington, and the Acting Commissioner responded a few weeks later:

> The pictures accompanying each write-up show, in a noticeable degree, the lack of attractive home surroundings. The making of a lawn, the planting of a few trees or shrubs, the laying of walks, the general cleaning up of the premises, require but little time and effort and the results of any attempts to better home conditions are always worth the little effort that may be necessary…. A coat of paint would seem to be a necessary addition to a great many of the Indian homes. It likewise appears that more of the Indian allotments should be fenced.[71]

The acting commissioner made it clear: when judging Indian "progress" toward "civilization," the ante was always going to go up. Whatever Indian people did, whatever their agents did for them or to them, it was never going to be quite good enough to merit self-determination. The ultimate irony of the photographs preserved in the Industrial Surveys is that the images profess to tell some truth about American Indians, that they were in the process of being "made over" in the image of civilization, but the federal government refused to acknowledge the evidence it had accumulated in its own surveys. That refusal is striking. Indian people had always known that the truth of "assimilation" and accommodation was much more complicated than what might be seen on the surface of a photograph, but how do we understand the acting commissioner's criticisms of the homes at Omaha? Both the situation at Havasupai and the scenario at Omaha boiled down to exercises of power. Captain Jim strategically out-flanked his agents in a moment of economic self-determination, but winning a single battle does not win a war. Federal correspondence about the Industrial Surveys at Omaha well illustrates the scale of the larger battleground: despite apparent evidence of Indian "progress," the government would refuse to easily surrender power over Indian peoples' lives. Native struggles to assert sovereignty and self-determination have always been hard-fought and hard-won.

Conclusion

The federal government set out to transform "the Indian home," and through a multitude of policies and practices—burning down traditional architectural forms, enveloping children in self-consciously grand school buildings, carefully orchestrating the organization of living, eating, and sleeping spaces, training young girls in practice cottages and young families in model homes, building "Connecticut Cottages" on reservations and sending out field matrons to write reports on peoples' housekeeping, restructuring agricultural practices, outlawing polygamy, and so on and so forth—the federal government accomplished many of its goals. Most domestic architecture in Indian country today resembles the homes of rural non-Native neighbors much more than it resembles "traditional" forms. Indian people may belong to a kiva or travel the powwow circuit, they may speak their language, have long hair or short, eat blue corn or commodity cheese, but chances are they live in a trailer, or a HUD house, or something close to it.[72] Reservation housing has been transformed, and the policies and practices designed and implemented at the turn of the last century continue to impact the way Indian people live today.

Notes

1. See Paul Chaat Smith, *Everything You Know about Indians Is Wrong.*

2. Earlier versions of this paper were presented April 1996 at the Museum of Natural History, University of Oregon, in conjunction with the exhibit *Living Traditions: Continuity and Resurgence of Native American Architecture*; and November 1996 at a session of the annual meeting of the American Society for Ethnohistory, Portland, Oregon.

3. See K. Tsianina Lomawaima, "Estelle Reel, Superintendent of Indian Schools, 1898–1910: Politics, Curriculum, and Land"; K. Tsianina Lomawaima and Teresa L. McCarty, "*To Remain an Indian*": *Lessons in Democracy from a Century of Native American Education.*

4. American Indian bodies were subjected to intense regimentation and discipline in school and reservation agency environments. In the boarding schools, in addition to learning how to walk up and down stairs, sit at desks, sleep in beds, and correctly thread needles, students were subjected to mandatory haircuts in homogenizing "styles," while men with long hair on reservations were shorn in accord with the Short Hair Order of 1903, and military units carried out physicians' orders to forcibly "dip" Native bodies to fight smallpox.

5. "Citizen dress" served to homogenize and transform Native bodies, transmitting visible markers of modesty, class, and gender.

6. Native populations were frequently characterized as inherently unhealthy and weak, in comparison to the more inherently vigorous white race (because of generations of "productive" labor and "high" morals) and black race (because of the "uplifting" labor training and discipline instilled by slavery). Samuel Chapman Armstrong, founder of Hampton Institute, a normal school for African Americans that accepted Native students in the late 1880s, commented on Indian health: "We have found the weak point of the race to be physical, not mental or moral. They can endure the hardships peculiar to the plains, but not ready work from day to day. They are swept away by measles and smallpox, being weakened by inherited disease; the lungs are their weakest point. They are sinewy but not muscular." See Samuel Chapman Armstrong, *The Indian Question,* 15.

7. Two important areas intersect in this domain: the production of foodstuffs through agriculture, horticulture, gathering, hunting, fishing, and their related technologies; and the

preparation of foods, the arena of menus, recipes, and cooking technologies. All were important markers of the boundary between savage and civilized. Even traits that appeared to be civilized were ruled out of bounds if they had been learned through home instruction. An alumna of Chilocco Indian Agricultural School recalled that in the 1930s she came to school knowing how to bake biscuits; she had to "relearn" biscuit-making according to the Cooking class recipe, however, to pass muster (Lomawaima, *They Called It Prairie Light: The Story of Chilocco Indian School*).

8. Where, when, how, and why men and women labor; toward what ends; and with what compensation.

9. "Buildings constructed at Hampton Institute between 1867 and 1887 were *symbols and tools* of General Samuel C. Armstrong's program of self-help for the freedmen and Indians through an industrial education with the primary goal of building character." See Thelma Robins Brown, "Memorial Chapel: The Culmination of the Development of the Campus of Hampton Institute, Hampton, Virginia, 1867–1887," 1. Emphasis added. Also see Jeff Mauger, "Shed Roof Houses at the Ozette Archaeological Site: A Protohistoric Architectural System," 230–234.

10. Two themes that consistently unify the domains are the refrains of cleanliness/orderliness, and the notion that Native societies were characterized by idleness or intermittent labor, while civilization's steady, daily, focused "work" subsumed all possible meanings of "productive" labor.

11. See Suquamish Tribe.

12. See Wayne Suttles, "The Shed-Roof House."

13. See Nabokov and Easton.

14. See Suttles, "The Shed-Roof House."

15. Archaeological evidence indicates Big Man House was about 530 feet long and varied from 40 to 60 feet in width. See Jeff Mauger, "Shed Roof Houses at the Ozette Archaeological Site: A Protohistoric Architectural System," 230–234.

16. See Leonard Forsman, "History of Western Washington Native Peoples," 208.

17. The analysis of photographs included in this chapter has benefited greatly from the input of students in class discussions. I am grateful to the undergraduate and graduate students in classes at the University of Washington (1989–1994) and the University of Arizona (1994–2009) who have thoughtfully and insightfully commented on these images.

18. See Samuel Chapman Armstrong, *Report of a Trip Made on Behalf of the Indian Rights Association to Some Indian Reservations of the Southwest*, 21.

19. National Archives, Record Group 75, Entry 762: Reports of Industrial Surveys, 1922–1929, Box 17: Greenville-Hoopa Valley, Grip File *Havasupai Indian School (Arizona) Industrial Survey*, p. 2, 1923.

20. See Armstrong.

21. See Marianna Burgess, *Stiya, a Carlisle Indian Girl at Home.*

22. See Amos Rapoport, *The Meaning of the Built Environment.*

23. See Susan Kent, *Domestic Architecture and the Use of Space: An Interdisciplinary Cross-cultural Study.*

24. See Amos Rapoport, "Systems of Activities and Systems of Settings," 17.

25. The *Uniform Course of Study* for Indian Schools stated categorically that food must *never* be kept in a room where people sleep. See Estelle Reel, 441.

26. See Bishop William Hobart Hare, *How the Church Schools in South Dakota Help Indian Boys and Girls*, 6.

27. The eventual name for the school that originated as the Salem [Oregon] Industrial

Training School, Chemawa, was alleged to be the "Indian" word for "Happy Home" (September 20, 1899, letter in the Estelle Reel Papers/Cheney Cowles Museum, now in the collections of the Northwest Museum of Arts & Culture/NWMAC). See also images and records from the Santa Fe Indian School, picture captioned "Mother's Day at the Hecha Kewa (Happy Home) home economics building, ca. 1930" and "Members of the Hecha Kewa Club were high achievers in the field of home economics. In the Pueblo spirit of hospitality, they gave special parties, entertained parents, and hosted picnics for public school home economics clubs. The club's motto was 'Glorify Work and Be Happy,' and its colors, red and white, symbolized friendship between races." See Sally Hyer, *One House, One Voice, One Heart: Native American Education at the Santa Fe Indian School*, 54.

28. See Society of Friends, *A Sketch…for Promoting the Improvement and Gradual Civilization of the Indian Natives*, 6–8.

29. Society of Friends, 10.

30. Armstrong, *Report of a Trip Made on Behalf of the Indian Rights Association to Some Indian Reservations of the Southwest*, 21.

31. Gilbert B. Morrison, "School Architecture and Hygiene," 411.

32. Ironically, this reality was as evident to Native students as to federal agents, given the archival and anecdotal evidence of student-initiated arson in the boarding schools. Lomawaima, *They Called It Prairie Light: The Story of Chilocco Indian School*.

33. For detailed discussion of student lives, creative activities, and resistance, especially as revealed in alumni memories, see Margaret L. Archuleta, Brenda J. Child, and K. Tsianina Lomawaima, *Away from Home: American Indian Boarding School Experiences*; Brenda J. Child, *Boarding School Seasons: American Indian Families*; Clyde Ellis, *To Change Them Forever: Indian Education at the Rainy Mountain Boarding School, 1893–1920*; Basil H. Johnston, *Indian School Days*; F. LaFlesche, *The Middle Five: Indian Schoolboys of the Omaha Tribe*; and Lomawaima, *They Called It Prairie Light: The Story of Chilocco Indian School*.

34. Chilocco was built in north-central Oklahoma, its northern boundary the Oklahoma-Kansas state line. It operated as the flagship school for agricultural instruction; the school was closed in 1980; see Lomawaima, *They Called It Prairie Light: The Story of Chilocco Indian School*. Haskell was built in Lawrence, Kansas, and by the mid-1900s operated as the flagship school for business and commercial instruction; many of its alumna went on to careers in the Bureau of Indian Affairs. The campus still operates as Haskell Indian Nations University.

35. Helen Ludlow, *Ten Years' Work for Indians at Hampton Institute, VA, 1878–1888*, 7.

36. See H. B. Frissell, "Hampton Institute," 129.

37. See Edith Armstrong Talbot, *Samuel Chapman Armstrong*, 159.

38. See Talbot, 161.

39. See Talbot, 161–162.

40. Richard Morris Hunt (1827–1895) was the first American architect to study at the École des Beaux-Arts in Paris. His work has been largely forgotten today, but in the late nineteenth century he was nationally famous as "the Vanderbilt architect," or "chateau builder to Fifth Avenue." See Paul R. Baker, "Richard Morris Hunt: An Introduction," 3–4; Talbot, 172–173.

41. See Thelma Robins Brown, "Memorial Chapel: The Culmination of the Development of the Campus of Hampton Institute, Hampton, Virginia, 1867–1887," 1.

42. See Brown, 13.

43. See William Hardin Hughes and Frederick Patterson, *Robert Russa Moton of Hampton and Tuskegee*, 25.

44. See Frances B. Johnston, *The Hampton Album*.

45. Johnston, 10; emphasis added.

46. Quoted in David Wallace Adams, *Education for Extinction: American Indians and the Boarding School Experience, 1875–1928*, 174.

47. *Talks & Thoughts*, April 1889, 1.

48. Rapoport, *The Meaning of the Built Environment.*

49. Brown, 158, citing Talbot, 185–186.

50. Placing Indian students in their own dorms was strongly motivated by beliefs that the races should be in close enough proximity that Indian students might benefit from exposure to the supposed superior work ethic and Christian morality of the blacks, but not so close as to encourage "mixing" or romantic entanglements.

51. "Winona, a Dakota word meaning eldest sister of a female, was the name given to the Indian girls' dormitory." See Cora Mae Folsom, *Twenty-Two Years; Work of the Hampton Normal and Agricultural Institute at Hampton, Virginia*, footnote on 58.

52. Mary Lou Hultgren and Paulette Molin, *To Lead and to Serve: American Indian Education at Hampton Institute, 1878–1923*, 33. Emphasis added.

53. In the same volume of *The Southern Workman*, another teacher, Miss Eustis, proclaimed: "The meaning of the new building to the Indian girls that night! Its meaning for Indian girls through all the coming years! We wish such things could be told" (November 1882, 107). Hampton's 1883 Annual Report credited Winona with doing "more in some ways than ten years school work." See Hampton Normal and Agricultural Institute, *Concerning Indians, Extracts from the Annual Report*, 12.

54. *The Southern Workman* (1879), 93.

55. Winona not only organized and furbished interior spaces: the front lawn was shaded by sycamores and maples, with room for croquet, tennis, and a patterned flower garden. See *Talks and Thoughts* (December 1893), 1–2.

56. W. Roger Buffalohead and Paulette Fairbanks Molin, "'A Nucleus of Civilization': American Indian Families at Hampton Institute in the Late Nineteenth Century."

57. Valerie Sherer Mathes, *Helen Hunt Jackson and Her Indian Reform Legacy*, 131.

58. Hultgren and Molin, 38.

59. See Adams, 251.

60. See Adams, 251.

61. "Industrial Status Reports" had been produced as early as 1912 (Entry 121, BIA Classified Files 1907–1939, Havasupai 24442–33–910 to 84615–13–920). Circular #1774 from the commissioner of Indian Affairs directed reservation superintendents to undertake surveys to document living conditions, especially progress in housing and agriculture. Box after box in the National Archives is filled with one-page forms reporting on living conditions on reservations. Forms from most agencies each have a photo of an Indian home attached. (There are some exceptions: very few photos appear in the files from the Hopi agency).

62. National Archives, Record Group 75, Records of the Education Division, Records of the Industries Section, Entry 762: Reports of the Industrial Surveys, 1922–1929.

63. The homes cost $150.00 apiece. John W. Atwater, Inspector. June 20–23, 1922. *Inspection Report: Havasupai Agency and School*, p. 3. National Archives, Record Group 75, Entry 121: Central Classified Files Havasupai, 56886 1922 Havasupai File No. 916.

64. National Archives, Record Group 75, Entry 762: Reports of Industrial Surveys, 1922–1929, Box 17: Greenville-Hoopa Valley, Grip File *Havasupai Indian School (Arizona) Industrial*

Survey, p. 13, 1923. The discourse about cleanliness was tied closely to notions about health. Indian agents were often distressed to discover that building "better" homes did not correspond to improvements in overall health. A Superintendent at Omaha noted: "It is the same old story, people accustomed to constant out-of-door life, suddenly finding themselves in modern environments": the story was, they sicken and die (National Archives, Record Group 75, Entry 121 Central Consolidated Files, Omaha). This quote shows how prevalent the idea of adaptation was. Different societies were "adapted to," in the sense of habituated to, certain patterns of living over the generations, so it made perfect sense to the Omaha Agent that you had to be civilized in order to survive civilization.

65. National Archives, Record Group 75, Entry 762: Reports of Industrial Surveys, 1922–1929, Box 17: Greenville-Hoopa Valley, Grip File *Havasupai Indian School (Arizona) Industrial Survey*, p. 17, 1923.

66. National Archives, Record Group 75, Entry 121: Central Consolidated Files, Havasupai, 1912.

67. Superintendent D. Clinton West to C.I.A., March 4, 1915. National Archives, Record Group 75, Entry 121: Central Consolidated Files 1907–1938, 29546 1915 Havasupai File No. 916.

68. Captain Jim Catagomer to C.I.A., March 13, 1915. National Archives, Record Group 75, Entry 121: BIA Consolidated Files 1907–1938, 29546 1915 Havasupai File No. 916.

69. Capt. Jim Catagomer to C.I.A., August 8, 1915. National Archives, Record Group 75, Entry 121: BIA Consolidated Files 1907–1938, 29546 1915 Havasupai File No. 916.

70. Federal powers on reservations were considerable, and should not be underestimated, but they were not total. By the same token, Native powers on reservations should not be overestimated; but they were not powerless.

71. Letter dated May 26, 1922. Acting Commissioner Meritt to Superintendent Lohmiller. National Archives, Record Group 75, Entry 762: Reports of Industrial Surveys, 1922–1929, Box 27: Omaha-Pawnee.

72. An intimately related issue that is beyond the scope of this chapter entails the economic and legal structures of American capital investment that have seriously handicapped home construction, home ownership, and other forms of economic development, such as small business ownership on reservations. Much of reservation property is held in trust by the federal government; this legal fact means that mortgages—the primary means most Americans use to finance home ownership—are not available to Native people who reside on trust lands. The administration of President William Clinton was the first to address this issue, and in the last decade some home loan programs have been developed on some reservations. The historic lack of mortgage loans has contributed to the "popularity" of trailer housing on many reservations. Being mobile, trailers and similar manufactured homes are repossessable by financing banks, which are willing to make loans for their purchase.

9 Encounters with Interculturalidad

Indigenous Education and the Politics of Knowledge in the Andes

María Elena García

In April 2007 I received an e-mail from Ana,[1] an Aymara community educator from Bolivia who had recently graduated from the Program for Training in Intercultural Bilingual Education for Andean Countries, or the PROEIB Andes. The PROEIB Andes is a master's program for indigenous students based in Cochabamba, Bolivia, and (until late 2007) supported by various international development agencies. Since 1996, this program has trained indigenous men and women from at least six different South American countries with the aim of creating a critical mass of indigenous professionals who will work toward the advancement of an intercultural bilingual education agenda in Latin America.[2] Ana, the Aymara woman I just mentioned, was responding to an e-mail in which I told her about my new research project: an exploration of the political impact of the PROEIB. She responded almost immediately, and with much enthusiasm. "For me," she wrote, "the PROEIB Andes marked a milestone in my life; it has helped me be a better Aymara, a better professional, and to open my heart and mind in order to take on life's diversity, including its conflicts and tensions."

I listened to a very different assessment of the PROEIB during a conversation earlier that same year with Carmen, another Aymara intellectual who was among the PROEIB's first students and who now teaches at an intercultural bilingual education program run through a different university in La Paz, Bolivia. Carmen described the PROEIB as a colonial institution where, in her view, non-indigenous academics imposed a discourse of *interculturalidad* (or interculturality) that was superficial, insincere, and folkloric. When I asked her to expand, she explained: "Interculturality. A matter of respecting he who is different, even if he steps on you. Even if he kills you, you must respect the other." And she added, "in such a racist and colonial country [Bolivia], to talk about cultural respect is suicide."

Taking these two visions as points of departure, in this chapter I explore the cultural politics of the PROEIB as both a transnational space (anchored in Bolivia) and a transnational project (promoting indigenous education throughout South America). In doing so, I pay particular attention to the encounters (between and among students, faculty, and indigenous leaders) that shape and shatter notions of indigeneity and inclusion at the PROEIB. Is the PROEIB an intercultural haven, or is it in fact another imperial endeavor? In trying to answer this question, it is useful to think about the PROEIB as a sort of "contact zone," a term borrowed from Mary Louise Pratt's discussion of colonial encounters in which, in her words, "peoples geographically and historically separated come into contact with each other and establish on-going relations, usually involving conditions of coercion, radical inequality, and intractable conflict."[3] The PROEIB's founders sought to turn this concept on its head and create a horizontal and democratic space where colonial legacies could be challenged, where knowledge could be decolonized, and where power relations and hierarchies could be minimized, if not erased. In other words, they sought to create an intercultural space, one that moved beyond simply the recognition of cultural difference—beyond multiculturalism—and instead promoted *intercultural* relationships and collaborations between indigenous and non-indigenous actors.

However, for a variety of reasons the program has found itself wrestling with the legacies of coercion, inequality, and conflict that tend to define relationships between indigenous and non-indigenous interlocutors in Latin America. It has been accused by many of training a certain kind of indigenous subject, the so-called "*indio permitido*" (or "authorized Indian"), who works within the parameters of what state (and international) entities deem "safe."[4] As Silvia Rivera, Rosabel Millamán, Charlie Hale, and others have detailed elsewhere, this kind of subject emerged in the era of multicultural reforms that were intimately aligned with neoliberal policies throughout Latin America. Indigenous activists working outside of these boundaries are thus deemed unsafe or subversive. The PROEIB is intimately connected to the neoliberal multicultural moment in Bolivia, and for many it is no more than an instrument of colonial and imperial projects inserted in the region as one way to manage and control (indigenous) difference. In other words, for critics of the program, it trains and crafts safe and compliant indigenous subjects who are then placed in positions of power at the level of government ministries, universities, international entities, and nongovernmental organizations. The election of Evo Morales, the first self-identified indigenous president of Bolivia, greatly challenged the PROEIB's vision and political significance, just as it has radically transformed politics and society in Bolivia today. However, here I focus on the PROEIB as it existed between 1996 and 2007.[5]

The contrasting impressions from the two Aymara women I cite at the beginning of this chapter demonstrate that the PROEIB's story has been a messy, complex, and contradictory one. What follows, then, is an examination of some of the ways in which progressive politics, colonial legacies, and pedagogical practices have come together in unexpected and often contradictory ways at the PROEIB. It is also an opportunity to think about the real impact that this space has had on the professional and political lives and identities of the approximately 150 indigenous students who (as of late 2007) attended and graduated from the program.[6] While in many ways we can think of the PROEIB as inspired by the imperialism of good intentions, the testimonies of students, even those who are highly critical of the program, push us to consider a more complicated understanding of the cultural politics and unintended consequences of this institution. And yet, even while taking such complexity into account, I argue that the counter-hegemonic possibilities at the PROEIB are limited. In this chapter I explore the production of indigenous subjects at the PROEIB by examining varying notions of interculturalidad, and the experiences of indigenous graduates of the program. Before diving into that discussion, I provide some background to the PROEIB and the research conducted in South America.

De-centering the PROEIB: Notes on Field Research and the Politics of Engagement

I began thinking about the political significance of the PROEIB Andes in 1998. At the time I was finalizing research and fieldwork for my PhD dissertation, which would focus on the connections between indigenous mobilization and intercultural bilingual education in Cuzco, Peru. I had heard about the program at various international conferences on intercultural bilingual education prior to 1998, but I arrived at the PROEIB that year, during the first term of the program.[7] I had traveled to Cochabamba to visit a friend who happened to be among the students participating in this first year of the program. While I have written elsewhere about that first encounter,[8] for years after that visit I contemplated the impact of the training at this program on indigenous graduates. Although I returned sporadically to Bolivia and the PROEIB during the next ten years, I was unable to conduct the kind of long-term research that would help me situate the PROEIB and its graduates within a broader discussion of indigenous politics in the region.

In 2007, the mutually agreed upon ten-year period of collaboration between international funders and the PROEIB came to an end. With this end period in mind, I applied for and received a fellowship that offered me the possibility of returning to Bolivia to conduct ethnographic research on the impact of the PROEIB. The moment was particularly significant given the changes in the political context. Bolivia now boasted its first self-identified indigenous president, and presumably the by now well-placed PROEIB graduates would be taking an active role in the much celebrated decolonization of society. The timing of my fellowship would allow research to take place between October 2006 and August 2007, one month before the official transition of the PROEIB from an internationally funded institute to a private Bolivian-administered foundation.

My original intention was to conduct comparative ethnographic research with PROEIB faculty, scholars and intellectuals, indigenous graduates, and indigenous leaders in Bolivia and Peru. However, when I met with the PROEIB directors of the program to discuss the scope of the study, both of them noted that it would be more useful for the program if I could conduct an evaluation of sorts of the PROEIB through an investigation of the trajectories of graduates of the program in the six affiliated countries. This meant traveling to and spending time in all of the countries officially affiliated with the PROEIB: Argentina, Bolivia, Chile, Colombia, Ecuador, and Peru.

I should note that I was sympathetic to the work conducted at the PROEIB, and more generally to the implementation of intercultural politics throughout Latin America. I wanted to help, and this would be an opportunity to "give back" to the PROEIB in some ways. Both directors of the program had been supportive of my previous work on intercultural education in Peru, and the program's doors had always been open to me. At the same time, I worried about the methodological implications of conducting the kind of research they needed me to do. Their request called for the kind of research and evaluative report that a consultant might prepare, and given my training as a cultural anthropologist and belief in the importance of long-term ethnographic research, I couldn't help but wonder if I would be able to conduct this short-term, multi-sited kind of research. In hindsight, after almost a year of traveling to multiple countries, cities, towns, and communities, and talking with a wide range of actors, directly or indirectly connected to the PROEIB and intercultural education politics in the region, I realized that one advantage of this kind of research, whatever its limitations, was that it offered the possibility of thinking about the PROEIB in a de-centered way,

180   *María Elena García*

understanding how ideas and debates that originated in the Cochabamba campus "traveled" (or did not) to a wide range of contexts. This kind of research also allowed me to see the Bolivian "center" of the PROEIB network as one of many nodes of a transnational network that linked students and faculty from multiple countries and indigenous communities with a wide number of ministries of education, universities, and indigenous organizations. Moreover, in each of the six countries, "the PROEIB" took on different valences as it entered different local contexts that varied in their acceptance of or hostility to ideas about intercultural education in general and the PROEIB in particular.

Some of the controversy about the PROEIB was also due to the context in which the PROEIB was created. While the program opened its doors in 1996, the idea of the PROEIB had been in the works for several years prior and emerged within the context of a region-wide increase in indigenous mobilization. National protests, marches, and uprisings (levantamientos) throughout Latin America had (peacefully but powerfully) placed the political and cultural demands of indigenous people on the agendas of national governments and international development organizations. Intercultural bilingual education (IBE) occupied a central role in these demands.[9] Initially, IBE was described as a more inclusive kind of education that would move beyond the assimilationist policies of the past. Among the goals of IBE is the revalorization of indigenous languages, and thus in its fullest form IBE would be designed not solely for indigenous children but it would involve a rethinking of education for all members of multilingual and pluri-ethnic societies.[10] While in practice, indigenous people remained the "target population" of IBE programs, these initiatives soon attracted the interest of an important set of international funding agencies that pushed for the development of cultural and bilingual education programs at all levels, programs that multiplied during the 1990s. Thus, the other important part of the constitutive moment of the PROEIB was the "mainstreaming" of policies of official multiculturalism in Latin America. Below I discuss in more detail the dangers of what Charles Hale has provocatively called the "menace of multiculturalism."[11] For now it suffices to say that the PROEIB emerged in the context of a contradictory political moment characterized by insurgent indigenous political projects ("from below") and state projects that sought to address, channel, and contain indigenous demands ("from above").

The selection of Bolivia as the main site of the PROEIB reflects, in part, these contradictory tensions. As one of the program directors, Luis Enrique López, noted in an interview,[12] Bolivian indigenous movements were among the strongest in the hemisphere, and the state response to their demands was also considered by many one of the more innovative approaches to indigenous recognition and inclusion. The educational reforms that have taken place since the 1990s have reflected changing dynamics between the Bolivian state and indigenous social movements. Though the multicultural reforms of the 1990s have been the subject of great debate (especially over whether the reforms were meant to empower or contain indigenous political projects), they reflected a new recognition of the importance of addressing indigenous social demands.[13] For López, the official commitment to interculturalism was an important step toward a more inclusive vision of Bolivian society. It should be pointed out that López, a Peruvian-born and Oxford-trained linguist who is considered one of the leading academic authorities on IBE in Latin America, was not only the director of the PROEIB but also part of the team that designed the new Bolivian education reforms during the multicultural opening of the 1990s. In addition to these links between PROEIB founders and Bolivia, the broad autonomy that the Bolivian state guaranteed the PROEIB within its university system led to its installation at the Universidad Mayor San Simon in Cochabamba, Bolivia.

Very quickly, the PROEIB became an obligatory point of reference for IBE in Latin America. The PROEIB is primarily known for its master's program tailored exclusively for indigenous teachers, intellectuals, and professionals from the six South American countries mentioned earlier, though increasingly students from other countries outside of the Andean region, such as Mexico, Guatemala, and Panama, are part of the student body.[14] At the PROEIB, these students are expected to receive theoretical and practical training (not to mention the academic credentials) enabling them to participate in their respective countries' educational reforms as administrators, technicians, curriculum designers, and policy makers. As of 2007, the PROEIB boasted five graduating classes of the master's program and two classes of a relatively new program in indigenous leadership training. With the support of international funders (the *Deutsche Gesellschaft für Technische Zusammenarbeit*, or GTZ, in particular), the PROEIB Andes has received the kind of economic, material, and human resources that are unusual for university programs in Latin America. Within the context of educational politics, the PROEIB is a significant part of the broader networks and processes of IBE at various levels, not only nationally (in ministries of education and through education reform), but also at local levels (in teacher training institutes, schools, communities, and other spaces). Politically, the training of indigenous leaders and intellectuals has accompanied and responded to indigenous movement demands and struggles. Socioculturally, the use and revitalization of indigenous languages and the promotion of a politics of interculturality has helped to make visible the colonial legacies that are an all too present part of Latin American realities.

According to the official PROEIB website,[15] the goal of the program is to "support the consolidation of intercultural bilingual education in the Andes, mainly through the formation of human resources that this new kind of education requires in order to move beyond the stage of pilot programs and experiments" in which IBE, to some degree, still finds itself. Moreover, the selection and training of new indigenous educators and intellectuals relies upon and strengthens an existing "network of indigenous organizations, ministries of education, and universities committed to the development of IBE." These networks also include international development agencies that fund IBE activities throughout the region. Thus, the goal of the PROEIB is not only training a critical mass of indigenous professionals but also connecting them with supporters and allies of IBE.

While the PROEIB is recognized locally and internationally as a prestigious institution, there are very few studies focused on the experiences of the graduates of the program and the impact these graduates have had on educational and intercultural politics in each of the six countries participating in the PROEIB network.[16] When I discussed the possibility of exploring the trajectories of PROEIB graduates with the program directors, I was encouraged by their eagerness to support this research. Their hope was clearly that this might be a way to provide a critical analysis of the educational, political, and sociocultural impact of the PROEIB in the region. And this is what I set out to do.

Over the course of eleven months, I tracked down as many PROEIB graduates as possible.[17] I talked with them about their personal and professional lives, and the impact of the PROEIB on their life and work. Additionally, I sought out as many as possible of the actors participating in the PROEIB network, including indigenous organizations, universities, and ministries of education. I spent, on average, between two and four weeks in each of the six PROEIB countries. Ordinarily, I would fly to capital cities, take trains and buses to smaller cities and towns, and travel by moto-taxi, cab, and/or foot to various communities. In each of my research trips, I interviewed a mix of former graduates, IBE professionals, university officials, and indigenous leaders. The advantage of interviewing a relatively large number of people in their home countries is that one is able to observe both the common challenges and the often stark differences that characterize IBE policies in the Andean republics. The disadvantage of covering so much ground lies in the difficulty of acquiring the kind of deep ethnographic understanding that comes with extended participant observation. Nevertheless, the interviews conducted for this study provided a broad set of views that offered some clear patterns and highlighted some persistent challenges. Moreover, interview data was complemented by preliminary phone conversations and e-mail correspondence with interviewees, focus-group interviews when a critical mass of graduates was available, and e-mail questionnaires.

Producing Indigenous Subjects: The PROEIB and Its Critics

As I began field research for this project in the fall of 2006, I sat down to speak with an administrator at the University of San Simon in Cochabamba, where the PROEIB is housed. Like all others before her, this administrator praised the work conducted at the PROEIB, and proudly announced that it was one of their only "star" programs. I thought back to the first time I was at the PROEIB, back in 1998 as I conducted dissertation fieldwork. I, too, saw this program as a fascinating and important space where individual and collective ideas about indigeneity were continuously negotiated, and where local politics (at both ideological and material levels) were deeply affected by the national and global dimensions of indigenous political struggles.[18] This was a place where men and women from over sixteen different South American indigenous groups gathered to share similarities and differences in their struggles and lives, and where they engaged and challenged both Western and indigenous forms of knowledge. This included learning and practicing English, Aymara, Quechua, and French; learning how to use computers and e-mail; and reading texts by Bourdieu, Foucault, and Bakhtin, among others.

I shared my first impressions with Cecilia (the administrator with whom I was speaking), and asked her what it was about the program that she admired most. Cecilia immediately said that the most important aspect of this program was the foreign influence that it brought to the campus, the university students, and in particular to the students at the PROEIB. She was referring specifically to the directors of the program (one is a well-known Peruvian intellectual, the other is an Austrian linguist), and to the many European and North American lecturers who walked the PROEIB's halls. I asked her what about this "foreign influence" was most significant in her view. It is worth quoting her answer at length:

> This influence will contribute...to [changing] a community. My hope is that the resentments [the students] have carried through generations disappear and instead turn into what we all want: a multilingual, intercultural country where different races...are not resentful of each other. At first I was scared of the students at the PROEIB. When I went there for the first time I felt rejected. My skin crawled from listening to them talk. But now these people seem to have changed. Of course, I always tell [the directors] that they must focus not only on pedagogy, but also on making these people understand that...we must forget what happened 500 years ago because I was not alive 500 years ago. That is interculturalidad: forgetting about all that from 500 years ago. These people need to understand, and they will

understand. But it takes time. [M]any of these people will end up in important places, like the ministry of education, and it is good that they will have a different attitude; a more open and welcoming attitude.

It is important to note that Cecilia's comments were made in the context of a tense and violent period in the history of Cochabamba. Only a week before this conversation took place the city had erupted in violent clashes that pit coca farmers and peasants from the countryside against white, mostly young and male, city dwellers. Cecilia had also referred to the recent election of Evo Morales with unease, proclaiming at one point in our conversation that "if [Morales] could, he would execute all of us [who are not indigenous]." It was clear that at least for this administrator, the PROEIB was an important step toward the production of a different kind of indigenous subject, one who would learn to let go of resentments and, she hoped, one who would signal a more "intercultural" future for Bolivia. While these sentiments are heavy with an old and problematic concern for civilizing and even taming potentially dangerous natives, they are hardly unique to this administrator and in less explicit forms have been expressed by other non-indigenous supporters of the program. Many university and government officials in Bolivia and beyond echoed her sentiments, particularly regarding what several (Bolivian, Chilean, Peruvian, and other Latin American) scholars referred to as "the shaping of indigenous minds for the future."

But what, then, does *interculturalidad* really mean? How one answers this question entails significantly different political consequences. According to two Chilean Mapuche graduates of the program, the PROEIB did not advocate a "true" interculturality. In the offices of a Chilean government agency for indigenous development, I spoke with David and Claudia, both of whom had been a part of the first graduating class. When I asked them what they meant by saying that the PROEIB did not promote true interculturalidad, David answered with the following statement: "The PROEIB is very clear. The directors and many of the teachers say, 'we will prepare these Indians to do something different'; but, they never really imagined that we could actually be leaders in the social and political developments of our countries." This comment reflects a widely shared view among students, that the PROEIB's heavy emphasis on all things academic (and particularly theoretical linguistics) and seeming lack of attention to the politics of struggle create a space that removes the political edge from indigenous cultural politics.

But is this critique fair? Can we really declare the PROEIB one more example of the imperialism of good intentions, another version of a civilizing project meant to transform indigenous subjects? There is clearly much debate around this question, but it is worth considering some alternative readings of the program. To begin with, it is important to note that this is not simply a case of non-indigenous voices speaking at indigenous students. While the PROEIB began with a clear division between indigenous students and non-indigenous faculty, since its first years the program has included several indigenous faculty members who have left their own mark on the pedagogical practices of the curriculum.[19]

One teacher, a Quechua intellectual whom I will call Fausto, has worked for decades on questions of indigenous education. Earning a PhD in England and having worked in various national and international programs, Fausto is hardly a cog in a colonial apparatus, but an important and independent voice in the formation of indigenous policies. Though he sees some problems in the current incarnation of indigenous education, as someone who has worked during times of military dictatorship and during times when there was no interest among international funders to support these kinds of initiatives, Fausto is hardly ready to declare the PROEIB a failure. Rather, he sees it as an opportunity to be seized, an opening to be pursued. His view of interculturality is also far from the pessimistic and cynical ones that many students expressed. Speaking in his office at the PROEIB, Fausto recalled a particular day in one of his workshops on indigenous language. In a space that included members of various language communities, students were asked to devote substantial energy to developing written and oral skills in their respective languages. Yet, when they came together, perhaps naturally, they felt it important to resort to a lingua franca, in this case the colonial language of Spanish, so that Aymaras, Mapuches, Quechuas, Guaranis, and others would understand what the particular speaker wanted to convey. As students switched to Spanish, however, Fausto demanded that they stop. He insisted that they speak only in their native languages. Though students objected that their peers would not understand what they were each saying, Fausto responded that this did not matter. The point, according to Fausto, is not to be always understood, but to know how to speak, without apology and without fear. For Fausto, interculturality was not about overcoming the cultural distance that separated different linguistic or racial groups; it was about enhancing the capabilities of all groups to have a voice and to find peace with the cultural distances that will inevitably be a part of plural societies. Interculturality, he seemed to say, was about the importance and democratic value of listening, even if one did not always understand. Fausto, who spoke to students about this in Spanish, was not opposed to building bridges to greater understanding. His comments, however, seem to suggest that the foundation for such bridges was provided by stronger indigenous voices and languages.

Another indigenous faculty member, whom I will call Mateo, offers an additional counter-example to the view that the PROEIB sought to take the politics out of indigenous education. Mateo heads a relatively new program at the PROEIB that is called the Indigenous Leaders Training Program. The goal of this program is to identify indigenous students from various Bolivian communities who would come to the PROEIB in order to develop education programs that would be implemented in their local communities. These students do not receive a degree, but are afforded the opportunity to come together and take courses in a prestigious university center, establish networks, and move between the classroom and community political organizations. This initiative was born out of a demand from community organizations, and Mateo has been a powerful advocate in institutionalizing this dialogue. As I sat in on one of the program's activities, students listened to the experiences and views of two older leaders of the indigenous movement, one from the Bolivian altiplano, the other from the Bolivian lowlands. While they had different interpretations of the current context of indigenous politics in Bolivia, by listening to these leaders' trajectories in the movement, the students understood the broader importance of the learning they were acquiring. As one leader passed around pictures of indigenous peoples in chains (photographs taken in the early twentieth century and which he recovered from an archive in Spain), students understood where his passion came from. As he passed around another photo of himself as a young man in the jungle, wearing only a loincloth, this leader joked that he didn't come to the PROEIB dressed in the same way as he was in the picture, because he did not want to, in his words, "scare the children." The laughter of the students allowed a transition to the more serious round of questions about the kind of everyday negotiations that indigenous people make to be members of their own local communities and of broader national and international ones.[20] Rather than suggest that students should simply become good intercultural technicians, these kinds of encounters seemed to encourage them to think more boldly about who they are and what the arc of indigenous activism could look like.

Even the more critical former graduates, those who accused the PROEIB of imperialistic paternalism, made those critiques from spaces within education ministries, international development agencies, and national universities. Malba, a Mapuche now working within the Chilean state, suggested that while some instructors wanted to "trap us within their [Western] logic," the PROEIB also gave her and others the tools to debate questions of colonization and identity, "internally and externally." This tension, between pedagogies of entrapment and liberation, was experienced and described in various ways by many program graduates. Their reflections offer a crucial opportunity to explore the ambivalences and ambiguities of interculturalisms.

One particularly powerful critique of the PROEIB was offered by Alvaro, who saw in the everyday workings and practices of the program some unsettling contradictions. For example, speaking with the director of the program, a British-educated, non-indigenous Peruvian linguist, was (for Alvaro) an unnecessarily complicated process. His description is not without some sarcasm:

> To speak with el jefe, one had to wipe one's feet, have one's arrival announced, and then have the trumpets sound, once he was ready to receive you, or something like that. The institutional message was incoherent, the [vertical] academic structure was inconsistent with the [horizontal] pedagogical proposal.... The link with colonial, official knowledge was intact. It pained me to learn about my culture from foreign experts. One is much closer to what one lives, experiences, than to that which is described by others. I don't dismiss my instructors, but in a program which claims to be about cultural revindication, these colonialist academic practices should be done away with. They didn't do that, and it is sad to see that the director of an indigenous educational program is a person from the city and rooted in the [Western] academy. The director of this program should be someone from the indigenous context, an indigenous person.... They are stuck in the same contradiction; they don't give an indigenous face to the academy.

In Alvaro's estimation the PROEIB continued to be a "contact zone" in just the way Pratt originally conceived of the term, as a place of radically unequal power relations that was constituted by and constitutive of the broader forces of colonialism. Such an interpretation has been rejected by many, including the director himself, but nevertheless these and other student views are helpful in exploring the challenges of an indigenous program that was created for indigenous people but not by them.[21]

Exploring the "Insides" of Indigeneity

Given the last set of remarks it is perhaps not surprising to note that none of the PROEIB students and graduates I spoke with were as positive in their comments about this program as Ana, the Aymara woman I cited at the beginning of this paper, who went as far as saying that being a student at the PROEIB had actually helped her become a "better Aymara." Yet, Ana's comments, just like Alvaro's, help us understand the various ways in which students negotiated and contested the meanings of indigenous education. During a telephone conversation, I asked Ana if she could expand on what she meant by the idea of becoming a "better Aymara." She told me that she simply meant that the PROEIB had given her the tools to anchor herself more firmly, historically and culturally, to her "Aymaraness." She had always had ethnic pride, she said, but after the PROEIB, she was not only proud of being Aymara, but she understood more clearly what that meant, what that identity category held inside it, and what that signified for her work as an indigenous professional. This "inside" and rooted notion of indigeneity was embedded within a broader sense of being a Latin American indigenous person. Indeed, "Aymaraness" made more sense for Ana in dialogue with other indigenous experiences.[22]

Even if not always as positive in their reflections of this program as Ana, most former students did cite the PROEIB as an important domain for the development of indigenous solidarity and of the creation of (in their words) a "more Latin American indigenous identity." For many, it was their first time encountering and engaging with students from different indigenous communities. This kind of engagement led many students to feel that they left the PROEIB with a deeper and wider understanding of indigeneity in their own countries, and in the Latin American region.[23] One student put it like this: "Having to live with other *compañeros* from other cultures opens a window into a broader Latin American vision. It is a lovely space, exciting [*apasionante*], where one confronts others, it is living in a microcosm of society; it is training for reality." But what *kind* of training did students expect to receive at the PROEIB? What *kind* of reality were indigenous students being shaped for? These questions have been at the heart of critiques of the PROEIB and institutions like it. They point to the tensions between what many students expected of the program (a space that privileged indigenous knowledge) and what they experienced once at the PROEIB (a space that was "too Western" and not "indigenous enough").

Clearly, student expectations of the program varied. Some students, for instance, emphasized their professional goals. It is worth underlining that all students enrolled in the PROEIB master's program have university degrees (e.g., in anthropology, education, linguistics) and are already considered indigenous professionals. However, while some of these students wanted to move further down the path of professionalization, many also saw the PROEIB as an opportunity to explore non-Western, *indigenous* forms of knowledge. As one student put it, "I sought to deepen my understanding of indigenous knowledge, which in my case, means the Aymara cosmovision, along with that of other indigenous peoples. In addition, I tried to delve more deeply in issues relating to the history and language [of indigenous people]."

The PROEIB, then, offered a chance to accumulate the cultural capital that indigenous people could use to navigate national and international networks of development while also acquiring cultural knowledge that they saw as part of their own world visions.[24] Yet, among the most consistent and profound critiques of the program is the dissatisfaction with what many described as the PROEIB's slant toward Western ideologies, and the marginalization of indigenous knowledge and politics at the institute.[25] While there are varying views on this, I was quite struck by the fact that this was a concern brought up (albeit in different ways and for different reasons) in all of the six countries affiliated with the PROEIB, and by the majority of the actors involved in the research and implementation of intercultural bilingual education. To be clear, in raising this concern, no one implied that the PROEIB should not ask students to engage Western theorists, or require strict academic standards. What they all seemed to be asking for was a balancing of the curriculum so that "alternative" forms of knowledge are also given their proper place and emphasis. As one Aymara student explained, in her view Western thinkers were important to the extent that they could provide tools with which to develop indigenous philosophies and intellectual approaches from indigenous points of view. This student echoes a point that other indigenous scholars have made about negotiating Western and indigenous forms of knowledge. A particularly useful account of these negotiations has been provided by Temagami political philosopher Dale Turner.

Dale Turner interrogates the role of indigenous intellectuals in Canadian discussions about sovereignty, nationhood, and indigenous rights.[26] He focuses particularly on the significance of "word warriors," indigenous intellectuals who have been educated in the universities of the dominant "Euro-American" world, in mediating between indigenous and non-indigenous ways of thinking. Turner makes a distinction between these word warriors (who in the terms of this analysis might be thought of as intellectual brokers of the contact zone) and *indigenous philosophers* who practice indigenous forms of knowledge outside the academy. According to Turner, word warriors' "primary function is to engage the legal and political discourses of the state."[27] The PROEIB mission is precisely the training of this kind of word warrior. Yet, many students complain that there needs to be a bigger role for indigenous philosophers as well.

To be fair, program administrators did indeed attempt to integrate alternative forms of knowledge into the program by inviting indigenous elders (*yachacs*, shamans, and so forth) to the PROEIB. Nevertheless, this did not please many of the students or even some of the faculty. The problem with this approach, some argued, was that indigenous elders were simply (and problematically) "inserted" into a non-indigenous context. One PROEIB graduate described the problem in the following terms:

> After we complained about the lack of indigenous knowledge, the directors decided to invite the indigenous elders [los sabios]. But it is not about "inserting" them, it is about having a context in which they can share their knowledge. Their knowledge can't be disconnected from the geographic and spiritual space in which it is learned. At first we thought that this was a good response to our complaint, but it turned out that this was only about "squeezing" them and extracting information.

Writing from his vantage point in Canada, Turner seems to come to an almost identical conclusion. Rather than seeing word warriors as privileging "Western" forms of knowledge that can later be deployed for "indigenous" ends, Turner suggests that word warriors must also connect to the worlds of indigenous philosophers. He puts it this way:

> [Word warriors] ought to assert and defend the integrity of indigenous rights and nationhood and protect indigenous ways of knowing within the existing legal and political practices of the dominant culture. However, their intellectual labour must be guided by indigenous philosophies; that is, indigenous philosophies—the wisdom of the elders—must inform and help shape the strategies word warriors use to engage European intellectual discourses. How they are to do so remains largely unresolved at this point in the relationship. What I am calling for is a kind of indigenous dialogue that protects the integrity of indigenous ways of knowing the world even while engaging the dominant intellectual culture in more empowering ways.[28]

Many also felt that the program did not make adequate use of the indigenous knowledge that students themselves brought with them, and spoke of missed opportunities. A program graduate expressed this frustration in the following terms:

> They didn't take advantage of the life experience of the students. I say that the PROEIB could be an academic steamroller. The life experience of students could not be explored because we had to complete courses and theses. And when I defended my thesis they said that it had too many signs of "orality." What is that about? Is this about ripping us out of our oral culture, our oral and indigenous identity?

Another Aymara student underlined the importance of privileging indigenous students' knowledge over and above that of Western theorists. It is important, she explained, not only to understand indigenous culture from "the office" or "the city." Instead, "a master's program in Intercultural Bilingual Education whose students are indigenous from the Andean countries provides a place in which to organize an educational curriculum that grows from those cultures. That is, it would be interesting to know the different forms of life and organization of different indigenous peoples rather than having to know and repeat certain theories."

Behind many of these objections was a discomfort with the theoretical critique of "essentialism," the idea that there were more or less enduring ideas, practices, and customs that could be considered authentically and timelessly indigenous. While students understood the importance of the Barthian critique of essentialism which shifts analysis from the "insides" of culture to the ways in which cultural boundaries were drawn and redrawn, many found that this left them poorly prepared to create forms of knowledge that they could claim as uniquely their own, non-Western expression. One student, whom I will call Vicente, expressed his frustration in this way:

> *I felt that Barth's theories were not the only ones that could be guides. I was hungry for other theories that replied to Barth. I understand what he says, about culture, about boundaries, whatever [que se yo]. But I argued that, without falling into essentialisms, I maintained that there something had to sustain me [algo tiene que sostenerme]; that I still am Quechua, that I still feel Quechua. If I stick to the dead letter [la letra muerta] of Barth's theories, then I could be in a situation where I would feel that "well, I can be Quechua there, but I can't be Quechua here." In any case, the whole emphasis on problematizing and questioning makes me strengthen my sense of identity. So I sought out other things that could help me interpret Barth, respond to him.*

Vicente and I spoke at length about his concerns and frustration and they are difficult to summarize. However, he seemed to be suggesting that Barth's situational and relational analysis of identity left him without a language of experience, a way of expressing the embodied reality and sense of self that was not simply a product of changing context or place, but a more sustained and continuous sense of subjectivity. This is close to what some scholars have termed "post-positivist realism,"[29] the idea that identity, while socially constructed, has real consequences (political, phenomenological) for people. Others describe this as an "anti-anti-essentialist" position, one that similarly understands the constructed nature of identities but nevertheless is reluctant to dismiss the experience and importance of claims to a "real" identity, one that is not subject to the authorization of others.[30]

Students at the PROEIB understand the theoretical framework of the social construction of indigenous identities, but they emphasize the importance of the lived experience of indigeneity.[31] Students have thus looked outside of the PROEIB for sources of inspiration that take seriously the experiential dimension of indigenous practices. For example, Vicente and other students found inspiration in the work of what some might call essentialist or Indianist organizations like the *Proyecto Andino de Tecnologías Campesinas* (PRATEC) in Peru. The PRATEC approach emphasizes the "de-professionalization" of knowledge, the practice of "ritual agriculture," and the opposition to Western industrial capitalism. Another interesting and oft-cited point of comparison was AGRUCO (Agroecología Universidad Cochabamba),[32] a program that many see as similar to the PROEIB, also nestled in the university in Cochabamba. Unlike the PROEIB, however, AGRUCO, according to faculty member Cesar Escobar, uses indigenous practices of agriculture as points of departure as opposed to the PROEIB, which began with Western models and sought to insert indigenous issues within that framework. "Interculturality," explained Escobar, "is about constructing a new society from an indigenous matrix," rather than assimilating indigenous elements into a Western frame.

The fact that many students sought out such ideas reflects the desire among indigenous students to develop indigenous ontologies and epistemologies rather than approaches that seek to problematize and unsettle them. One interesting comment along these lines, from a PROEIB graduate, was that, in her view, at the PROEIB there was a "wasted richness; a cultural and historical matrix that was not taken advantage of." Another student noted that the program reinscribed a pedagogical coloniality that he described in the following terms:

> The [PROEIB] model assumed that indigenous people were empiricists but not theorists. So they felt they had to fill us up with theories, and they assume that as indigenous people, we had no theories. Our knowledge was not theoretical because according to their models, theory only comes from the West, from the academy in Europe, the US, whatever, what do I know? But this is insulting to human beings. Why can't a person be both empirically and theoretically engaged? We must be holistic.

I should point out that many of the non-indigenous (and even some of the indigenous) instructors of the program would dispute the idea that the West is the only site of theoretical production and that indigenous people are incapable of theorizing their own reality. Some have even noted that these critiques by indigenous students can serve as testimony to how the PROEIB has succeeded in helping forge a new generation of indigenous intellectuals capable of critiquing the worlds in which they move. Despite the dialectical possibilities that these dynamics suggest, however, it remains important to be attuned to the limitations of this extremely well-funded program that is seen by some as the "gold standard" of indigenous post-graduate education. If such problems and critiques have emerged in this "model" program, one suspects that similar dynamics may also be at work in the multiple spaces of indigenous education across the Americas.

Concluding Thoughts

In an article about the "menace" of multicultural neoliberalism and the emergence of the so-called "authorized Indian," anthropologist Charles Hale states:

> Far from eliminating racial inequity, as the rhetoric of multiculturalism seems to promise, these [multicultural neoliberal] reforms reconstitute racial hierarchies in more entrenched forms. While indigenous movements have made great strides over the past two decades, it is now time to pause and take stock of the limits and the political menace inherent in these very achievements.[33]

This article is an attempt at doing just that. It is also an attempt at reflecting critically about the nature of the "contact zone" represented by the PROEIB. Like the colonial zone Pratt has in mind, the PROEIB is hardly a "natural" space but one structured by the legacies of unequal social and political conditions and the particular choices of specific political actors. While the existing constraints of Latin American societies make it difficult to envision any space that is entirely free from the coloniality of power,[34] by designing an academic program that is heavily entrenched in Western academic models, practices, and idioms, the PROEIB constrains the very transformative project it promises. As the critiques of various students suggest, the program arguably reinscribes colonial relations by emphasizing a top-down model of inclusion and interculturality, one that endorses the official multiculturalist vision of state recognition of indigenous subjects. Additionally, many of the practices at the PROEIB—though certainly not all—continue previous patterns of exclusion. For instance, while the publication of student theses was a laudable project, examining the various works reveals a remarkable rigidity about "what counts" as knowledge, as student projects take very similar forms and, aside from short indigenous-language summaries, make few concessions to indigenous forms of knowing. Similarly, the guest lectures by indigenous *sabios* were an effort at inclusion that nevertheless reinforced a clear separation between indigenous intellectuals who can manage Western forms of knowledge and indigenous elders who remain in their own space. This reproduces an indigenous-Western binary rather than dismantling it.

More generally, the PROEIB's emphasis on professionalization and the placement of graduates in centers of power suggests a somewhat cautious approach in striking a balance between the necessities of accommodation and the project of transformation. As Turner argues, as long as we privilege academic models in which "indigenous peoples are required to explain themselves within the discourses of the dominant culture, there will be a need for specially educated indigenous people to generate the required explanations. It must be remembered that the need to explain ourselves to the dominant culture arises primarily for political reasons and only secondarily from a desire to attain some kind of rich cross-cultural understanding of indigenous philosophies."[35] Using Turner's terms, the PROEIB seems to have been designed with a different mix of "political" and "cross-cultural understandings" in mind. Stressing the importance of interculturality as a guiding principle and seeking to place students within official state and international development spaces, the politics of the PROEIB seem to be more about the governance and management of difference than the cultivation of insurgent subjectivities and knowledge.

While it is important to complicate the stark distinction made between "safe" and "unsafe" indigenous subjects; between colonial and decolonizing spaces, we should also take seriously the dangers inherent in these kinds of efforts. Can any attempt at institutionalizing interculturalism or cultural sensitivity ever escape hierarchies and unequal power relations? Is it too simple to dismiss a program like the PROEIB because it is funded, directed, and largely controlled by non-indigenous "outsiders"? It is easy to be critical of this kind of intercultural project. At the same time, it is hard to ignore what former students, almost invariably, say: that regardless of the problems, the PROEIB changed their lives and offered them opportunities they would have otherwise not had. While we need to look carefully at the selection of these students, and think about the role of indigenous elites in representing community demands, we should not dismiss the possibility that even despite their contradictions, these kinds of programs can be part of often dramatic social change.

The fact that this program has produced radicalized indigenous intellectuals who are now positioned in strategic points of transnational activism and education seems to suggest that the possibilities for change are very much alive in the wake of a decade of indigenous intercultural education at the PROEIB Andes. And yet at the same time, many of the PROEIB graduates I spoke with felt silenced in their current positions, tokens placed strategically in ministries or universities, symbolically in positions of power, but politically not (yet?) able to challenge current policies.

Over the last decade, indigenous students have been using the PROEIB to craft alternative imaginings of indigenous politics. These imaginings include what social scientists might label essentialist understandings of indigeneity. Yet, these understandings should not be dismissed as simply one more set of discourses that await academic deconstruction. Indigenous students at the PROEIB are themselves frustrated by the limitation of an analytical language that offers a choice between constructs or essences, and little guidance for their efforts at framing the contents of indigenous identities. Such a task is in obvious tension with the well-known Barthian call to explain identities by watching their boundaries (or outsides) and not simply interrogating their contents (or insides). Yet, indigenous students are well aware of these debates and find themselves struggling to give shape to their claims for alternative memberships and ways of knowing. In some scholars' formulation, these students are "anti-anti-essentialists,"[36] who, given the constructivist thrust of anthropology and the PROEIB, are left ill-equipped to produce accounts of the cultural "insides" of indigeneity. Similarly, Joanne Rappaport's work in Colombia with Nasa intellectuals (and others) is also an attempt at better understanding these cultural visions and imaginings, what she sees as part of the forging of "intercultural utopias."[37] For many students at the PROEIB, this linking of interculturality and utopia is problematic, as interculturality has become less a utopian space than an actual set of policies and practices that continue to constrain indigenous imaginings. However, these students are also engaged in the active cultural and political work of decolonizing spaces in society, a process that, while uneven and contradictory, offers the possibility of finding new ways to rethink and remake societies. Yet, unless the curriculum is significantly revised, and student critiques of the program incorporated, the PROEIB will continue to reproduce hierarchies its founders hoped to challenge.

I would like to conclude with some thoughts that add yet another layer of complexity. During the week in January 2007 when I arrived in Bolivia, there had been a major shake-up in President Evo Morales's cabinet. The Minister of Education, an outspoken and "radical" Aymara sociologist, was sacked by the president. While I cannot discuss at length all the reasons for his removal, it is crucial to note that his replacement, Víctor Cáceres, did not come from the world of indigenous movements and intellectuals, but rather from the urban teachers' union, a powerful part of President Morales' constituency. The new minister and the union he represents have never been friendly to the project of indigenous bilingual intercultural education, seeing it as a part of the neo-liberal baggage of previous presidents. Other voices from the Trotskyist urban teachers union are skeptical about culturalist claims that, for them, misdiagnose the essentially economic nature of Bolivia's fragmentation.[38] This cabinet change (which did not last long, there have been several other ministers since Cáceres) accompanied other education initiatives like literacy programs run by Cuban educators. These programs may have a strong popular and leftist component, but they leave behind any discussion of cultural difference and colonial legacies. As for the numerous indigenous professionals who were at the ministry working for the previous minister, as often happens, they too found themselves out of work. One PROEIB graduate, the critical Aymara professional who equated interculturality with cultural suicide, could not help but see the removal of an indigenous education minister as a step backward. Almost not believing her own words, she declared "things were better for us [indigenous people] with the neoliberals. Who would have thought they would be more open?"

Notes

1. To respect the privacy of interviewees and informants, I have changed the names of those who spoke with me about this project unless they explicitly told me that I could use their real name.

2. The program now also includes indigenous students from Mexico and various Central American countries.

3. See Mary Louise Pratt, *Imperial Eyes: Studies in Travel Writing and Transculturation*, 4.

4. See Charles Hale, "Rethinking Indigenous Politics in the Era of the 'Indio Permitido'"; Charles Hale and Rosamel Millamán, "Cultural Agency and Political Struggle in the Era of the *Indio Permitido*." See also Goodyear-Kaopua (chapter 2, this volume) for a fascinating discussion of the Kamehameha Schools for Boys in Hawai'i, the intersection of "pedagogies of domestication" and imperial projects, and the production of "safe" indigenous subjects.

5. In September 2007, the German development agency *Deutsche Gesellschaft für Technische Zusammenarbeit*, or GTZ, ended its funding of the PROEIB's master's program. While the program still exists as a part of the San Simón University in Cochabamba, it counts with significantly reduced resources.

6. I spent eleven months (between October 2006 and September 2007) conducting interviews and participant-observation research in the six countries affiliated with the PROEIB: Argentina, Bolivia, Chile, Colombia, Ecuador, and Peru. This research was supported by a Mellon postdoctoral fellowship.

7. While the PROEIB officially opened its doors in 1996, faculty members were given eighteen months to design the curriculum and prepare for the arrival of the first class of students in 1998.

8. See María Elena García, *Making Indigenous Citizens: Identities, Education, and Multicultural Development in Peru*.

9. See Laura R. Graham and Flor Ángela Palmar Barroso (chapter 11, this volume) for a discussion of IBE and indigenous politics in Venezuela.

10. For more on IBE, see Albó, *Iguales aunque diferentes: Hacia unas políticas interculturales y lingüísticas para Bolivia*; Albó and Anaya, *Niños alegres, libres, expresivos: La audacia de la educación intercultural bilingüe en Bolivia*; Godenzzi, *Educación e interculturalidad en los Andes y la Amazonía*; Hornberger, *Indigenous Literacies in the Americas: Language Planning from the Bottom Up*; and López, *De resquicios a boquerones: La educación intercultural bilingüe en Bolivia*.

11. See Hale, "Does Multiculturalism Menace? Governance, Cultural Rights, and the Politics of Identity in Guatemala."

12. See López, interview in *Fondo Indígena*.

13. A more detailed discussion of the multicultural reforms of the 1990s in Bolivia is beyond the scope of this paper. See Bret Gustafson, *New Languages of the State: Indigenous Resurgence and the Politics of Knowledge in Bolivia*, and Rosaleen Howard, "Education Reform, Indigenous Politics, and Decolonisation in the Bolivia of Evo Morales," for more on these reforms, and for terrific discussions of indigenous education and political mobilization in both highland and lowland Bolivia.

14. The PROEIB also has a few other non–degree granting programs like its indigenous leadership program, and different degree tracks for education planning and management.

15. See PROEIB Andes ORG. http://www.proeibandes.org/.

16. Some of these studies about the PROEIB include recent works by Aurolyn Luykx, Sarela Paz, and Solange Taylor.

17. I was able to speak with 56 of the 109 graduates. Additionally, I spoke with various university officials and administrators from the six affiliated countries, representatives from ministries of education, scholars and public intellectuals working in the field of intercultural bilingual education, PROEIB faculty (current and former) and current students, indigenous leaders from all six countries, and several known critics of the PROEIB Andes, both in Bolivia and beyond.

18. The PROEIB was founded in 1996, what may be considered a high point of the "neoliberal multicultural" moment in Latin America as new programs of "ethno-development" and indigenous education were supported by national government and international organizations that also

supported liberalizing economic reforms such as privatization. The PROEIB was funded largely by German development assistance but its emergence in Bolivia during the neoliberal presidency of Gonzalo Sánchez de Lozada has served to, rightly or not, associate this program with that period of Bolivian history.

19. The inclusion of indigenous faculty like Fausto was in part a response to student critiques about the lack of indigenous representation among the faculty. Specifically, previous courses in indigenous languages had been taught by non-indigenous US visiting faculty who did not speak indigenous languages.

20. See Laura R. Graham, "How Should an Indian Speak? Amazonian Indians and the Symbolic Politics of Language in the Global Public Sphere."

21. This does not mean that students at the PROEIB have not been actively involved in shaping the program. Indigenous faculty are also crucial actors in the continuous reshaping of pedagogies and methodologies used at the PROEIB.

22. It is beyond the scope of this essay to provide a full discussion of indigenous or even Aymara cosmovisions. However, students at the PROEIB did provide many examples of themes and values such as the significance of complementarity (between men and women, individual and community, human and nature). Students often spoke about the importance of spiritual and social understandings of the *pachamama* (Earth Mother) and *apus* (mountain deities). These and other ideas challenged what students saw as Western ontological and epistemological commitments to individualism which was part of the project of colonialism.

23. See Laura R. Graham and Flor Ángela Palmar Barroso (chapter 11, this volume) for a similar discussion about the significance of pan–Latin American indigenous activism, especially around IBE in Venezuela.

24. See Castellanos (chapter 4, this volume) for a discussion of how some Maya parents utilize boarding schools in Mexico as a path for upward mobility in segmented national economies. Though the context in the case of the PROEIB is different, the concern with education as a resource for negotiating national and global economies is a common one in debates over indigenous education.

25. This debate about the place of indigenous education at universities raises larger normative questions about whether universities *should* be the privileged site of indigenous education. Such territorialization of knowledge production is the hallmark of colonial projects, and thus its reterritorialization would be crucial to decolonizing projects.

26. See Dale Turner, *This Is Not a Peace Pipe: Towards a Critical Indigenous Philosophy.*

27. Turner, 72.

28. Turner, 74.

29. See Paula Moya and Michael R. Hames-García, *Reclaiming Identity: Realist Theory and the Predicament of Postmodernism.*

30. I am grateful to Brian Klopotek for bringing the work of Paula Moya and Michael Hames-García to my attention. For discussions of "anti-anti-essentialism" see Aurolyn Luykx, "Theory into Practice: Intercultural Pedagogy, Academic Socialization, and Anti-anti-Essentialism," and Maximilian Forte, "Indigenism and Essentialism 2."

31. This debate over identity at the PROEIB forms part of a larger debate over race that has haunted the Atlantic World for centuries. While this is not the place to explore all the possible connections, there are importance resonances with the work of Frantz Fanon, specifically with an important chapter of *Black Skins, White Masks*, translated as "The Fact of Blackness." As many critics have noted, a better translation of the title would have been "The Lived Experience of

Blackness," as this chapter is one of Fanon's most powerful statements about the phenomenology of race. It is also a direct rebuttal to Jean-Paul Sartre's *Black Orpheus*, who suggests that the racialism of negritude (what Sartre calls "anti-racist racism") is a necessary step on the way to a more universal humanism. While sharing the concern with a "new humanism" that would not be confined to the racial categories of colonialism, Fanon (135) replies: "Jean-Paul Sartre, in this work, has destroyed black zeal. In opposition to historical becoming, there had always been the unforeseeable. I needed to lose myself in negritude...." Though understanding and echoing the theoretical arguments for seeing racial categories as social constructions and dialectical possibilities, Fanon emphasizes the importance of lived experience and rejects the paternalistic path that Sartre has charted for "blacks." I am thankful to José Antonio Lucero for the suggestion of looking for connections between indigenous identity politics and the theorizing of Fanon. For an interesting discussion of the dialogue between Bolivian *indianista* intellectual Fausto Reinaga and Fanon, see José Antonio Lucero, "Fanon in the Andes: Fausto Reinaga, Indianismo, and the Black Atlantic."

32. See Agroecología Universidad Cochabamba. http://www.agruco.org/.

33. See Hale, "Rethinking Indigenous Politics in the Era of the 'Indio Permitido.'"

34. See Aníbal Quijano, "Coloniality of Power, Eurocentrism, and Latin America."

35. See Turner, 73.

36. See Luykx, Forte, or, following Moya and Hames-García, post-positivist realists.

37. See Rappaport, *Intercultural Utopias: Public Intellectuals, Cultural Experimentation, and Ethnic Pluralism in Colombia.*

38. See Howard, 590–591.

10 Canadian Law Schools and Indigenous Legal Traditions

John Borrows

Indigenous peoples' historic experiences with Canadian residential schools did not recognize or affirm their abilities to construct lives in accordance with indigenous values, aspirations, and traditions. This was symptomatic of many policy initiatives that indigenous peoples have been exposed to over the years. We have been contained, constrained, retrained, and detained in others' visions of how we should live in the world. The editors of this volume have asked us to imagine alternatives where indigenous peoples create their own educational goals. In my view, such a task requires critique, creativity, and plain hard work. Educational reform involves precisely calibrated resistance and carefully constructed collaboration. The cultivation of our own educational visions is a multifaceted endeavour. Education is not just about ideas. It occurs through practices that actively create and reproduce our social worlds.

Education always takes place within contested political spaces. In fact, we should be wary when political struggles seem invisible within educational circles. It is during such moments that we will most likely find that a particular faction or ideology disciplines and dominates the field. In these instances indigenous action is needed to replace or transform repressive institutions that replicate unexamined appeals to questionable sources of authority. Law schools are one particularly important site of educational struggle because of the role they play in sustaining and critiquing systems of legal authority, which ignore and suppress indigenous peoples' physical well-being and political aspirations.

University law schools often stand at the crossroads of political formation and formulation in Canadian society. They train future lawyers, bureaucrats, judges, legislators, and parliamentarians. What law schools regard as authoritative is often transmitted through the rest of society. Legal culture is also continually formed and reformed with each cohort of students. Indigenous peoples must take part in shaping these cultures to create spaces within society to pursue their own objectives. As such, this chapter will examine what indigenous peoples might do in Canadian law schools to create new educational trajectories to better negotiate future interactions within our constantly changing, complex world. In the following pages I explore how indigenous legal traditions might be more fully understood by law students and law professors in Canada, and thus might more broadly influence policy makers and legislators to see indigenous laws as containing standards by which our other educational and political choices can be measured.[1]

Knowledge about Canada's legal options and educational opportunities are incomplete if Canadians do not understand indigenous legal traditions. Indigenous legal education could greatly impact how students eventually learn and practice law in Canadian society. If done properly, it could significantly influence how institutions such as law societies, courts, legislatures, band councils, Metis organizations, Inuit governments, and other relevant public organizations view indigenous legal traditions. If indigenous laws were more fully understood, accepted, and applied, they could help suggest answers to pressing questions related to nation-state/indigenous relations.[2] This has occurred to a limited extent even under Canada's current framework. For example, indigenous pressure in Canadian legal practice has been influential in opening greater space for supportive reform in the fields of criminal law, environmental law, and tort law. In the criminal law context, legislation and cases now require that the courts take account of the "special circumstances" of indigenous peoples who appear in them.[3] In the environmental realm indigenous peoples' legal traditions have been incorporated into administra-tive decision-making procedures.[4] In the realm of Canadian tort law, indigenous peoples' activism prompted lawyers to develop legal theories that successfully challenged abuse by government and church employees in Canadian residential schools.[5] If indigenous peoples continued to press their interests and further developed legal traditions within Canada, this could have a great impact on how indigenous educational initiatives were received in the broader public sphere.

Describing Indigenous Legal Traditions[6]

Canada is a legally pluralistic state: civil law, common law, and indigenous legal traditions regulate behaviour and organize dispute resolution in our country in different ways. Although there are similarities between traditions, each has its own distinctive methods for development and application. The root origin of the word *tradition* is from the Latin verb *tradere,* which means "to transmit." "Traditions must be both given *and* received to have any chance of application in a contemporary context. The relational nature of traditions means that they must constantly be retaught and reinscribed in people's lives through an active process of conveyance, reception, reformulation, and application."[7] Furthermore, tradition must relate to peoples' contemporary lives to have continuing relevance; it must speak to all our concerns: past, present, and future. The development of tradition must therefore concern itself with the question of power. Thus, in teaching legal traditions educators must ensure that their application does not support or replicate inequalities, stereotypes, or other discriminatory ideas or practices that are contrary to contemporary concerns within indigenous communities.[8] Tradition as a living practice must not be used as an excuse to oppress people on the basis of gender, age, religion, or in any other way.[9] When recognized, provided with resources, and given jurisdictional space, each Canadian legal tradition is applicable in a modern context, and therefore has a place in the law school setting. While Canadian law schools should never be the exclusive or even the most authoritative bearers of tradition, the teaching of living legal traditions is an important task for the legal academy, particularly if it is done in accordance with indigenous legal protocols and procedures. As Pelikan writes, "A mark of an authentic and living tradition [is] that it points us beyond itself."[10] Each of Canada's major legal traditions remains vibrant, and continues to grow amid changing circumstances.

In my experience, indigenous laws are those procedures and substantive values, principles, practices, and teachings that reflect, create, respect, enhance, and protect the world and our relationships within it. There are many sources of law within indigenous communities: sacred, environmental, deliberative, positivististic, and customary, which will briefly be discussed in their turn.[11] While not an exhaustive list, these categorizations establish a sufficient analytical lens through which to explore indigenous legal traditions, and to encourage their further study and application, as urged in subsequent sections of this article.

Sources of Indigenous Law

First, as in other legal traditions, some indigenous laws have sacred sources.

Laws can be regarded as sacred if they stem from the Creator, creation stories, or revered ancient teachings that have withstood the test of time. When laws exist within this category they are often given the highest regard and deference. Legal traditions based on spiritual principles form an important part of most every culture's legal inheritance.[12] Nevertheless, because of their claims to sovereignty and their constitutional character within Canada, the civil law, common law, and indigenous legal traditions are distinguished from other legal orders that have religious roots.[13]

Laws that are held to be sacred may also be used in secular functions.[14] For example, in common law systems the receipt of evidence and the test for truth often rest on appeals to the divine.[15] The Canadian constitution's preamble states that Canada is "founded on principles that recognize the supremacy of God."[16] Indigenous legal traditions also contain sacred laws that operate in a similar way. For instance, the laws surrounding Canada's formation through treaties in many indigenous territories are a form of sacred law. Treaties brought new people into indigenous territories to initiate new relationships, and are thus a unique type of creation story.[17] In this light treaties are meant to encourage the spiritual, moral, and legal capacities of all who would live together in these spaces. The sacred nature of the treaties is one reason why many First Nations would not consider abandoning them despite generations of government neglect. Fortunately, despite problems in their formation and interpretation, many things, including treaties, can be considered sacred even if they are not given the respect they deserve. For example, treaties can also be viewed as the product of fraud, duress, and manipulation, designed to separate Indians from their lands and resources for the lowest possible price. In this light, creation is not always "pure." Creation thus can be flawed in some respects, even if it is still regarded as sacred. Many sacred stories contain similar ambiguities: Jacob's receipt of God's blessings in Genesis was the product of his deception and trickery, Nanaboozhoo's sacred naming of the Ojibway world involved the deception of many humans, animals, and supernatural beings.[18] The fact that Canada's creation was not always positive, or universally regarded as flowing from a pure source, does not undermine the laws of those First Nations who see things differently. For some First Nations, treaties are regarded as sacred creation stories about Canada's formation, even if such creation is trickster inspired, and thus entangled with real and metaphorical serpents, briars, and thorns.

A second source of indigenous law is environmental. This approach to legal interpretation attempts to develop rules for regulation and conflict resolution from a study of the world's behavior.[19] When considering laws from this source, it is often necessary to understand how the earth maintains functions that benefit us and all other beings.[20] Law, in this vein, flows from the consequences of creation—the continual re-creation of the "natural" world or environment. Indigenous peoples who practice this form of law may watch how a plant interacts with an insect, how an insect relates to a bird, or how a bird interrelates with an animal or another bird, and draw legal principles or standards for judgment from that experience. There may also be analogies drawn from the behaviors of watersheds, rivers, mountains, valleys, meadows, or shorelines to guide legal actions.[21] These observations can also incorporate scientific insights about the "nature" of the world. As such, these laws may be regarded as literally originating from the earth.[22]

Anishinaabe law is thus closely connected to where we live. Anishinaabe-akiing, our land, surrounds the North American Great Lakes and includes places that are now also called Ontario, Manitoba, Saskatchewan, North Dakota, Minnesota, Wisconsin, and Michigan. The Ojibway, or Chippewa, as we are sometimes called, attempt to correlate our highest laws to the natural world throughout this territory. The Anishinaabe word for constitutional law is *kiki-nawaezhiwaewin* and refers to the guidelines or precepts we follow to constitute ourselves. Dr. Basil Johnston, an elder from the Chippewas of the Nawash (my reserve), says this word refers to "living in balance within our inner worlds and in harmony with the outer world." Another Ojibway word related to constitutional law is *chi-inaakonigewin*, which means to regulate or to place ourselves in proper order. Both of these concepts can be interpreted to mean that legal order best comes from aligning ourselves with the world's larger patterns. Since these patterns are found first in our environment the Ojibway learn important legal principles from observing the seasons.

For example, seasonal observations can be related to general obligations parents owe to their children.[23] The Anishinaabe word for spring is *ziigwan*, which comes from the word for "to flow." When we are born our blood starts to run on its own. When we leave our mother's womb our lives slip into the stream of time and begin their flow. Many stories within Ojibway legal tradition seek to encourage this flow to sustain a young person's healthy growth and development.[24] Unfortunately, there are also times when proper flows are blocked. Sometimes children are limited by inappropriate parental control or abuse. When this occurs, Ojibway people have developed laws to address this problem.[25] At other times children's growth is staunched through their own improper actions. When this occurs, parents have a duty to ensure their own frustrations do not further stifle a child's growth. Ojibway people learn these important legal lessons from the environment.

For instance, there is a time in the Ontario spring when cold and warm air masses intermingle and cause fine mists to rise over the earth. The word used to describe this phenomenon is *aabawaa*, which means "warm and mild." At these moments winter starts to loosen her grip on the land. The snows melt and waters start to flow. Sap begins running through the trees and the bear cubs are born.[26] Interestingly, our word for forgiveness is related to this moment in time; the Ojibway word for forgiveness is *aabawewenimaa*. Thus, forgiveness is to loosen one's thoughts toward others; to let our relationships flow more easily without restriction. Forgiveness is a state of being warm; it signifies having a warming trend toward another. This may seem like a vague legal standard, but it is no more ambiguous than the duty of care in Canadian tort law. An Ojibway "reasonable person" standard requires that parents apply abaawewenimaaa and meet this high standard of care in raising their children. Thus, when the Anishinaabe think about the legal obligations we have toward children, one can see how the combination of ideas about spring (relating to the flow surrounding birth and subsequent growth) and forgiveness (relating to flows surrounding obligations related to that growth) can be used to regulate parental behavior when dealing with wayward children. This is merely one small example of how indigenous peoples might use observations relating to their environment to create law.[27]

A third, especially broad source of indigenous legal tradition is formed through processes of persuasion, deliberation, council, and discussion.[28] While sacred and environmental law may sometimes form the backdrop against which debate occurs, the proximate source of most indigenous law is developed through people talking with one another. Deliberation occurs in feast halls, circles, band councils, potlatches, lodges, tribal courts, and kin and clan gatherings. The human dimension of these laws means that recognition, enforcement, and implementation make them subject to re-examination and revision through the generations. Indigenous law is not static and can move with the times. The deliberative nature of many indigenous laws means they can be continuously updated and remain relevant in the contemporary world. When indigenous people have to persuade one another within their traditions, they must do so by reference to the entire body of knowledge to which they have access, which includes ancient and modern understandings of human rights, due process, gender equality, and economic considerations. While contemporary concepts will modify and be modified by very old principles and processes, they will also remain distinct by virtue of their particular cultural and legal contexts.[29] Thus, since deliberative indigenous laws draw upon historical and current legal ideas, they can likewise explicitly take account of and incorporate practices and standards from other legal systems. They can be harmonized with or distinguished from the laws around them based on what counts as persuasive to the group involved in the debate. Since no indigenous person or community is completely detached from the world, many influences will be brought to bear on indigenous legal developments. Deliberation aimed at making indigenous law can occur in formal and informal meetings and gatherings; in these settings laws can be constructed through highly structured or ad hoc means.

Many Anishinaabe people deliberate and reach legal conclusions with the help of stories.[30] Stories open us to the world of interpretation because their meaning is not always immediately apparent, especially when one is dealing with tales of our trickster, Nanaboozhoo. Nanaboozhoo wanders from place to place engaged in actions that can be simultaneously mean and kind, charming and cunning, selfish and selfless. Listeners are encouraged to see themselves in his behavior and recognize the fact that all humans are complex, shifting characters, capable of great acts of generosity and cruelty. When these stories are told, they are also related against the backdrop of a constantly changing context. Thus a story told in the 1830s might have a different meaning if told in the present day. This makes our "cases" capable of speaking in the present day. They contain ideas that can be interpreted as law, capable of continual development and contemporary application.[31] In fact, stories can only be fully understood and applied through a contemporary process of transmission, discussion, deliberation, and debate, even as we do our best to understand their past meanings. Like most cases they are not self-enforcing and thus require a process of discursive development to bring them into each generation's life. When related by experienced indigenous and other appropriately accredited practitioners, Anishinaabe and other indigenous stories are a rich source of case law for community problem solving. In this light, they can also be an important source of legal knowledge in Canadian legal education.

A fourth source of indigenous law is found in the proclamations, rules, regulations, codes, teachings, and axioms that bind or regulate people's behavior.[32] The laws to which I refer here are somewhat distinct from those discussed above because they do not necessarily depend on appeals to the Creator, the environment, or deliberative processes to possess force. Legal traditions in this mode have weight because proclamations are made by a person or group regarded by a sufficient number of people within a community as authoritative. Individuals who are seen to possess such power may be hereditary chiefs, clan mothers, headmen, sachems, or band leaders.[33] Their proclamations may be regarded as positivistic laws because they rely more on the authority of those who issue them than on notions of creation, nature, or community deliberation. Philosopher John Austin referred to legal positivism as being based upon command. He wrote that binding legal authority stems from "determinate rational being[s] or bod[ies] that the other rational beings are in the habit of obeying."[34] Rationality is of course present in every community, and laws that flow from trusted individuals and groups are given due regard as a result.[35] In an indigenous context, positivistic laws may be formally proclaimed in feast halls, council houses, wampum readings, band council chambers, and other such public settings. In announcing these laws, ancient and contemporary legal ideas also mingle together and become the basis for bylaws, statutes, conventions, and protocols.

One example of positivistic law in an Anishinaabe context (which understandably draws together sacred, deliberative, and customary legal sources) is contained in many Anishinaabe constitutions, codes, and tribal court decisions. Constitutions are quite common amongst Anishinaabe people. In the following paragraphs I focus on one particular community, the Little River Band of Indians, to provide examples of their constitution, code, and tribal court. The preamble to their constitution reads, in part:

We, the Little River Ottawa people have asserted our sovereignty throughout history including in the Treaty of Chicago [August 29, 1821; 7 Stat 218], the Treaty of Washington [March 28, 1836; 7 Stat 491], and the Treaty of Detroit [July 31, 1855; 11 Stat 621].

Between the last treaty and the present day, the Grand River Ottawa people who became the Little River Band of Ottawa Indians were known and organized under several names, including members of "Indian Village" on the Manistee River, residents of the Pere Marquette Village or "Indian Town," Unit No. 7 of the Northern Michigan Ottawa Association, the Thornapple River Band, and finally the Little River Band of Ottawa Indians.

On September 21, 1994, Public Law 103–324 [108 Stat 2156] was enacted, reaffirming federal recognition of and confirming the sovereignty of the Grand River Bands comprising the Little River Band of Ottawa Indians (referred to as the Tribe or Little River Band).

As an exercise of our sovereign powers, in order to organize for our common good, to govern ourselves under our own laws, to maintain and foster our tribal culture, provide for the welfare and prosperity of our people, and to protect our homeland we adopt this constitution, in accordance with the Indian Reorganization Act of June 18, 1934, as amended, as the Little River Band of Ottawa Indians.[36]

This constitution shows the contemporary "mixed" nature of Anishinaabe positivistic constitutional law. Its authority is rooted in pre-existing rights, treaty agreements, federal recognition, and contemporary tribal law, governance, and culture. Similarly, the Little River Band of Indians Tribal Code is also a syncretic document and draws on many federal, state, and indigenous sources.[37] The band has enacted detailed legislative rules involving issues such as government operations, government entities, membership, judiciary, law and order, environment, construction, employment, business, finance, and family. Finally, positivistic law in this community is also found in rulings of the Little River Band Tribal Court. The Court hears a wide range of civil matters, including divorces, personal injury issues, child custody disputes, domestic violence cases, and various small claim issues.

One of my favorite decisions from this court involves a tribal court judge who was convicted of attempted fraud.[38] The case draws its authorities from Anishinaabe stories, Western legal principles, and the tribe's own democratically derived code. It is an excellent example of the type of case that could be taught to students in Canadian or US law schools. The following brief excerpt from the judgment illustrates the positivistic yet complex nature of Anishinaabe law:

> There are many trickster tales told by the Anishinaabek involving the godlike character Nanabozho. One story relevant to the present matter is a story that is sometimes referred to as "The Duck Dinner." See, e.g., John Borrows, Recovering Canada: The Resurgence Of Indigenous Law 47–49 (2002); Charles Kawbawgam, Nanabozho in a Time of Famine, in Ojibwa Narratives of Charles and Charlotte Kawbawgam and Jacques LePique, 1893–1895, at 33 (Arthur P. Bourgeios, ed. 1994); Beatrice Blackwood, Tales of the Chippewa Indians, 40 Folklore 315, 337–38 (1929). There are many, many versions of this story, but in most versions, Nanabozho is hungry, as usual. After a series of failures in convincing (tricking) the woodpecker and muskrat spirits into being meals, Nanabozho convinces (tricks) several ducks and kills them by decapitating them. He eats his fill, saves the rest for later, and takes a nap. He orders his buttocks to wake him if anyone comes along threatening to steal the rest of his duck dinner. During the night, men approach. Nanabozho's buttocks warn him twice: "Wake up, Nanabozho. Men are coming." KAWBAWGAM, supra, at 35. Nanabozho ignores his buttocks and continues to sleep. When he awakens to find the remainder of his food stolen, he is angry. But he does not blame himself. Instead, he builds up his fire and burns his buttocks as punishment for their failure to warn him. To some extent, the trick has come back to haunt Nanabozho—and in the end, with his short-sightedness, he burns his own body.
>
> The relevance of this timeless story to the present matter is apparent. The trial court, per Judge Brenda Jones Quick, tried and convicted the defendant and appellant, Hon. Ryan L. Champagne, a tribal member, an appellate justice, and a member of this Court, of the crime of attempted fraud. Justice Champagne's primary job during the relevant period in this case was with the Little River Band of Ottawa Indians. Part of his job responsibilities included leaving the tribal place of business in his personal vehicle to visit clients. While on one of these trips, Justice Champagne took a personal detour and was involved in an accident. The Band and later the trial judge concluded that his claim for reimbursement from the Band was fraudulent. Judge Quick found that Justice Champagne "attempted to obtain money by seeking reimbursement from the Tribe for the loss of his vehicle by intentionally making a false assertion that he was on his way to a client's home at the time of the accident." People v. Champagne, Opinion and Judgment at 6, No. 06–131-TM (Little River Band Tribal Court, Dec. 1, 2006) (Champagne III). Justice Champagne was neither heading toward the tribal offices nor toward a client's home.
>
> Like Nanabozho, Justice Champagne perpetrated a trick upon the Little River Ottawa community—a trick that has come back to haunt him. It would seem to

*be a small thing involving a relatively small sum of money, but because the Little
River Ottawa people have designated this particular "trick" a criminal act, Justice
Champagne has burned himself.*

While the Tribal Court draws on many sources of authority to uphold the
trial judge's conviction, the Court is always attentive to Anishinaabe culture,
language, and stories in sustaining the Anishinaabe legal order. As such, the
judgment demonstrates the importance of creatively deploying many community legal resources to address actions that are contrary to peace and good
government in the Little River Band. The case also shows that Anishinaabe
people have law, not because we are above conflict, but because—like other
people—we are also kind *and* mean, selfless *and* selfish, charming *and* cunning. The ability to apply and teach Anishinaabe law is important in helping
us deal with the ever present challenges caused by such conflicting behaviors.
Canadian law schools could benefit from the insight generated by these practices and principles.

The final source of indigenous law discussed in this article relates to
laws formed through custom.[39] "Custom" is the label that most people would
likely give indigenous law if they were unfamiliar with the complexity of
these societies' social organization.[40] Of course, customary law is not peculiar
to indigenous societies.[41] The common law, the civil law, and international
law also rely on custom as a source of binding obligation for those subject to
their operation.[42] Customary law can be defined as those practices developed
through repetitive patterns of social interaction that are accepted as binding
on those who participate in them.[43] Customary laws are often inductive, and
the obligations they produce are regularly implied from a society's surrounding context.[44] An effective way of learning operative customs within a community would involve examining or living specific routines and procedures
associated with conduct within that community and talking to people about
why they feel obliged to act in a particular manner. Such an investigation
might lead one to conclude that customary law rests heavily on an individual's unspoken agreement about how rights and obligations will be regulated
between community members. The communally developed and individually
intuitive nature of this legal form means that disputes are often regulated
through social pressures that distribute incentives and disincentives to act or
refrain from acting in certain ways. Since customary laws are not always as
explicit as other forms of law, their recognition, interpretation, and enforcement are often initially more difficult to achieve when other sources of law
intervene. However, this does not mean that they cannot be studied, rendering their implicit norms explicit.[45] The law school setting offers one example
where this can be achieved. It does not have to be frozen, codified, and

bureaucratized in order for us to teach and live its precepts.[46] Customary law can be a creative source of law in its own right, and in its proper context can be very effective in producing strong and healthy community relationships.

Indigenous Law: A Living System of Social Order

It should be noted that the distinctions between the different sources of law outlined above are formalistic and artificial. In reality, indigenous legal traditions usually involve the interaction of multiple sources that are difficult to separate from one another. Furthermore, it is easy to see how the sources of law would change as indigenous communities worked with them. For example, some aspects of customary law could become positivistic if codification is undertaken. A positivistic law could take on a deliberative source if debate occurs about the appropriateness of rules derived from custom. Similarly, sacred law may influence environmental law if people relate to the Creator through natural processes. My point in making the distinctions using these classifications is to illustrate the complex nature of indigenous law; indigenous peoples have choices when they turn to their laws for answers. While complexity and choice might make working with the law appear more complicated, it should also provide greater opportunities for those interested in recognizing, studying, interpreting, enforcing, and implementing these laws. Recognizing that laws are founded upon environmental, deliberative, positivistic, or customary sources may help dispel the mistaken notion that indigenous legal traditions are static. This will create a much greater space for the application and development of indigenous law in modern Canada.

Furthermore, to fully appreciate the complexity of indigenous law we must recognize that indigenous peoples hold many different views about law's character and practice, within and across categories. Disagreement is an important part of the law where there are sufficient convergences to produce ongoing and continuous interim settlements.[47] In fact, there would be no such thing as indigenous law if these communities did not experience conflict. As discussed above, law is present in indigenous societies because there will always be dissent and disagreement.[48] Like the civil and common law traditions, the indigenous legal tradition is enhanced by deep philosophical disputes about its nature and sources. Differences of opinion are a part of the vibrancy and strength of "Western" law because they provide for shifting appeals to legitimacy over time, or even within a single case.[49] When working with indigenous legal traditions one must take care not to oversimplify their character. Indigenous legal traditions are as varied and diverse as Canada's other legal traditions, although they are often expressed in their own unique ways. Law, like culture, is not frozen.[50] Legal traditions are permeable and subject to crosscutting influences.[51]

Thus, indigenous peoples compare, contrast, accept, and reject legal standards from many sources, including their own.[52] This is an important aspect in continually remaking indigenous law into a living system of social order. Some might label the contemporary and comparative nature of indigenous law as revisionist, and thereby seek to undermine indigenous law by regarding these developments as inauthentic or potentially non-aboriginal. This criticism would be unfortunate and inaccurate. Legal systems are at their healthiest when they are susceptible to evolution. Law is boldly "presentist" in its orientation. The practice of law draws deeply from its historical roots, but it is deployed because some current issue needs resolution. As a result most legal systems use the past as a resource to answer present questions. Legal traditions must continually be reinterpreted and reapplied in order to remain relevant amidst changing conditions.[53] Indigenous law is no different, and should not be held to unrealistic, historical, or timeless standards. It would thus be healthy to teach these traditions in a law school setting, so that they could be compared and contrasted with other authorities, including other indigenous legal orders.

Experience Teaching Indigenous Legal Traditions

I have experienced the importance of learning indigenous legal traditions in a law school setting. When the territory of Nunavut was created, there was an expressed desire to have more Inuit people work in all levels of the territorial public service.[54] Nunavut is Canada's newest territory, created in 1999, with an Inuit majority comprising 85 percent of the population. The territory covers over one-fifth of Canada's land mass and was created through twenty years of negotiation, which culminated in a constitutionally protected land claim agreement and a legislatively recognized Inuit government. Article 23 of the *Nunavut Land Claims Agreement* has as its stated objective "to increase Inuit participation in government employment in the Nunavut Settlement Area to a representative level," which applies to "all occupational groupings and grade levels" within the government.[55] Article 23 presupposes that initiatives will be taken to increase educational opportunities to allow more Inuit to work within all levels of government.[56] The Nunavut government, along with the Akitsiraq Law School Society, determined that this objective could be pursued in part by creating a law school in the territory. The Akitsiraq Law School Society approached the Faculty of Law at the University of Victoria to set up such a school. They soon partnered with the Nunavut Arctic College and a four-year program was created to allow students to earn a University of Victoria law degree. The Department of Justice of Canada and the Gordon Foundation provided substantial financial support for the initiative. Andrew Petter, former dean of the University of Victoria Law School and former attorney general of British Columbia, was particularly key to the program's development. Its success was dependent on many visionary Inuit elders, legislators, and educators. The Nunavut judiciary and the Arctic College were also integral to the initiative. This innovative legal education program was called the Akitsiraq Law School.

One of the goals of the new law school was to make Inuit law more intelligible and accessible to students, and by extension to citizens of the territory and Canada as a whole. Thus, in its first instantiation, the program worked to assist the residents of Nunavut to articulate their ancient laws and present-day legal traditions in contemporary terms. The Akitsiraq Law School respected legal pluralism in the North by integrating traditional Inuit law with the requirements of Canada and the territory's constitutional and legislative provisions. Students received all their classes in Iqaluit, the capital of Nunavut, and at the end of four years earned a law degree from the University of Victoria. Inuit law was a vital part of this education, as taught by elders and community leaders. This aspect of the program grew in strength as the four years progressed. Students also interacted with Southern legal academics, judges, and lawyers to ensure that Inuit law fit the needs of the residents of the new territory.

When I taught at the Akitsiraq Law School, I found the class was better equipped to understand law's cultural contours than is the case with most Southern law students. They were already bilingual and bicultural before the program began, and Akitisiraq prepared them to be bijuridical. They were outstanding students, and it was the best formal educational experience I have ever had. They became grounded in both the common law and Inuit law during their time at the school. The use of Inuit law and language infused their courses at each step along the way. For example, when I taught Contract Law and Remedies, the students supplemented their understanding of the common law of obligations with the Inuit law of obligations. After I taught a concept, the students would often talk among themselves in Inuktitut to clarify and deepen their comprehension of what I was saying. In this way they took more active control of their legal education than is typical in a conventional law school. In the classroom, we all felt a responsibility for translating common law concepts into an Inuit linguistic and cultural framework, although we as Southern faculty were often secondary to this endeavor. The faculty did their best to introduce Inuit cases, context, and Nunavut legislation in each class. I sought to demonstrate the dialogue between Anishinaabe law, the constitution, legislation, and the common law to provide analogies of how students might work with Inuit law. However, the common law–trained teachers recognized that our efforts were somewhat inadequate to the students' needs when it came to their own legal traditions.

Fortunately, students were able to complement their classes with an Inuit law and language class under the direction of Inuit elders. In this setting, they learned the law of obligations and other concepts within an Inuit legal framework. They also further explored the lessons of their common law education under the guidance of experts more knowledgeable in Inuit law than their Southern-trained law professors. Lucien Ukaliannuk was exceptional in leading students through the interaction between Inuit legal traditions and the common law. Students relayed that his classes were both theoretically beneficial and highly relevant to their eventual practice of law in the North. They talked about legal traditions related to *pijitsirniq* (serving); *aajiiqatigiinniq* (decision making); *pilimmatsaniq* (passing knowledge and skills through observation, action, and practice); *piliriqatigiinniq* (working together for a common cause); *avatittinnik kamattiarnik* (environmental stewardship); *oanuqtuurniq* (creative, resourceful problem solving); *tunnganarniq* (openness, acceptance, and inclusivity); *ippigusuttiarniq* (caring for others); *angiqatigiinniq* (proceeding forward with clear understanding); *ikajuqatigiinniq* (assistance and cooperation without barriers); *oaujimautittiarniq* (information sharing); *uppiriqattautiniq* (fair treatment); *tukisiumaqatigiinniq* (conscious understanding of others as the basis of mutual relationships); *ilainnasiunnginniq* (sensitivity to difference); *ilajjuttigiinniq* (encouragement of others); *aaqqiumatitsiniq* (keeping order in place); *iqqaqtuijjiqattariaqannginniq* (restraint on personal judgment); *piviqaqtittiniq* (opportunity for participation and contribution); *silatuniq* (wisdom to know how to apply your knowledge); and *ajuqsatittinginniq piviqarialinnik* (support for growth, development, and success).[57] Their exploration of frameworks for integration and separation of the traditions made greater sense when it started from an Inuit worldview.[58]

The Akitsiraq Law School is a prominent example of the type of institution that may be established elsewhere in Canada to facilitate the development of legal processes and reasoning appropriate to indigenous norms and needs. In case there are questions about the relevance of indigenous legal traditions in southern Canada, I should also note that I have taught Anishinaabe law at the University of Minnesota Law School and the southern campus of the University of Victoria Faculty of Law. For example, in the class offered at the University of Minnesota Law School, students learned Anishinaabe common law, alongside Anishinaabe legislative code and tribal court jurisprudence.[59] Students wrote an appellate Anishinaabe Tribal Court judgment, on appeal from a past or forthcoming case from the Supreme Court of the United States. The assignment instructed students to apply Anishinaabe law to pursue questions raised in cases such as, inter alia, *Brown v. Board of Education*,[60] *Roe v. Wade*,[61] and *Bush v. Gore*.[62] Other students used the assignment to address pressing questions facing Anishinaabe communities, including adoption,[63] domestic violence,[64] and indigenous employment laws.[65] This gave students an opportunity to use Anishinaabe law in a contemporary context. Anishinaabe law is not frozen in time but deals with contemporary challenges with all their complexities and nuance.

When students work with indigenous legal traditions they move away from stereotypes of these laws as being relegated to the past and one dimensional. Indigenous people possess a great variety of opinions about the proper principles to apply to resolve specific issues. They use their laws in different ways to arrive at conclusions that best suit their communities in the present day. Indigenous peoples mingle ancient ideas with contemporary concerns and teachings. When indigenous legal traditions are taught in a law school setting, it is possible to see how these laws can be harmonized with other legal systems in the country.[66] Indigenous legal traditions become more accessible to a greater number of people when they are taught in open and transparent ways. When the transmission and acquisition of legal knowledge is supported by law schools, these legal traditions are more fully seen as constituting a necessary part of the fabric of Canadian law. When this occurs on a wider scale, indigenous legal traditions will be seen more fully as an integral part of Canadian life and Canada's constitution.[67]

The Role of Law Schools in Indigenous Legal Education

Law is a practice, not just an idea.[68] The practical exercise of teaching law requires the allocation of sufficient resources and the development of appropriate relationships.[69] Therefore, in the remainder of this chapter I will place an increasing emphasis on the details of developing a program of indigenous legal education, though I hope not to lose sight of the animating ideas of the law. It is important to understand both abstract *and* pedestrian issues related to teaching indigenous law to appreciate the nature and scope of what is being proposed. I call this approach a physical philosophy,[70] one that takes guidance from the metaphysical realm of ideas, but gives priority to constructing decentered genealogies of knowledge,[71] developed from specific grounded practices.[72]

Since law is also a practice, universities could work with indigenous peoples on developing the neglected dimensions of Canada's legal pluralism within the law school context. The richness of such a multijuridical curriculum could enhance students' civic engagement in a legally pluralistic and diverse world. It would better prepare students to practice law in a global context, where conflict among legal cultures is a particularly vexing issue.[73] I should reemphasize that such engagement could be even further enhanced if indigenous law was taught in other countries, too, throughout Latin America, Central America, and the United States. Students would learn how to compare and contrast sources of authority within legal systems that are committed to unity by understanding, critiquing, and applying deep jurisprudential diversity. A hemispheric approach to indigenous legal education would further strengthen the teaching of indigenous law within particular countries. Indigenous legal analogies and pedagogies would be enhanced as indigenous peoples learn from one another in bringing our laws to light in law school settings. A multijuridical approach to legal education would also highlight the choices available to students in further constructing our communities. Individuals and societies would benefit from people who know what is required to navigate many different traditions. In this way, indigenous law schools would effectively prepare students for future research or practice in Canada's legal traditions.

As requires repeated emphasis, multijuridical indigenous law schools would teach indigenous legal traditions alongside the common law or civil law. Professors and students would learn from elders, practitioners, and communities about the contours of historic legal ideas in a contemporary setting. They would study indigenous law in great depth and from a perspective that gives these traditions the respect they deserve. Of course, the respectful examination of any legal order includes critique alongside appreciation and constructive application. This process helps to avoid oppressive fundamentalism; it challenges those who hold a narrowly defined set of beliefs that are closed to the influence of other traditions. The desire of elders, educators, practitioners, and students to improve indigenous and other legal traditions would lead to recommendations for both reform and retrenchment.[74] However, intense intellectual debate over the strengths and weaknesses of a particular law does not have to be socially disagreeable.[75] As is the case within existing law schools, indigenous law schools would work closely with their constituencies to ensure that law is taught in a way that is attentive to both procedural and substantive concerns. Exposure to indigenous law alongside other traditions would lead students to develop a broader, more refined understanding of the rule of law in Canada, and beyond.

While the creation of indigenous law schools would facilitate learning without having to overcome potentially entrenched common law or civil law biases, it may be difficult to generate the resources to establish them. The money needed for administrators, professors, support staff, and students is not currently allocated to the task of teaching indigenous law. Therefore, in the short term, existing law schools may be in the best position to develop multijuridical programs. As the University of Victoria's experience in Nunavut demonstrates, Canadian law schools already possess some experience working with indigenous issues. It would be possible for some of these schools to build upon their successes to create new courses and programs.

Existing law schools could more readily introduce indigenous law into legal education than could new law schools, as they already possess significant resources and enjoy broader credibility with the bench, bar associations, and other interested parties. The academic rigor and scholastic reputation of an existing law school could enhance the legitimacy of studying indigenous law and ensure that such traditions are more widely understood. On the other hand, an established school might have a more difficult time changing its culture to accommodate some of the unique approaches involved in teaching indigenous law. As has been stressed throughout this piece, indigenous law must be taught in accordance with indigenous legal procedures. While there is always room for creativity, change, and challenge in relation to accepted ways of understanding and practicing indigenous law, strict attention must also be paid to ensuring that it is taught in an anti-colonial context. In this vein, while an unaffiliated indigenous law school might initially have difficulty establishing its reputation with relevant constituencies, resulting in a devaluation of its program, it may better create an environment that would be more supportive of indigenous practices and aspirations. Furthermore, a strong investment in financial, physical, and human resources is absolutely necessary to ensure its success. Until that day arrives, however, steps must be taken in the present environment to bolster indigenous legal education in Canada. The timing of an indigenous law school's formation, and the resources devoted to it, must be carefully calibrated to ensure future success.

In the meantime, the potential contours of indigenous legal education can be explored in greater detail in a contemporary law school setting. In the last twenty years, some law schools have nurtured growing relationships and expertise in working with indigenous communities.[76] Other law schools have developed admissions criteria and programs to facilitate indigenous student success.[77] Furthermore, most Canadian law schools already teach courses that examine how Canadian law affects indigenous peoples; a few even specialize in training graduate students in this field and have hired professors who can teach both indigenous law and the common law. These people, programs, and courses have helped to increase student interest in, and scholarship about, indigenous issues more generally.[78] They have also encouraged a number of indigenous academics to gain knowledge of their own legal traditions and pursue post-graduate legal training in a common law or civil law field. Furthermore, nonindigenous academics with similar qualifications are also increasingly beginning to possess these skills. These experiences and

216   John Borrows

initiatives have created a fertile ground for the future cultivation of indigenous legal education.[79]

Living Traditions: Toward an Indigenous Law Curriculum

Building on existing practices, the day will soon arrive when a Canadian law school will develop a degree program focused specifically on indigenous legal traditions in a contemporary setting. For those wishing to understand how I envision teaching indigenous legal traditions alongside other laws, I have written about lesson plans for teaching first-year Canadian Constitutional Law in an Anishinaabe context.[80] For example, in "Living Law on a Living Earth" I describe Anishinaabe constitutional principles relating to a particular piece of land and demonstrate how Anishinaabe people use their law in a contemporary setting to resolve a dispute.[81] After outlining indigenous law in this fashion, I compare and contrast the Supreme Court of Canada's potential treatment of this same issue under section 2 of the *Canadian Charter of Rights and Freedoms* and subsection 35(1) of the *Constitution Act, 1982*. The information in this piece lends itself to expansion and development in the classroom because of the detail about the relationship of legal systems found therein.[82] Similarly, in an article about the *Indian Act* I wrote about how parliamentary legislative initiatives could benefit from an infusion of Anishinaabe law.[83] This article could serve as the basis for a first-year multijuridical constitutional law class, as it discusses how Canadian legislation could be written from a legally pluralistic perspective. There is much that could be done in the classroom to challenge conventional legal pedagogies and introduce students to indigenous legal traditions.

Furthermore, it should be noted that students would be best served by also learning indigenous law outside of the classroom in an applied context. Immersion is important: a program would absolutely fail to adequately teach indigenous law if it did not provide rigorous learning opportunities within indigenous communities. While there is great value in formal classroom instruction, indigenous law must also be learned in an applied and practical context within community settings.[84] Indigenous laws are often the product of specific relationships to land, plants, animals, water, and people. To fully appreciate indigenous law, students need to live with the people whose law they want to understand. This immersion must also be intensive, and focused on one tradition at a time in order to expose students to each tradition's depth and complexity. Students' education in indigenous law will be incomplete if they do not delve deeper into legal traditions of their choice for either three summer terms or one final year.

Whatever methods are chosen, it is currently possible to teach indigenous legal traditions within a conventional law school setting if curricular reform is undertaken.

Looking Beyond a Conclusion: Deciding the Future of Legal Education

This chapter has discussed how law schools might take further steps to encourage a healthier conception of Canada's legal system. My "work-in-progress"[85] proposal is offered to generate further discussion about the possibilities and limitations of offering indigenous legal education in Canadian law schools. The recovery and regeneration of any legal tradition involves working in a collective context, while being attentive to the larger philosophies and ideas of groups and individuals who participate in and are affected by that context.[86] It is my belief that law schools throughout the hemisphere (and Canada's legal system more generally) would greatly benefit from the significant challenge offered by the ideas in this article. The rule of law can be enhanced if the continent's legal traditions are brought into authoritative conversation with one another to resolve pressing disputes that lie before us as a country. Positive change could occur in a law school setting if professors and administrators were committed to seeing legal education develop beyond its current cultural constraints. In fact, those who work with indigenous legal traditions may find that such broadened knowledge makes them better common law or civil law theoreticians and practitioners in certain contexts. They may be more attentive to the assumptions and contrasts available within the law when they are teaching, writing about, or practicing in a specific doctrinal field. This awareness could highlight where choices between alternatives are colonially constructed, and therefore not as universal or neutral as may be presented in common law or civil law discourse. As multijuridical elders, professors, and law students bring their insights to bear on pressing problems, they may be in a better position to articulate solutions that enjoy persuasive resonance in common law, civil law, and indigenous legal traditions. While far from comprehensive or perfect, this result could greatly assist in searching for constructive solutions to remedying the injustice underlying Canadian/indigenous relations.

Acknowledgments

The author would like to thank Ben Berger, Gillian Calder, Sakej Henderson, Rebecca Johnston, Brian Klopotek, Hester Lessard, Constance MacIntosh, Erin Morgan, Andrew Petter, Stefan Szpajda, Jim Tully, Val Napoleon, Jeremy Webber, and Doug White for their helpful comments and encouragement.

Notes

1. This chapter summarizes arguments made in my book *Canada's Indigenous Constitution*. As such, this chapter is not an entirely original piece of work; in some instances it is a "cut and paste" reproduction of some of my most recent work. However, readers may nevertheless find value in this chapter as I do attempt to synthesize arguments developed over almost five hundred pages in this short piece. By so doing I hope to make my arguments more accessible to readers interested in broader educational issues as they relate to law and legal education. I hope that by standing beside other works on indigenous education readers will see the following ideas in a broader light.

2. For a discussion of how indigenous peoples and ideas have influenced Canada in other ways, see David Newhouse, Cora Voyageur, and Dan Beavon, eds., *Hidden in Plain Sight: Contributions of Aboriginal Peoples to Canadian Identity and Culture*. For a popularized examination of this idea, see John Ralston Saul, *A Fair Country: Telling Truths about Canada*.

3. R v. Gladue, [1999] 1 S.C.R. 688, sets out the parameters of section 718.2(e) of the Criminal Code regarding the sentencing of offenders, and in particular, aboriginal offenders. "Perhaps the most prominent example of Indigenous legal traditions being used in a Canadian urban context is found in the experiences of Aboriginal Legal Services of Toronto (ALST). ALST was established on February 21, 1990, following years of deliberation, debate and discussion within Toronto's Indigenous communities. A number of exceptionally knowledgeable and supportive non-Aboriginal people such as Jonathon Rudin also contributed to the development of ALST. The Native Canadian Centre of Toronto compiled the results of community consultations in the mid-1980s through a Needs Assessment Report. Later in the process, prominent yet humble Indigenous Elders gave ALST's founders an important set of traditional teachings and principles to guide their work. As a result, ALST was established to strengthen the capacity of the Aboriginal communities and their citizens to deal with justice issues and provide Aboriginal-controlled and culturally based justice alternatives. It is instructive to note that ALST's existence flows from an inspiring combination of Indigenous and western legal concerns and knowledge that developed through persuasion, counseling together, and consensus-building." See Borrows, *Canada's Indigenous Constitution*, 40.

4. For example, in Canada's newest territory, Nunavut, *Inuit Qaujimajatuqangit*, is used to inform resource use decisions; see Martha Dowsley, "The Value of a Polar Bear: Evaluating the Role of a Multiple-Use Resource in the Nunavut Mixed Economy," 39.

5. Blackwater v. Plint, [2005] 3 S.C.R. 3; for a more critical view see Bruce Feldthusen, "Civil Liability for Sexual Assault in Aboriginal Residential Schools: The Baker Did It," 61.

6. Ideas in this section are drawn from John Borrows, "Indigenous Legal Traditions in Canada," 167, 174–175; John Borrows, *Canada's Indigenous Constitution*.

7. John Borrows, *Canada's Indigenous Constitution*, 271.

8. For an excellent illustration of this point, see Goodyear-Ka'ōpua, chapter 2, this volume, "Domesticating Hawaiians: Kamehameha Schools and the 'Tender Violence' of Marriage," which describes how the Kamehameha School trustees reproduced discriminatory stereotypes in running their schools.

9. I am including the common law and civil law traditions in this observation.

10. Jaroslav Pelikan, *The Vindication of Tradition*, 54.

11. For a more developed discussion of these classifications, see Borrows, *Canada's Indigenous Constitution*, above note 9.

12. See generally Michael L. Hadley, ed., *The Spiritual Roots of Restorative Justice*; R. H. Helmholz, *The Spirit of Classical Canon Law*; Wael B. Hallaq, *The Origins and Evolution*

of Islamic Law; N. S. Hecht et al., eds., *An Introduction to the History and Sources of Jewish Law*; Werner F. Menski, *Hindu Law: Beyond Tradition and Modernity*; Rebecca Redwood French, *The Golden Yoke: The Legal Cosmology of Buddhist Tibet*; Yongping Liu, *Origins of Chinese Law: Penal and Administrative Law in Its Early Development*.

13. Political entrenchment gives indigenous legal traditions an authority within Canadian life beyond what can be claimed by other traditions. See Patrick Macklem, *Indigenous Difference and the Constitution of Canada*.

14. For a discussion of how religion affected the common law and civil law, see Harold J. Berman, *The Interaction of Law and Religion*; Peter Radan, Denise Meyerson, and Rosalind F. Croucher, eds., *Law and Religion: God, the State, and the Common Law*; Brian Young, *The Politics of Codification: The Lower Canadian Civil Code of 1866,* 113–120.

15. See M. H. Ogilvie, *Religious Institutions and the Law in Canada*, 2nd ed., c. 7.

16. Constitution Act, 1982, being Schedule B to the Canada Act 1982 (U.K.), 1982, c. 11. See, for example, Jonathon W. Penney and Robert J. Danay, "The Embarrassing Preamble? Understanding the 'Supremacy of God' and the *Charter*"; George Egerton, "Trudeau, God, and the Canadian Constitution: Religion, Human Rights, and Government Authority in the Making of the 1982 Constitution," 90.

17. See Harold Cardinal and Walter Hildebrandt, *Treaty Elders of Saskatchewan: Our Dream Is That Our Peoples Will One Day Be Clearly Recognized as Nations*; Office of the Treaty Commissioner, *Treaty Implementation: Fulfilling the Covenant*; Arthur J. Ray, Jim Miller, and Frank Tough, *Bounty and Benevolence: A History of Saskatchewan Treaties*; James Miller, *Compact, Contract, Covenant: Aboriginal Treaty-Making in Canada*.

18. There are many stories related to the deception and gifts Nanaboozhoo gives to other animals: see "Nanabush and the Skunk," Verna Patronella Johnston, *Tales of Nokomis*, 5; "Nanabushu Breaks the Necks of Dancing Geese," William Jones, *Ojibwa Texts*, 101; Basil Johnston, *Ojibway Heritage*.

19. An interesting example of how environmental law might develop and be operative within indigenous communities is found in the writings of Julie Cruikshank. See Julie Cruikshank, *Do Glaciers Listen? Local Knowledge, Colonial Encounters, and Social Imagination*. See also William Robinson, as told by Walter Wright, *Men of Medeek*, 2nd ed.; Jo-Anne Fiske and Betty Patrick, *Cis Dideen Kat (When the Plumes Rise): The Way of the Lake Babine Nation*; Kiera L. Ladner, "Governing within an Ecological Context: Creating an AlterNative Understanding of Blackfoot Governance," 150; James (Sa'ke'j) Youngblood Henderson, "Mikmaw Tenure in Atlantic Canada," (1995) 218; John Borrows, "Living Law on a Living Earth: Aboriginal Religion, Law, and the Constitution," 161.

20. Chief Wayne Roan of the Mountain Cree speaks about nature's laws from a Cree perspective. See Roan, http://www.abheritage.ca/natureslaws/index2.html. See also *Aboriginal Online Teachings and Resource Centre,* http://www.fourdirectionsteachings.com.

21. For a more general discussion of analogical reasoning, see Cass R. Sunstein, "On Analogical Reasoning."

22. See Nancy J. Turner, *The Earth's Blanket: Traditional Teachings for Sustainable Living,* 11–40 and following, on the Nlaka'pmx's respectful use of natural resources.

23. For an extended discussion of this issue, embedded within an entire book, see John Borrows, *Drawing Out Law: A Spirit's Guide*.

24. This is one of the reasons laws are given as stories, so that they are understandable to young and old alike. For a detailed recounting of these stories in the context of such support see Basil Johnston, *Ojibway Heritage*.

25. For an example of these laws within one community see the Children's Code, Title 10 of the Grand Traverse Band Code: Statutes of the Grand Traverse Band of Ottawa and Chippewa Indians. http://www.narf.org/nill/Codes/gtcode/10.pdf. For Tribal Court interpretations of this Code enhancing children's safety see In re D.D., No. 97–11–083-CV-DR; People v. Schocko, No. 97–06–003-ICW (Grand Traverse Band Tribal Ct., October 21, 1999).

26. Some elders teach that these mists are the mother bear's afterbirth.

27. Other examples could be developed but space does not permit a fuller explanation in this survey article. Those wanting to learn more could consider a further study of other Ojibway seasonal descriptions. For example, our word for summer is *niibin*, which comes from the word *neebina* and means "plenty." This conveys expectations about how we should live this as teenagers and young adults; we are encouraged to grow and draw from the richness around us. The Ojibway word for fall is *tikwaagi* and derives from the word *tik-ayaa*, meaning "cool." As we reach late adulthood, the autumn of our lives, we are encouraged to draw less from the world. Growth slows and we are encouraged to prepare for a period of sustained reflection and observation. If we live by this guidance we can become Elders, or those who know and live the laws with sufficient depth that they are regarded as authoritative. Finally, the Ojibway word for winter is *biiboon*, and comes from the words '*abi*, which means "here," and '*boon*, which means "where growth is suspended." Thus, winter describes what happens as we die, physically our growth is suspended for a season. These laws could be taken to apply to an entire lifetime but they could also relate to how we should pattern our lives each day: as we wake and experience a flowing of energy (ziigwan), then most of our day we partake of and develop practices that build on nature's plenty (niibin), and then we get ready for bed and slow down during the evening (tikwagi), and a certain kind of suspension occurs as we sleep every night (biiboon).

28. See Karl N. Llewellyn and E. Adamson Hoebel, *The Cheyenne Way: Conflict and Case Law in Primitive Jurisprudence*; E. Adamson Hoebel, *The Law of Primitive Man: A Study in Comparative Legal Dynamics*; Max Gluckman, *Politics, Law, and Ritual in Tribal Society*; Rennard Strickland, *Fire and the Spirits: Cherokee Law from Clan to Court*; Antonia Curtze Mills, *Eagle Down Is Our Law: Witsuwit'en Law, Feasts, and Land Claims*.

29. Each indigenous legal system integrates the past and the present in a unique way. See Peter Nabokov, *A Forest of Time: American Indian Ways of History*. For an example of how this is done in one indigenous legal system, see Raymond D. Austin, *Navajo Courts and Navajo Common Law: A Tradition of Tribal Self-Governance*. For a discussion of how this is done in the common law, see Gerald J. Postema, "On the Moral Presence of Our Past."

30. This point is explored in some detail in John Borrows, *Recovering Canada: The Resurgence of Indigenous Law*; see particularly chapters 1 to 3.

31. Though they have other applications, these stories are "cases" which contain guidance about how the Anishinaabe should act when they encounter conflict; see John Borrows, *Recovering Canada: The Resurgence of Indigenous Law*, chapter 1.

32. Indigenous law creates relationships between people by addressing the consequences of their actions. For further discussion on the relational aspects of law and obligation, see Arthur Ripstein, "Justice and Responsibility." For an application of this idea in an indigenous context, see Kathleen O'Reilly-Scanlon, Christine Crowe, and Angelina Weenie, "Pathways to Understanding: 'Wâhkôhtowin' as a Research Methodology"; Robert Brightman, *Grateful Prey: Rock Cree Human-Animal Relations*, ("*pāstāhōw* [verb] 'someone brings retribution on himself,'" 103).

33. Respected elders can be an explicit source of positive law. See Jake Thomas, *The Great Law*; Mariano Aupilaarjuk et al., *Interviewing Inuit Elders: Perspectives on Traditional Law*. Indigenous

courts can also serve to communicate positive law. See Cathy E. Bell, *Contemporary Métis Justice: The Settlement Way.*

34. John Austin, *Lectures on Jurisprudence or the Philosophy of Positive Law*, 88.

35. See Aharon Barak, "Judicial Philosophy and Judicial Activism," who writes, "The world is filled with law. Every human behavior is subject to a legal norm. Wherever there are living human beings, law is there. There are no areas in life which are outside of law," 483.

36. Constitution and Ordinances of the Little River Band of Indians of Manistee, Michigan. https://www.lrboi-nsn.gov/council/docs/Constitution%20-%202004%20Amendments.pdf.

37. See https://www.lrboi-nsn.gov/council/ordinances.html.

38. Champagne v. Little River Band of Indians, Case No. 06–178-AP, June 2007, Little River Band of Indians Court of Appeal.

39. See *The Oxford English Dictionary*, 2nd ed., under the word "custom." ("The body of rules, whether proceeding from formal enactment or from custom, which a particular state or community recognizes as binding on its members or subjects.") For articles on First Nations' law, see Bradford W. Morse and Gordon R. Woodman, *Indigenous Law and the State*; Michael Coyle, "Traditional Indian Justice in Ontario: A Role for the Present?" 605. Compare Roger F. McDonnell, "Contextualizing the Investigation of Customary Law in Contemporary Native Communities"; Delgamuukw v. British Columbia: "what the Gitksan and Wet'suwet'en witness[es] describe as law is really a most uncertain and highly flexible set of customs which are frequently not followed by the Indians themselves," 447. For criticism of this view, see Michael Asch, "Errors in *Delgamuukw*: An Anthropological Perspective," 221. For a fuller description of Wet'suwet'en law, see Mills, above note 44.

40. For further information about indigenous diversity in Canada, see Tim Schouls, *Shifting Boundaries: Aboriginal Identity, Pluralist Theory, and the Politics of Self-Government.*

41. The laws of England largely operated through custom until precedent and consolidation took place through the 1700s. See H. Patrick Glenn, "The Common Law in Canada." Even today, the common law method uses customs and traditions to fill gaps when interpreting written rules. See Reference re Secession of Quebec, [1998] 2 S.C.R. 217, 161 D.L.R. (4th) 385 [Secession Reference cited to S.C.R.].

42. See Rudolf Schlesinger, et al., *Comparative Law*, 669–670, 690–694; Stephen C. McCaffrey, *Understanding International Law*, 44–55.

43. For a general definition of customary law, see James Brierly, *The Law of Nations: An Introduction to the International Law of Peace*, 59; *Black's Law Dictionary*, under "customary law."

44. See Gerald J. Postema, "Implicit Law," 255.

45. For a discussion of how implicit law can be made explicit, see Postema, "Implicit Law." For a historical analysis of implicit law, see Janna Promislow, "Toward a Legal History of the Fur Trade: Looking for Law at York Factory, 1714–1763." For an insightful series of case studies that make indigenous legal traditions more explicit, see Catherine Bell and Val Napoleon, eds., *First Nations Cultural Heritage and Law: Case Studies, Voices, and Perspectives.*

46. For further explanation see John Borrows, *Canada's Indigenous Constitution*, 51–55.

47. See Jeremy Webber, "Legal Pluralism and Human Agency."

48. In this respect, counsel can be taken from the words of the Supreme Court of Canada: "Inevitably, there will be dissenting voices. A democratic system of government is committed to considering those dissenting voices, and seeking to acknowledge and address those voices in the laws by which all in the community must live" (*Secession Reference,* above note 57 at paragraph 68).

For further discussion about the role of dissent in democracy, see James Tully, *Public Philosophy in a New Key: Democracy and Civic Freedom,* vol. 1, 198–199.

49. For an illustration, see Philip Bobbitt, "Constitutional Law and Interpretation," 126; Philip Bobbitt, *Constitutional Interpretation.*

50. As James Tully has observed:

> Cultures are interdependent, overlapping and internally complex. Cultures exist in dynamic processes of interaction, negotiation, internal challenge and reinterpretation, and transformation. As a result, humans are always members to varying degrees of more than one culture. They experience misunderstandings and differences within their first cultures, such as between genders, generations and classes, that are not completely different in kind from misunderstandings and differences across cultures. Cultural understanding and identity is thus enormously more complex, open-textured, interactive and dynamic than the old vision of closed and homogeneous cultures presupposed.
>
> So, when Aboriginal and non-Aboriginal partners meet on the middle ground, they are not trapped in closed and mutually incommensurable world-views.... Interaction has shaped the cultural identities of both in complex ways. [above note 67 at 240]

51. See Clifford Geertz, *Local Knowledge: Further Essays in Interpretive Anthropology,* 167.

52. See James Clifford, "Indigenous Articulations."

53. In Canada the most prominent metaphor for legal fluidity is the living tree. The Judicial Committee of the Privy Council wrote: "The B.N.A. Act planted in Canada a living tree capable of growth and expansion within its natural limits. The object of the Act was to grant a Constitution to Canada" (Reference re Section 24, B.N.A. Act, [1930] 1 D.L.R. 98 at 106–107, [1930] A.C. 124). It then quoted Sir Robert Borden: "'Like all written constitutions it has been subject to development through usage and convention'" (107). See also Reference re Same-Sex Marriage, (2004) 3 S.C.R. 698, 246 D.L.R. (4th) 193. ("The 'frozen concepts' reasoning runs contrary to one of the most fundamental principles of Canadian constitutional interpretation: that our Constitution is a living tree which, by way of progressive interpretation, accommodates and addresses the realities of modern life"; S.C.R. at paragraph 22.)

54. See Kelly Gallagher-Mackay, "Affirmative Action and Aboriginal Government: The Case for Legal Education in Nunavut."

55. Agreement between the Inuit of the Nunavut Settlement Area and Her Majesty the Queen in Right of Canada, S.C. (1993), c. 29 [Nunavut Land Claims Agreement].

56. See Thomas Berger, "Letter to Minister Prentice,"http://www.nunavutliteracy.ca/english /research/reports/Berger%202006%20PL%200907.pdf.

57. See Research and Statistics Division, *Review of the Nunavut Community Justice Program: Final Report,* http://www.justice.gc.ca/eng/rp-pr/aj-ja/rr05_7/index.html, cited in John Borrows, *Canada's Indigenous Constitution,* 103–104.

58. When students graduated from the Akitsiraq law school most secured excellent articling experiences, including one student who clerked at the Supreme Court of Canada. Though it is still early in their career they make a significant contribution to the profession as young lawyers in the territory of Nunavut.

59. The course at the University of Minnesota Law School is called "Tribal Courts in the United States: An Introduction to Indigenous Peoples Law." The course description reads as follows:

> Tribal Courts flow from legal traditions and a sovereignty that stands outside of the US Constitution. Despite this unique base, Tribal Courts most often operate in conjunction with Federal

and State Courts, and apply both "common law" and "Indigenous" legal principles. This course will explore the many facets of tribal courts in the United States, including their use of diverse legal justifications and sources. Among the topics will be the inherent power of tribal courts, judicial independence, separation of powers within tribal governments, inter-tribal appellate courts, and the interplay among federal, state, and tribal courts. We will also analyze the fundamental characteristics of tribal courts and their function in the context of cutting edge cases involving jurisdictional issues, Indian civil rights, the use of tribal custom and tradition, criminal law, torts, and family law. This course is intended to familiarize students not only with traditional and contemporary aspects of the internal law of tribes, but also to consider the complex interrelationship between the two. The course will also devote significant attention to Chippewa (Ojibwe or Anishinaabe) law and legal history in exploring these issues.

60. 347 U.S. 483 (1954). For information on Anishinaabe education laws, see Grand Traverse Band Code, Title 16, Education and Culture, http://www.narf.org/nill/Codes/gtcode /index.htm.

61. Roe v. Wade, 410 U.S. 113 (1973). While there are many opinions for and against abortion amongst the Anishinaabe, at least one Anishinaabe community has prohibited abortion. On September 17, 2008, the Turtle Mountain Chippewa Tribal Council enacted the following resolution: "…absolutely under no circumstances will abortions be performed and allowed within any private or public facility within the boundaries of the Turtle Mountain Indian Reservation and other lands under the jurisdiction of the Tribe. The governing body faithfully believes that life is sacred and begins at the moment of conception between a man and a woman and life to be protected at all levels affirming environmental law and reasoning…pro-life is a universal issue of common sense, moral righteousness for the common good of life." For more information see *News from Indian Country*; http://indiancountrynews.net.

62. Bush v. Gore, 531 U.S. 98 (2000). For an Anishinaabe Tribal Court decision that deals with electoral issues see Lenoir v. Monette, No. CIV-02–0039 (Turtle Mountain, June 28, 2002) at http://www.tribal-institute.org/opinions/2002.NATM.0000002.htm.

63. The leading United States Supreme Court case that deals with adoption is *Mississippi Choctaw Indian Band v. Holyfield*, 490 U.S. 30 (1989). If I taught this class in a Canadian context I would offer students an opportunity to appeal *Racine v. Woods*, [1983] 2 S.C.R. 173, 1 D.L.R. (4th) 193 to an Anishinaabe Tribal Court to explore how Anishinaabe law would deal with questions of adoption.

64. In examining this question the student, Katherine Belzowski, debated the question of domestic violence within Anishinaabe communities such as the Little Traverse Odawa Band of Indians, in a moot in Traverse City, Michigan. Title IX of the *Waganakising Odawa Tribal Code: Little Traverse Bay Bands of Odawa Indians* defines "domestic violence" as:

> [t]he occurrence of one or more of the following acts by a family or household member, but does not include acts of self-defense:

> 1. Attempting to cause or causing physical, emotional or mental harm to another family or household member;
> 2. Placing a family or household member in fear of physical harm; or
> 3. Causing a family or household member to engage involuntarily in sexual activity by force, threat of force, or duress. (9.703(A))

> The crime of domestic violence occurs when a family or household member commits one of the listed offenses in 9.703(A) against "family or household members" as defined in 9.703(B).

65. The case appealed from was *Greene v. Commissioner of Minnesota Dept. of Human Services*,

733 N.W. 2d 490, 497 (MN 2007), and *San Manuel v. National Labor Relations Board*, 475 F. 3d 1306 (D.C. Cir. 2007).

66. Harmonization in the United States is accomplished through full faith and credit provisions between courts or as expressed in Tribal Codes. For an Anishinaabe example from the Sault Ste. Marie Tribe of Chippewa Indians Tribal Code, see Enforcement of Foreign Judgments, Chapter 86 at http://www.saulttribe.com/images/stories/government/tribalcode/chaptr86.pdf. For discussions about harmonization in a Canadian context see Borrows, above note 9 at 215–220.

67. Canada's law is evolutionary and is best facilitated when it promotes self-government, accommodates cultural and group identities, appeals to moral values, requires a continuous process of discussion, compromise, negotiation, and participation, and rests on a legitimate legal foundation. For a discussion of these values in Canadian law, see Secession Reference, above note 57 at paragraphs 63–69.

68. Rawls says the question is "political not metaphysical" (Tully, above note 64 at 175 citing John Rawls, *Political Liberalism*).

69. I acknowledge that teaching indigenous law in present circumstances is not an ideal situation. Despite our best efforts, it will be "shot through with relations of inequality, force and fraud, broken promises, failed accords, degrading stereotypes, misrecognition, paternalism, enmity and distrust" (Tully, 240). However, there never will be an ideal moment for any initiative, including teaching indigenous law to a wider audience. The best one can do "is to give oneself the rules of law, the techniques of management, and also the ethics, the *ethos,* the practice of the self, which would allow these games of power to be played with a minimum of domination"; see Michel Foucault, *The Final Foucault,* 18, cited in Tully, above note 64, 121.

70. I have developed this idea in another context. See John Borrows, "Physical Philosophy: Mobility and the Future of Indigenous Rights," 403.

71. See Michel Foucault, *Discipline & Punish: The Birth of the Prison.* In the education context Foucault wrote the following, which I believe has application to law schools as presently constituted:

> [T]here are also "blocks" in which the adjustment of abilities, the resources of communication, and power relations constitute regulated and concerted systems. Take for example an educational institution: the disposal of its space, the meticulous regulations which govern its internal life, the different activities which are organized there, the diverse persons who live there or meet one another, each with his own function, his well-defined character—all these things constitute a block of capacity-communication-power. The activitiy which ensures the apprenticeship and the acquisition of aptitudes of types of behavior is developed there by means of a whole ensemble of regulated communications (lessons, questions and answers, orders, exhortations, coded signs of obedience, differentiation marks of the "value" of each person and of the levels of knowledge) and by the means of a whole series of power processes (enclosure, surveillance, reward and punishment, the pyramidal hierarchy). [Michel Foucault, "The Subject and Power," 218–219.]

These power processes are what is being challenged by this proposal. A challenge of this magnitude requires a detailed account of another alternative model of legal education.

72. See Rorty, "The Priority of Democracy to Philosophy," 178 (arguing that "a liberal democracy" does not need philosophical justification).

73. Teaching multijuridically could lead students to international and comparative law practices, as well as national and local practice. The initiative could also provide ideas for other countries searching for models to better deal with indigenous law. For example, Robert Husbands at the Rule of Law and Democracy Unit, of the Office of the High Commission for Human Rights

(OHCHR) in Geneva, is working on this issue at the international level. For more discussion from an international perspective of indigenous legal traditions relations to other state laws, see Van Cott, "A Political Analysis of Legal Pluralism in Bolivia and Colombia"; Stavenhagen, in "Report of the Special Rapporteur on the Situation of Human Rights and Fundamental Rights of Indigenous Peoples," states:

> Indigenous peoples have the right to promote, develop and maintain their institutional struc-
> tures and their distinctive customs, spirituality, traditions, procedures, practices and, in the cases
> where they exist, juridical systems or customs, in accordance with international human rights stan-
> dards (art. 34).

For more discussion on indigenous peoples at the international level, see James (Sa'ke'j) Youngblood Henderson, *Indigenous Diplomacy and the Rights of Peoples: Achieving UN Recognition*; James Anaya, *Indigenous Peoples in International Law*.

74. I want to be clear that my proposal to teach law in a multijuridical context is *not* a proposal for the assimilation of any legal tradition within another. Traditions can be harmonized. When music is harmonized individual notes retain their distinctiveness and resonance. The synchronicity I propose requires measured integration, as well as the maintenance of indigenous societies, and envisions their future growth and strength. See John Borrows, "A Separate Peace: Strengthening Shared Justice," 343.

75. In fact, a variety of indigenous legal processes might be followed in schools to explore different ways to vigorously yet respectfully disagree. For example, in a Great Lakes context, this could lead to classroom discussions that seek for "peace, friendship and respect" (*Gus Wen Tah* treaty values) in the midst of profound and deep-seated disagreement. For a discussion of these values, see John Borrows, "Constitutional Law From a First Nation Perspective: Self-Government and the Royal Proclamation." For an excellent review of the intertwining aspects of wampum belts in the past and present, see Kathryn V. Muller, "The Two 'Mystery' Belts of Grand River: A Biography of the Two Row Wampum and the Friendship Belt," 129.

76. For example, Osgoode Hall Law School has an excellent clinical program that allows students to work with aboriginal communities around the world; see Intensive Program on Aboriginal Lands, Resources, & Governments, http://www.osgoode.yorku.ca/clinics-experiential /clinical-education/aboriginal-lands-resources-governments. There have been many develop-ments in the United States in a similar pattern; see Heidi Estes and Robert Laurence, "Preparing American Indians for Law School: The American Indian Law Center's Pre-Law Summer Institute." There are now three graduate LL.M. programs in Indigenous Legal Studies in the United States (University of Arizona, Arizona State University, and University of Tulsa), with numerous JD pro-grams specializing in Indian law (New Mexico, Arizona State University, Washington, Wisconsin, Kansas, Iowa, South Dakota, Vermont) or Indian law clinics (Colorado, Idaho, Montana). Other countries with indigenous populations have also developed indigenous focused programs: the University of Waikato in New Zealand was created for the purpose of advancing Maori legal stud-ies in a bicultural environment, though it has been slow in establishing itself. The University of New South Wales has an Indigenous Law Centre. The University of Tromso, in Norway, has led the way in teaching Sami legal issues.

77. For comments on different indigenous law programs in Canada, see Roger Carter, "The University of Saskatchewan Native Law Centre"; Donald J. Purich, "Affirmative Action in Canadian Law Schools: The Native Student in Law School"; Hugh MacAulay, "Improving Access to Legal Education for Native People in Canada: Dalhousie Law School's I.B.M. Program in Context." The Native Law Centre has both a research and teaching mission. It offers a pre-law summer program for indigenous students interested in admission to law schools. It also publishes the Canadian

Native Law Reporter, theoretical and technical legal texts, and has an excellent resource library. The University of British Columbia's First Nations Legal Studies Program has operated since 1975. Originally an admissions program, it has assisted over 230 indigenous law students to graduate from its school. The University of British Columbia has a Centre for International Indigenous Legal Studies to further its mission, with two community research projects focused in indigenous legal traditions and governance. Akitsiraq is a law program offered by the University of Victoria to Inuit people in Canada's newest territory, Nunavut. Fourteen Inuit students are studying entirely at home in their own territory, and will graduate with a law degree in four years. The University of Victoria also offers a joint law degree and Masters of Indigenous Governance at its main campus. Osgoode Hall Law School at York University has offered the Intensive Program in Lands, Resources and First Nations Governments since 1994. This clinically based program immerses students in an indigenous legal experience for all their credits over an entire semester. The June Callwood Program at the University of Toronto provides graduate scholarships for advanced indigenous legal studies. It also facilitates internships and applied educational experiences with Indigenous communities. The Faculty of Law at the University of Alberta also has an Indigenous Law Program that has director and student support.

78. See John Borrows, "Fourword: Issues, Individuals, Institutions, and Ideas," [ix]. For reflections of indigenous law students' experiences in law school, see Patricia A. Monture, "Now That the Door Is Open: First Nations and the Law School Experience"; Tracy Lindberg, "What Do You Call an Indian Woman with a Law Degree? Nine Aboriginal Women at the University of Saskatchewan College of Law Speak Out"; Leah Whiu, "A Maori Woman's Experience of Feminist Legal Education in Aotearoa."

79. For example, the University of Victoria has extensive experience dealing with indigenous legal education, including working with indigenous communities in a law school context as evidenced through the law school's experience with the Akitsiraq Law School. Some of the initiatives at the school during the time the degree was being discussed included:

(1) An Endowed Chair in Aboriginal Economic Development cross-appointed in the law and business school;

(2) A Law Foundation Endowed Professorship in Aboriginal Justice and Governance;

(3) A Graduate Program focused on indigenous legal issues;

(4) An indigenous student population that is approximately 9 percent of the law school;

(5) Four indigenous teachers employed full time by the faculty (Heather Raven, Maxine Matilpi, James Hopkins, and John Borrows);

(6) A Summer Intensive Program in Indigenous Legal Studies held every third year;

(7) Successful completion of the Akitsiraq Law School Program for Inuit students in Nunavut;

(8) Six courses focused on indigenous legal issues and many others which include components dealing with indigenous legal issues;

(9) An exchange program with the law school at Arizona Sate University to facilitate comparative Indigenous Legal Studies;

(10) An annual Aboriginal Awareness Camp in which approximately one-quarter of the University of Victoria entering first year class participate;

(11) An excellent Academic and Cultural Support Program;

(12) A large and active Indigenous Law Club;

(13) Annual participation in the National Kawaskimhon Aboriginal Moot;

(14) A Faculty Aboriginal Equity Plan;

(15) A joint Aboriginal Restorative Justice Program with the Victoria Native Friendship Centre;

(16) An Environmental Law Clinic with strong aboriginal participation and content;

(17) Frequent national and international Visitors on Indigenous issues; and

(18) Active research support for indigenous issues (Trudeau Fellows and Mentors, Social Sciences and Humanities Research Council Major Collaborative Research Initiatives, Virtual Scholar in Residence Award, British Columbia Law Foundation grants, Western Economic Development funding, and others).

The depth of the university's resources at the time, along with the critical mass of students and faculty, provides a strong enough base to take initial steps in developing a joint JD/JID Program. Other law schools may be in a similar position, or could develop similar strength through the coming years.

80. I have written two books on this subject. See John Borrows, *Drawing Out Law: A Spirit's Guide*; John Borrows, *Canada's Indigenous Constitution*, above note 9.

81. Borrows, *Canada's Indigenous Constitution*, above note 9.

82. Incidentally, my approach to multijuridical teaching does not wholly dispense with territoriality and borders. In my view, teaching indigenous legal traditions alongside the common law or civil law could challenge the idea that such an endeavor is "nomadic" with no fixed home, as claimed by Nicholas Kasirer. See Nicholas Kasirer, "Legal Education as *Métissage*," 491.

83. See Borrows, "Stewardship and the First Nations Governance Act."

84. See Cody and Sue Green, "Clinical Legal Education and Indigenous Legal Education: What's the Connection?"

85. For my views on Canada as a work in progress, see John Borrows, "Measuring a Work in Progress: Canada, Constitutionalism, Citizenship, and Aboriginal Peoples," 222.

86. See, for example, John Borrows, *Recovering Canada: The Resurgence of Indigenous Law*.

11 "Yaletüsü Saaschin Woumain (Glory to the Brave People)"

Flor Ángela Palmar Barroso's Creative Strategies to Indigenize Education in Venezuela

Laura R. Graham and Flor Ángela Palmar Barroso

Flor Ángela Palmar Barroso, a Wayuu woman of the Iipuana clan, was born May 15, 1957, in Kalimiisirou (near Parouralapü, Colombia) on the northernmost tip of the Guajira Peninsula, an arid strip of land that juts into the Caribbean Sea from the South American continent.[1] Palmar was the third of eleven children born to Emelina Barroso (Iipuana clan) and Emiliano Palmar (Epieyu clan).[2] Like most Wayuu men in the Guajira region at that time, Emiliano made a living herding goats and sheep, a primary form of Wayuu currency in the traditional pastoral economy. Emelina was noted for her skill at weaving hammocks and *süsü* handbags that provided supplemental income. Like many Wayuu from the Alta Guajira (Upper Guajira Peninsula) beginning in the 1940s, Palmar's family moved south across the border that divides the nation-states of Venezuela and Colombia into the Venezuelan state of Zulia on the eastern side of the peninsula to take advantage of economic and educational opportunities for their children. As members of the Wayuu nation, some 438,000 individuals who contiguously inhabit the Guajira Peninsula and adjacent areas, they do not recognize this international border.

Palmar's experiences in what she calls "the identity castrating" project of the Venezuelan state schools of her youth and her frustration with their assimilationist curriculum spurred her to pursue a professional career as an educator. Teaching in one-room schools in the Guajira Peninsula and poor urban neighborhoods of Zulia's large capital, Maracaibo, where Wayuu make up a significant percentage of the total urban population, Palmar pioneered innovative tactics for indigenous education within a system designed to divest indigenous peoples of their identity and transform them into "good citizens"—undifferentiated national subjects.[3] Through her work she became a leading figure in Wayuu education and eventually, during the presidency of Hugo Chávez Frías, in the national effort to develop bilingual intercultural education for Venezuela's diverse indigenous peoples. From 2006 to 2007 Palmar worked in the Ministry of Education as Coordinator of Programs in the National Office of Bilingual Intercultural Education and served as a member of the National Commission on Curriculum within the Ministry of Education. Continuing her life's work, Palmar dedicated herself to the national project to develop curricula for Venezuela's forty-one distinct indigenous groups.[4] In 2011–2012, Palmar worked as a member of the Technical Academic Team at the national Simón Rodriguez Experimental University in the Masters Graduate Program in Bilingual Intercultural Education,[5] carrying on her lifelong efforts to incorporate indigenous language, knowledge, and ways of teaching and learning into the university curriculum, and to gain broader recognition for indigenous forms of knowledge and practices within professional arenas. In 2013, as this book goes to press, Palmar is involved in developing policy related to the implementation of Venezuela's Cultural Law (Ley de Cultura) and the Special Law for Intercultural Bilingual Education, along with helping to establish a group called the Organization of Indigenous Educators of Venezuela.

Flor Palmar's experiences as an indigenous student and her subsequent professional trajectory capture important components of indigenous educational history in Venezuela. Her creative involvement in the grassroots struggle to develop bilingual indigenous education and curricula in Venezuela during the top-down assimilationist period of the late twentieth century reveals the challenges, victories, and sacrifices that have been made in this effort. Palmar's life also exemplifies the involvement of indigenous leaders and educators in national policy during a new era inaugurated in 1999 under President Hugo Chávez, through the adoption of Venezuela's new multicultural and populist constitution. Palmar is one of several notable Wayuu women who—through their dedicated efforts to promote indigenous rights to education, health care, and political representation—have emerged as leading figures in regional, national, and international arenas.[6]

As a pioneering and dedicated educator, Palmar has worked outside, within, against, and alongside different political and administrative institutions as an advocate for bilingual intercultural education.[7] She has utilized numerous creative strategies—from designing her own laminate workbooks to involvement in community organizing to strategically deploying the national anthem in the Wayuu language—to achieve her goals. This chapter traces Palmar's path from small Guajira schools in Yaguasirú and Yosipa, in Zulia state, to the ministry of education in the nation's capital of Caracas. The rural to urban path Palmar followed mirrors the movement of many Wayuu from remote areas of the Guajira to the urban sectors of Venezuela's second largest city, Maracaibo. It shows her participation in the consciousness-raising efforts around indigenous rights during the 1980s that developed through interaction with socialist intellectuals and educational activists. This activity led to her eventual work within the state system during a historical moment when national leaders and policy makers sought to transform the national educational system into one that validates and reinforces indigenous languages, culture, and knowledge—a system that would be tailored to suit the needs and desires of individual communities within unique geographic locations and social circumstances. Before turning to these, however, it will be helpful to have some historical perspective on the state's policies toward indigenous education and basic ethnographic contextualization on Wayuu and Venezuela's indigenous populations. We also briefly comment below on our collaborative process in producing this text, as it may be of interest to some readers.

Our Collaborative Process

This chapter developed out of ethnographic research, conversations, interviews, and a process of dialogic editing between the European-American anthropologist Laura R. Graham and the indigenous education professional Flor Palmar.[8] Graham observed and participated in events that Palmar organized in 2006, accompanied her in her work on and off over a period of one year, and returned in July and August 2007 for follow-up research. As part of this effort Graham conducted an extensive open-ended interview with Palmar focusing on her life history and professional work. This conversation forms the basis of much of what appears in this chapter. At Graham's request, Palmar supplemented these discussions and an earlier draft of this chapter with an overview of the history of indigenous education in Venezuela, parts of which we have incorporated into the body of this text.

Throughout the writing process Graham and Palmar maintained ongoing dialogue. Graham drafted the essay in its academic form, consulting frequently with Palmar via e-mail and Skype calls; she highlighted Palmar's voice through extensive quotations drawn from the 2007 interview and other conversations. Words and phrases that appear in quotations are direct quotations of Palmar's speech, unless otherwise noted. In addition to these more visible quotations, Palmar's voice is woven seamlessly throughout the narrative as a result of our collaborative process. Our work resembles, in some ways, Ruth Behar's presentation of Esperanza's story in *Translated Woman*.[9] Palmar, however, took an active role in the writing process itself. For example, Palmar provided drafts of historical sections and reviewed, commented on, and edited the draft manuscript. Palmar's eldest son, David Hernández Palmar, provided invaluable assistance and translation, especially so that Palmar could read Graham's English draft, make corrections, and comment on it. Unlike Behar or Feld's "dialogic editing," in which Kaluli commented on an already completed and published ethnographic monograph, Palmar was an active participant in the crafting of this multivocal text.[10]

Education of Indigenous Peoples in Venezuela: A Brief Historical Overview

Debate over language, specifically the question of which language would be used in official politics of the Spanish Empire in the conquered territories of the Americas, dates to the sixteenth century. Parties close to the Spanish crown considered whether Spanish would be the political language of the empire and deliberated whether the crown should energetically force a policy of "castilianization," imposing the language of the Spanish region of Castile, or if it would allow use of local languages.[11] Catholic missionaries, typically the vanguard of imperial presence, opted for the latter since evangelization was more effective in indigenous languages. Missionaries' knowledge of local languages enabled them to exercise more exclusive control over the colonized peoples, thus giving them an advantage over the crown's secular representatives in their ongoing battle for authority.[12] In many parts of Latin America, including Venezuela, Spanish colonizers favored castilianization for official business and resented the advantages and power that the clergy derived from its linguistic monopoly. Conflict between the clergy and the crown over the issue of language persisted through the eighteenth century.

During the nineteenth century, when revolutionary movements in the Americas sought independence from Spain, nationalist leaders saw the castilianization of indigenous populations as an effective means to integrate and consolidate the populations of their emergent republics.[13] Early state efforts to enforce Castilian Spanish on the nation's Native peoples had varied success; new leadership in the nascent states that followed independence controlled the educational systems in the metropole, while the Catholic church and evangelical groups dominated education in more remote areas inhabited by indigenous peoples. The Venezuelan state, which earned its independence from Spain and established the first republic in 1811, was not particularly successful in enforcing castillizination throughout its territory.

The Ley de Misiones (Mission Law), and its further specification in 1921 known as the "Reglamento," outlined a framework for assimilating into the nation-state indigenous populations, as well as campesinos (small scale farmers of mixed or African descent and/or indigenous ancestry, and anyone raised in, living in, or working the land in agricultural zones). It introduced the rural school system, first to campesinos in 1921, and then in 1922 to indigenous communities. With these laws, the Venezuelan state structured a juridical and legal framework for minimizing indigenous cultural identity, since the stated explicit goal of the Ley de Misiones was "to organize, to civilize, and to evangelize the aboriginal population."[14] It delegated responsibility for this to the Catholic Church and designated the Capuchin religious order to exercise guardianship, vigilance, representation, and education of indigenous populations. It encouraged "civilizing" strategies, including the promotion of Spanish literacy, Christianization, and the adoption of "modern" economic practices, such as Western-style agriculture.[15] Article 13 of the Ley de Misiones imposed the Spanish language as the sole language of instruction in indigenous primary education and expressly forbade students from speaking their native languages at each center that was established for indigenous education.

In 1952, the Venezuelan state entered into agreements with missionaries of various religious orders (primarily Capuchin as well as Franciscan), and granted them jurisdiction over the indigenous groups in designated regions.[16] Missionaries from various orders, including evangelical Protestants, worked in Wayuu communities. This system lasted until the end of the 1970s, when the Ministry of Education assumed responsibility for indigenous education.[17] Over time, the government gradually assumed greater responsibility for providing education for campesinos and indigenous groups in rural zones, and began to train "civil teachers" for its programs. It charged the Ministry of Justice with the responsibility for dealing with the needs of indigenous peoples, including education.[18]

In the late 1970s and early 1980s growing progressive movements throughout Latin America generated ideas that propelled innovations in popular education, such as the approaches of Paulo Freire, adherents of Liberation Theology, and other progressive social movements. Emerging from these ideologies was the vision of bilingual intercultural education. Agitation for changes led Venezuelan President Luis Herrera Campins, in 1979, to sign Presidential Decree 283, which mandated the implementation of bilingual intercultural education for all schools located in indigenous communities.

It decreed indigenous languages, complemented by Spanish, as the medium of instruction and also mandated the development of native language and bilingual pedagogical materials as well as resources for teacher training and instruction. In March 1982, the state adopted a single alphabet, developed by a team of linguists, for writing indigenous languages.[19] Known as the Alphabet of Indigenous Languages of Venezuela (ALIV), this alphabet was recognized as a national standard for writing indigenous languages, and it allowed for more consistent translation and development of curricular materials.[20] Experimental bilingual programs were implemented in sixty-eight indigenous schools within six states that have large native populations: Amazonas, Apure, Bolívar, Anzoategui, Delta Amacuro, and Zulia. Indicative of its large population, forty-five of these sixty-eight schools were in Wayuu communities.

Following Presidential Decree 283, the Department of Indigenous Affairs (Dirección de Asuntos Indígenas) sponsored the first workshop on the implementation of bilingual intercultural education for primary level teachers. This forum brought indigenous leaders together to discuss ideas about bilingual intercultural education that were then circulating throughout Latin America, especially in Mexico and Bolivia (see, for example, García chapter 9, this volume). These programs raised the hopes of indigenous educators like Flor Palmar, who had great expectations for further advances during the 1980s.

However, despite Presidential Decree 283 and several Ministry of Education resolutions that offered tremendous promise and raised hopes for more innovative programs, state policy and support for programs in bilingual intercultural education atrophied from the mid-1980s through most of the 1990s. Substantive support as well as policy for the development of indigenous education by successive governmental administrations was lacking for several reasons. First, it relied exclusively on academic linguists and anthropologists and did not involve indigenous educators and community members in any part of the process. Second, it was imposed from the top and did not include participation or support from local communities. Third, there was little political will to carry out programs, train teachers, and produce pedagogical materials. The Ministry of Education failed to develop a plan for the implementation of bilingual intercultural education, in part because it was understaffed and did not have a team of trained experts with the capacity for planning or implementing programs. Also there was little technical information about the languages, cultures, and pedagogical methods appropriate for communities where bilingual intercultural education was to be implemented. Fourth, the majority of the nation's indigenous peoples and communities were not aware of the educational project since they were neither informed nor trained regarding its sociocultural importance and potential.

The participation and support of local communities therefore was not secured. Fifth and finally, policy makers had a strikingly inadequate understanding of processes and challenges involved in the transition from orality to literacy. Thus, bilingual intercultural education during the 1980s until the end of the 1990s was, as Palmar calls it, an "orphaned politics."

In most cases, the education that was implemented in indigenous towns and communities during the 1980s and 1990s was neither intercultural nor bilingual. It continued to reproduce what Palmar calls "the deficient, assimilationist, segregationist traditional education" of the national curriculum. Thus while Presidential Decree 283 and the Ministry of Education's official posture appeared to offer support for indigenous peoples, there was, in fact, very little actual support and virtually no follow-through. With the exception of the sixty-eight pilot schools, the curriculum in schools in indigenous communities remained unchanged and, even in these, the government drew upon the expertise of nonindigenous linguists and anthropologists to determine what should be included as "indigenous content" rather than asking indigenous peoples themselves. The purpose of state schools in indigenous communities continued to be the formation of national subjects and "good" Venezuelan citizens. The curriculum was both homogeneous and homogenizing.

Bilingual intercultural education was not resuscitated until after the 1998 presidential election of populist Hugo Chávez. His new government made efforts to implement sweeping social reforms, including major educational reforms throughout the nation. The new constitution of 1999 and Chávez's explicit support for multiculturalism renewed discussions for indigenous educators and ushered in a period of reforms for bilingual intercultural education at local as well as national levels. We turn to these more specifically later.

Wayuu

Flor Palmar is one of approximately 438,000 Wayuu who live in a broad region extending from the area around Lake Maracaibo in Venezuela up through the Guajira Peninsula, the Wayuu homeland.[21] Since independence from Spain, the Guajira Peninsula has been politically divided between the nation-states of Venezuela and Colombia (see map, figure 11.1).[22] Wayuu people are the most numerous indigenous group in both Venezuela and Colombia. According to the Venezuela census of 2011, Wayuu make up 58 percent of the nation's total indigenous population.[23] Their large numbers, relative to the population of other indigenous groups in both Venezuela and Colombia, make Wayuu stand out as exceptional. Wayuu may claim dual

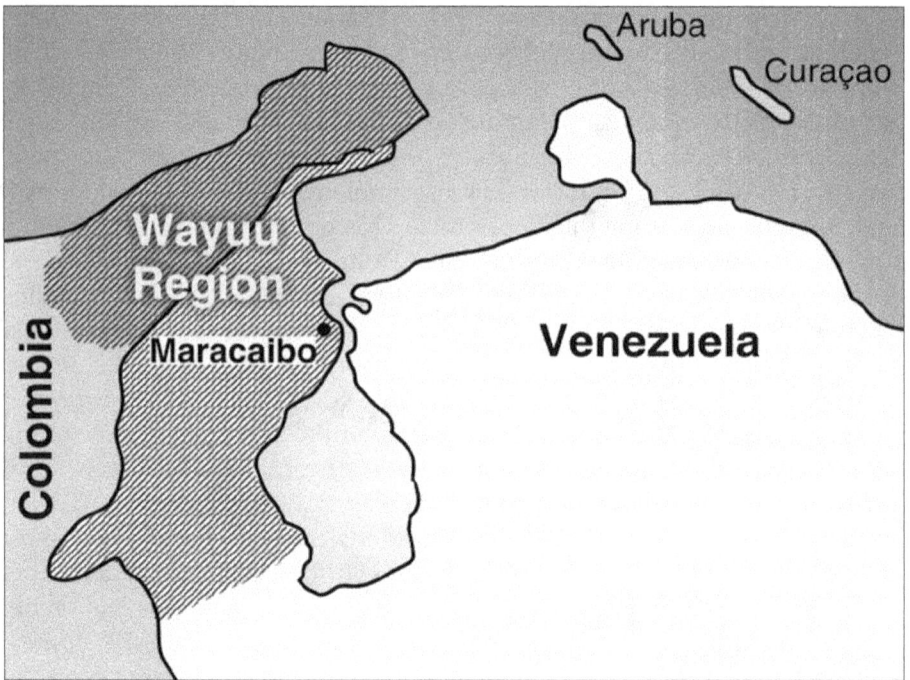

Figure 11.1. Map of Wayuu homeland from the film *Owners of the Water: Conflict and Collaboration over Rivers*. Dirs. L. Graham, D. Hernández Palmar, and C. Waiassé. Watertown, MA: Documentary Educational Resources, 2009.

citizenship, and many frequently traverse the international border to visit relatives, to engage in commerce, or to access services, such as medical care in Maracaibo. In Zulia state, Wayuu make up more than 10 percent of the total population, and half of these are found in the city of Maracaibo.

In the Guajira, Wayuu traditionally lived in dispersed and highly mobile pastoral settlements. Today, the majority has abandoned the semi-nomadic pastoral lifestyle. Palmar's family is representative. Two of her four brothers live in the Guajira and maintain goat and sheep herds; two other brothers, as well as her three sisters and herself, all live in Maracaibo. Upholding a pattern that is typical of contemporary Wayuu, they all move fairly frequently between the rural Guajira Peninsula and urban Maracaibo. Similarly, as Sara Jamieson points out, "a steady flow of material goods, food items, and animals also moves back and forth between the Guajira and Maracaibo."[24] Most Wayuu who live in the northern section of Maracaibo earn their living working in the informal sector. Among the younger generations, however, as Jamieson notes, there is a steady trend toward proletarianization.[25]

It is important to underscore that Wayuu are very heterogeneous; some are quite wealthy, and a significant number of Wayuu youth now attend and graduate from university. Well over one thousand Wayuu currently attend the University of Zulia (LUZ) in Maracaibo.[26] Many of these students follow in Palmar's footsteps, entering the educational profession, aspiring to become primary or secondary school teachers or to work in state-sponsored social programs, such as Misión Robinson, a secondary equivalency program implemented in poor neighborhoods, or Misión Guaicaipuro, created in 2003, to provide services directly to benefit indigenous peoples, including restoring land titles, protecting indigenous lands from resource speculation, and preserving the human rights of indigenous communities. Others benefit from Misión Cultura, established in 2005 by the national government, to promote cultural identity and community integration through a university-level teaching degree specializing in Venezuelan culture and diversity.[27]

Palmar's native language, Wayuunaiki (Wayuu speech), is an Arawakan language, and belongs to one of the major lowland South American language families.[28] Historical reconstructions based on linguistic and archaeological data suggest that the predecessors of contemporary Wayuu (whom linguists identify as Proto-Maipuran/Arawakan speakers) originated in the central Amazon region. Sometime between 1200 BCE and 900 BCE, Palmar's Wayuu ancestors moved northward into the Barquisimeto Plateau and Maracaibo Basin, an area to the south of Guajira Peninsula.[29] Palmar's ancestors have lived in the Guajira region for nearly three thousand years, and this is the area where they encountered the first Spanish explorers in the sixteenth century.[30]

Compared to the status of women in many other lowland South American groups, Wayuu women have considerable social status and prestige. Women are especially valued as perpetuators of the matriline.[31] Wayuu society is, nevertheless, patriarchal, and women are subject to patriarchal gender ideologies. Many women still today are compelled into forced marriages, for example. At marriage, the groom's family offers gifts—animals and precious stones—to the bride's parents, which anthropologist Maria Barbara Watson-Franke termed "bridal payment."[32] In addition to speaking of these as "gifts," Palmar, like most Wayuu, considers these also to be expressions of the groom's family's blessing upon the marriage. Men are chiefs and headmen of dispersed segmentary groups (there is no overarching political structure); however, male chiefs frequently share leadership and decision making with their sisters.[33] As this suggests, Wayuu women are often politically influential and frequently occupy other significant political roles. Wayuu women can, for example, become *piache*, or *outs* (shamans), as well as *puitchipü*, political intermediaries who are recognized for their eloquent speaking abilities and knowledge of Wayuu's extensive system of customary law.[34] Wayuu women such as Flor Palmar and Noeli Pocaterra, a Wayuu woman who is one of four indigenous members of the Venezuelan National Congress, have extended women's influence beyond Wayuu communities into regional and national arenas. Strong and assertive, these women are extremely capable advocates for indigenous rights.

An Educational Journey: From Parouralapü, Colombia, to Maracaibo, Venezuela

Palmar's parents, Emelina Barroso and Emiliano Palmar, attended primary school in the Alta Guajira, in Colombia.[35] In the early 1960s, when they moved their family south into Venezuela, they followed a migration that many Wayuu from the Alta Guajira had been making especially since the discovery of oil in 1910 in the Maracaibo Basin. Beginning in the decade following 1910, many Wayuu settled in the outskirts and then barrios of Maracaibo in search of jobs in the burgeoning oil industry. As many scholars note, this migration gained considerable momentum over the last four decades as many Wayuu, seeking labor and educational opportunities, settled in Maracaibo's predominantly Wayuu-populated neighborhoods.[36] Today, approximately one hundred thousand Wayuu live in Maracaibo, making up approximately 5.3 percent of the city's total population.[37] Maracaibo's northern zone is distinctively Wayuu.[38] Many Wayuu neighborhoods, such as 23 de marzo and el Mamón, where goats and chickens amble in the unpaved streets, feel more rural than urban despite their location within Maracaibo's city limits. These spaces, in fact, can be thought of as transitional zones between highly urban Maracaibo and rural Guajira.

The Palmar Barroso family did not, however, move to the urban zones of Maracaibo. Instead Emelina and Emiliano chose to remain in the Guajira and settled in the town of Yaguasirú (*Yawaasiru*, in Wayuunaiki, means "watering place of the *yaguazos*," or wild ducks), in what is now the Guajira municipality (formerly Páez). A short walk from their home in Yaguasirú was a state elementary school, Centro Piloto de Educación Indígena Yaguasirú, established in the mid-1950s.[39] Emiliano got a job in construction and facility maintenance at the school and was able to continue herding his animals; Emelina supervised the large family garden and household. Along with her brothers and sisters, Flor Palmar attended primary school in Yaguasirú (see figure 11.2). Lessons from the national curriculum were taught in Spanish, by *alijuna* (nonindigenous) teachers. The shock of the language, curriculum, and behavior policy was tremendous.

Figure 11.2. The Palmar Barroso family at their home in Yaguasirú, circa 1973. Flor Palmar is back row center. Photo courtesy of Flor A. Palmar and the Palmar Barroso family archive.

The teachers forced us to speak Spanish. If we spoke Wayuunaiki, our language, we were physically punished. They teased us and belittled our language directly to our faces. They said we couldn't speak Wayuunaiki because it wasn't a language. It was not Spanish. This is what our teachers said.

During recess we would speak Wayuunaiki. All of us would speak it to communicate among ourselves. Since the teachers weren't present, we would speak it while we played. But when we spoke to the teachers, we had to speak Spanish, even if we spoke poorly.

Children who didn't speak Spanish were beaten. They told us we had to speak Spanish well. If we needed something, we had to ask for it in Spanish. They punished us if we didn't. We were afraid to make any kind of request. Many children wet their pants just because they were afraid to make a mistake in Spanish.

The Centro Piloto de Educación Indígena Yaguasirú school was a Venezuelan state institution created by the Ministry of Justice. This pilot project was one of the few indigenous schools that, during the 1950s and 1960s, was not entirely run by any religious order. It exemplifies the state's effort to reassert its control over public schools in rural areas. At first, the classes were held in a shelter; eventually construction workers like Emiliano built several little houses for separate classrooms. This pilot school's mission, part of a national politics for social integration, was to socially and economically assimilate Wayuu into the region's *criolla* (mixed) population.[40] The curriculum emphasized basic academics (reading, writing, math) for all, and vocational training in diverse areas, according to gender. For boys, this meant masonry, carpentry, electrical training, agriculture, ironwork, and animal husbandry. For girls, Wayuu women called "Home Demonstrators" (demostradoras del hogar) offered classes teaching skills such as sewing and embroidery. Palmar states that "the academic training had nothing to do with Wayuu life. It was completely divorced from Wayuu reality and everything was in Spanish."

To advance in school, Wayuu children like Palmar learned Spanish. Because Spanish was the medium of instruction in school, it slowly crept into everyday use in the Palmar Barroso family home.[41]

> Little by little I started learning Spanish in school. With time our Spanish improved. By the time we reached high school, we managed to speak it much better.

Catholic priests came once a week during the 1960s, to, as Palmar states, "indoctrinate" the Wayuu students. Flor Palmar and her siblings were excused from these sessions because her parents had converted to evangelical Protestantism and Emiliano convinced the teachers to excuse the Palmar Barroso children from the catechism. Palmar's experience as a child in the Ministry of Justice's pilot educational project of indigenous education illustrates how the Church and the state cooperated in the assimilationist mission of the 1950s and 1960s.[42] As elsewhere in the Americas, religious indoctrination, language of instruction, and intimidation—both physical and psychological—were primary means of achieving this, even outside the boarding school experiences of North America.[43]

Despite this oppressive atmosphere, Palmar discovered that she was good at schoolwork. She recalls, "I helped my brothers and sisters with their homework." While this provided a source of satisfaction, Palmar found the mistreatment of Wayuu children in the pilot school disturbing. She dates her earliest recognition of the need for indigenous educators who use native language as the medium of instruction to this early experience. "I realized how important it is for teachers to understand the students they teach, to understand *Wayuunaiki* (Wayuu speech). I realized the need for indigenous teachers."

While Palmar was in primary school, the Peruvian linguist Marta Hildebrandt came to Yaguasirú. As part of her work on the Wayuu language, Hildebrandt developed some workbooks using an orthography she developed for her Guajiro-Spanish dictionary.[44] The orthography she used provides the foundation for what is now known as the Alphabet of Indigenous Languages of Venezuela (ALIV). The Ministry of Justice, which ran the pilot educational project, published several of Hildebrandt's workbooks and Palmar notes that these are the basis for the workbooks used in Wayuu schools today.

Hildebrandt and her linguistic work inspired young Palmar, who was determined to continue her education. She was intrigued that the linguist could *write* Wayuunaiki, when her teachers at school were telling her that her native tongue was not even "a language." Palmar decided early on that she wanted to become a teacher, and she saw her Wayuu language and culture as assets for teaching other Wayuu children. In Yaguasirú, however, there were no educational opportunities beyond primary school. "I had to stay out for almost two years after sixth grade because there was no school near where we lived." Then two years later, when a high school was established in Paraguaipoa, about an hour from Yaguasirú, Palmar attended it, finishing seventh, eighth, and ninth grades at that school. Palmar next looked for scholarships to support her further study.

> When some scholarships became available to study elementary education, I took the entrance exams. I had to leave home to study in Maracaibo at the Alejandro Fuenmayor High School.[45] First I lived with an aunt, then when my sister Nora got married, I lived with her for a while. Later I lived in a rented room until I graduated in 1978.

Like other Wayuu from the Guajira who sought higher education during this period, Palmar had to leave her family and move to Maracaibo to live with relatives. Life in the city was expensive; Palmar's schooling demanded sacrifices of her and her family. Flor Palmar had no money for food or books and this caused her to nearly drop out several times. Recognizing her dedication and potential, administrators responded to her pleas for help and awarded her a scholarship to the cafeteria, equivalent to approximately twenty dollars a month, so that she could eat one hot meal a day (lunch, the primary meal in Venezuela) and another that totaled about five dollars per month for supplies and transportation. Because this was insufficient to cover her expenses, Palmar began selling her homework to classmates who were not as good at academics as she was. She also did other students' homework so that she could purchase bus tickets to get home from school. When there was a drought and Palmar's father's herds in the Guajira suffered, things got worse. The family could spare no money for Palmar's expenses. Flor Palmar adapted by doing chores in her classmates' homes. She washed dishes and helped them with their homework. "These girls got the best grades. My work suffered because I did their homework first. I was tired by the time I could do my own." In 1978 Palmar graduated from the Alejandro Fuenmayor Normal School, earning the title of Normal School Teacher (Maestra Normalista).

Today, there are more opportunities for Wayuu to attend secondary school in the Guajira, but Maracaibo continues to be a destination for many Wayuu who seek post-secondary education. Many Wayuu send their children to live with relatives to attend secondary school or university in Maracaibo. Palmar's niece—whose family lives in Yaguasirú, where her father, Luis, maintains goat and sheep herds—is living with Palmar's youngest brother in the el Mamón neighborhood while she attends university. She hopes to become a medical doctor. Wayuu make up the great majority of the nearly two thousand indigenous students who attend the University of Zulia, and the majority of these are young women. Jameison points out that urban Wayuu women are attaining university degrees in numbers disproportionate to men and are increasingly pursuing professional careers in education, community activism, and regional government.[46] The fact that these women have considerable autonomy and may be relatively independent in comparison with women in many other lowland South American indigenous societies may help explain why so many Wayuu women are able to seek postsecondary degrees.[47] Wayuu also attend other universities in Maracaibo. Palmar's eldest son, David Hernández Palmar, for example, is completing his education at Universidad Dr. Rafael Belloso Chacín (URBE). Her daughter, Anggie Hernández Palmar, completed a degree in Business Administration in 2013 at Instituto Universitario Pedro Emilio Coll and, also in 2012, was a recipient of a fellowship from the United Nations Indigenous Fellowship Programme (IFP) (see figure 11.3). Palmar's youngest sons, Daniel and Renny, completed high school and are now undergraduate students at the URBE. Wayuu also attend universities in neighboring Colombia, primarily in Maicao, Riohacha, Barranquilla, Medellín, and Bogotá.

As an increasing number of Wayuu earn advanced degrees, they follow in the footsteps of pioneers such as Noeli Pocaterra, who received a PhD in sociology (her father was the first Wayuu to become a teacher) and Nemesio Montiel Fernández who earned a PhD in anthropology and now teaches at the Universidad de Zulia (LUZ). Growing numbers of Wayuu are also becoming professionals, earning degrees and practicing as lawyers and medical doctors. Palmar's younger brother Yan Josué, for example, is a veterinarian; her younger sisters Nancy and Naffi are nurses. Naffi was recently awarded a scholarship to Italy to study palliative care and bone-marrow transplant nursing. While many Wayuu, such as the Palmar Barroso children, have advanced in Venezuela's educational system, the great majority live in areas with few educational opportunities, in remote areas of the Guajira or the poorly served urban neigborhoods of Maracaibo. Serving these Wayuu and other children in such communities has been Palmar's life work, which, when reflecting on the creative strategies she has employed throughout her career, she refers to as "her art."

Figure 11.3. Flor Ángela Palmar with her daughter, Anggie Hernández Palmar, on the occasion of Flor Palmar's graduation Magíster Scientiarum in Basic Education Adminstration, Rafael María Baralt Experimental University. Photo courtesy of David Hernández Palmar, 2011.

Teaching, Educating, and Community Organizing

After receiving her teaching degree, Palmar returned to the Guajira, through an appointment from the Regional Office of Indigenous Affairs of Zulia state (Oficina Regional de Asuntos Indígenas, ORAI) and the Ministry of Education, to a town called Yosipa, not far from her hometown, Yaguasirú. This was a time, in the late 1970s, when the state was opening up a number of schools for Wayuu children throughout the region. Palmar's charge was to establish an elementary school in Yosipa and teach the national curriculum.[48]

> But since I didn't have supervision there, and I remembered my experiences and how I suffered in the flesh as an indigenous child—how my identity was negated, how it was castrated—I understood the indigenous children who were there perfectly well. I did not have any problem teaching in my language, in Wayuunaiki, which made it easy to work with them. I explained everything perfectly in Wayuunaiki—counting, reading, and reciting poems. Anything they wanted to know, I explained in Wayuunaiki. I didn't force them to speak Spanish. And when they wanted to ask me something, to know how to say something in Spanish, they would ask me, "Teacher, how do you say this in Spanish?" And I would reply, "Well, this is how you say it."

So the children felt really good about having an indigenous teacher, speaking to them in their native language, telling them everything.

Palmar's training and familiarity with the different pedagogical methods she had studied in school did not prepare her for the work of a bilingual teacher in rural areas with no resources. She developed her own style, teaching in Wayuunaiki, and in Spanish when students were ready and requested it. She also developed a strategy for teaching multiple grade levels in a one-room school. Palmar divided the fifty-six students in the Yosipa school into various groups and taught them separately, in sequence. "At eleven o'clock I would let the first group go, the littlest ones, at noon the second group, the third group at one o'clock, and the fourth group when I was almost ready to go, when the truck passed and I could get a ride." Palmar taught in this way for two years in Yosipa.

Prior to this experience in the Guajira, however, after her graduation in 1978 from Alejandro Fuenmayor, Palmar spent one year working as substitute teacher in Maracaibo, in a school that had "many problems."[49] During this time she gained formative experience under the mentorship of Solanda García, a Wayuu educator who was affiliated with the Liga Socialista (Socialist League). The national socialist movement was active in poor neigborhoods in Maracaibo and among Wayuu, because they make up a large segment of the urban population and therefore have the potential to be a significant political and economic force. Through García, Palmar was exposed to socialist ideas. She also participated in socialist-led campaigns to educate both Wayuu and nonindigenous children in Maracaibo's poorest neighborhoods.[50] Other young and idealistic Wayuu intellectuals also participated in these activities, and this is where Flor Palmar met her future husband, David Julio Hernández.

We went to those neighborhoods—Chino, Julio, el Mamón—to teach. Nobody told us how they were going to pay us, or even if they were going to pay us. This was social work! I had my first experience there with my friend who was a teacher, Solanda García. She taught her art there, her pedagogy, even though she wasn't trained to teach in indigenous communities.

Palmar's experience with Solanda García and the socialist educational campaigns in the poor Wayuu neighborhoods of Maracaibo provided a model for the indigenous pedagogy she has developed throughout her professional career. From Solanda García, Palmar learned how to work directly from the children's experiences and to make "homemade" books for teaching. She assembled children's drawings, based on words they found interesting, and laminated (plasticized) these to form the pages of her "text books."

Solanda García and I both spoke Wayuunaiki and she was the experienced teacher. To teach reading and writing, she asked the children, "What would you like to draw to make your pages? What do you want to talk about?" "Animals!" "So what animals are from the Guajira?" And we would start to name them, the animals in the Guajira. We would write in our beginner Wayuunaiki, because it didn't have standardized spelling yet. Solanda would write the names of all the animals [in Spanish] and we would write them in Wayuunaiki too. That is how we did it, little by little.

This is how I began to teach using a name as a basis, a concrete object that children could develop. For example, I would ask, "What is this?" "Oh. Well, this is an animal. Its color is this. Its name is this. It eats this kind of food. It eats insects."

Palmar, García, and the students wrote five books using "sight words" familiar to Wayuu and used these as a basis for teaching Wayuu literacy skills. "The children would learn to read little by little and every day we would put together a laminated sheet. Each laminated sheet was what the students would learn in one day, quickly." In the excerpt above, Palmar mentions that she wrote in "beginning Wayuunaiki." At this time, during the late 1970s, as she and her colleagues were experimenting with written forms of the native language, linguists were also experimenting with orthography, developing what, in 1979, became ALIV.

In 1979, after Presidential Decree 283 mandated the implementation of bilingual intercultural education in all schools located in indigenous communities, Flor Palmar enrolled in the first seminar for the implementation of bilingual intercultural education in indigenous communities held in Carrizal, Miranda state. This class, which took place in 1980, broke new ground: it was led by indigenous teachers. Organized by the Department of Indigenous Affairs, it was designed for teachers who taught in the sixty-eight experimental schools in different indigenous communities from among the nine that had been designated to have bilingual programs. These were the first classes to bring indigenous educators from across the nation together. For Flor Palmar and other participants, the discussions were exciting and invigorating. In the first session they deliberated over the very idea of bilingual intercultural education: what was it and why was it necessary? Conversations and debates like these were occurring elsewhere in Latin America, in countries such as Bolivia and Mexico.[51] Participants considered how these ideas could be adapted and implemented among the thirty-four distinct indigenous populations that were recognized by the Venezuelan state at that time.[52]

During this first seminar, conversation focused on elementary education. As Palmar says, "at that time no one was thinking about preschool." This was the first time that indigenous people were included in the process of developing educational curriculum. It resulted in some study plans that were used in sixty-eight experimental indigenous schools across the nation, including schools among Wayuu and Yukpa in Zulia state.[53] Unfortunately, as Palmar notes, "after these programs were implemented, there was no follow-through. There was no political will. Teachers had to come up with their own ways of teaching, in Spanish, because there was no support for bilingual programs."

In 1980 Palmar was transferred to a different school, in Puerto Aléramo, close to Paraguaipoa, the seat of the Guajira municipality where she had attended first through sixth grades. Palmar's time at this school energized her developing ideas about indigenous education, especially her ideas about the use of traditional expressive forms such as song, dance, and other art forms for pedagogical purposes. Her experience in Paraguaipoa also introduced her to the potential of using these expressive forms, and the Wayuunaiki language, as political instruments. She learned that Wayuunaiki can be harnessed to advance the indigenous education mission beyond the classroom.[54]

Along with other new teachers at the Puerto Aléramo school, including one who Palmar recalls as "especially conscious of her indigenous identity," Palmar and her colleagues founded a cultural group. Students in this group performed Wayuu dances as a means to validate cultural identity as well as Wayuu expressive forms themselves. "We worked a little with the art," Palmar commented, "and also tried to write in Wayuunaiki." The most courageous and provocative act of this group of teachers was to translate the first verse and the chorus of the Venezuelan national anthem into Wayuunaiki. They did this so that their Wayuu students could sing the national anthem, albeit an incomplete version, in their own language, as part of the official celebrations commemorating the city of Paraguaipoa's bicentennial anniversary.

This was, as Palmar commented, "a daring act" and also a powerful assertion of Wayuu identity in the national arena, for the national anthem is a paramount sign of national unity. Prior to this the national anthem was exclusively sung at official events in Castilian Spanish. Singing it in Spanish could not but help remind native indigenous language speakers of their remove, both geographically and linguistically (symbolically), from the nation's power centers. Since all Venezuelan children, regardless of what language they speak in their homes and communities, sing the national anthem at the beginning of the school day, their having to sing it in Spanish signals the dominance of the Spanish language (and culture) over other languages that are spoken in Venezuela.

Attempts had been made by a number of individuals to translate parts or all of the national anthem into Wayuunaiki as early as the 1950s. There was, however, no agreed upon or officially recognized version until 2006. (We discuss this below.) When the Wayuu school children sang even just the anthem's chorus in Wayuunaiki at the celebration in Paraguaipoa, the effect on the mostly Wayuu crowd was powerful:[55]

Yaletüsü saaschin woumain
aja'ttitka mülia
kojutuin akua´ipa
süma wayuwaa.

Glory to the brave people
who threw off the yoke that burdened them,
the law respecting[56]
virtue and honor.

For nonindigenous Venezuelans, these words refer to the overthrow of the Spanish colonizers. For Palmar and many other Wayuu, in Wayuunaiki these words may take on a more immediate significance.

The Paraguaipoa school children's performance of the national anthem's first verse and chorus in Wayuunaiki asserted—and acoustically inserted—Wayuu language, culture, and identity into the national public sphere. Palmar, her colleagues, and their students used language in the national anthem to make a powerful statement against the dominance of Spanish language and culture in Venezuelan national public space. Singing at least part of the anthem in Wayuunaiki affirmed Wayuu language and identity, enabled Wayuu to claim the national anthem, and also strengthened the use of the native language in the local schools.

By 1988 bilingual intercultural education in Venezuela was nearly paralyzed. Palmar attributes this primarily to lack of political commitment. During the doldrums for bilingual intercultural education of the late 1980s up through the late 1990s, until Hugo Chávez was first elected, there were, however, a few workshops and state-sponsored courses to train indigenous educators in bilingual education. With support from the Ministry of Education, one initiative to train indigenous teachers took place in the Rural Pedagogical Institute, "El Macaro," in Aragua state; this was the second intensive course on bilingual intercultural education. Palmar recalls that all of the indigenous teachers who wanted to promote bilingual education enrolled. In the first phase, in 1981, there were spots for only thirty teachers. This number was increased and, in 1997, when she graduated with a degree in bilingual intercultural education, there were more than four hundred indigenous participants.

Because their successes in the late 1970s and early 1980s were followed by stagnation and lack of state support in the late 1980s and the decade that followed, this program was refreshing and energizing to Palmar and other indigenous educators. In fact, this training provided "an awakening," according to Palmar. The experience of gathering so many indigenous educators together in one place was especially powerful because not all of the indigenous participants spoke their native languages. Among the majority of indigenous teachers who were committed to bilingual education, the event prompted what Palmar labels a "renewed consciousness" of the importance of teaching in the native language. Participants expressed tremendous enthusiasm, and Palmar recalls expressions of their tenacious spirit: "We have to fight for bilingual intercultural education!" It was not, however, until the new constitution of 1999, according to a central pledge of the Chávez presidency, that the state demonstrated any consistent, long-term commitment to developing bilingual intercultural curriculum for Venezuela's indigenous groups. This is, in fact, the first Venezuelan constitution that guarantees the nation's indigenous peoples the right to bilingual intercultural education.

From Puerto Aléramo in the mid-1980s, Palmar moved to the Escuela Básica Nacional La Resistencia (National Primary School of the Resistance) in Maracaibo. Part of her attraction to this school was that all of the teachers were Wayuu. "It was exhilarating. We were developing bilingual intercultural education on our own. No one told us how to do it." With some resources and knowledge based on experience, the teachers developed a program that combined national curriculum with Wayuu education. But Palmar soon found that the physical conditions in this school were not conducive to her methods. The desks were too close together; she could not move about the classroom. "I am a teacher who walks all through the classroom, between the chairs. I am speaking. I am telling. I am encouraging. I put my hand on the students' heads, on their shoulders. I teach them how to write with their little hands." Palmar also incorporated Wayuu culture and performance into students' educational experience, and this became a hallmark of her pedagogy. Some parents, however, complained that she took students out of the classroom to a nearby cultural center to see Wayuu dance performances and hear music. In fact, her receptiveness to activities involving the cultural center eventually opened more doors along her pedagogical path.

The performers at the cultural center at the time were from a predominantly Wayuu neighborhood known as 23 de marzo (March 23rd). This neighborhood was extremely poor and had no school. Palmar recalls that just when she was feeling particularly frustrated and constrained in the La Resistencia school, an opportunity presented itself to build a school in 23 de marzo. She recalls,

> One day in the cultural center some people came to look for me. "Profesora Flor, we need your support so that you can guide us to start a school." I went there and it was a perfect environment for me. It was spacious and there were many children. I went there and told them we could begin on Saturday. I asked them, "How do you envision this school?"

Thus dialogue and much hard work began in this community which had few material resources but whose residents possessed a great deal of determination. Palmar marshaled the skills she had acquired as a volunteer organizer and teacher through her work with the Socialist League. She discovered resources that others did not realize could be tapped. All her work starting the school in 23 de marzo was voluntary, since she was still working in La Resistencia. Her example inspired a spirit of volunteerism among community members.

> I told them, "There is no water here. The first thing we have to build is a tank so that we can have water." I discovered a hospital that had an extra. That tank was the first thing we built there, in 1991. Then there was water for the school and the whole community!
>
> We began with 380 students and a plot of land 500 feet long. There was no infrastructure. There were five cuji trees; that was a classroom. We had to get plastic chairs. Next I got some used desks from a private school that was getting new ones. That's how we began.
>
> Each year we had a new project. I began to apply for funds to manage construction. Inspections began in 1992. In 1994, the first three rooms were built. We continued to hold classes: one group in the bushes and another group—the privileged ones, the first grades—in the classrooms. Each year we asked, "What do we need next?"

Working as the project coordinator for the 23 de marzo school in a severely underprivileged neighborhood of Wayuu and Colombian immigrants,[57] Palmar began dealing with higher level administrators, school superintendents, the mayor's office, and the mayor. She even took the school's projects directly to the governor. She learned the intricacies of interacting with municipal and state administrators. In these dealings, Palmar deployed creative tactics to garner material and political support for the school, and she got results. In this excerpt from her narrative, Palmar recounts how, once again, she used the national anthem sung in Wayuunaiki as a productive strategy for achieving the goals of bilingual intercultural education.

> We already knew all the little tricks: how to access the administrative offices, the governor's staff, when meetings are held, and with whom to communicate. I learned about all of the processes, including how to take over the governor's office.
>
> Once we did take over the governor's office. We didn't arrive as a single group. We had five or six different fronts. When the staff least expected it, they were surrounded. They said, "What does this mean?!" Someone shouted, "Let's sing the national anthem in Wayuu!" We sang and then made our requests. "We need this and this and this! We want to talk to the governor!" We did this again and again until one day the governor agreed to meet with us. Eventually we didn't need to go anymore. They knew us already.

> Another time, when we didn't get a response to our request, we wrote to the mayor's office. We worked for the mayor. We told him, "Listen, in this community, we need civic action and support from you. It is almost Mothers' Day."[58] And the mayor responded by providing food at affordable prices, and medical and dental care. We also requested a basketball court. That was the last thing I did there.

Palmar's activities as director of the 23 de marzo school, as her last comment indicates, went far beyond the role of school administrator. She worked as a community organizer to attain many forms of support for the community, such as medical and dental care, in addition to attempting to improve the school. She was flexible, and considered alternative forms of support that financially strapped parents could provide in lieu of payments for school improvements. When she needed to collect donations she had lined up from private schools and universities—desks, chalkboards, stands, telephones, even toilets and garbage cans—she did not expect families who donated their time and trucks to contribute financially toward other expenses.

Palmar began the 23 de marzo school as an experiment in bilingual intercultural education. When the classes began, in 1991, she served as both project coordinator and teacher. There were four other teachers, and none of them were indigenous. Having no other indigenous teachers was, Palmar recalls, "my first mistake. I should have had at least some indigenous teachers. Once I began to incorporate indigenous teachers the project started to make sense." As they began to work as a team of bilingual intercultural educators, Palmar mentored the younger teachers. She developed an evaluation scheme to assess and help the younger teachers progress. These teachers had no pedagogical training; they had only recently graduated from high school and did not have any postsecondary degrees.

Initially this work began with identity, Wayuu history, and how to talk about race and ethnicity. For these young indigenous people, this was consciousness-raising. Palmar and her Wayuu teacher-students discussed "what should and should not be said about Indians. What is beneficial as well as what is harmful. We talked about all of the pejorative terms that refer to the indigenous community." She gave each of the teachers a topic to research and then, after they had done the research, each presented his or her findings to the group. Eventually these projects were so successful that Palmar invited a municipal supervisor to participate. Following the supervisor's suggestion, Palmar invited two institutions to collaborate, the University of Zulia and the Pediatric Specialization Hospital Foundation (Funcación Hospital Especialidades Pediátricas). Together they developed workshops that provided a space for young Wayuu educators to learn how to do research, to develop as workshop leaders, and to incorporate into the curriculum language, culture, and experiences that were meaningful for their students.

I remember a beautiful experience when the children began to paint the basketball court for a project on traffic signals. They painted stoplights and cross walks. One boy played a blind person who had a live dog. He walked with a little white cane. The dog guided him across the street. Some children played the role of Wayuu from La Guajira who don't understand traffic signals. They saw the cars, wanted to turn back, tried to cross again and more cars came—wooden cars that went "beep, beep." It was very funny!

While Palmar recalls many productive and educational experiences such as this one, her work in the 23 de marzo school was not always positive. There were plenty of disagreements. Some parents objected to Palmar's method of sometimes incorporating multiple grades into one class. Others thought that children should not be taught in Wayuunaiki. There were too many students for the small facility; the number reached over one thousand at one point. "We suffered. We had many difficult experiences." Reflecting on her time as director of this school, Palmar says that she learned that bilingual intercultural education "should have continuity, tolerance, perseverance, permanence, and a presence even in the most trying times, as well as in the most satisfactory."

Together with the lessons that she had learned as a student and teacher in the Guajira, Palmar took these insights with her in 2002 when she was promoted to regional coordinator of bilingual intercultural education, becoming a member of the pedagogical team that was working to reform education in Zulia state. Her experiences and vision contributed to her eventual promotion in 2006 to the position of academic and administrative assistant in the General Directorate of Bilingual Intercultural Education in the Ministry of Education in Caracas.

Indigenous Education within Bolivarian Educational Reform

For Flor Palmar, Venezuela's National Constitution of 1999, adopted in the second year of President Hugo Chávez's first presidential term, signaled a "new beginning" for the Venezuelan state and for indigenous education in the nation.[59] To differentiate the state from its predecessors and to signal its alignment with the ideals of Simón Bolívar, a leading figure in the Hispano-American movement for independence from colonial Spain, the constitution renamed the state "the Bolivarian Republic of Venezuela." Palmar speaks of this constitution as "an achievement that marked an historic page in Venezuelan social policy." The 1999 constitution validates the nation's sociocultural and linguistic diversity, including indigenous peoples, and recognizes Venezuela as a multiethnic, pluricultural, democratic society. Chapter VIII specifically grants indigenous peoples full constitutional rights, including rights to land, language, and culture, and guarantees the right to bilingual intercultural education. In accordance with the constitution, various laws favorable to indigenous peoples were subsequently passed. Among these are the Organic Law of Indigenous Peoples and Communities, the Law of Demarcation of Indigenous Lands and Habitats (2002), the Law of Indigenous Languages (2008), the Law of Cultural Patrimony of Indigenous Peoples and Communities (2009), and the Law of Indigenous Artists (2009). Elements of these various laws are related, and they guarantee rights to intercultural bilingual education for indigenous peoples and communities.

The new constitution marks a radical shift from postures of previous governments toward indigenous education. Even though, in 1998, the Department of Indigenous Affairs carried out needs assessments with the goal of relaunching the project of bilingual intercultural education that had foundered during the 1980s and 1990s, it was not until the beginning of 2001, with the creation of the Department of Indigenous Education (Dirección Nacional de Educación Indígena), that a plan of action to develop an appropriate program was fleshed out. From 2001 to 2003, within the framework provided by the 1999 constitution and the National Simón Bolívar Project (also known as the "First Socialist Plan"[60]), educational needs assessments were carried out at the regional level and throughout the nation.

After the failed coup against President Chávez of April 11, 2002, politically progressive forces redoubled their efforts, and educational reform accelerated in Zulia state and across the nation. In Zulia, administrators in the Department of Education sought to identify someone with the proper credentials and experience to lead the task of designing and implementing bilingual intercultural education in the state. Palmar rose to the top among potential candidates. She was the only indigenous person qualified for this position and, although she felt that she had not completed her work at the 23 de marzo school, she was highly motivated to participate in the greater project of national indigenous educational reform. She stepped into her new position as regional coordinator of bilingual intercultural education in the Zulia Educational Zone in 2002 and held this position until 2006.

Palmar's first act was to bring in a linguist, Luis Beltrán, who is also Wayuu. The two of them worked together to coordinate meetings for the discussion of bilingual intercultural education *inside* communities of each of the state's five indigenous groups: Wayuu, Añu, Barí, Yukpa, and Japreria. Discussions of this nature were taking place in indigenous communities across the nation. Administrators and educators such as Palmar faced a tremendous job: they were charged with explaining the concept of bilingual intercultural education to local communities—to educators, parents, leaders, artisans, indeed anyone with an interest in education. Only after these kinds of discussions took place, when communities began to envisage what kind of education they wanted, could the task of *beginning* to discuss and then design curriculum commence.

> *In community meetings we asked many questions. What form should indigenous education take in this town? What would education look like so that children are happier, so that they feel better?*
>
> *Elders, women, leaders, indigenous painters and artists took part. They participated saying, for example, "in painting, this must be done; in history, these topics must be covered." They also discussed supplies: "these kinds of traditional, natural resources must be used so our children become familiar with them."*

Palmar and Luis Beltrán worked well together, facilitating what were for them and other participants tremendously exciting and empowering workshops about locally designed indigenous curriculum. The process was conceptualized as dialogic, beginning with discussions at the local level. They noted participants' comments and returned to communities for follow-up discussions. Palmar states, "This is how we did this work."

Along the way they encountered significant challenges. Among these were problems associated with writing. For languages that have no agreed-upon orthography, community members often disagreed over which writing system should be used.[61] "This is an issue that has to be decided at the community level," Palmar asserts. It is not appropriate for state-level administrators to say, "You should write like this, or like that." Further, they found that written reports of meeting proceedings often distorted discussions and decisions that had taken place in native languages; writing and translation into Spanish often transformed participants' intended meanings.

> *When we took reports back to the assemblies to be validated, we realized many things. The majority of what we picked up was written and transferred into Castilian, so a great deal of the contextual meaning, such as the richness of elders' speech, was lost. When we read the written reports, the meanings had been transformed. People said, "This isn't what I said! This is not what was said here!" And so, corrections were made.*

In some cases, people were resistant to change. Some people and groups opposed education in the native language.

> *Some said, "Don't use Wayuunaiki in school because we speak it at home." People don't understand the danger of this. Native culture is undermined every time a child is subjected to education where the native language is not spoken. Parents often don't understand this.*

But gradually, with sustained dialogue and consciousness-raising, such attitudes are beginning to change. Palmar is generally optimistic: "We all feel that our indigenous education can be based on our own educational processes. Then it will truly be our education." While Palmar acknowledges that resistance persists in some towns, she attributes this primarily to a lack of follow-through and long-term commitment.

During each year of her tenure as regional coordinator of bilingual intercultural education in the Zulia Educational Zone, Palmar's work advanced the indigenous educational project. In 2002, she developed a state-level plan that included completing a census of schools in indigenous communities. During 2003, a sociolinguistic evaluation of teaching staff and students in these schools was completed. Teachers also received basic linguistic training and educational supervision. All of these programs represent major improvements in attention to indigenous schools, where previously teachers were largely unsupervised and had little or no training in indigenous education or in issues specific to indigenous populations. In 2004, Palmar organized pedagogical workshops in each of the twenty-one municipalities throughout Zulia state. In preparation for their participation in these workshops, teachers participated in a series of meetings that brought together teachers from different schools in their regions. In 2005, Palmar's office developed a systematic proposal for intercultural bilingual education to be implemented in each indigenous school; supervised teacher training was a major component. This was followed, in 2006, with an evaluation of staff and pedagogy along with the development of bilingual texts and translations of texts, including the national anthem and other songs.

In 2006, Palmar was promoted to become a member of the Technical Pedagogical Team for Bilingual Intercultural Education in the National Commission for Curriculum within the Ministry of Popular Power of Education,[62] a position she held until the end of 2007. Palmar's work thus expanded from Zulia state to the national level. She continued to work on the same sorts of projects that she had organized and been involved in at state and local levels: organizing conferences, workshops, and courses for those involved in bilingual intercultural education, and continuing to work on teacher preparation. A primary objective of these activities was explaining the principles of bilingual intercultural education to educators and other sectors within specific indigenous communities, and facilitating exchange and discussion of these. Palmar said, "I consider a big part of my job to be a messenger; I take the idea of bilingual intercultural education to each and every one of the communities." Palmar observes that once communities are convinced that education, especially primary education, should take place in indigenous languages, discussions about curriculum development become easier. This is because "it is in their language. The cultural content is there. It exists within the communities."

Palmar was also responsible for collating, organizing, and summarizing curriculum proposals and materials from communities, based on discussion in local assemblies, that came to the national office. Collecting materials that adequately represented these discussions, and any consensus that may have been achieved, was not a simple, straightforward process. In many cases where there was no systematized orthography, partisan debates erupted. And, as in the case of many community meetings in Zulia that Palmar noted above, problems emerged when oral discussions were transformed into writing, and into Spanish. People contested that their words and positions had been misrepresented. Many discussions had to be repeated, and Spanish translations themselves were debated. Palmar notes that sessions in which bilingual intercultural education are discussed in communities need to be videotaped and that this is what is being done now.

Palmar cites lack of training and sustained technical support (ranging from linguistics and pedagogy to technology, from the operation of cameras to tractors) that is pertinent to the needs of specific communities as primary reasons that indigenous educational reform still faces challenges.

> For example, in the state of Bolívar, where a majority of Venezuela's indigenous peoples reside, there are seventeen indigenous groups. The coordinator there does not have a team. He should have seventeen teams, one for each group. It is complicated where there are different languages, different cultures. We go whenever we can to give feedback and support to communities that are developing programs, thanks to their own initiative and will.

Currently in Venezuela, according to Palmar, because Venezuela's indigenous groups themselves are undergoing a process of education regarding intercultural bilingual education; they are experimenting with various aspects of such programs, including language and language arts, culture, identity, cosmology, geography, math, science, music, dance, ecology and environment, health and medicine, and Spanish. Given the extent of experimentation, the novelty of the concept of bilingual intercultural education, and the limitations of training and technical support, a concrete educational curriculum has yet to be developed for any indigenous group. Developing uniquely tailored curricula is a long process, as Palmar's work and examples illustrate. It involves sustained efforts with each individual community, and must be informed from the ground up. Given that the goal of educational reform is to achieve a "democratic curriculum," one that is fundamentally designed by and tailored to meet the needs and desires of each community, the process entails dialogue at the local level, as well as between community members and experts such as Palmar, and back and forth at every stage.

Educational leaders at the national level face distinct challenges when working with multiple indigenous groups to promote and facilitate the construction of culturally specific bilingual intercultural curricula. As we noted above, many groups, especially smaller ones, do not have systematic orthographies. Larger nations, such as the Wayuu, may have orthographies as well as an emerging set of educational professionals who are trained (or are training) to think about pedagogy. Many smaller groups, in contrast, are just beginning discussions about what and how their children should learn in school. A further complication is that larger groups, such as the Wayuu, are extremely heterogeneous: some Wayuu communities are urban, others are rural; some are bilingual, others are monolingual; some Wayuu economies are primarily pastoral, others depend on fishing, while others deal in commerce. Each of these diverse Wayuu communities have specific needs and demands. This makes the development of "a Wayuu curriculum" particularly challenging. Regardless of differences between communities, Palmar notes that for bilingual intercultural education to work, teachers must embrace the "art" of intercultural pedagogy; this entails appreciating and building upon their communities' local knowledge as the basis for a general education.

According to Palmar, a landmark stage in the process of curriculum development is the production of what are known in Venezuela as a "Pedagogical Guides," "Manuals," or "Cultural Guides" for specific communities. These are large volumes, about 1.5 inches (4 centimeters) thick, that provide information about each indigenous group's language, culture, location, geography, economy, and so forth. As of June 2006, six pedagogical guides had been completed, one each for Warao, Yekuana, Chaima, Warekena, Joti, and Kariña people. Notably, these are groups that have standardized orthographies. The Wayuu guide is still in progress.[63] Groups that do not yet have guides are working in piecemeal fashion, discussing orthography and standardization, for example. Some are developing reading cards or encyclopedias for first and second grades. Thus, as of yet, discussion of formalizing "an indigenous curriculum" would be premature.

Yaletsü Saascjom Woumain (The National Anthem of the Bolivarian Republic of Venezuela in Wayuunaiki)

Nourishing a seed that had been planted during her years teaching in Puerto Aléramo when, as part of a group of teachers, she and other teachers "dared" to translate the national anthem for school children to sing at the city's municipal bicentennial anniversary, as an administrator in both the Zulia Educational Zone and in the national Ministry of Education, Palmar continued to develop an official Wayuu version of the national anthem. In addition to the group of teachers at Puerto Aléramo mentioned above, a number of other Wayuu had been experimenting with translation since the 1950s. In fact, by 2005 there were fourteen different Wayuunaiki versions of the national anthem. Some were incomplete, and many were full of errors. None was definitive or officially recognized. One of Flor Palmar's primary missions during her employ within the Ministry of Education in 2006–2007 was to produce a definitive version of the entire national anthem so that Wayuu people could sing and assert their unique identity as members of the Venezuelan nation-state. Speaking of the significance of this, Palmar asserts:

> For my people it is very important to have a Wayuunaiki translation of the national anthem. This song is sung at the beginning of each school day; it is also used to mark the opening of various official activities that take place in our communities. Singing the national anthem in Wayuunaiki forms part of a pedagogical strategy to familiarize students with bilingual translations, to strengthen their identity and resist ethnic shame. Singing the national anthem in Wayuunaiki is also a way to strengthen our native language as part of daily practice.

To accomplish this, Palmar endeavored to contact the individuals who had attempted the existing translations. She reached the authors of twelve of the fourteen translated versions that she was aware of and asked each to sing her their work. "Most sang out of the rhythm. The words didn't fit." But these different versions offered a place to start.

As general coordinator of this project, Palmar first convened an open meeting for discussion and consideration of proposals. Some two hundred individuals attended. She then devoted two months to meetings with groups of teachers and convening round tables. She asked each group to come up with and submit its preferred version. Palmar then assembled a team of ten experts[64] consisting of seven Wayuu and three non-Wayuu and including a musician, linguist, and historian. For each proposed version, these experts considered lyrics, poetics, semantics,[65] and how different phraseology fit with the anthem's rhythmic structures. "We looked for synonyms for each word, considering which would best fit into the musical and literary/poetic structures."

When the final version of the national anthem in Wayuunaiki was released on July 21, 2006, it garnered a great deal of media publicity. The leading news daily in Maracaibo, *Panorama*, did a special feature and published the entire text in Wayuunaiki. This project was the first state-level effort to translate the national anthem into an indigenous language. Many Wayuu celebrate this accomplishment and take pride in the national anthem in Wayuunaiki, especially on occasions when it is sung to dignitaries, as it was on October 12, 2006, when President Hugo Chávez visited the Guajira to celebrate what in Venezuela is called "National Indigenous Resistance Day" (Día de la Resistencia Indígena, or, as it is known elsewhere, "Columbus

Figure 11.4. Wayuu children singing the national anthem in Wayuunaiki. Photo courtesy of David Hernández Palmar, 2011.

Day"). Furthermore, this project has inspired other indigenous groups to do the same. For example, as part of their broader project to rescue their language and culture, the neighboring Añu, who no longer speak their language, are building on the Wayuu project to translate the national anthem into Añu. Other groups, such as the Warao, are also following this inspiration.[66]

At the end of 2007, for a complex set of personal reasons having to do with the arduous commute between Maracaibo, where her family remained, and the nation's capital of Caracas, Palmar resigned from her high-level position in the Ministry of Education. Her resignation does not mean that she resigned from the struggle to implement bilingual intercultural education in Venezuela, nor does it signify her rejection to participate in state projects. On the contrary, Palmar currently works to advance bilingual intercultural programs at all levels of the educational spectrum, from promoting programs within state-sponsored Bolivarian early childhood education centers, known in Venezuela as "Simóncitos," to consulting for the Bolivarian University in Maracaibo.[67] She also recently served as an advisor on the new Federal Law for Intercultural Bilingual Education, which was approved by the National Assembly on May 21, 2012.

As a consultant to developing the master of arts curriculum in intercultural bilingual education at the state-run Simón Rodriguez Experimental University, Palmar sought to promote the value and importance of traditional knowledge in bilingual intercultural education. She advocates for professional recognition of traditional forms of indigenous knowledge, including indigenous vocations and trades. She lobbies administrators, teachers, and policy makers to implement policy and accreditation programs that will certify indigenous elders to teach Wayuu students Wayuunaiki as well as history, artistry, health and healing, law and mediation, and other forms of traditional knowledge, including vocations such as herding and fisheries management. Palmar asserts that those who practice traditional arts or vocations, or provide culturally recognized services such as healing or mediating, deserve full professional recognition. These professionals should be able to earn licenses that entitle them to the same social security and other economic benefits that are enjoyed by other Venezuelan professionals and skilled workers, such as plumbers and electricians. For Palmar, accreditation programs in state schools are one path toward ending social and professional discrimination, as is the organization of indigenous educators, a project she has undertaken more recently.

Conclusion

Flor Palmar has dedicated her life to promoting and advancing bilingual intercultural education in Venezuela by working within, outside of, against, and alongside official structures. At every step of her career she has adapted to contemporary social and political realities while developing creative pedagogical and political strategies to advance the cause of bilingual intercultural education. Like many of her indigenous compatriots, Palmar has been agitating and organizing on behalf of indigenous rights and education in Venezuela over the last thirty-five years. Her educational and professional trajectory demonstrates that the project of developing bilingual intercultural education in Venezuela is a long-term, dialogic, and emergent process.

Palmar does not feel, as some of the activists noted in García's chapter in this volume suggest, that her work within the national educational system has "co-opted" her energy and efforts or prevented her from advancing the goals she aspires to achieve. She feels assured that, with the new 1999 constitution, the rights of Venezuela's indigenous peoples to education with culturally and linguistically specific curricula are legally guaranteed. She is optimistic that these rights will continue to become a reality. While holding fast to the ideals of bilingual intercultural education, Palmar is also a realist. She recognizes, and indeed her professional trajectory demonstrates, that to be effective, indigenous educational leaders must be flexible. They must engage in dialogue, develop creative strategies, take multiple approaches, adapt to new circumstances and possibilities, and work both within and outside of state and national administrations, depending on where they feel their efforts will have greatest impact.

Flor Palmar's life's work, her "art," illustrates clearly that committed indigenous educators are often political activists and, in fact, that they often have few alternatives to becoming engaged in various forms of political activism. Palmar's educational and activist repertoire has included innovative pedagogical and creative civic actions, from developing homemade laminated workbooks and incorporating expressive practices into her classroom, to developing community infrastructure as part of building schools, to occupying the governor's office and translating the national anthem into Wayuunaiki so that all Wayuu, from school children to elders, can sing it to signal and affirm Wayuu identity within the Venezuelan nation-state. Working both against and within state and national administrative institutions, Palmar's life and career underscore that dedication, creativity, and often a healthy dose of activism are required of indigenous teachers to be able to bring about the positive changes they desire in individual lives, schools, communities, and the nation.

Notes

1. Although Flor Palmar was born in the Alta Guajira, Colombia, her official documents indicate that she is from Malimai, Venezuela. This is where she was registered after her parents moved south to the Venezuelan part of the Guajira Peninsula.

2. Emiliano completed primary school at the "Internado de Nazareth" (Nazareth Boarding School).

3. De Certeau's notion of "tactics" emphasizes specific strategies employed in expressing resistance. See Michel de Certeau, *Practice of Everyday Life*.

4. Prior to the national census of 2001 (XIII Censo General de Poblacifon y Vivienda), the Venezuelan state recognized thirty-four distinct indigenous groups. The 2001 Census identified seven additional indigenous groups, bringing the total number of indigenous groups in Venezuela to forty-one and the total indigenous population to 536,863, or 2.3 percent of the nation's total population (see Vicariato Apostolico de Machiques, http://servidor-opsu.tach.ula.ve/alum/pd_4/vica_a_m/html/indive.html). A number of these newly identified groups were peoples who, because of discrimination, had not previously openly disclosed their indigenous identities. Venezuela's 1999 multicultural constitution validates cultural difference and many individuals and groups who previously hid their indigenous identity to avoid discrimination are now asserting or reclaiming it. According to the most recent census of 2011, Venezuela's indigenous population further increased to 725,141. For 2011 census data, see http://www.ine.es/inebmenu/mnu_cifraspob.htm; for indigenous figures specifically, see http://www.ine.gov.ve/documentos/Demografia/CensodePoblacionyVivienda/pdf/PrimerosResultadosIndigena.pdf.

5. Equipo Técnico Académico de la Universidad Nacional Experimental Simón Rodríguez, Programa de Post-Grado, Area: Maestría en Educación Intercultural Bilingüe.

6. Noeli Pocaterra, a Wayuu woman who is one of three indigenous representatives to the National Assembly, President of the Permanent Commission of Indigenous People, and Coordinator of the National Council of Indigenous Peoples of Venezuela, has been a leading figure in regional, national, and international movements for indigenous rights. For more on Pocaterra's leadership, see Sara Jamieson, "Female Initiation Rituals among Urban Wayuu in Hugo Chávez's Multicultural Venezuelan Republic"; Natasha Blanchet-Cohen, "A Portrait of Noeli: A Defender of La Guajira," 38.

7. "Intercultural bilingual education" is the term used in Venezuela, and elsewhere in Latin America (see García, chapter 9, this volume, and *Making Indigenous Citizens: Identities, Education, and Multicultural Development in Peru*; also Nancy Postero, *Now We Are Citizens: Indigenous Politics in Postmulticultural Bolivia*, for multicultural curricula that are provided in native languages. Conforming to local usage, we use this term in this chapter. In Venezuela, bilingual intercultural education is to be developed in collaboration with representatives from indigenous communities, based on traditional forms of knowledge and education for each indigenous group, and designed to complement the national curriculum according to the specific sociocultural and linguistic contexts of each indigenous community. According to the 2009 Organic Law of Education, intercultural bilingual education is obligatory and inalienable in all educational centers located in regions with indigenous populations, from pre-school through secondary education, including secondary technical schools. Intercultural bilingual education is governed by a specific law. In addition to Articles 9 and 121 of the Constitution of the Bolivarian Republic of Venezuela and the Organic Law of Indigenous Peoples and Communities (Ley Organica de Pueblos e Comunidades Indígenas, LOPCI) other legislative instruments guarantee intercultural education for indigenous peoples. Among them are the Organic Law for the Protection of Children and Adolescents (Ley Organica de Proteccion de Niños, Niñas, e Adolescentes, La LOPINA), the Law of Indigenous Languages of LOPINA (Ley de Idiomas Indígenas La LOPINA), and the Organic Law of Education. Bilingual intercultural education is an educational model grounded in the culture, values, norms, languages, traditions, and realities of each indigenous community, with administrative structures specific to individual communities, including curricular design, calendar, pedagogical materials, and teachers who specialize in bilingual intercultural education. This model acknowledges the scientific, technological, and humanistic contributions of each group and integrates those contributions with the cultural heritage of the Venezuelan nation and of humanity. Generally instruction is given exclusively in the native language until third grade, when instruction in Spanish begins. In some cases, where a majority of students are bilingual or speak only Spanish, Spanish is the medium of instruction beginning in first grade.

8. With support from a Fulbright Foundation Lecture-Research Fellowship to the Universidad de los Andes in Mérida, anthropologist Laura Graham carried out ethnographic work among Wayuu during 2006 and worked closely with Flor Palmar's family. She greatly appreciates the support of the extended Palmar Barroso family who embraced her and her study and friends in Maracaibo and Yaguasirú, as well as students and colleagues, especially Nelly Velasquez and José Vila Lobos, at the Universidad de los Andes (ULA) in Mérida, Venezuela. Graham extends special thanks to Lilette and the late Roberto Lizaraldi for their hospitality and stimulating discussions about Venezuela's indigenous peoples. She is grateful to Brian Klopotek, Elizabeth Martinez, Sara Jamieson, and T. M. Scruggs, who read and provided helpful comments on earlier drafts of this chapter, and especially to Brenda Child for encouraging and inspiring her to write about Flor Palmar and her work with indigenous education in Venezuela. Graham also thanks

Charles Briggs for conversations about scholarship on indigenous education in Venezuela. She gives special thanks to David Hernández Palmar for transcribing interviews, for finding photographs, and for the indispensable role he played in mediating the translation of the final text; he graciously answered innumerable questions and is a steadfast friend. Above all, Graham thanks Flor Palmar for her generosity, friendship, and professional collaboration.

Flor Palmar gives thanks to her Wayuu people and is thankful for being part of the Wayuu nation. She also thanks her parents, Emiliano and Emelina, for nurturing her with Wayuu and human values. In addition Palmar is grateful to many friends and advisors who have offered their support and contributions to her work and study. She thanks her children, especially David Hernández Palmar, for his tireless support with transcriptions, translations, and images for this chapter. Additionally, Flor Palmar gives thanks to life (*gracias a la vida*) for meeting Laura Graham, for the learning and opportunities she provided, and for the experiences Palmar shared with Graham's family. She appreciates Graham's humility, her willingness to engage in intercultural exchange, and a friendship that transcends all social, political, and cultural barriers.

9. Ruth Behar, *Translated Woman: Crossing the Border with Esperanza's Story*.

10. Steven Feld describes the interaction he had with Kaluli interlocutors when he read and received their comments on his published book as "dialogic editing." See Steven Feld, "Postscript, 1989," 239–268. For Bakhtin all texts and speech are dialogic and multivocal; see Mikhail Mikha lovich Bakhtin, "Discourse in the Novel," in *The Dialogic Imagination: Four Essays*, 259–422.

11. John Haviland describes the debate of language between the Spanish Crown and the Catholic church, "El problema de la educación bilingüe en el área Tzotzil," 150–151.

12. See Guillermo Bonfil Batalla, *México profundo: Una civilización negada*, 134–135; in *Converting Words: Maya in the Age of the Cross*, Hanks teases out the complexities of the missionaries' endeavor to "systematize" Mayan languages through the creation of "Maya reducido" as well as how Mayans used new language forms for their own ends.

13. See Villalón, *Educación para indígenas en Venezuela: una crítica razonada*.

14. The Spanish verb *reducir* (to reduce) here translates to "organize." For an excellent discussion of Spanish efforts to "reduce"—systematize or organize—language as well as other aspects of indigenous society and culture among Mayans in the Yucatan region, see William Hanks's *Converting Words: Maya in the Age of the Cross*.

15. See Jamieson, "Female Initiation Rituals among Urban Wayuu in Hugo Chávez's Multicultural Venezuelan Republic," 78.

16. See Carmen Laura Paz, "Las políticas indigenistas en el marco del nuevo Ideal Nacional (1953–1958)," 365–390, also Jamieson, 78.

17. See Adrián Setién Peña, *Realidad indígena venezolana*, 29.

18. At the national level, the Department for Indigenous Affairs (Dirección de Asuntos Indígenas) was made responsible for attending to indigenous peoples. At the regional level, this fell to the Regional Office for Indigenous Affairs (Oficina Regional de Asuntos Indígenas, ORAI).

19. Esteban Emilio Mosonyi coordinated the team of linguists that developed the Alphabet of Indigenous Languages of Venezuela (ALIV). This writing system is also used in Colombia.

20. Ministry of Education Resolution 83, passed by the Department of Indigenous Affairs of the Ministry of Education and signed on March 15, 1982, authorizes the use of indigenous languages for each indigenous group in intercultural education institutions. For discussion, see Zaida Perez Gonzalez, "Reseña de 'Manual de lenguas indígenas de Venezuela' de Esteban Emiliano Mosonyi y Jorge C. Mosonyi," 124–127; also Dirección de Asuntos Indígenas, "Régimen de educacíon intercultural bilingüe: Diagnósticos e propuestas, 1998–2008," Ministerio de Educación,

Caracas; and the Dirección de Asuntos Indígenas report, "Informe final de la comisión de diagnóstico del Decreto 283 Educación Intercultural Bilingüe." For further discussion of indigenous education in Venezuela, see, for example, Quispe and Moreno, "La educacíon intercultural bilingüe en un contexto de transformación social," 118–127; Ministerio de Educación Superior, "Educacíon superior indígena en Venezuela: Una aproximación"; and Ricardo Colmenares Olívar, n.d. http://www.iidh.ed.cr/comunidades/diversidades/docs/div_enlinea/el%20derecho%20a%20 %20la%20%20propia%20cultura.htm.

21. Wayuu have also been called Guajiro by non-Wayuu; they prefer to be called by their own name, "Wayuu."

22. The most recent national censuses identify the Wayuu population at 293,777 in Venezuela (La Oficina Central de Estadística e Informática 2001) and 144,003 in Colombia (DNP-INCORA 1997, http://www.ine.gob.ve/fichastecnicas/censo/censoindigena.htm).

23. To view 2011 census results for Venezuela's indigenous population, see http://www.ine .gov.ve/documentos/Demografia/CensodePoblacionyVivienda/pdf/PrimerosResultadosIndigena.pdf.

24. Jamieson, 27.

25. Jamieson, 28.

26. Approximately two thousand indigenous students are currently attending LUZ, and the majority are Wayuu (Alí Fernandez, personal communication).

27. The Chávez government implemented various programs designed to deliver social services (medical care, housing, education) directly to underserved populations. These are discussed in Steve Ellner, *Rethinking Venezuelan Politics: Class, Conflict, and the Chávez Phenomenon*, and Gregory Wilpert, *Changing Venezuela by Taking Power: The History and Policies of the Chávez Government*. Several were directly relevant to indigenous peoples: Misión Robinson, a secondary equivalency program, Misión Ribas, a secondary and high school equivalency program implemented in poor neighborhoods, and Misión Guaicaipuro, created in 2003, to provide services directly to benefit indigenous peoples, such as restoring land titles, protecting indigenous lands from resource speculation, and to preserve the human rights of indigenous communities. Misión Cultura, established in 2005, promotes cultural identity and community integration through a university-level teaching degree specializing in Venezuelan culture and diversity. See Jamieson, 18, for further discussion of this program.

28. The other major lowland South American language families are Carib, Tupi-Guarani, and Gê. For further discussion of scholarly reconstructions of Proto-Maipuran/Arawakan speakers' movements see José R. Oliver, 487–499. For further scholarly information on Wayuunaiki, see Richard Mansen and David Captain, "El idioma wayúu (o guajiro)," 795–810, and Richard Mansen, *Aprendamos guajiro: Gramática pedagógica de guajiro*; see also Jean-Guy Goulet and Miguel Angel Jusayu, *El idioma guajiro; sus fonemas, su ortografía, su morfología*.

29. José R. Oliver, "The Archaeological, Linguistic, and Ethnohistorical Evidence for the Expansion of Arawakan into Northwestern Venezuela and Northeastern Colombia," 488; also Jamieson, 25.

30. Remedios Fájardo Gomez, "The Systematic Violation of the Human Rights of the Indigenous People, Black People, and Campesinos by the Coal Mining Multinationals in the Department of La Guajira, Colombia," 16–28.

31. Wayuu is a matrilineal society. Thus Palmar and her siblings belong to their mother's clan, Iipuana. Wayuu clans, which are made up of multiple matrilineages, are each associated with a totemic animal and, historically, with specific geographic areas. They are now large, diffuse, and lack corporate functions. For further discussion, see Jamieson, 430. Matrilineages are exogamous,

meaning that individuals must marry "outside," preferably to someone belonging to one of the approximately thirty other Wayuu clans. Palmar's four children, like those of her sisters, are also Iipuana while her brothers' children are members of their wife's matriline. Like many contemporary Wayuu, one of Palmar's sisters married an *alijuna*, or non-Wayuu, and her sons are all Iipuana. In cases where a Wayuu man marries an *alijuna* woman, his children have no matrilineal or clan identity or membership. Many individuals in this category consider themselves, and are considered by others, to be Wayuu. In Venezuela or Colombia, as elsewhere in Latin America, there is no such thing as a blood quantum measurement that is used as an official metric for determining an individual's membership or exclusion from indigenous tribes. For further discussion of Wayuu social organization see, for example, Lawrence Craig Watson,"Marriage and Sexual Adjustment in Guajiro Society."

32. Maria Barbara Watson-Franke, "To Learn for Tommorrow: Enculturation of Girls and Its Social Importance among the Guajiro of Venezuela," 203.

33. Olga Mejía Mendoza, *Conceptos de la sexualidad wayúu: Espresados en los mitos, leyendas, y tradiciones*; see also Jamieson.

34. Wayuu anthropologist Weildler Guerra Curvelo has written extensively about Wayuu customary law and *puitchipü,* known in Spanish as *"palavreros"* (men of words), who are legal experts, in *La disputa y la palabra: La ley en la sociedad wayúu.*

35. Emiliano Palmar completed primary school at the "Internado de Nazareth" (Nazareth Boarding School), which celebrated its one hundredth anniversary in July 2011.

36. A number of scholars discuss Wayuu migration patterns, for example, Jamieson, 26; Lawrence Craig Watson, *Guajiro Personality and Urbanization*; also Nemesio Montiel Fernández, *Movimiento Indígena en Venezuela.*

37. This is an approximate figure calculated from the city's estimated Wayuu population of 100,000 and Maracaibo's total population of 1,891,800 from the 2001 census. See http://www .citypopulation.de/Venezuela.html#Stadt_gross. Readers should consider this figure and the total Wayuu population in Maracaibo to be general estimates, given that Wayuu population in Maracaibo is highly fluid. As has been mentioned, people come and go for healthcare, to attend school, and to visit relatives. Wayuu are highly mobile both in the Guajira and in and out of Maracaibo.

38. In recent years, poor Colombian immigrants fleeing violence and seeking opportunities in Venezuela have gravitated to Wayuu neighborhoods in Maracaibo.

39. Before moving to Yaguasirú, the family moved to Malimai (Venezuela, "place of the toothless people"), which was better for the animals. From Malimai, the Palmar Barroso family moved to Yaguasirú.

40. "Criolla" is the term used to denote Venezuela's mixed heritage, which combines peoples of indigenous, African, and European descent.

41. Palmar notes that even before she started school, her father had taught her some Spanish, but this language was never used in the home before the children were exposed to it in school.

42. Within the Venezuelan state, the Ministry of Justice was the organ responsible for indigenous peoples, including indigenous education, until the mid-1960s. At the national level the responsible department was the General Department for Indigenous Affairs (Dirección General de Asuntos Indígenas), which was terminated in 2007. It was replaced, in 2007, by the General Department of Intercultural Bilingual Education (Dirección General de Educación Intercultural Bilingue); at the regional level the Regional Department for Indigenous Affairs (Regional de Asuntos Indígena, ORAI), which was also terminated in 2007, was directly responsible.

43. For example, see K. Tsianina Lomawaina, *They Called It Prairie Light: The Story of Chilocco Indian School*; Child, *Boarding School Seasons: American Indian Families, 1900–1940*.

44. Martha Hildebrandt, *Diccionario Guajiro-Español*.

45. Palmar was also offered a scholarship to study in the state of Tachira, much farther from home than Maracaibo and in a mountainous area. Fearing that she would be cold in the mountains, her father discouraged her from going there.

46. Jamieson, 39.

47. Sara Jamieson makes this observation, 53–54.

48. The school started in a shed that had been used for tanning leather. It was in the middle of the savannah, exposed to the elements. "When the wind blew, your face got full of dust and sand. We would all come back after class full of sand. We had a little room where we would go when the dust blew and we would all get inside.... When it rained it became a clay pit. In the summer the wind would blow. We would have to run out when the wind blew, cover the desks until it passed, because we had desks there. After a year's time they covered all that up and set up the school. It [the school] doesn't exist anymore."

49. Palmar taught forty-five students in a classroom that was literally a chicken coop. Despite the many challenges and students with serious problems, she had some rewarding experiences. For example, she taught one third-grade boy, Rixio, to read during recess in three months.

50. Nemesio Montiel Fernández observes that Wayuu in Maracaibo have been active as community organizers since the early 1940s and mobilized some of the nation's first indigenous movements. Wayuu formed the Junta Indígena de Mutuo Auxilio (Indigenous Committee of Mutual Support) in response to their forced removal from several Maracaibo neighborhoods in the early 1940s during a period of rapid urban expansion (Montiel Fernández, *Movimiento indígena en Venezuela*, 20). As a result of Wayuu mobilization, in 1944 the national government authorized the construction of the Ziruma neighborhood on the northern margins of the city; see also Jamieson, 9–10.

51. Bilingual intercultural education is the term used in Latin America for bilingual multicultural curricula, see María Elena García, chapter 9, this volume, and *Making Indigenous Citizens: Identities, Education, and Multicultural Development in Peru*; also Aurolyn Luykx 1999; Nancy Postero 2007.

52. See note 3: seven additional indigenous groups were identified after the 2001 Census; until then, Venezuela recognized thirty-four distinct indigenous groups.

53. Two of the five indigenous groups in Zulia state had experimental schools (Wayuu and Yukpa); there were no bilingual schools for the Bari, the Añu, or the Japreria.

54. Laura Graham discusses the "symbolic power" of language and its uses by indigenous spokespersons for political purposes in "How Should an Indian Speak? Brazilian Indians and the Symbolic Politics of Language Choice in the International Public Sphere," 181–228. Conklin discusses indigenous uses of other forms of bodily decoration in identity politics in "Body Paint, Feathers, and VCR's: Aesthetics and Authenticity in Amazonian Activism."

55. These chorus lyrics are from the version that was officially recognized on July 21, 2006, not what was actually sung in Paraguaipoa.

56. The Law referred to is the new 1810 constitution of the First Republic, newly independent from Spain.

57. In addition to Wayuu from the Guajira, many poor Colombians immigrated to Maracaibo seeking refuge from that nation's violence and economic hardship.

58. Palmar used Mothers' Day as a rhetorical device to play to politicians' awareness of their

constituents' desperate needs and public relations sensibilities. The mayor used this opportunity to hold a public relations event at the school for the entire neighborhood: mobile medical and dental offices were brought to the school and provided services free of charge; the governor's office subsidized prices at adjacent stores so that staple goods were available at reduced prices.

59. It is important to point out that elaboration of educational projects for indigenous people and the processes of curricular construction for bilingual intercultural education are considered to be strategic and indispensable elements for building Venezuela's new educational system.

60. Ministerio del Poder Popular para el Despacho de la Presidencia, 2000, see Hugo Chávez, Corazón de mi patria, http://www.chavez.org.ve/temas/noticias/se-le-dara-continuidad-al-primer-plan-socialista-nacion/; see also Wilpert 2007, http://www.reclaimthemedia.org/communications _rights/chavez_to_nationalize_venezuelan_telecommunications_energy_industries.

61. Wayuu were in no way unique; disagreements over orthography are common in the development of indigenous writing. Among indigenous groups throughout Venezuela, there were differences over criteria for defining an alphabet. This was especially true among communities where alphabets have been imposed, by New Tribes missionaries or the Capuchins. In Zulia state, there were some disagreements among Yukpa and Bari, as well as Wayuu.

62. All government ministries in Venezuela are titled "Ministry for the Popular Power for..." ("Ministerio del Poder Popular para...").

63. Various sections are being compiled in different Wayuu communities and this will represent the great diversity among Wayuu people. Wayuu already have substantial materials such as workbooks and books, whereas many other groups have fewer resources.

64. Members of this expert team included Modesto Horias (poet/literary scholar), José Pepo Alvarez (linguist), Luis Beltrán (linguist), and Dora Palmar (educator).

65. Palmar recalls that some lyrics were interpreted in ways that were humorous. For example, one individual suggested that the first line, "Gloria bravo pueblo" (Glorious brave people), should be translated as "Glorious angry people" to signal the anger and hostility of the European conquerors. This interpretation stems from the fact that the Spanish "bravo" has two meanings: 1) brave; 2) angry. Another line of the anthem calls for the Venezuelan people to "cast off their neck chains," pointing to colonial experience of Spain's oppression. One Wayuu lyric interpreted this line in the Wayuu context of the prized golden or coral necklaces that Wayuu women wear to signal wealth. This proposed translation read, "Cast off your golden necklaces."

66. For example, see "Himno de la República Bolivariana de Venezuela en Warao." http://www.youtube.com/watch?v=715ylT7bTrE.

67. The Chávez government has inaugurated a new system of public universities throughout the nation known as Bolivarian universities. These are specifically designed to make higher education more accessible to previously underserved populations.

12 The Boarding School as Metaphor

Brenda J. Child

For many in our society, the role of parenting was halted by boarding schools. Our great-grandparents were prevented from being parents. Both my grandmother and my grandfather were sent away. Then their kids were brought up in a regimented, abusive system of boarding schools. What that system has done to our grandparents, our parents, and then to us and our children is put holes in the fabric of our society.—Ingrid Washinawatok—El Issa

Over the years, thousands of Native children have learned the message that is implicit in boarding school education: that Native people are children of the devil who are condemned by God. This sense of worthlessness, of evil, of unlovability because they were Native was turned inward, internalized, becoming the root for some of the profound dysfunction later in life.
 —Diane Wilson, from Beloved Child: A Dakota Way of Life

They are something tangible—mnemonic benchmarks—that, as with sites of Australian Aboriginal mytho-geography, one can point to and say "it happened there." A visit to the school can provide a trigger or cue that takes one back to the past almost as if there again—a redemptive pilgrimage to an Aboriginal Auschwitz. Perhaps is it all a bit too easy.—Michael G. Kenny

The boarding school experience remains a burning historical memory for American Indian people in the United States. This despite the fact that most federal Indian boarding schools closed in the 1930s, or had by then adopted policies that rejected assimilation and were more in tune with contemporary ideas about race and progressive education. While scholarly studies have espoused resistance and resilience in the historical record of students who survived an assimilationist education, boarding school is increasingly conceptualized by many American Indians as a uniquely Native usable past that links tribal people of diverse backgrounds today to a devastating common history, one that must be evoked, many argue, to understand our present conditions and social problems. Boarding school is now the ancestor in a direct genealogical line of terrible offspring—alcohol abuse, family and sexual violence, and other social dysfunction.

It is not necessarily the job of the historian to explain how Indian people today remember the past. But the intensity with which Indian people in the present day explain and respond to the role of boarding school in the broader history of their families and communities suggests that for many, boarding school is also a useful and extraordinarily powerful metaphor for colonialism. Perhaps, like the Trail of Tears or Wounded Knee, the boarding school as an institution is symbolic of American colonialism at its most genocidal. Boarding schools did, after all, align federal authority with the zealotry of religious missions, and suppress Indian cultures in an English-only way while opening the door to alienation from land and the extension of everyday Anglo-American culture into the lives and souls of Indian people. Not to mention the important fact that for the boarding school system to become established, it depended on those in power at the national and local level, sometimes police, to abduct and remove children from their parents, ostensibly rendering them powerless. The introduction of boarding schools coincided with the end of the Indian Wars, and the most famous school, Carlisle, was a former military establishment. The extraordinary part of the boarding story emerges because Indians, even children, refused to act powerless.

Scholars including me have been fascinated by the complexity of Indian people's experiences with boarding school, examples of which range from the Flandreau graduate who reminisced about his school as "my Shangri-la" to countless others who were tolerant of school, without forgetting that many students suffered—whether from loneliness, extreme prejudice, violence, or even death. As key players in the boarding school narrative, Indian people offered no single prevailing opinion, nor did they share a universal experience. At times, the views and actions they express in historical documents or recollections contradict our deepest assumptions about an education for assimilation. Case in point—federal archives reveal government officials fielded an astonishing number of requests from children and families seeking enrollment in boarding school. Moreover, it was not unusual for Indian families to effusively praise teachers and superintendents, or to spill over with pride when a child graduated from Haskell or Flandreau, while a fair number of other parents challenged boarding school policies or felt a desperate alienation from the people and schools that educated their children.

During the course of my research in the Bureau of Indian Affairs records in the National Archives for a book titled *Boarding School Seasons: American Indian Families, 1900–1940*, I became a witness to my own people's perseverance, particularly the young, impressionable, and vulnerable students, as they were besieged by assimilation on all fronts. My book was inspired by the life of my grandmother, an Ojibwe woman from the Red Lake Reservation in Minnesota who attended boarding school during her girlhood in the 1920s, and returned home afterward to re-embrace her culture, language, and community. She and other students, most of whom I encountered in documents and letters, made it impossible to view this history as one of simple victimization. In the end, what impressed me most about the boarding school story was *the strength of Ojibwe family and community life*, a deep and abiding commitment to children, demonstrated time and time again by parents and others at home, that outlasted and outmaneuvered a failed educational idea.[1]

It is worth examining how Indian people remember the history of boarding school, perceptions of which have no doubt changed over time. I have been influenced by my grandmother's observations about school as well as other elders from my community, who shared with me memories of youthful friendships and the drama of a time passed within a fusion of tribal backgrounds. For my generation, we heard stories from our grandparents and other relatives who lived the experience of assimilation—how they worked as maids and farm laborers, ran away from boarding school, and were sometimes rebellious. These stories were popular among Indians, and are the most prevalent memory of boarding school passed down by families. The expanding body of literature on the history of Indian education in the United States, beginning with Tsianina Lomawaima's *They Called It Prairie Light: The Story of Chilocco Indian School*, David Wallace Adams's *Education for Extinction: American Indians and the Boarding School Experience*, my own *Boarding School Seasons*, and other scholarly works and memoirs, has depicted the history of Indian education as far more multifaceted and untidy than a simple story of federal policy and assimilationist practice. The focal point of these studies is foremost the resistant and resilient Indian students who attended federal boarding schools run by the US government during the assimilation years, not the separately organized mission schools.[2]

Great differences as well as profound parallels exist between the residential school histories of Canada and the boarding schools of the United States, both created out of a colonial desire for indigenous assimilation and lands. Complementing work by American scholars, Canadian Ojibwe writer Basil Johnston has left a significant mark on the literature about the history of Indian education for his insistence on representing the survival humor of students at his Ontario residential school run by Jesuits in the 1930s, while narrating a broader strategy of resistance on the part of students and their families.[3] Canadian residential schools outlasted their US counterparts, declining but not disappearing in the late 1950s, and were at their core a component of Canadian religious organizations, to the detriment of several generations of First Nations children and youth who were silenced and abused within their walls.[4] As a consequence, Canadian residential school history is remembered more intensely today by First Nations peoples, where the concept of "residential school syndrome" is a recognized malady of some former students, and the Assembly of First Nations has referred to residential schools as "total institutions."[5]

In Canada, a national dialogue on residential school history emerged, led by charges of abuse from former students, while in the United States it remains a distant and relatively unknown chapter for non-Indians. The Canadian government approved the Indian Residential Schools Settlement Agreement in 2006, the largest class action arrangement in that nation's history. The settlement initiated a process for former students to apply for a modest financial compensation for each year of school attendance, with extra provisions for those victimized by physical or sexual abuse. Additionally, the agreement set up a Truth and Reconciliation Commission to address the legacy of the residential school system in Canada. In 2008, the Canadian Prime Minister issued an unprecedented formal apology on behalf of the government, which included a statement publicly saying the "legacy of Indian Residential Schools has contributed to social problems that continue to exist in many communities today."[6] Yet, some First Nations people believe the measures do not go far enough, and one outspoken former (non-Native) United church minister has maintained that thousands of Native children died or disappeared at residential schools across Canada, and that an investigation of crimes against humanity is necessary to comprehend and address what must be labeled an aboriginal holocaust.[7]

Boarding schools in the United States and Canada originated in the same colonial project, one that espoused extending Christianity, private property, and incorporation into the nation, at a time when indigenous land holdings and resources were still viewed as ripe for plunder. Canadian residential schools farmed out education to Roman Catholic, Anglican, Presbyterian, and United church organizations, a practice that ended in the United States with the establishment of the first government-run boarding school in 1879, the Carlisle Indian Industrial School in Pennsylvania. Fifty years later, the impoverishment and dispossession of American Indians was complete, and it was no longer necessary to maintain Indians in separate and segregated government boarding schools. As a consequence, American progressive educators found little resistance to their idea for Indian integration into public schools. This emphasis on public school education for Indians during the 1930s is why historians (though not necessarily American Indians) see an end to the boarding school era, though demand for the schools by impoverished American Indians was high throughout the Great Depression.

In the United States, some American Indians remember the government boarding school era as lasting decades longer than it actually did, perhaps failing to differentiate between US and Canadian indigenous history, or including assorted mission schools privately operated by churches, who continued to spread their faith among Indian students. Or are they making a very reasonable suggestion: that assimilation lasted longer as a practice than as policy? Even American Indian educators and professionals in fields including social work seem to have made the assumption that later Indian schools had the same policies as their nineteenth-century predecessors, which they did not. The proportionally small number of children who continued in Indian boarding schools or mission schools throughout the second half of the twentieth century was born after an era when assimilation dominated federal policy making toward Indians. Maria Yellow Horse Brave Heart, a professor of social work in the United States, has worked to address issues of historical trauma and unresolved grief for American Indians today, viewing their experiences as much like those of survivors of the Jewish Holocaust. Unlike historians, she extends the boarding school era from "1879 through the 1970s," when "federal policy included the forced removal of Lakota children from home and their abusive institutional treatment."[8] For those who work in the field of social work and not history, it may be constructive when helping clients who suffer unresolved grief to have a more straightforward explanation for the complexities of the colonial past, and so the boarding school is a usable metaphor that crosses eras and tribal differences.

Social work and education were the first fields to indentify boarding school as the primary explanation for social dysfunction and adverse conditions on reservations and communities, and educators and specialists in human service fields now repeat the idea that boarding schools disrupted indigenous child rearing so permanently that "institutionalized behavior resulted" and "young people grew into adults who did not know how to parent children."[9] Psychologist Joseph Gone has observed the trend of "increasingly attributing the mental health problems of American Indians to *historical trauma*" as "an alternative to established psychiatric disorders" by health care providers and clinicians. Gone notes that American Indian historical trauma "has been described as the collective, cumulative, and intergenerational psychosocial disability resulting from massive group-based oppression, such as forced relocation, political subjugation, cultural domination, and genocide," yet he questions the lack of nuance within the historical trauma construct, while acknowledging the very real problem of "enduring mental health disparities" in the American Indian population.[10]

The historical trauma construct has gained a wide following. Writer Diane Wilson, in finely written and tender biographical essays of contemporary Dakota people, also singles out boarding school as a defining experience to explain the presence of "historical trauma that is a consequence of our unacknowledged history." Like Yellow Horse Brave Heart, she oversimplifies by melding mission and government boarding schools histories, along with fosterage and adoption, to position a long chronology of child removal based on the beginning of compulsory attendance laws established for Native children in 1891, stating, "This policy remained in place until 1978."[11] Also like Yellow Horse Brave Heart, she disregards critical evidence that the majority of American Indians integrated public schools fairly early in the twentieth century. For Wilson, boarding school is a usable past that still speaks to Indian people today, who must learn and remember the experiences of their parents and grandparents, so that the consequences of this history are not passed down as a terrible legacy to future generations in the form of "suicide, alcoholism, depression, and poverty."[12]

The generation who experienced schooling during the peak years of assimilation policies in the United States, the late nineteenth and early twentieth centuries, has now passed away. Public school education surpassed boarding schools as the foundation of US Indian education in the 1930s, and the smaller number of boarding schools that remained primarily existed to offset the poverty of Indian families during the Great Depression, when Indian demand for the schools was so widespread that the 1930s became the decade of highest enrollment. American Indians suffered greatly through hard times and extraordinary deprivation during the Depression, only weathering these years with great difficulty. There is not a strong historical memory of the notion that Indian people themselves repeatedly sought out government boarding schools as a strategy of family preservation, except among the generation who lived through the Great Depression.

The memoir of Ojibwe artist George Morrison, born in Chippewa City along the north shore of Lake Superior, represents the changing role of boarding school for American Indian families during the Great Depression. For Morrison and two brothers, the Hayward Indian School in Wisconsin was a place of refuge against extreme poverty during the early Depression years, and when Hayward closed in 1933, most students transferred into local public schools. Morrison entered Hayward at the age of nine, and later wrote of his experience.

The Hayward, Wisconsin, Indian school helped people with big families. It was available to a lot of poorer families during the Depression. Things got hard for us, especially during the Depression. I remember eating plain rice, or rice and potatoes together. Sometimes those old staples were the only things around. Now, my brother Mike and I kid about pork grease and potatoes....

There were maybe fifty to seventy-five boys and the same number of girls, on opposite sides of the campus. There was a central dining room; the meals were adequate. It gave us a good place to eat.

When September came, the school provided transportation, either with a government car or by paying the bus fare for a group of young children. We stayed at the school during the whole nine-month period, and we never did see our parents.

That's an awfully long time. I guess my parents were too poor to come—they didn't have a car and they couldn't pay to travel by bus. They never came to see us. As I recall, we accepted it, we kept busy with the activities, school, and playing. We were in it, so we weren't lonesome.

The Morrisons' family story is not unlike the experience of many Indian families during the Great Depression, forced to make practical decisions for the well-being of their children, which may have included boarding school. Reflecting on the place of boarding schools in American Indian life, Morrison was well aware of their reputation, saying, "I've heard stories of the teachers in certain schools being very cruel to Indians," though his own experience during the Depression reflected Washington's changing policies away from assimilation in the 1930s. Indigenous languages were no longer stifled, and teachers were not callous to students, Morrison remembered: "Many of the kids probably spoke Indian. The school didn't repress it or stop it the way I've heard was done in some schools," and "as I recall, the teachers at Hayward were fairly decent. They all got along with the students and were liked by the students, too. It was all right."[13]

Teachers at the school supported Morrison's emerging talent, as he remembered, "I was always chosen to do posters and things like that." Fewer numbers of American Indians attended boarding school after the Great Depression, and the institutions evolved from their nineteenth-century origins. In this later era of Indian education during the 1930s and 1940s, the superintendent of the Flandreau Indian Boarding School was so highly regarded by students and the local Dakota community that they adopted him into their tribe.[14] Forced attendance was a thing of the past, but students in the schools continued to miss their families at home, undergo conflicts with teachers, and run away. Their memories of school are not so unlike those of children who lived in institutions like orphanages. The Minnesota Ojibwe writer Jim Northrup attended Pipestone in the postwar years, and remembered beatings by both teachers and other Indian students. Is what he suffered, and other Indian students institutionalized in those years suffered, simply racism, bullying, and lonesomeness, rather than the forced acculturation experienced by the early generations of Carlisle or Haskell students?

Another Ojibwe memoir, Peter Razor's remarkable *While the Locust Slept*, about life in a Minnesota state orphanage in the 1930s, is an indicting commentary on the violence of his institution, where he remembered all non-white students were mistreated. Razor spent his childhood in the orphanage from the age of seventeen months, finally leaving in 1944, the year before it closed. The state orphanage was a sterile and cruel environment for child rearing, and Razor was more than once beaten to unconsciousness by an employee.[15] For both Razor and Northrup, dormitory life at the orphanage and the boarding school was often unbearable and lacked the warmth and security of a home, and students suffered. Night times were particularly miserable for young children, and Northrup spoke of waves of weeping that would begin "at one end of the dormitory and come traveling down until the boy in the next bed was crying and I was sobbing too." He eventually ran away from school simply because he missed his mother, though he was found and returned to Pipestone, where he "toughed it out" and "survived."

It is little wonder that Indian people explain and rationalize the existence of social problems in their communities as a legacy of boarding schools. The suggestion that students in schools were left without Indian parental role models while being exposed to violence and cultural repression is a compelling explanation for contemporary social ills so at odds with Indian values. Yet, parents and families refused to allow government boarding schools to supplant their essential roles in child rearing, which, along with student resistance, put limits on the assimilative intentions of the institution. I worry that to suggest otherwise considerably underestimates American Indian families, and the historical record is unambiguous in the way it demonstrates how they also shaped and defined the boarding school era.

What do we make today of boarding school narratives that might be described as happy? Letters written by Indian people decidedly show there were those who supported education, with many on the reservations eager to attend an Indian boarding school. Even during the height of the assimilation campaign in 1913, George White Bull, a fifth grader from Porcupine, South Dakota, had heard so many positive things about Flandreau from other Lakota children, he impatiently waited for word that he could also enroll, making plans to join the school band. Boarding school letters and oral histories indicate there were countless students who not only survived, but flourished and emerged satisfied.

Or what of parents who willingly sent their children away? Were those who spoke out in favor of education or heartily approved of boarding school education for their children naïve and uninformed, or persuaded by the promises of assimilation? In today's jargon, were they colonized minds? What was the Oneida mother thinking as she wrote to the school's administrators with heartfelt gratitude in 1924, terribly disappointed she would miss her daughter's graduation from Flandreau?

> I am very thankful to you people for all good you have taught my daughter while she was in school and that she is a graduate girl now. I am proud of her. I am sorry I can't be there on the Graduating exercise oh I would like to have been there. When will you send the Oneidas home?[16]

Narratives of boarding school life include students who found happiness or refuge in the schools, while clearly others were abused and suffered—and so we have learned that there is a wide-ranging continuum of Indian experiences. As Philip Deloria has suggested, Indian people do unexpected things in unexpected places. Indian people in American history continually made the best out of socially ambiguous situations, and it does not mean Indians in the boarding school era sacrificed their identity and ideals as they incorporated Western education into their own or their children's lives.[17]

Scholars, especially American Indian scholars, must try to make sense of that surprising continuum, and search for historical context for the decisions that students and parents made, to show how Indian people actively shaped the boarding school era. Learning of happy students and satisfied parents—Indians who liked boarding school—can be mystifying, even troubling to Indian people today. Teaching a course on the history of Indian education at the University of Minnesota a few years back, two terrific Indian students in the class set out to interview Dakota elders and their eighty-nine-year-old former teacher, Father Stan of the Grey Cloud Mission, a Benedictine school near Sisseton, South Dakota. One student was the granddaughter of a Grey Cloud Mission female alumna who had played on the basketball team at school, and she was initially puzzled by the reflections of her grandmother and the elders they interviewed at Sisseton. They were not expecting to find elders so strongly identified with the mission school or with such fond memories of Father Stan. How do we remember the legacy of all of these boarding and even mission schools, if this legacy also included well-adjusted and thankful alumni and families?

For Indians, our historical memory of the boarding school era is clouded—confused and impaired by terrible losses for our families, communities, and cultures—the disruptive processes of settler colonialism. The years after 1879 were a time when Indian people moved to reservations and witnessed the environmental destruction of land and resources in the post-allotment mayhem. Treaty rights were abused at the local level as states intruded on tribal sovereignty, and in federally issued orders, Indians contended with religious discrimination and the suppression of their spiritual practices and other traditions. Even with the decline of assimilation, problems continued unabated, especially economic hardship on reservations. The Great Depression was a catastrophe for Indian people already coping with poverty, insidious diseases like tuberculosis, and new social ills. Cultural practices collapsed under the weight of Christianity, and migrations to towns and cities had a significant impact on Native language retention and other social formations. Perhaps most disturbing, these problems appeared to be permanent. Is the boarding school era so clouded by overlapping categories of colonialism, hardship, trauma, and drastic change that it is unfeasible for Indian people to begin to sort it all out? History is so deliberately confusing we may lean on the ready explanation, especially when one defining memory is endorsed by so many Indian people.

Is there still opportunity to narrate another sort of boarding school story, an alternative to what has become a vastly oversimplified history? A man from my reservation, Alex Everwind, went away to government boarding school in the early years of the twentieth century. He was the child of a stable and solid Ojibwe family, and remembered being indulged as a child growing up in Ponemah as the only boy with two sisters. Sadly, Everwind's older sister became sick and died before he went to boarding school. There were several students from Ponemah at Carlisle, and Everwind first thought of attending school in the east. Instead, he was sent to the Tomah Boarding School in Wisconsin as a teenager. In the fall of 1914, he left for Tomah with a friend, Russell Wind, who very soon became sick and died. Everwind stayed on, and worked hard in the school's boiler house half the day, shoveling coal and cleaning out ashes, but years later he shared no memories of mistreatment, simply recalling the vocational prospects at school. In four years, Everwind only came home from school twice, once in the early spring of 1918, when his younger sister, Eliza, died. Everwind never forgot the day a telegraph arrived at Tomah with this unbearably sad news. Decades later, he would recall in detail his subsequent journey home by train and somber arrival on the reservation, and finding the familiar landscape of Red Lake still frozen.

> I walked. I walked this lake on foot, on snow. That evening when I got off at Redby, I didn't have no supper and I walked right straight across [the lake to Ponemah] and I landed down here about a mile on the east here. Then my aunt was living here. I got off there and then she grabbed me and says, "I hear you come home." I says, "Yes." And I asked her, "How's my folks?" She says, "They're all right. I don't think they knew you were coming," she says. "You will kinda surprise them when you come in." So, she gave me a little bread and what she had, and a little meat that she had and fed me. I had to walk about half a mile, I guess. Folks jumped up when I got there,

so I kinda surprised them. Well, you know what they told me? They says, "Well, we lost your sister." I says, "That's what they told me."[18]

Everwind's devastated parents spoke about his sister's courageous demeanor on her deathbed, the story of which they related in detail when he returned to Ponemah from boarding school. Even as an older man, Everwind remembered and still cherished Eliza's last words, "Ma, don't cry for me, when I gone, don't cry. I'll be all right. I'm going to have a good time when I leave here." Eliza said the same thing to her father, "Don't cry. Just go ahead and bury me and I'll go and have a good time. Don't be sad because I am leaving." Everwind said, "And then she turned and died, that was the last breath she took."

The year of his sister Eliza's death, Everwind completed the program at Tomah and decided to go on for further vocational training at the Wahpeton School in North Dakota. He arrived at Wahpeton in the fall, just as the flu epidemic of 1918 grew deadly and was breaking out in the government school, and hundreds of students were violently ill. Everwind made the best of his situation and ran the boiler house and power at Wahpeton while the student body recovered, a time when every available hand was needed. His attitude about the flu was, "If I'm going to get it, I'm going to get it anyway," though fortunately, said Everwind, "I never got it." In his short life, Everwind had experienced firsthand too much death, even before witnessing young people dying in the flu epidemic of 1918. When he related this story as an older man, he spoke firmly of going away to boarding school as his own decision. Everwind never complained once about learning English or his time at school, but the vivid, some might say traumatic, memories of his boarding school years were permanently imprinted on his life. Alex Everwind was highly respected in our community, and even as a young man was asked to travel as part of the Red Lake 1919 delegation to Washington, DC, and in later years he worked as a tribal judge. His boarding school narrative is at first glance an ordinary story about one young Ojibwe man and his family's internal struggles, but its greater significance may possibly be what it expresses about the human suffering that complicated and further destabilized Ojibwe and other Indian communities in these same years, when grief was a relentless presence.

Is the boarding school experience overly remembered? Is it remembered at the expense of other significant events, tragedies, and practices of settler colonialism that also dramatically shaped American Indian peoples' lives? Sadly, my tribe's history has many examples of colonial intrusion, violence, and death before and after the establishment of government boarding schools. During the first years of the organization of new political entities in Ojibwe

Country—Wisconsin and Minnesota—12 percent of Lake Superior Ojibwe people died in an event sometimes called the "Sandy Lake Tragedy," though today it should be appropriately identified as ethnic cleansing. Minnesota Territorial authorities trapped Ojibwe people hundreds of miles from home in winter with the promise of annuity payments, leading to six weeks of starvation when food and annuities failed to arrive. This was an immediately devastating population loss, but also an episode with profound psychological and economic consequences for the next generation of Ojibwe people. These same events coincided with an era of treaty agreements that resulted in large portions of our homeland being opened to new settlers.

When the United States passed the General Allotment Act of 1887 calling for individual property ownership on reservations, a collection of circumstances opened the floodgates to land loss for Ojibwe and other American Indians. Reservations including White Earth were plundered for land and resources by timber companies and their allies in business and politics during the boarding school and allotment era. Along with these challenges, Ojibwe living in states including the newly established Wisconsin and Minnesota were systematically harassed for over a century by citizens and local law authorities when they exercised treaty rights by hunting, fishing, and gathering in their homelands. One Lake Superior leader, Joe White or Gishkitawag, was clubbed and murdered by a game warden and deputy in Washburn County, Wisconsin, in December 1894, after shooting a deer out of season, and a local all-white jury found the two men innocent of all charges the following year. Ojibwes were frequently the victims of local law authorities bent on Indian harassment and expulsion during this era, and in one notorious 1902 case the Mille Lacs County Sheriff forced Ojibwes off their lands near Isle, Minnesota, marched the band members to a public highway, and set their houses on fire. Many devastating episodes in Ojibwe history paralleled the boarding school era.

Our problems and tribulations as Indian people did not end with the decline of government boarding schools. My public talks about the history of education present many opportunities for people to remember and to tell their own stories. I have conducted workshops with Ojibwe elders from the US and Canada, in addition to my regular work with college students. After I concluded a presentation on a college campus about boarding school history, an Ojibwe woman in the audience commented that her mother had been forcibly sterilized in a reservation border town in Minnesota. At first glance, boarding school history and the more recent history of forced sterilization of Indian women, which has been documented as a practice of the Indian Health Service in the 1960s and 1970s, are not necessarily intertwined, unless viewed as part of a broader pattern of colonial violence.[19] Clearly, this

Ojibwe woman found a strong association between boarding school and forced sterilization, since both were practices implicated in this kind of state interference into Indian family life, especially in relation to the bearing or rearing of children.

After many years of listening to Indian people respond in discussions about boarding school and interpret that legacy for their own families and communities, I am beginning to understand how insightfully Indian people use boarding school as a metaphor. When Indian people talk about boarding school, they are not always exclusively referring to the education for assimilation designed for them by colonizing nations. They tell other stories. At times, they express discontent, frustration, or horror with a broader colonial experience. This broader experience may comprise personal exploitation or the state interference into family life, as in forced sterilization of women, or a more widespread exploitation of tribal land or resources, in addition to misguided educational efforts. Does all state interference into family life—forced sterilization or placing Indian children in white foster homes—resonate as boarding school? Is this why tribal elders can simultaneously have fond memories of Father Stan and support their local mission school's activities, yet view boarding schools as the reason for epidemic social problems in their communities today?

Has boarding school become an adaptable metaphor Indian people in the United States use to describe and encapsulate many different forms of colonialism and historical oppression? To recap and remember all the negative experiences is simply unfeasible in day to day life, and boarding school may be the one encounter that is most allegorical of the deeper inequality of power that characterized the relationship between Indians and the United States government. Surely, boarding school is easier to name than the duplicitously layered assimilation campaign that unfolded in the late nineteenth and early twentieth century US, which manipulated federal and state policy to get at Indian lands and resources, while stomping on tribal political and cultural sovereignty. Indian history is never uncomplicated or simple, and boarding school might be the best metaphor for the vast chain reaction of events that worked against the well-being of American Indian families, communities, and nations.

A Canadian scholar has observed that perhaps one-third of Native Canadians attended residential schools, and yet the discourse about colonialism and violence seems focused on residential school history in recent years.[20] Similarly, not all Indian people in the United States attended government boarding school during the assimilation years, just as in Canada the majority of students attended day schools on reservations. In my community at Red Lake, also about one-third of the reservation population had spent time at one of the schools when a survey was conducted in the 1930s. Many of the non–federally recognized Indian tribes in the US were never compelled to send their children to boarding schools. Yet today, boarding school is the institution singled out and remembered for the decline of Native languages and other traditions.

My mother, Florence Auginash Child, attended a public school on the Red Lake Reservation during the 1940s and 1950s that was located only five miles from her home. Just as today, her generation of rural children was bused to school. On school days she was immersed in English. For her, the bus represented a transitional passage between home and school, where children still spoke Ojibwe. Once at school, she spoke English until the bus ride home at the end of the day, when students resumed speaking the Ojibwe language. Eugene Stillday, a Navy veteran of the Korean War, also from Red Lake, described punishment for children like him and my mother, who were caught speaking Ojibwe at the reservation public school. Public school education, on reservations and off, was as much an agent of language transformation as boarding school.

Every family affected by boarding school has their own story. I am the granddaughter of Ojibwe people who were sent to Carlisle and Flandreau during the prime years of cultural assimilation. Fortunately for us, Carlisle and Flandreau have never been defining chapters in our larger family narrative, which is far more deeply intertwined with the cultural life and Ojibwe landscape of northern Minnesota. We do still remember our great-grandfather as a Carlisle athlete, one who played professional football in later years with Jim Thorpe. He returned to his small village on the reservation to marry and raise a family. He sent his own daughter, my grandmother Jeanette Auginash, to the Flandreau boarding school. In our family she was a beloved figure, and we all knew how critically important the Ojibwe language was to her. Even though the Ojibwe man she married did not speak English, for her, a bilingual boarding school graduate, speaking Ojibwe with her children was a conscious decision. She raised her own children, including my mother, to always speak the Ojibwe language at home, even though she was well aware it would not be part of their school days. My own research into the history of boarding school education, which began with her, taught me about my own family and community's history, but also about the larger narrative of the persistence of Indian people and their ways of life.

When I was researching in the archives one day, I came across a powerful story of Ojibwe people from the small village at Ponemah on Red Lake who forcefully resisted the introduction of a new school in their midst in 1900. We have many relatives from Ponemah, and I like to think that some of them participated in these events. This community's determined and swift reaction to the establishment of a reservation boarding school in their midst, known as the Crosslake Boarding School, was shocking to government authorities at the time. On July 11, 1900, the government overseer stationed on the Red Lake Reservation telegraphed an alarming message to his supervisor, William Mercer, Acting Indian Agent and Captain in the 7th Cavalry, who was stationed about seventy miles away at the Leech Lake Agency. The sparse telegram read, "Come at once, serious outlook ahead."

> The school site is located on the south shore of the peninsula which extends westward from the main land and nearly divides upper and lower Red Lake. This peninsula, as may be seen from a glance at the map of Red Lake Reservation, is quite an extensive bit of territory, and is isolated from the rest of the reservation, and is occupied by a band of unprogressive, pagan Indians, who desire nothing more than to be separated, both from the other Indians and from the white people. They have never had any discipline and never recognized any authority, refuse to sign all treaties and to take payments, have declared they would never permit schools, missionary buildings, or the advent of improvements of any kind on what they consider their territory, which is the peninsula described above.[21]

Workmen had recently arrived in the Ojibwe village "*on what they consider their territory*" to begin the construction of a new on-reservation government boarding school. The agent in charge warily described the independent spirit of Ponemah residents, "*their refusal to recognize any authority*," and the position of sovereignty from which they countered this colonial intrusion. When Ponemah residents took a stand, an armed stand, against the establishment of a new school, they defended their right to control the education of their own children on their own homeland—a determination they had never once considered was not theirs to make. US government officials interpreted their intervention as a rebellion. After a great deal of dialogue with the people of Ponemah and concessions from US representatives, the school was eventually built.

I continue to be inspired by all forms of rebellion—the students in boarding school who would not bend to the will of administrators and the scores of resilient parents who insisted on remaining parents, staying in touch with their children who lived hundreds of miles from home. We as Indian people, who share a common experience with colonial education, must also remember the resistance of our ancestors that came in the form of tribal communities actively refusing to go along with Western education, including the Hopi men imprisoned at Alcatraz or the Iowa tribe of northeastern Kansas who harbored boarding school runaways from Haskell. Most Indian people, like the villagers at Ponemah, eventually sent their children to boarding schools or public schools, or allowed for schools in their communities, and often *did so on their own terms.* Differences will continue to exist between how scholars write about boarding school history and how American Indian people remember that experience, which is a tension between history and memory.

It makes sense to implicate boarding schools. Boarding school has become the most tangible symbol of the widespread turmoil that sprang from the allotment and assimilation era; for some indigenous people boarding school may be the "mnemonic benchmark," or even an "aboriginal Auschwitz." Native people today are overwhelmed by the array of social problems in their urban and reservation communities—alcoholism, unemployment, low test scores, high drop-out rates, and family violence. In their own family lineages, they recognize how these problems are attended by cultural losses such as the decline of speaking Native languages and indigenous spiritual practices. Indian people understand that the reasons social problems disproportionately appear in our communities reside somewhere in our troubled historical experiences with American settler colonialism, which devoured our land and resources with the greed of a Windigo.[22] Until a better day, boarding school is with us.

Boarding school history, like all of American Indian history, is also about agency, resistance, survival, and the sometimes heroic actions of people both young and adult who had lost significant freedoms. Without that, as Basil Johnston suggests, there is no story. As a historian and an Ojibwe person, I am dedicated to learning more about the multiple experiences and diverse perspectives of indigenous people throughout the history of Indian education in the United States. I also know that boarding school is not the only window from which to view our colonial past or present. Scholars tell us that history and memory are both part of a changing landscape—that historians and all the rest of us can be selective about how we remember, even though historians have the privilege of publishing books. For many important reasons, some that historians might find to agree or disagree, the boarding school era continues to hold great meaning for Indian people today. Boarding school history offers a plausible explanation for how and why colonialism has been destructive to American Indian community life, with the resulting losses to tradition and especially to the Native languages of North America.

On a visit to central Michigan recently, I drove past the campus of the former Mount Pleasant Indian School, which had educated the children of dispossessed and impoverished Ojibwe, Ottawa, and Potawatomi people for fifty years before closing in 1933. Today the school is a state historic landmark and, as luck would have it, the style of architecture is described as "Colonial Revival." The campus was built on land confiscated from the Ojibwe and unsympathetically sited directly over their traditional burial grounds. The shade trees that one superintendent, in 1902, remarked on the planting of now tower along the perimeter of boarded brick buildings. Just across town, the Saginaw Chippewa Tribe operates a beautiful new cultural center and museum that interprets the history of the boarding school, in addition to their very successful casino and hotel. Asked to tell something of his experience at the Mount Pleasant School, a former student recollected in one exhibit, "If it wasn't for this school, I would've starved to death," and so the contradictions that make up the history of Indian boarding schools persist. If boarding school is the best way Indian people have to sum up the complexities of colonial encounters, surely the architecture of boarding school is also our best monument to the history of colonial cruelty and dispossession, but one with the power to educate us about Indian survival, both past and present.

Notes

Epigraphs: Ingrid Washinawatok-El Issa, *Women of the Native Struggle: Portraits and Testimony of Native American Women*, 48; Diane Wilson, *Beloved Child: A Dakota Way of Life*, 133; Michael G. Kenny, "A Place for Memory: The Interface between Individual and Collective History," 436.

1. Brenda J. Child, *Boarding School Seasons: American Indian Families, 1900–1940*.

2. David Wallace Adams, *Education for Extinction: American Indians and the Boarding School Experience, 1875–1928*; K. Tsianina Lomawaima, *They Called It Prairie Light: The Story of Chilocco Indian School*.

3. Basil Johnston, *Indian School Days*.

4. Exposing residential school violence and pedophile rings has been a significant part of the testimony of former students. See Celia Haig-Brown, *Resistance and Renewal: Surviving the Indian Residential School*; Milloy, *"A National Crime": The Canadian Government and the Residential School System, 1879 to 1986*.

5. See "Breaking the Silence: An Interpretive Study of Residential School Impact and Healing as Illustrated by the Stories of First Nation Individuals."

6. See Paulette Regan, *Unsettling the Settler Within: Indian Residential Schools, Truth Telling, and Reconciliation in Canada*.

7. Kevin Annett has authored two books, produced a documentary film, *Unrepentant: Kevin Annett and Canada's Genocide*, and hosts a radio show to publicize his claims of mass child murders in postwar Canadian residential schools.

8. Maria Yellow Horse Brave Heart-Jordan has numerous articles dealing with historical trauma, including M. Y. H. Brave Heart-Jordan and Lemyra DeBruyn, "So She May Walk in Balance: Integrating the Impact of Historical Trauma in the Treatment of Native American Indian Women," 345–368; M. Y. H. Brave Heart-Jordan and Lemyra DeBruyn, "The American Indian Holocaust: Healing Historical Unresolved Grief"; Brave Heart-Jordan, "Gender Differences in the Historical Trauma Response among the Lakota," 1–21; Brave Heart-Jordan, "The Historical Trauma Response among Natives and Its Relationship with Substance Abuse: A Lakota Illustration," 7–13.

9. Thomas Peacock and Marlene Wisuri, *Ojibwe Waasa Inaabidaa: We Look in All Directions*, 81.

10. Joseph P. Gone, "Reconsidering American Indian Historical Trauma: Lessons from an Early Gros Ventre War Narrative."

11. Wilson, *Beloved Child: A Dakota Way of Life*, 35.

12. Wilson, 6.

13. George Morrison as told to Margot Fortunato Galt, *Turning the Feather Around: My Life in Art*, 37–38.

14. The superintendent was Bryon Brophy; see Child, *Boarding School Seasons: American Indian Families, 1900–1940*.

15. Peter Razor, *While the Locust Slept: A Memoir*.

16. Bureau of Indian Affairs, Record Group 75, Records of the Flandreau Indian School, Parent Letter, 1924.

17. Philip Deloria, *Indians in Unexpected Places*.

18. Everwind was interviewed at Red Lake and his record is part of the Doris Duke Oral History Collection. A copy of his transcript is in the Red Lake Tribal Archives.

19. A classic review essay is Rayna Green, "Native American Women"; see also Jane Lawrence, "The Indian Health Service and the Sterilization of Native American Women."

20. Paulette Regan, *Unsettling the Settler Within: Indian Residential Schools, Truth Telling, and Reconciliation in Canada*.

21. Bureau of Indian Affairs, Record Group 75, Records of the Leech Lake Agency, The Crosslake Boarding School, July 1900.

22. In Ojibwe traditions of storytelling the Windigo is a cannibal, and used to symbolize insatiability and greed.

About the Contributors

William J. Bauer Jr. is an associate professor in the Department of History at the University of Nevada–Las Vegas. He earned his PhD in history at the University of Oklahoma and has written extensively on California Indian history. His first book, *"We Were All Like Migrant Workers Here": Work, Community, and Memory on California's Round Valley Reservation, 1850–1941* (2009), examined the ways in which Native people from the Round Valley Reservation used migrant labor to maintain a sense of community in late nineteenth- and early twentieth-century California. He is currently writing a book that uses California Indian oral traditions to tell and interpret California history. Bauer was born on the Round Valley Reservation where he is a citizen.

John Borrows is a professor and Robina Chair in Law and Society at the University of Minnesota Law School. He earned the BA, MA, JD, LLM (Toronto), PhD (Osgoode Hall Law School), and FRSC. His publications include *Recovering Canada: The Resurgence of Indigenous Law* (Donald Smiley Award for best book in Canadian Political Science, 2002), *Canada's Indigenous Constitution* (Canadian Law and Society Best Book Award, 2011), and *Drawing Out Law: A Spirit's Guide*. Borrows is a recipient of the Aboriginal Achievement Award in Law and Justice; a fellow of the Trudeau Foundation; and a fellow of the Academy of Arts, Humanities, and Sciences of Canada (RSC), Canada's highest academic honor. He also received the honorary Indigenous Peoples Counsel (IPC) designation from the Indigenous Bar Association for his service to indigenous communities around the world. He is Anishinaabe and a member of the Chippewa of the Nawash First Nation in Ontario, Canada.

M. Bianet Castellanos is an associate professor in the Department of American Studies at the University of Minnesota. She received her PhD in anthropology from the University of Michigan. Her book *A Return to Servitude: Maya Migration and the Tourist Trade in Cancún* (2010) examines the role indigenous communities have played in tourism development and nation-building projects. Her co-edited volume with Lourdes Gutiérrez Nájera and Arturo Aldama, *Comparative Indigeneities of the Américas: Toward a Hemispheric Approach* (2012), analyzes indigenous experiences across the Américas to promote a broader understanding of the relationships between Native and mestiza/o (mixed race) peoples in the hemisphere. Her current projects focus on indigenous struggles for property rights in Cancún and efforts to build communities of sentiment in Southern California.

Brenda J. Child is an associate professor in the Department of American Studies at the University of Minnesota. She received her PhD in history at the University of Iowa and was a Katrin Lamon Fellow at SAR. Her first book, *Boarding School Seasons: American Indian Families, 1900–1940* (1998), won the North American Indian Prose Award. Her scholarship focuses on gender and labor among the American Indian people of the Great Lakes and the history of indigenous education. She is the author of *Holding Our World Together: Ojibwe Women and the Survival of Community* (2012). Her work in public history includes service on the boards of the Minnesota Historical Society and the National Museum of the American Indian at the Smithsonian; and membership in a research group that developed a new digital humanities project, the Ojibwe People's Dictionary. At the University of Minnesota, she was a recipient of the President's Award for Outstanding Community Engagement. Child was born on the Red Lake Ojibwe Reservation in northern Minnesota where she is a citizen.

María Elena García is an associate professor in the Comparative History of Ideas and the Jackson School of International Studies at the University of Washington. She received her PhD in anthropology at Brown University and has been a Mellon Fellow at Wesleyan University and Tufts University. Her first book, *Making Indigenous Citizens: Identities, Development, and Multicultural Activism in Peru* (2005), examines indigenous politics and multicultural activism in Peru. Her work on indigeneity and interspecies politics in the Andes has appeared in multiple edited volumes and journals such as *Anthropology Now*, *Anthropological Quarterly*, *International Journal of Bilingual Education and Bilingualism*, *Journal of Latin American and Caribbean Anthropology*, *Latin American Perspectives*, and *Latin American and Caribbean Ethnic Studies*. Her second book project, *Cuy Politics*, explores the cultural politics of guinea pig lives and deaths in Andean communities, breeding farms, laboratories, and markets.

Noelani Goodyear-Ka'ōpua is an associate professor of indigenous and Hawaiian politics in the Department of Political Science at the University of Hawai'i at Mānoa. Noelani is a Kanaka 'Ōiwi who was born and raised in Hawai'i. The ethics and practices of aloha āina guide her academic and community work, as she seeks to document, analyze, and proliferate the ways people are transforming imperial and settler colonial relations through indigenous political values and initiatives. For example, her research has focused on the politics of designing and implementing indigenous culture– and land–based educational initiatives within and against settler state structures. Her book *The Seeds We Planted: Portraits of a Native Hawaiian Charter School* (2013) discusses some of these tensions and the ways educators and students navigate them. Noelani also teaches and writes about indigenous social movements, participatory and activist research methods, and Hawaiian sovereignty. Her second book, *Ea: Hawaiian Movements for Life, Land and Sovereignty* (forthcoming), is a collection co-edited with Ikaika Hussey and Kahunawai Wright that explores late twentieth and early twenty-first century Hawaiian organizing for justice and self-determination.

Laura R. Graham is an associate professor of anthropology at the University of Iowa. Her research focuses on politics of indigenous language and representation, concentrating on indigenous peoples of lowland South America, specifically Xavante of central Brazil and Wayuu of Venezuela and Colombia. She is executive producer and co-director with David Hernández Palmar (Wayuu) and Caimi Waiassé (Xavante) of the film *Owners of the Water: Conflict and Collaboration over Rivers* (2009). Her book *Performing Dreams: Discourses of Immortality Among the Xavante Indians of Central Brazil* (1995) won the Chicago Folklore Prize (1996), the Hans Rosenhaupt Memorial Book Award (1997), and Honorable Mention in the Victor Turner Prize for ethnographic writing (1996).

Roy M. Huhndorf has long been a prominent leader in Native issues in Alaska and nationally. He served for twenty-one years as president and CEO of Cook Inlet Region, Inc., one of the regional corporations established under the 1971 Alaska Native Land Claims Settlement Act, and he is a former co-chair of the Alaska Federation of Natives. He was instrumental in the establishment of the Alaska Native Justice Center, the Alaska Native Heritage Center, Koahnic Broadcast Corporation, and the CIRI Foundation. He has also served on the Board of Regents of the Smithsonian Institution and the Board of Directors of the Institute for American Indian Arts. He holds an honorary doctorate of law from the University of Alaska. Now retired, he remains active in Native political and social causes in Alaska.

Shari M. Huhndorf received her PhD in comparative literature from New York University, and she is currently a professor of Native American Studies and Comparative Ethnic Studies at UC Berkeley. She is the author of two books, *Going Native: Indians in the American Cultural Imagination* (2001) and *Mapping the Americas: The Transnational Politics of Contemporary Native Culture* (2009); and co-editor of *Indigenous Women and Feminism: Politics, Activism, Culture* (2010), winner of the Canadian Women's Studies Association prize for Outstanding Scholarship. Currently she is working on a manuscript tentatively entitled "Indigeneity and the Politics of Space: Gender, Geography, Culture." She served for a decade on the board of directors of the CIRI Foundation, which supports educational and cultural endeavors for Alaska Natives in her home community.

Brian Klopotek is an associate professor in the Department of Ethnic Studies at the University of Oregon. He received his PhD in American studies at the University of Minnesota in 2004, winning the Gabriel Prize from the American Studies Association for his dissertation on federal recognition of Indian tribes in Louisiana. His first book, *Recognition Odysseys: Race, Indigeneity, and Federal Recognition Policy in Three Louisiana Indian Communities* (2011), explores the ways Native Louisianans have responded to various conceptions of race and indigeneity in culture and policy over the past one hundred and fifty years. He is currently an NEH residential fellow at the Huntington Library in San Marino, California, where he is conducting research on the Choctaw-Apache Tribe's history for a book on constructions of Indians and Mexicans in the United States and Mexico. Klopotek is a Choctaw with roots in Sabine Parish, Louisiana.

K. Tsianina Lomawaima (Muskogee) is a professor of American Indian Studies at the University of Arizona. Her research sprang from an interest in Native peoples' experiences in federal Indian boarding schools, work which appeared in *They Called It Prairie Light: The Story of Chilocco Indian School* (1994). Twenty years of research and teaching about the history of American Indian education led to *"To Remain an Indian": Lessons for Democracy from a Century of Native American Education* (2006). Her current research focuses on how notions of American Indian citizenship, sovereignty, and economic development have developed from the early twentieth century to the early twenty-first century.

Alyssa Mt. Pleasant is an assistant professor in the American Studies program and the Department of History at Yale University. She received her PhD in history and American Indian studies at Cornell University in 2007. Her scholarship focuses on early modern Haudenosaunee (or Iroquois) history. She is completing a manuscript about the Buffalo Creek Reservation in western New York State that examines the community's development in the midst of the Revolutionary War and considers its place in the social, political, and diplomatic world of Haudenosaunee people and the early American republic. She served as co-chair of the host committee for the 2012 annual meeting of the Native American and Indigenous Studies Association. Mt. Pleasant, who grew up in Syracuse, New York, is Tuscarora on her paternal side.

Flor Ángela Palmar Barroso is Wayuu (Iipuana clan) and a leading indigenous educator in Venezuela. She is among the first group of indigenous Venezuelans to receive a degree in bilingual intercultural education (Aragua State Rural Pedagogical Institute, 1997). She also holds advanced degrees in education administration and supervision (Universidad Nacional Experimental Rafael Maria Baralt, Maracaibo, 2010; Instituto Pedagógico Latinoamericano y Caribeño, Caracas, 2007). Palmar has taught in rural schools in the Wayuu homeland, La Guajira, and in Maracaibo's urban schools, where she founded La Resistencia school in the impoverished neighborhood of 23 de marzo. From 2002 to 2005 she was Regional Coordinator of Bilingual Intercultural Education in the Zulia Educational Zone and from 2005 to 2007 held the position of Academic and Administrative Assistant in the General Directorate of Bilingual Intercultural Education in the Ministry of Education in Caracas. She served as an advisor on the new Federal Law for Intercultural Bilingual Education, consultant for the Bolivarian University in Maracaibo, and as a member of the Technical Academic Team in the Masters Graduate Program in Bilingual Intercultural Education at the National Experimental University Simón Rodriguez in Maracaibo, Venezuela. She currently works as a policy advisor for bilingual intercultural education and cultural patrimony legislation.

References

Abler, Thomas S., and Elisabeth Tooker. "Seneca." In Vol. 15, *Northeast* of *Handbook of North American Indians,* edited by William C. Sturtevant and Bruce G. Trigger, 505–517. Washington, DC: Smithsonian Institution, 1978.

Aboriginal Online Teachings and Resource Centre. FourDirectionsTeachings.com. http://www .fourdirectionsteachings.com, accessed June 10, 2013.

Adams, David Wallace. "Beyond Bleakness: The Brighter Side of Indian Boarding Schools, 1870–1940." In *Boarding School Blues: Revisiting American Indian Educational Experiences,* edited by Clifford E. Trafzer, Jean A. Keller, and Lorene Sisquoc, 35–64. Lincoln: University of Nebraska Press, 2006.

———. *Education for Extinction: American Indians and the Boarding School Experience, 1875–1928.* Lawrence: University Press of Kansas, 1995.

———. "Education in Hues: Red and Black at Hampton Institute, 1878–1893." *The South Atlantic Quarterly* 76, no. 2 (1977): 159–176.

Agreement between the Inuit of the Nunavut Settlement Area and Her Majesty the Queen in Right of Canada, S.C. (1993), c. 29 [Nunavut Land Claims Agreement].

Agroecología Universidad Cochabamba. http://www.agruco.org/, accessed June 10, 2013.

Aguilar Padilla, Héctor. *La educación rural en México.* Mexico: Secretaría de Educación Pública, 1988.

Alaska Native Knowledge Network. *Alaska Native History Timeline.* UAA Institute of Social and Economic Research, University of Alaska Anchorage. http://www.alaskool.org/cgi-bin /java/interactive/timelineframe.html, accessed June 10, 2013.

Albó, Xavier. *Iguales aunque diferentes: Hacia unas políticas interculturales y lingüísticas para Bolivia.* La Paz: CIPCA, 1999.

Albó, Xavier, and Amalia Anaya. *Niños alegres, libres, expresivos: La audacia de la educación intercultural bilingüe en Bolivia.* La Paz: UNICEF, CIPCA, 2003.

Alden, Timothy. *An Account of Sundry Missions Performed among the Senecas and Munsees; in a Series of Letters.* New York: J. Seymour, 1827.

Aleut Story. Directed by Marla Williams. Aleutian Pribilof Heritage Group, 2005. Film.

Allen, Helena G. *The Betrayal of Liliuokalani: Last Queen of Hawaii, 1838–1917*. Honolulu: Mutual Publishing, 1982.

Anaya, James. *Indigenous Peoples in International Law*, 2nd ed. Oxford: Oxford University Press, 2004.

Anders, Gary C. "Theories of Underdevelopment and the American Indian." *Journal of Economic Issues* 14 (September 1980): 681–701.

Anderson, James D. *The Education of Blacks in the South, 1860–1935*. Chapel Hill: University of North Carolina Press, 1988.

Andrews, Thomas. "Turning the Tables on Assimilation: Oglala Lakotas and the Pine Ridge Day Schools, 1889–1920s." *Western Historical Quarterly* 33 (Winter 2002): 407–408.

Annett, Kevin. *Unrepentant: Kevin Annett and Canada's Genocide*. Documentary film. http://www .youtube.com/watch?v=88k2imkGIFA, accessed September 12, 2012.

Archuleta, Margaret L., Brenda J. Child, and K. Tsianina Lomawaima. *Away from Home: American Indian Boarding School Experiences, 1879–2000*. Phoenix, AZ: The Heard Museum, 2000.

Ariès, Philippe. *Centuries of Childhood*. Translated by Robert Baldick. London: Jonathan Cape, 1962.

Armitage, Andrew. *Comparing the Policy of Aboriginal Assimilation: Australia, Canada, and New Zealand*. Vancouver: University of British Columbia Press, 1995.

Armstrong, Samuel Chapman. *The Indian Question*. Hampton, VA: Normal School Steam Press, 1883.

———. *Report of a Trip Made on Behalf of the Indian Rights Association to Some Indian Reservations of the Southwest*. Philadelphia: Indian Rights Association, 1884.

Asch, Michael. "Errors in *Delgamuukw*: An Anthropological Perspective." In *Aboriginal Title in British Columbia: Delgamuukw v. The Queen*, edited by Frank Cassidy. Lantzville, BC: Oolichan Books; Montreal: Institute for Research on Public Policy, 1992.

Aupilaarjuk, Mariano, et al. *Interviewing Inuit Elders: Perspectives on Traditional Law*, vol. 2. Iqaluit: Nunavut Arctic College, 1999.

Austin, John. *Lectures on Jurisprudence or the Philosophy of Positive Law*. St. Clair Shores, MI: Scholarly Press, 1977.

Austin, Raymond D. *Navajo Courts and Navajo Common Law: A Tradition of Tribal Self-Governance*. Minneapolis: University of Minnesota Press, 2009.

Baas Lara, Mario Alberto, Pedro Antonio Sánchez Escobedo, and Francisco Rafael Mena Chiu. "Papel de los albergues escolares en el desempeño escolar del niño de la zona rural de Yucatán." *Educacion y Ciencia* 4, no. 7 (2000): 23–35.

Baca, Lawrence R. "*Meyers v. Board of Education*: The *Brown v. Board* of Indian Country." *University of Illinois Law Review* 5 (2005): 1155–1180.

Bacon, David. "Rev. David Bacon's Visits to Buffalo, in 1800 and 1801." *Buffalo Historical Society Publications* 6 (1903): 183–186.

Baker, Paul R. "Richard Morris Hunt: An Introduction." In *The Architecture of Richard Morris Hunt*, edited by Susan R. Stein, 3–4. Chicago: University of Chicago, 1986.

Bakhtin, Mikhail Mikhaĭlovich. *The Dialogic Imagination: Four Essays*, edited by Michael Holquist, translated by Caryl Emerson and Michael Holquist. Austin: University of Texas Press, 1981.

Barak, Aharon. "Judicial Philosophy and Judicial Activism." *Tel Aviv University Law Review* 17.3 (1993): 477.

Barker, Adam. "The Contemporary Realism of Canadian Imperialism: Settler Colonialism and the Hybrid Colonial State." *American Indian Quarterly* 33, no. 3 (Summer 2009): 325–352.

Barman, Jean, Yvonne Hebert, Don McCaskill, "The Legacy of the Past: An Overview." In *Indian Education in Canada.* Vol. 1, *The Legacy,* 1–23. Vancouver: University of British Columbia Press, 1986.

Barnhardt, Carol. A History of Schooling for Alaska Native People. *Journal of American Indian Education* 40, no. 1 (2001): 1–30.

Barrington, John. *Separate but Equal? Maori Schools and the Crown, 1867–1969.* Wellington: Victoria University Press, 2008.

Bartell, Ernest J. "Opportunities and Challenges for the Well-being of Children in the Development of Latin America: An Overview." In *The Child in Latin America: Health, Development, and Rights,* edited by E. J. Bartell and A. O'Donnell, xiii–xxxi. Notre Dame: University of Notre Dame Press, 2001.

Basham, Leilani. "Awaiaulu ke aloha: The Ties That Bind Hawaiian Gender, Sexuality, and Marriage." Paper presented at the Indigenous Sexualities Symposium, University of Illinois, Urbana-Champaign, 2009.

Basso, Keith. *Wisdom Sits in Places: Language and Landscape among the Western Apache.* Albuquerque: University of New Mexico Press, 1996.

Bauer, Jr., William J. *"We Were All Like Migrant Workers Here": Labor, Community, and Survival on California's Round Valley Reservation, 1850–1941.* Chapel Hill: University of North Carolina Press, 2009.

Beamer, B. Kamanamaikalani. "Na wai ka mana? *ʻŌiwi Agency and European Imperialism in the Hawaiian Kingdom.*" PhD diss. in geography. University of Hawaiʻi, 2008.

Beaulieu, David. "Native American Education Research and Policy Development in an Era of No Child Left Behind: Native Language and Culture during the Administrations of Presidents Clinton and Bush." *Journal of American Indian Education* 47, no.1 (2008): 10–45.

Behar, Ruth. *Translated Woman: Crossing the Border with Esperanza's Story.* Boston: Beacon Press, 1993.

Bell, Catherine, and Val Napoleon, eds. *First Nations Cultural Heritage and Law: Case Studies, Voices, and Perspectives.* Vancouver: University of British Columbia Press, 2008.

Bell, Cathy E. *Contemporary Métis Justice: The Settlement Way.* Saskatoon: Native Law Centre, 1999.

Benham, Maenette K. P., and Ronald H. Heck. *Culture and Educational Policy in Hawaiʻi: The Silencing of Native Voices.* Sociocultural, Political, and Historical Studies in Education. Mahwah, NJ: L. Erlbaum Associates, 1998.

Benson, Todd. "The Consequences of Reservation Life: Native Californians on the Round Valley Reservation, 1871–1884." *Pacific Historical Review* 60 (May 1991): 221–244.

Beresford, Quentin. *Reform and Resistance in Aboriginal Education: The Australian Experience.* Crawley: University of Western Australia Press, 2003.

Berger, Thomas. "Letter to Minister Prentice." March 6, 2006. Conciliator's Final Report: Nunavut Land Claims Agreement Implementation Planning Contract Negotiations for the Second

Planning Period. http://www.nunavutliteracy.ca/english/research/reports/Berger%20 2006%20PL%200907.pdf, accessed June 10, 2013.

Berkhofer, Robert F., Jr. *Salvation and the Savage: An Analysis of Protestant Missions and American Indian Response, 1787–1862*. Lexington: University of Kentucky Press, 1965.

Berkley, Anthony Robert. "Remembrance and Revitalization: The Archive of Pure Maya." PhD diss. University of Chicago, 1998.

Berman, Harold J. *The Interaction of Law and Religion*. New York: Abingdon Press, 1974.

Beyer, Carl Kalani. "Female Seminaries in America and Hawaii During the 19th Century." *Hawaiian Journal of History* 37 (2003): 91–118.

———. "Manual and Industrial Education During Hawaiian Sovereignty: Curriculum in the Transculturation of Hawai'i." PhD diss. in education. University of Illinois at Chicago, 2004.

———. "The Connection of Samuel Chapman Armstrong as Both Borrower and Architect of Education in Hawai'i." *History of Education Quarterly* 47, no. 1 (2007): 23–48.

Bishop, Bernice Pauahi. "Last Will and Codicils of the Late Hon. Mrs. Bernice P. Bishop." Honolulu: Hawai'i State Archives, 1883. *Kamehameha Schools*. http://www.ksbe.edu /pauahi/will.php, accessed March 14, 2011.

Bishop, Charles R. Address about the Purpose of the Schools. *Handicraft* 1, no.1 (1889).

Black, Cobey, and Kathleen Dickenson Mellen. *Princess Pauahi Bishop and Her Legacy*. Honolulu: Kamehameha Schools Press, 1965.

Black's Law Dictionary, 9th ed. St. Paul, MN: West Group, 2009.

Blackhawk, Ned. *Violence over the Land: Indians and Empires in the Early American West*. Cambridge, MA: Harvard University Press, 2006.

Blackwater v. Plint, [2005] 3 S.C.R. 3.

Blanchet-Cohen, Natasha. "A Portrait of Noeli: A Defender of La Guajira." *Akwe:kon* 14, no. 3 (1997): 40–43.

Blount, James. *Foreign Relations of the United States, 1894: Affairs in Hawai'i*. Report of the Commissioner to the Hawaiian Islands. 53rd Cong., 3rd sess., 455–456. Washington: Government Printing Office, 1895. University of Hawai'i at Minoa Library. http://libweb .hawaii.edu/digicoll/annexation/blount/br0443.html, accessed June 10, 2013.

Bobbitt, Philip. "Constitutional Law and Interpretation." In *A Companion to Philosophy of Law and Legal Theory,* edited by Dennis Patterson. Cambridge, MA: Blackwell, 1996.

———. *Constitutional Interpretation*, rev. ed. Cambridge, MA: Blackwell, 2006.

Bonfil Batalla, Guillermo. *México profundo: Una civilización negada*, 134–135. Ciudad de México: Grijalbo y Consejo Nacional para la Cultura y las Artes, 1989.

Borrows, John. "A Separate Peace: Strengthening Shared Justice." In *Intercultural Dispute Resolution in Aboriginal Contexts*, edited by Catherine Bell and David Kahane. Vancouver: University of British Columbia Press, 2004.

———. *Canada's Indigenous Constitution*. Toronto: University of Toronto Press, 2010.

———. "Constitutional Law from a First Nation Perspective: Self-Government and the Royal Proclamation." *U.B.C.L. Rev.* 28 (1994): 1.

———. *Drawing Out Law: A Spirit's Guide.* Toronto: University of Toronto Press, 2010.

———. "Fourword: Issues, Individuals, Institutions and Ideas." *Indigenous L.J.* 1 (2002): [ix].

———. "Indigenous Legal Traditions in Canada." *Wash. U.L.J. L. & Policy* 19 (2005): 167, 174–175.

———. "Living Law on a Living Earth: Aboriginal Religion, Law, and the Constitution." In *Law and Religious Pluralism in Canada,* edited by Richard Moon. Vancouver: University of British Columbia Press, 2008.

———. "Measuring a Work in Progress: Canada, Constitutionalism, Citizenship and Aboriginal Peoples." In *Box of Treasures or Empty Box: Twenty Years of Section 35*, edited by Ardith Walkem and Halie Bruce. Penticton, BC: Theytus Books, 2003.

———. "Physical Philosophy: Mobility and the Future of Indigenous Rights." In *Indigenous Peoples and the Law: Comparative and Critical Perspectives,* edited by Benjamin J. Richardson, Shin Imai, and Kent McNeil. Portland, OR: Hart, 2009.

———. "Stewardship and the First Nations Governance Act." (2003) 29 *Queen's L.J.* 103.

———. *Recovering Canada: The Resurgence of Indigenous Law.* Toronto: University of Toronto Press, 2002.

Boxberger, Daniel. *To Fish in Common: The Ethnohistory of Lummi Indian Salmon Fishing.* Seattle: University of Washington Press, 2000.

Brave Heart-Jordan, M. Y. H. "Gender Differences in the Historical Trauma Response among the Lakota." *Journal of Health & Social Policy* 10, no. 4 (1999): 1–21.

———. "The Historical Trauma Response among Natives and Its Relationship with Substance Abuse: A Lakota Illustration." *Journal of Psychoactive Drugs* 35, no. 1 (2003): 7–13.

Brave Heart-Jordan, M. Y. H., and Lemyra DeBruyn. "So She May Walk in Balance: Integrating the Impact of Historical Trauma in the Treatment of Native American Indian Women." In *Racism in the Lives of Women: Testimony, Theory, and Guides to Antiracist Practice,* edited by J. Adelman and G. Enguidanos, 345–368. New York: Haworth, 1995.

———. "The American Indian Holocaust: Healing Historical Unresolved Grief." *American Indian and Alaska Native Mental Health Research* 8 (1998): 56–78.

"Breaking the Silence: An Interpretive Study of Residential School Impact and Healing as Illustrated by the Stories of First Nation Individuals." Ottawa: Assembly of First Nations, 1994.

Brierly, James. *The Law of Nations: An Introduction to the International Law of Peace*, 6th ed. Oxford: Oxford University Press, 1963.

Brightman, Robert. *Grateful Prey: Rock Cree Human-Animal Relations.* Berkeley: University of California Press, 1993.

Britton, June. Interview by William Bauer, Covelo, CA, March 19, 2002. Tape and transcript in the possession of William Bauer.

Brooks, James. *Captives and Cousins: Slavery, Kinship, and Community in the Southwest Borderlands.* Chapel Hill: Published for the Omohundro Institute of Early American History and Culture by the University of North Carolina Press, 2002.

Brother, Farmer's, and Red Jacket. *Indian Speeches; Delivered by Farmer's Brother and Red Jacket, Two Seneca Chiefs.* Canandaigua, NY: James D. Bemis, 1809.

Brown v. Board of Education, 347 U.S. 483 (1954).

Brown, Deidamia Covell. *Memoir of the Late Rev. Lemuel Covell, Missionary to the Tuscarora Indians and the Province of Upper Canada Comprising a History of the Origin and Progress of Missionary Operations in the Shaftsbury Baptist Association, Up to the Time of Mr. Covell's Decease in 1806*. Brandon, VT: Telegraph, 1839.

Brown, Thelma Robins. "Memorial Chapel: The Culmination of the Development of the Campus of Hampton Institute, Hampton, Virginia, 1867–1887." Master's thesis, School of Architecture, University of Virginia, 1971.

Budka, Metchie J. E., trans. and ed. "Journey to Niagara." *New-York Historical Society Quarterly* 44, no. 1 (1960): 73–113.

Buffalohead, W. Roger, and Paulette Fairbanks Molin. "'A Nucleus of Civilization': American Indian Families at Hampton Institute in the Late Nineteenth Century." *Journal of American Indian Education* 35, no. 3 (Spring 1996): 59–94.

Bureau of Indian Affairs. Central Correspondence File 25436–31–150; General Services, Record Group 75, National Archives.

———. Correspondence of Interior Secretary Hitchcock, Leech Lake Agency, July 20, 1900. Record Group 75, National Archives.

———. File 68776–1931–800; Part I, Record Group 75, National Archives.

———. Record Group 75, Records of the Flandreau Indian School. National Archives.

———. Record Group 75, Records of the Leech Lake Agency. National Archives.

Burgess, Marianna. *Stiya, a Carlisle Indian Girl at Home*. Cambridge: Riverside, 1891.

Burns, Allan. *An Epoch of Miracles: Oral Literature of the Yucatec Maya*. Austin: University of Texas Press, 1983.

Bush v. Gore. 531 U.S. 98 (2000).

Campisi, Jack, and William A. Starna. "On the Road to Canandaigua: The Treaty of 1794." *American Indian Quarterly* 19, no. 4 (1995): 467–490.

Cardinal, Harold, and Walter Hildebrandt. *Treaty Elders of Saskatchewan: Our Dream Is That Our Peoples Will One Day Be Clearly Recognized as Nations*. Calgary: University of Calgary Press, 2000.

Carpio, Myla. "Countering Colonization: Albuquerque Laguna Colony." *Wicazo Sa Review* 19, no. 2 (Autumn 2004): 61–78.

Carranco, Lynwood, and Estle Beard. *Genocide and Vendetta: The Round Valley Wars of Northern California*. Norman: University of Oklahoma Press, 1981.

Carter, Roger. "The University of Saskatchewan Native Law Centre." (1979–1980) 44 *Sask. L. Rev.* 135.

Case, David S., and David A. Voluck. *Alaska Natives and American Laws*, 2nd ed. Fairbanks: University of Alaska Press, 2002.

Certeau, Michel de. *Practice of Everyday Life*, translated by Steven Rendell. Berkeley: University of California Press, 1984.

Champagne v. Little River Band of Indians, Case No. 06–178-AP, June 2007, Little River Band of Indians Court of Appeal.

Chapin, Dr. [Cyrenius]. Red Jacket to Cram a Missionary, 1805, B00–2, Box 1, Folder 1, Buffalo and Erie County Historical Society, Buffalo, NY.

Chapin, Helen Geracimos. *Shaping History: The Role of Newspapers in Hawai'i*. Honolulu: University of Hawai'i Press, 1996.

Chávez, Hugo. Corazón de mi patria. n.d. http://www.chavez.org.ve/temas/noticias/se-le-dara -continuidad-al-primer-plan-socialista-nacion/, accessed June 10, 2013.

Chazanof, William. *Joseph Ellicott and the Holland Land Company: The Opening of Western New York*. Syracuse, NY: Syracuse University Press, 1970.

Child, Brenda J. *Boarding School Seasons: American Indian Families, 1900–1940*. Lincoln, NE: University of Nebraska Press, 1998.

———. *Holding Our World Together: Ojibwe Women and the Survival of Community*. New York, NY: Viking, 2012.

Children's Code, Title 10 of the Grand Traverse Band Code: Statutes of the Grand Traverse Band of Ottawa and Chippewa Indians. http://www.narf.org/nill/Codes/gtcode/10.pdf, accessed February 18, 2011.

Chun-Lum, Sharlene, and Lesley Agard. *Legacy: A Portrait of the Young Men and Women of Kamehameha Schools, 1887–1987*. Honolulu: Kamehameha Schools Press, 1987.

Clarfield, Gerald H. *Timothy Pickering and the American Republic*. Pittsburgh, PA: University of Pittsburgh Press, 1980.

Clifford, James. "Indigenous Articulations." *The Contemporary Pacific* 13, no. 2 (2001): 468.

Clinton, Dewitt. "Private Canal Journal, 1810." In *Life and Writings of Dewitt Clinton*, edited by William W. Campbell. New York: Baker & Scribner, 1849.

Cody, Anna, and Sue Green. "Clinical Legal Education and Indigenous Legal Education: What's the Connection?" (2007) *International Journal of Clinical Legal Education* 51.

Cole, Terrence M. "Jim Crow in Alaska: The Passage of the Alaska Equal Rights Act of 1945." In *An Alaska Anthology: Interpreting the Past*, edited by Stephen W. Haycox and Mary Childers Mangusso, 314–335. Seattle: University of Washington Press, 2002.

Collier, George. *Basta!: Land and the Zapatista Rebellion in Chiapas*. Oakland: First Food, 1999.

Colmenares Olívar, Ricardo. El derecho de la propia cultura de los pueblos indígenas en Venezuela, n.d., http://www.iidh.ed.cr/comunidades/diversidades/docs/div_enlinea/el%20 derecho%20a%20%20la%20%20propia%20cultura.htm, accessed May 23, 2013.

Conklin, Beth A. "Body Paint, Feathers, and VCR's: Aesthetics and Authenticity in Amazonian Activism." *American Ethnologist* 24, no.4 (1997): 711–737.

Constitution Act, 1982, being Schedule B to the Canada Act 1982 (U.K.), 1982, c. 11.

Constitution and Ordinances of the Little River Band of Indians of Manistee, Michigan. https:// www.lrboi-nsn.gov/council/docs/Constitution%20-%202004%20Amendments.pdf. https://www.lrboi-nsn.gov/council/ordinances.html.

Cos-Montiel, Francisco. "Sirviendo a las mesas del mundo: Las niñas y niños jornaleros agrícolas en México." In *La infancia vulnerable de México en un mundo globalizado*, edited by Norma del Río Lugo, 15–38. Mexico: Universidad Autónoma Metropolitana; UNICEF, 2001.

Cott, Nancy F. *Public Vows: A History of Marriage and the Nation*. Cambridge: Harvard University Press, 2000.

Cotton, Stephen E. "Alaska's 'Molly Hootch Case': High Schools and the Village Voice." *Educational Research Quarterly* 8, no. 4 (1984): 30–43.

Covell, Lemuel. "Visit of Rev. Lemuel Covell to Western New York and Canada." *Buffalo Historical Society Publications* 6 (1903): 207–216.

Coyle, Michael. "Traditional Indian Justice in Ontario: A Role for the Present?" (1986) 24 *Osgoode Hall L.J.* 605.

Cruikshank, Julie. *Do Glaciers Listen? Local Knowledge, Colonial Encounters, and Social Imagination.* Vancouver: University of British Columbia Press, 2005.

Cusick, David. *David Cusick's Sketches of Ancient History of the Six Nations (1828)*, edited by Paul Royster. Lincoln, NE: DigitalCommons@University of Nebraska, 2006. http://digitalcommons.unl.edu/libraryscience/24/, accessed June 10, 2013.

Daiker, Fred. "Inspection Report 5–358," handwritten note on Roy Nash's report on Louisiana Indians (June 12, 1931), August 7, 1931. BIA Central Correspondence File 25436–31–150, General Services, Record Group 75, National Archives.

Dauenhauer, Richard. "Two Missions to Alaska." *The Pacific Historian* 26 (1982): 29–41.

Dawson, Alexander S. *Indian and Nation in Revolutionary Mexico.* Tucson: University of Arizona Press, 2004.

———. "'Wild Indians,' 'Mexican Gentlemen,' and the Lessons Learned in the Casa Del Estudiante Indigena, 1926–1932." *The Americas* 57, no. 3 (2001): 329–361.

Delgamuukw v. British Columbia (1991), 79 D.L.R. (4th) 185, [1991] 3 W.W.R. 97 (B.C.S.C.).

Deloria, Philip. *Indians in Unexpected Places.* Lawrence: University Press of Kansas, 2004.

———. *Playing Indian.* New Haven: Yale University Press, 1998.

Deloria, Jr., Vine, and Clifford M. Lytle. *The Nations Within: The Past and Future of American Indian Sovereignty.* Austin: University of Texas Press, 1984.

Dennis, Matthew. *Cultivating a Landscape of Peace: Iroquois-European Encounters in Seventeenth-Century America.* Ithaca, NY: Cornell University Press, 1993.

Densmore, Christopher. *Red Jacket: Iroquois Diplomat and Orator.* Syracuse, NY: Syracuse University Press, 1999.

Deur, Douglas. "A Most Sacred Place: The Significance of Crater Lake among the Indians of Southern Oregon." *Oregon Historical Quarterly* 103, no. 1 (Spring 2002): 18–49.

Dirección de Asuntos Indígenas. "Régimen de educacíon intercultural bilingüe: Diagnósticos e propuestas 1998–2008." Ministerio de Educación, Caracas, 2008.

———. Informe final de la comision de diagnóstico del Decreto 283 Educación Intercultural Bilingüe. Dirección General Sectoral de Programas Especiales del Ministerio de Educación, 1–9 April, 1981.

Dougherty, Michael. *To Steal a Kingdom: Probing Hawaiian History,* 1st ed. Waimanalo Hawaiʻi: Island Press, 1992.

Dowsley, Martha. "The Value of a Polar Bear: Evaluating the Role of a Multiple-Use Resource in the Nunavut Mixed Economy." *Arctic Anthropology* 47, no.1 (2010): 39–56.

Driskill, Qwo-Li, et al., eds. *Queer Indigenous Studies: Critical Interventions in Theory, Politics, and Literature.* University of Arizona Press, 2011.

Eckermann, Anne-Katrin. "Aboriginal Education in Rural Australia: A Case Study in Frustration and Hope." *Australian Journal of Education* 43, no. 1 (April 1999): 5–23.

Egerton, George. "Trudeau, God, and the Canadian Constitution: Religion, Human Rights, and Government Authority in the Making of the 1982 Constitution." In *Rethinking Church, State, and Modernity: Canada between Europe and America,* edited by David Lyon and Marguerite Van Die. Toronto: University of Toronto Press, 2000.

Eiss, Paul K. "Deconstructing Indians, Reconstructing Patria: Indigenous Education in Yucatan from the *Porfiriato* to the Mexican Revolution." *Journal of Latin American Anthropology* 9, no. 1 (2004): 119–150.

Ellicott, Joseph. "Map of Morris's Purchase or West Geneseo in the State of New York: Exhibiting Part of the Lakes Erie and Ontario, the Straights of Niagara, Chautauque Lake, and All the Principal Waters, the Boundary Lines of the Several Tracts of Land Purchased by the Holland Land Company, William and John Willink, and Others, Boundary Lines of Townships, Boundary Lines of New York and Indian Reservations, Laid Down from Actual Survey, Also a Sketch of Part of Upper Canada, 1804." Map Division, New York Public Library, Holland Land Company, New York City.

Ellis, Clyde. *To Change Them Forever: Indian Education at the Rainy Mountain Boarding School, 1893–1920.* Norman: University of Oklahoma, 1996.

———. "'We Had a Lot of Fun, but of Course, That Wasn't the School Part': Life at the Rainy Mountain Boarding School, 1893–1920." In *Boarding School Blues: Revisiting American Indian Educational Experiences,* edited by Clifford E. Trafzer, Jean A. Keller, and Lorene Sisquoc, 65–89. Lincoln: University of Nebraska Press, 2006.

Ellner, Steve. *Rethinking Venezuelan Politics: Class, Conflict, and the Chávez Phenomenon.* Boulder and London: Lynne Rienner Publishers, 2008.

Engelbrecht, William. *Iroquoia: The Development of a Native World.* Syracuse, NY: Syracuse University Press, 2003.

Erdoes, Richard, and Alfonso Ortiz. *American Indian Trickster Tales.* New York: Viking, 1998.

Estes, Heidi, and Robert Laurence. "Preparing American Indians for Law School: The American Indian Law Center's Pre-Law Summer Institute." (1992) 12 *N. Ill. U.L. Rev.* 278.

Everwind, Alex. Doris Duke Oral History Collection. Copy on file at Red Lake Tribal Archives, Redlake, Minnesota.

Eyre, Kāwika. "Suppression of Hawaiian Culture at Kamehameha Schools." Ka'iwakiloumoku Hawaiian Cultural Center: Kamehameha Schools, 2004. http://kaiwakiloumoku.ksbe.edu/, accessed June 10, 2013.

Fájardo Gomez, Remedios. "The Systematic Violation of the Human Rights of the Indigenous People, Black People, and Campesinos by the Coal Mining Multinationals in the Department of La Guajira, Colombia." *The People Behind the Colombian Coal: Mining, Multinationals, and Human Rights,* edited by Aviva Chomsky, Garry Leech, and Steve Striffler, 16–28. Colombia: Casa Editorial Pisando Callos, 2007.

Fallaw, Ben. "Rethinking Mayan Resistance: Changing Relations between Federal Teachers and Mayan Communities in Eastern Yucatan, 1929–1935." *Journal of Latin American Anthropology* 9, no. 1 (2004): 151–178.

Fanon, Frantz. *Black Skins, White Masks.* New York: Grove Press, 1967.

Feld, Steven. "Postscript, 1989." In *Sound and Sentiment: Birds, Weeping, Poetics, and Song in Kaluli Expression,* 2nd ed., 239–268. Philadelphia: University of Pennsylvania Press, 1990.

Feldthusen, Bruce. "Civil Liability for Sexual Assault in Aboriginal Residential Schools: The Baker Did It." (2007) 22 *Canadian Journal of Law and Society* 61.

Fenton, William N. "Structure, Continuity, and Change in the Process of Iroquois Treaty Making." In *The History and Culture of Iroquois Diplomacy: An Interdisciplinary Guide to the Treaties of the Six Nations and Their League,* edited by Francis Jennings et al., 3–36. Syracuse, NY: Syracuse University Press, 1985.

_____. *The Great Law and the Longhouse: A Political History of the Iroquois Confederacy.* Norman: University of Oklahoma Press, 1998.

Fischer, Ann. "History and Current Status of the Houma Indians." In *The American Indian Today*, edited by Stuart Levine and Nancy O. Lurie, 212–234. Baltimore: Penguin Books, 1968.

Fiske, Jo-Anne, and Betty Patrick. *Cis Dideen Kat (When the Plumes Rise): The Way of the Lake Babine Nation.* Vancouver: University of British Columbia Press, 2000.

Folds, Ralph. *Whitefella School: Education and Aboriginal Education.* Sydney: Allen & Unwin, 1987.

Foley, Neil. "Becoming Hispanic: Mexican Americans and Whiteness." In *White Privilege,* edited by Paula S. Rothenberg, 49–59. New York: Worth Publishers, 2008.

_____. *The White Scourge: Mexicans, Blacks, and Poor Whites in Texas Cotton Culture.* Berkeley: University of California Press, 1997.

Folsom, Cora Mae. *Twenty-Two Years; Work of the Hampton Normal and Agricultural Institute at Hampton, Virginia.* Hampton: Normal School Press, 1893.

For the Rights of All: Ending Jim Crow in Alaska. Directed by Phil Lucas. Blueberry Productions, 2009. Film.

Forsman, Leonard. "History of Western Washington Native Peoples." In *A Time of Gathering: Native Heritage in Washington State,* edited by Robin K. Wright, 205–210. Seattle: University of Washington Press for the Burke Museum, 1991.

Forte, Maximilian. "Indigenism and Essentialism 2." Zero Anthropology, 2007. http://openanthropology.wordpress.com/2007/11/24/indigenism-and-essentialism-2/, accessed June 10, 2013.

Foucault, Michel. Interview by Raúl Fornet-Betancourt, Helmut Becker, and Alfredo Gomez-Müller. In *The Final Foucault,* edited by James Bernauer and David Rasmussen. Translated by J. Gauthier. Cambridge, MA: MIT Press, 1988.

_____. *Discipline & Punish: The Birth of the Prison,* translated by Alan Sheridan. New York: Vintage Books, 1977.

_____. "The Subject and Power." Afterword to *Michel Foucault: Beyond Structuralism and Hermeneutics,* by Hubert Dreyfus and Paul Rabinow. Chicago: University of Chicago Press, 1982.

Freeman, Marian (Arvella). Interview with William J. Bauer, Jr., Covelo, CA, June 20, 2002. Tape and transcript in the possession of William Bauer.

French, Rebecca Redwood. *The Golden Yoke: The Legal Cosmology of Buddhist Tibet.* Ithaca: Cornell University Press, 1995.

Frissell, H. B. "Hampton Institute." In *From Servitude to Service,* 115–152. New York: Negro Universities Press, 1969. First published 1905 by American Unitarian Association.

Gallagher-Mackay, Kelly. "Affirmative Action and Aboriginal Government: The Case for Legal Education in Nunavut." (1999) 14 *C.J.L.S.* 21.

Galt, Margot Fortunato. *Turning the Feather Around: My Life in Art.* St. Paul: Minnesota Historical Society Press, 1998.

Galuteria, Peter. *Heart of a Hero: Charles Reed Bishop.* Honolulu: Bishop Museum Press, 2009.

Ganter, Granville, ed. *The Collected Speeches of Sagoyewatha, or Red Jacket.* Syracuse, NY: Syracuse University Press, 2006.

García, María Elena. "Indigenous Education in Peru." In *The Routledge International Companion to Multicultural Education,* edited by James A. Banks, 276–287. New York: Routledge, 2009.

———. "The Politics of Community: Education, Indigenous Rights, and Ethnic Mobilization in Peru." *Latin American Perspectives* 30, no. 1 (January 2003): 70–95.

———. *Making Indigenous Citizens: Identities, Education, and Multicultural Development in Peru.* Stanford: Stanford University Press, 2005.

Geertz, Clifford. *Local Knowledge: Further Essays in Interpretive Anthropology.* New York: Basic Books, 1983.

Getches, David H. "Law and Alaska Native Education: The Influence of Federal and State Legislation upon Education of Rural Alaska Natives." Center for Northern Educational Research, University of Alaska Fairbanks, September 1977.

Gibson, Campbell, and Kay Jung. "Historical Census Statistics on Population Totals by Race, 1790 to 1990, and by Hispanic Origin, 1970 to 1990, for the United States, Regions, Divisions, and States." Working Paper Series, no. 56, United States Census Bureau, Washington, DC, 2002. http://www.census.gov/population/www/documentation/twps0056/twps0056.html, accessed August 26, 2009.

Gilbert, Matthew Sakiestewa. *Education Beyond the Mesas: Hopi Students at Sherman Institute, 1902–1929.* Lincoln, NE: University of Nebraska Press, 2010.

Giordani, Lourdes, and María Eugenia Villalón."An Expansion of Citizenship in Venezuela." *NACLA Report on the Americas,* 35 no. 6 (2002): 44–45.

Giordani, Lourdes. "Llegó la hora del Indio, ¿si o no?: The Election of Three Indigenous Representatives to Venezuela's National Constituent Assembly." *Social Justice: Anthropology, Peace, and Human Rights* 3, no. 1–2 (2002): 63–95.

Glenn, H. Patrick. "The Common Law in Canada." (1995) 74 *Can. Bar Rev.* 261–292.

"Glossary of Figures of Speech in Iroquois Political Rhetoric." In *The History and Culture of Iroquois Diplomacy: An Interdisciplinary Guide to the Treaties of the Six Nations and Their League,* edited by Francis Jennings et al., 115–124. Syracuse, NY: Syracuse University Press, 1985.

Gluckman, Max. *Politics, Law, and Ritual in Tribal Society.* Chicago: Aldine, 1965.

Godenzzi, Juan Carlos, ed. *Educación e interculturalidad en los Andes y la Amazonía.* Cusco: Centro Bartolomé de las Casas, 1996.

Goldsmith, Sara Sue, with Risa Mueller. *Nations Within: The Four Sovereign Tribes of Louisiana.* Baton Rouge: Louisiana State University Press, 2003.

Goldsmith, Sara Sue. "The Jena Band: Choctaw Traditions Keep Tribe Together." *Baton Rouge Advocate Magazine,* June 2, 1996, 16.

Gone, Joseph P. "Reconsidering American Indian Historical Trauma: Lessons from an Early Gros Ventre War Narrative." *Transcultural Psychiatry*, forthcoming.

Gonzalbo Aizpuru, Pilar. Historia de la educación en la época colonial: El mundo indígena. Mexico City: El Colegio de Mexico, 1990.

Goodman-Draper, Jacqueline. "The Development of Underdevelopment at Akwesasne: Cultural and Economic Subversion." *American Journal of Economics and Sociology* 53 (January 1994): 41–56.

Goulet, Jean-Guy, and Miguel Angel Jusayu. *El idioma guajiro; sus fonemas, su ortografía, su morfología.* Caracas: Universidad Católica Andrés Bello, 1978.

Graham, Laura R. "How Should an Indian Speak? Amazonian Indians and the Symbolic Politics of Language in the Global Public Sphere." In *Indigenous Movements, Self-Representation, and the State in Latin America,* edited by Kay B. Warren and Jean E. Jackson, 181–228. Austin: University of Texas Press, 2002.

Grand Traverse Band Code, Title 16, Education and Culture. http://www.narf.org/nill/Codes /gtcode/index.htm, accessed May 14, 2013.

Grant, J. W. "Elkanah Holmes (1744–1832)." *Dictionary of Canadian Biography,* vol. 6, 1821–1835.

Graymont, Barbara. *The Iroquois in the American Revolution.* Syracuse, NY: Syracuse University Press, 1972.

Greaves, Cecilia L. "Entre la teoría educativa y la práctica indigenista: La experiencia en Chiapas y la Tarahumara (1940–1970)." In *Educación rural e indígena en Iberoamérica,* edited by Pilar Gonzalbo Aizpuru. Mexico: El Colegio de México, 1999, 161–178.

Greene, Candace S., and Russell Thornton. *The Year the Stars Fell: Lakota Winter Counts at the Smithsonian.* Lincoln: University of Nebraska Press, 2007.

Green, Rayna. "Native American Women." *Signs* 6, no. 2 (1980): 248–267.

———. "The Pocahontas Perplex: The Image of Indian Women in American Culture." *The Massachusetts Review* 16, no. 4 (1975): 698–714.

Greene v. Commissioner of Minnesota Dept. of Human Services, 733 N.W. 2d 490, 497 (MN 2007).

Greenwald, Emily. *Reconfiguring the Reservation: The Nez Perces, Jicarilla Apaches, and the Dawes Act.* Albuquerque: University of New Mexico Press, 2002.

Gregory, Hiram F. "The Jena Band of Louisiana Choctaw." *American Indian Journal* 3, no. 2 (1977): 2–16.

Griswold, Rufus Wilmot. *The Biographical Annual: Containing Memoirs of Eminent Persons, Recently Deceased.* New York: Linen and Fennell, 1841.

Guerra Curvelo, Weildler. *La disputa y la palabra: La ley en la sociedad wayúu.* Bogotá: Ministerio de la Cultura, 2002.

Gustafson, Bret. *New Languages of the State: Indigenous Resurgence and the Politics of Knowledge in Bolivia.* Durham: Duke University Press, 2009.

Guzman, Mireya Maritza Peña. "Legal Pluralism as an Approach to Indigenous and Tribal Peoples' Rights." In *Human Rights in Development, Yearbook,* edited by Lone Lindholt and Sten Schuamburg-Müller. Leiden: Martinus Nijhoff, 2003.

Hadley, Michael L., ed. *The Spiritual Roots of Restorative Justice.* Albany: State University of New York Press, 2001.

Haig-Brown, Celia. *Resistance and Renewal: Surviving the Indian Residential School.* Vancouver: Tillacum Library, 1988.

Hale, Charles. "Does Multiculturalism Menace? Governance, Cultural Rights, and the Politics of Identity in Guatemala." *Journal of Latin American Studies* 34, no. 3 (August 2002): 485–524.

———. "Rethinking Indigenous Politics in the Era of the 'Indio Permitido.'" *NACLA* 38, no. 2 (September/October 2004): 16–21.

Hale, Charles, and Rosamel Millamán. "Cultural Agency and Political Struggle in the Era of the *Indio Permitido.*" In *Cultural Agency in the Americas,* edited by Doris Sommer. Durham: Duke University Press, 2005.

Halfpenny, Rex. "Michigan Home Brewing during Prohibition." Michigan Beer Guide. http://www.michiganbeerguide.com/news.asp?articleid=24, accessed August 2, 2003.

Hall, Lisa Kahale'ole. "Strategies of Erasure: U.S. Colonialism and Native Hawaiian Feminism." *American Quarterly* 60, no. 2 (2008): 273–280.

Hallaq, Wael B. *The Origins and Evolution of Islamic Law.* Cambridge: Cambridge University Press, 2005.

Hampton Normal and Agricultural Institute. *Concerning Indians, Extracts from the Annual Report.* Hampton, VA: Normal School Press, 1883.

Hanks, William. *Converting Words: Maya in the Age of the Cross.* Chicago: University of Chicago Press, 2010.

Hare, Bishop William Hobart. *How the Church Schools in South Dakota Help Indian Boys and Girls.* Pamphlet No. 618. New York: Church Missions House, 1909.

Harmon, Alexandra. "American Indians and Land Monopolies in the Gilded Age." *Journal of American History* 90 (June 2003): 106–133.

Harris, G. H. "The Life of Horatio Jones." In Vol. 6, *Buffalo Historical Society Publications (381–526),* edited by Frank H. Severance. Buffalo, NY: Buffalo Historical Society, 1903.

Harris, Thompson S. "Journals of Rev. Thompson S. Harris, Missionary to the Senecas, 1821–1828." *Buffalo Historical Society Publications* 6, no. 8 (1903): 281–378.

Hauptman, Laurence M. *Conspiracy of Interests: Iroquois Dispossession and the Rise of New York State.* Syracuse, NY: Syracuse University Press, 1999.

Haviland, John. "El problema de la educación bilingüe en el área Tzotzil." *América Indígena,* no. XLII (1982): 147–170.

Hawaiian Kingdom. *Biennial Report of the President of the Board of Education to the Hawaiian Legislature of 1864. Report of Mataio Kekuanaoa.* Honolulu, 1864.

———. *Biennial Report of the President of the Board of Education to the Hawaiian Legislature of 1866. Report of Mataio Kekuanaoa.* Honolulu: Government document, 1866.

———. *Biennial Report of the President of the Board of Education to the Legislature of 1874.* Honolulu, 1874.

———. *Biennial Report of the President of the Board of Education to the Legislature of 1878.* Report of Charles R. Bishop. Honolulu, 1878.

———. *Biennial Report of the President of the Board of Education to the Legislature of 1884*. Report of Walter Murray Gibson. Honolulu, 1884.

———. "Civil Code of the Hawaiian Islands. Title 5, Of Laws Affecting the Domestic Relations." n.d. http://www.hawaiiankingdom.org/civilcode/CHAPTER_XXVIII_ART_LIII.shtml, accessed June 10, 2013.

———. *Report of the Minister of Public Instruction Read Before the King to the Hawaiian Legislature*. Report of Richard Armstrong on April 14, 1852. Honolulu: Government document, 1852.

Hawaiian Mission Children's Society. *Missionary Album: Portraits and Biographical Sketches of the American Protestant Missionaries to the Hawaiian Islands*. Honolulu: Hawaiian Mission Children's Society, 1937.

Haycox, Stephen W. "'Races of a Questionable Ethnical Type': Origins of the Jurisdiction of the US Bureau of Education in Alaska, 1867–1885." *Pacific Northwest Quarterly* 75 (1984): 156–63.

———. "Sheldon Jackson in Historical Perspective: Alaska Native Schools and Mission Contracts, 1885–1894. *The Pacific Historian* 28, no. 1 (1984): 18–28.

Haycox, Stephen W., A. J. McClanahan, Veldee Hall, and Larry Persily. *Alaska Scrapbook: Moments in Alaska History, 1816–1998*. Anchorage, AK: CIRI Foundation, 2007.

Hecht, N. S., et al., eds. *An Introduction to the History and Sources of Jewish Law*. Oxford: Oxford University Press, 1996.

Helmholz, R. H. *The Spirit of Classical Canon Law*. Athens: University of Georgia Press, 1996.

Henderson, James (Sa'ke'j) Youngblood. *Indigenous Diplomacy and the Rights of Peoples: Achieving UN Recognition*. Saskatoon: Purich, 2008.

———. "Mikmaw Tenure in Atlantic Canada." (1995) 18 *Dal. L.J.* 196.

Hensley, William L. Iggiagruk. *Fifty Miles from Tomorrow: A Memoir of Alaska and the Real People*. New York: Farrar, Straus and Giroux, 2009.

Hernández Murrillo, Ricardo, and Marjorie Thacker. *Diagnóstico de salud y nutrición en albergues escolares para niños indígenas*. Mexico: Fideicomiso para la Salud de los Niños Indígenas de Mexico, 1992.

Herndon, Ruth Wallis, and Ella Wilcox Sekatau. "The Right to a Name: The Narragansett People and Rhode Island Officials in the Revolutionary Era." *Ethnohistory* 4, no. 3 (1997): 433–462.

Hildebrandt, Martha. *Diccionario Guajiro-Español*. Caracas: República de Venezuela, Ministerio de Justicia, Comisión Indigenista, 1963.

Hill, Henry W., ed. *Municipality of Buffalo, New York: A History*, vol. 1. New York: Lewis Historical Publishing Co., Inc., 1923.

Himno de la República Bolivariana de Venezuela en Warao. http://www.youtube.com/watch?v=715 ylT7bTrE, accessed June 9, 2012.

Hoebel, E. Adamson. *The Law of Primitive Man: A Study in Comparative Legal Dynamics*. Cambridge, MA: Harvard University Press, 2006.

Holmes, Elkanah. "Mr. Holmes' Letter." *New-York Missionary Magazine, and Repository of Religious Intelligence* 2, no. 1 (1801).

_____. "Letters of Rev. Elkanah Holmes from Fort Niagara in 1800." *Buffalo Historical Society Publications* 6, no. 8 (1903): 187–206.

Hornberger, Nancy H., ed. *Indigenous Literacies in the Americas: Language Planning from the Bottom Up.* New York: Mouton de Gruyter, 1997.

Horsman, Reginald. *Expansion and American Indian Policy, 1783–1812.* East Lansing: Michigan State University Press, 1967.

_____. *Race and Manifest Destiny: The Origins of American Racial Anglo-Saxonism.* Cambridge, MA: Harvard University Press, 1981.

Hosmer, Brian. *American Indians in the Marketplace: Persistence and Innovation among the Menominees and Metlakatlans, 1870–1920.* Lawrence: University Press of Kansas, 1999.

Hosmer, Brian, and Colleen O'Neill, eds. *Native Pathways: American Indian Culture and Economic Development in the Twentieth Century.* Boulder: University of Colorado Press, 2004.

Howard, Rosaleen. "Education Reform, Indigenous Politics, and Decolonisation in the Bolivia of Evo Morales." *International Journal of Educational Development* 29, no. 6 (2009): 583–593.

Hoxie, Frederick E. *A Final Promise: The Campaign to Assimilate the Indians, 1880–1920.* Lincoln: University of Nebraska Press, 2001.

_____. "Retrieving the Red Continent: Settler Colonialism and the History of American Indians in the U.S." *Ethnic and Racial Studies* 31, no. 6 (2008): 1153–1167.

Hughes, William Hardin, and Frederick Patterson. *Robert Russa Moton of Hampton and Tuskegee.* Chapel Hill: University of North Carolina, 1956.

Huhndorf, Roy M. *Reflections on the Alaska Native Experience: Selected Articles and Speeches by Roy M. Huhndorf,* edited by A. J. McClanahan. Anchorage, AK: The CIRI Foundation, 1991.

Hultgren, Mary Lou, and Paulette Molin. *To Lead and to Serve: American Indian Education at Hampton Institute, 1878–1923.* Virginia Beach, VA: Virginia Foundation for the Humanities, 1989.

Hyde, Jabez Backus. "A Teacher among the Senecas: Narrative of Rev. Jabez Backus Hyde, 1811–1820." *Buffalo Historical Society Publications* 6, no. 8 (1903): 239–274.

Hyer, Sally. *One House, One Voice, One Heart: Native American Education at the Santa Fe Indian School.* Santa Fe: Museum of New Mexico Press, 1990.

In re D.D., No. 97–11–083-CV-DR (Grand Traverse Band Tribal Ct., February 1, 1998).

Instituto Nacional Indigenista (INI). *Instituto Nacional Indigenista, 1989–1994.* Mexico: INI, SEDESOL, 1994.

Intensive Program on Aboriginal Lands, Resources & Governments. Osgoode Hall Law School. http://www.osgoode.yorku.ca/clinics-experiential/clinical-education/aboriginal-lands-resources-governments, accessed May 14, 2013.

Iverson, Peter. *Diné: A History of the Navajos.* Albuquerque: University of New Mexico Press, 2002.

Jacket, Red. "Speech to Secretary of War on Behalf of the Six Nations, February 15, 1810." Letters received by the Secretary of War relating to Indian Affairs, 1800–1823, M271, Roll 1, National Archives and Records Administration, Washington, DC.

Jacobs, Margaret D. "Maternal Colonialism: White Women and Indigenous Child Removal in the American West and Australia, 1880–1940." *Western Historical Quarterly* 36 (Winter 2005): 453–476, 460.

Jamieson, Sara. "Female Initiation Rituals among Urban Wayuu in Hugo Chávez's Multicultural Venezuelan Republic." PhD diss., University of New Mexico, 2009.

Jemison, G. Peter, and Anna M. Schein, eds. *Treaty of Canandaigua, 1794: 200 Years of Treaty Relations between the Iroquois Confederacy and the United States.* Santa Fe, NM: Clear Light Publishers, 2000.

Jennings, Francis. *The Invasion of America: Indians, Colonialism, and the Cant of Conquest.* New York: Published for the Institute of Early American History and Culture by W. W. Norton, 1975.

Jennings, Francis, William N. Fenton, Mary A. Druke, and David R. Miller, eds. *The History and Culture of Iroquois Diplomacy: An Interdisciplinary Guide to the Treaties of the Six Nations and Their League.* Syracuse, NY: Syracuse University Press, 1985.

Johnson, Elias. *Legends, Traditions, and Laws of the Iroquois.* Lockport, NY: Union Printing and Publishing Co., 1881.

Johnston, Basil H. *Indian School Days.* Norman: University of Oklahoma Press, 1988.

———. *Ojibway Heritage.* Toronto: McClelland and Stewart, 1976.

Johnston, Frances B. *The Hampton Album.* New York: The Museum of Modern Art, 1966.

Johnston, Verna Patronella. *Tales of Nokomis.* Toronto: Stoddart, 1975.

Jones, William. *Ojibwa Texts.* New York: E. J. Brill, 1917.

Josephson, Jyl. "Citizenship, Same-Sex Marriage, and Feminist Critiques of Marriage." *Perspectives on Politics* 3, no. 2 (2005): 269–284.

Justice, Daniel Heath, Mark Rifkin, and Bethany Schneider. "Introduction to Special Issue on Sexuality, Nationality, Indigeneity." *GLQ: A Journal of Lesbian and Gay Studies* 16, no.1 (2010): 5–39.

Kamakau, Samuel Manaiakalani. *Ruling Chiefs of Hawaiʻi.* Rev. ed. Honolulu: Kamehameha Schools Press, 1992.

Kameʻeleihiwa, Lilikalā. *Native Land and Foreign Desires: Pehea Lā E Pono Ai?* Honolulu: Bishop Museum Press, 1992.

Kanahele, George S. *Pauahi: The Kamehameha Legacy*, 1st ed. Honolulu: Kamehameha Schools Press, 1986.

Kaomea-Thirugnanam, Julie. *Women of Kamehameha: A Collection of Oral Histories Commemorating the 100th Anniversary of the Founding of the Kamehameha School for Girls.* Honolulu: Kamehameha Schools Bernice Pauahi Bishop Estate, 1995.

Kasirer, Nicholas. "Legal Education as *Métissage.*" (2003) 78 *Tul. L. Rev.* 481.

Kauanui, J. Kēhaulani. "Native Hawaiian Decolonization and the Politics of Gender." *American Quarterly* 60, no. 2 (2008): 281–287.

Keahiolalo-Karasuda, RaeDeen. "A Genealogy of Punishment in Hawaiʻi: The Public Hanging of Chief Kamanawa II." *Hūlili: Multidisciplinary Research on Hawaiian Well-Being* 6 (2010): 154.

Keller, Jean. *Empty Beds: Indian Student Health at Sherman Institute, 1902–1922.* East Lansing: Michigan State University Press, 2002.

Kelsay, Isabel. *Joseph Brant, 1743–1807: Man of Two Worlds.* Syracuse, NY: Syracuse University Press, 1984.

Kenny, Michael G. "A Place for Memory: The Interface between Individual and Collective History." *Society for Comparative Study of History* 4, no. 3(July 1999): 436.

Kent, Harold Winfield. *Charles Reed Bishop, Man of Hawaii.* Palo Alto: Pacific Books, 1965.

Kent, Susan, ed. *Domestic Architecture and the Use of Space: An Interdisciplinary Cross-cultural Study.* Cambridge: Cambridge University Press, 1990.

Ketchum, William. *An Authentic and Comprehensive History of Buffalo.* 2 vols. Buffalo, NY: Rockwell, Baker & Hill, Printers, 1865. Reprint, Bowie, MD: Heritage Books, 2002.

Kleinfeld, Judith. "Alaska Native Education: Issues in the Nineties." Fairbanks: University of Alaska, 1992.

Klinck, Carl F., and James J. Talman, eds. *The Journal of Major John Norton, 1816.* Toronto: Champlain Society, 1970.

Klopotek, Brian. *Recognition Odysseys: Indigeneity, Race, and Federal Tribal Recognition Policy in Three Louisiana Indian Communities.* Durham, NC: Duke University Press, 2011.

Kramer, Karen L. *Maya Children: Helpers at the Farm.* Cambridge, MA: Harvard University Press, 2005.

Krout, Mary H. *The Memoirs of Hon. Bernice Pauahi Bishop.* New York: The Knickerbocker, 1908.

Kuykendall, Ralph S. *The Hawaiian Kingdom.* Vol. 1, *Foundation and Transformation.* Honolulu: University of Hawai'i Press, 1938), 347–348.

———. *The Hawaiian Kingdom.* Vol. 2, *Twenty Critical Years (1854–1874).* Honolulu: University of Hawaii Press, 1938.

Ladner, Kiera L. "Governing within an Ecological Context: Creating an AlterNative Understanding of Blackfoot Governance." *Studies in Political Economy* 70 (2003): 125.

LaFlesche, F. *The Middle Five: Indian Schoolboys of the Omaha Tribe.* Lincoln, NE: University of Nebraska Press, 1978. Bison Book edition. Reprint of University of Wisconsin Press 1963 edition; original work published 1900.

Laux, Wilma. "The Village of Buffalo, 1800–1832." In *Adventures in Western New York History.* Vol. 3. Buffalo, NY: Buffalo and Erie County Historical Society, 1960.

Lawrence, Charles R., III. "The Id, the Ego, and Equal Protection: Reckoning with Unconscious Racism." *Stanford Law Review* 39 (1987): 317.

Lawrence, Jane. "The Indian Health Service and the Sterilization of Native American Women." *American Indian Quarterly* 24, no. 3 (2000): 400–419.

Lenoir v. Monette, No. CIV-02–0039 (Turtle Mountain, June 28, 2002). http://www.tribal-institute .org/opinions/2002.NATM.0000002.htm, accessed June 10, 2013.

Lewis, David Rich. *Neither Wolf nor Dog: American Indians, Environment, and Agrarian Change.* New York: Oxford University Press, 1997.

Life. "Chicago 'Super' Battles for Trade Schools," December 13, 1937: 59–60.

Lincoln, Doran. Interview by Acklan Willits, April 25, 1990. Round Valley Oral History Project (RVOHP), Round Valley Public Library, Covelo, CA.

Lincoln, Randolph. Interview by Les Lincoln, April 9, 1990. Round Valley Oral History Project (RVOHP), Round Valley Public Library, Covelo, CA.

Lindberg, Tracy. "What Do You Call an Indian Woman with a Law Degree? Nine Aboriginal

Women at the University of Saskatchewan College of Law Speak Out." (1997) 9 *C.J.W.L.* 301.

Lindsey, Donal F. *Indians at Hampton Institute, 1877–1923.* Blacks in the New World. Urbana: University of Illinois Press, 1995.

Lipsitz, George. *The Possessive Investment in Whiteness: How White People Profit from Identity Politics.* Philadelphia: Temple University Press, 1998, revised and expanded, 2006.

Littlefield, Alice. "Indian Education and the World of Work in Michigan, 1893–1933." In *Native Americans and Wage Labor: Ethnohistorical Perspectives,* edited by Alice Littlefield and Martha Knack, 100–121. Norman: University of Oklahoma Press, 1996.

———. "Learning to Labor: Native American Education in the United States, 1880–1930." In *The Political Economy of North American Indians,* edited by John Moore, 43–59. Norman: University of Oklahoma Press, 1993.

———. "Native American Labor and Public Policy in the United States." In *Marxist Approaches in Economic Anthropology,* edited by Alice Littlefield and Hill Gates, 219–231. New York: University Press of America, 1991.

Liu, Yongping. *Origins of Chinese Law: Penal and Administrative Law in Its Early Development.* Hong Kong: Oxford University Press, 1998.

Llewellyn, Karl N., and E. Adamson Hoebel. *The Cheyenne Way: Conflict and Case Law in Primitive Jurisprudence.* Norman, OK.: University of Oklahoma Press, 1941.

Lomawaima, K. Tsianina, and Teresa L. McCarty. *"To Remain an Indian": Lessons in Democracy from a Century of Native American Education.* Multicultural Education Series. New York: Teachers College Press, 2006.

Lomawaima, K. Tsianina. *They Called It Prairie Light: The Story of Chilocco Indian School.* Lincoln, NE: University of Nebraska Press, 1994.

———. "American Indian Education: *by* Indians versus *for* Indians." In *A Companion to American Indian History*, edited by Philip J. Deloria and Neal Salisbury, 422–440. Malden, MA: Blackwell Publishing, 2004.

———. "Estelle Reel, Superintendent of Indian Schools, 1898–1910: Politics, Curriculum, and Land." *Journal of American Indian Education* 35, no. 3 (1996): 5–31.

López, Luis Enrique. *De resquicios a boquerones: La educación intercultural bilingüe en Bolivia.* La Paz: PROEIB Andes, Plural, 2005.

———. Interview. *Fondo indígena,* June 22, 2007.

Louisiana Act 220 of 1920. La. Civ. Code. (1920).

Low, Esther Rutgers. "Narrative of Esther Rutgers Low, 1819–1820." *Buffalo Historical Society Publications* 6 (1903): 275–280.

Loyo Bravo, Engracia. "Los centros de educación indígena y su papel en el medio rural (1930–1940)." In *La educación rural e indígena en Iberoamericana,* coordinated by Pilar Gonzalbo Aizpuru and Gabriela Ossenbach, 139–159. Mexico: El Colegio de Mexico, 1996.

Lucas, Paul Nahoa. "E ola mau kākou i ka ōlelo makuahine: Hawaiian Language Policy and the Courts." *Hawaiian Journal of History* 34 (2000): 3–4.

Lucero, José Antonio. "Fanon in the Andes: Fausto Reinaga, Indianismo, and the Black Atlantic." *International Journal of Critical Indigenous Studies* 1, no. 1 (2008): 12–21.

Ludlow, Helen. *Ten Years' Work for Indians at Hampton Institute, VA, 1878–1888.* Hampton, VA: Normal School Press, 1888.

Luykx, Aurolyn. *The Citizen Factory: Schooling and Cultural Production in Bolivia.* Albany: State University of New York Press, 1999.

———. "Theory into Practice: Intercultural Pedagogy, Academic Socialization, and Anti-anti-Essentialism." N.d. Unpublished MS.

MacAulay, Hugh. "Improving Access to Legal Education for Native People in Canada: Dalhousie Law School's I.B.M. Program in Context" (1991) 14 *Dal. L.J.* 133.

Macklem, Patrick. *Indigenous Difference and the Constitution of Canada.* Toronto: University of Toronto Press, 2001.

Mansen, Richard, and David Captain. "El idioma wayúu (o guajiro)." *Lenguas indígenas de Colombia: Una visión descriptiva,* edited by María Stella González de Pérez and Maria Luisa Rodríguez de Montes, 795–810. Bogotá: Instituto Caro y Cuervo, 2000.

Mansen, Richard. *Aprendamos guajiro: Gramática pedagógica de guajiro.* Bogotá: Editorial Townsend, 1984.

Marshall, Orsamus H. *The Niagara Frontier: Embracing Sketches of Its Early History, and Indian, French and English Local Names.* Buffalo, NY: Joseph Warren & Co., 1865.

Mathes, Valerie Sherer. *Helen Hunt Jackson and Her Indian Reform Legacy.* Austin: University of Texas, 1990.

Mauger, Jeff. "Shed Roof Houses at the Ozette Archaeological Site: A Protohistoric Architectural System." PhD diss., Washington State University, 1978.

McCaffrey, Stephen C. *Understanding International Law.* Newark: LexisNexis, 2006.

McClintock, Anne. *Imperial Leather: Race, Gender, and Sexuality in the Colonial Contest,* 1st ed. New York: Routledge, 1995.

McDonnell, Roger F. "Contextualizing the Investigation of Customary Law in Contemporary Native Communities." (1992) 34 *Can. J. Crim.* 299.

Mejía Mendoza, Olga. *Conceptos de la sexualidad wayú: Espresados en los mitos, leyendas, y tradiciones.* Fondo Mixto para la Promoción de la Cultura y las Artes de La Guajira: Programa Estímulo de la Investigación Cultural y Artística del Departamento de La Guajira. La Guajira, Colombia: Departamento de La Guajira, 2001.

Menski, Werner F. *Hindu Law: Beyond Tradition and Modernity.* New Delhi: Oxford University Press, 2003.

Menton, Linda K. "Review of *Pauahi: The Kamehameha Legacy.*" *Hawaiian Journal of History* 21 (1987): 177–179.

———. "Christian and 'Civilized' Education: The Hawaiian Chiefs' Children's School." *History of Education Quarterly* 32, no. 2 (1992): 213–252.

Merry, Sally Engle. *Colonizing Hawai'i: The Cultural Power of Law.* Princeton Studies in Culture/Power/History. Princeton, NJ: Princeton University Press, 2000.

Meyer, Melissa. *The White Earth Tragedy: Ethnicity and Dispossession at a Minnesota Anishinaabe Reservation, 1889–1920.* Lincoln: University of Nebraska Press, 1999.

Miller, James. *Compact, Contract, Covenant: Aboriginal Treaty-Making in Canada.* Toronto: University of Toronto Press, 2009.

Milloy, John S. "*A National Crime*": *The Canadian Government and the Residential School System, 1879 to 1986.* Winnipeg: University of Manitoba Press, 1999.

Mills, Antonia Curtze. *Eagle Down Is Our Law: Witsuwit'en Law, Feasts, and Land Claims.* Vancouver: University of British Columbia Press, 1994.

Ministerio de Educación Superior. "Educacíon superior indígena en Venezuela: Una aproxi-macíon." Caracas: República Bolivariana de Venezuela and the Instituto Internacional para la Educación Superior en América Latina y el Caribe, December 2004. http://www .aulaintercultural.org/IMG/pdf/Informe_20final_20educacion_20indigena_20Venezuela. pdf, accessed May 26, 2013.

Minnesota Department of Education, Advisory Task Force on Minnesota American Indian Tribes and Communities and K–12 Standards-Based Reform, Report to the Legislature, as required by MN Law Chapter 146—H.F. No. 2245, Section 41, May 15, 2009.

Mississippi Choctaw Indian Band v. Holyfield, 490 U.S. 30 (1989).

Modiano, Nancy. *Indian Education in the Chiapas Highlands.* New York: Holt, Rinehart and Winston, 1973.

Momaday, N. Scott. *The Names: A Memoir.* New York: Harper and Row, 1976.

Montiel Fernández, Nemesio. *Movimiento indígena en Venezuela.* Maracaibo: Ediciónes de la Secretária de Cultura, Gobernación del Estado Zulia, 1993.

Monture, Patricia A. "Now That the Door Is Open: First Nations and the Law School Experience." (1990) 15 *Queen's L.J.* 179.

Morehouse, Thomas A. "The Dual Political Status of Alaska Natives under US Policy." Institute of Social and Economic Research, University of Alaska Anchorage, March 1992.

Morgensen, Scott Lauria. "Settler Homonationalism: Theorizing Settler Colonialism within Queer Modernities." *GLQ: A Journal of Lesbian and Gay Studies* 16, no.1 (2010): 105–131.

Morrison, Gilbert B. "School Architecture and Hygiene." In *Education in the United States,* Nicholas Murray Butler. New York: American Book Co., 1910.

Morse, Bradford W., and Gordon R. Woodman, eds. *Indigenous Law and the State.* Dordrecht: Foris, 1988.

Moya, Paula, and Michael R. Hames-García, eds. *Reclaiming Identity: Realist Theory and the Predicament of Postmodernism.* Berkeley: University of California Press, 2000.

Mt. Pleasant, Alyssa. "After the Whirlwind: Maintaining a Haudenosaunee Place at Buffalo Creek, 1780–1825." PhD diss., Cornell University, 2007.

———. "Debating Missionary Presence at Buffalo Creek: Haudenosaunee Perspectives on Land Cessions, Government Relations, and Christianity." In *Ethnographies and Exchanges: Native Americans, Moravians, and Catholics in Early North America,* edited by A.G. Roeber, 175–192. University Park, PA: Pennsylvania State University Press, 2008.

Mt. Pleasant, Jane. "The Iroquois Sustainers: Practices of a Longterm Agriculture in the Northeast." *Northeast Indian Quarterly* 6, no. 1–2 (1989): 33–39.

Muller, Kathryn V. "The Two 'Mystery' Belts of Grand River: A Biography of the Two Row Wampum and the Friendship Belt." *American Indian Quarterly* 31, no. 1(2007): 129–164.

Nabokov, Peter. *A Forest of Time: American Indian Ways of History.* Cambridge, MA: Cambridge University Press, 2002.

Nabokov, Peter, and Robert Easton. *Native American Architecture*. New York: Oxford University Press, 1989.

Nash, Roy. "Indians of Louisiana." June 12, 1931, BIA Central Correspondence File 25436–31–150, General Services, Record Group 75, National Archives.

National Archives and Records Administration. Archives I, Record Group 75, Central Classified Files, 1907–1939, Round Valley Agency (CCF).

National Archives and Records Administration. Record Group 75, Reports of Industrial Surveys, 1922–1929. Preliminary Inventory of the Records of the Bureau of Indian Affairs, Entry 762, Box 17: Greenville, Hayward, Havasupai, Hoopa Valley. Grip File *Havasupai Indian School (Arizona) Industrial Survey*.

National Archives and Records Administration. Record Group 75, Entry 121: Central Consolidated Files, Havasupai, 1912.

National Archives and Records Administration–Pacific Region (Laguna Niguel). Record Group 75, Records of the Sherman Institute, Student Case Files (SCF).

———. Record Group 75, Records of the Sherman Indian Institute, Record of Student Outings (RSO).

National Archives and Records Administration–Pacific Region (San Francisco). Record Group 75, Records of the Round Valley Agency, 1859–1930, Correspondence of Agent/Superintendent to the Commissioner of Indian Affairs, 1873–1914 (CACIA).

———. Record Group 75, Records of the Round Valley Agency, Administrative Files, 1908–1924 (AF).

———. Record Group 75, Sacramento Area Office, Coded Records, 1910–1958, Box 34, Folder: Round Valley Sub-Agency, Mr. Peter Clark [No. 3].

National Archives and Research Administration, San Bruno, CA. Record Group 75, Sacramento Area Office, Tribal Group Files, 1915–1975.

National Resource Center. "'Voices of Our Elders': Boarding School and Historical Trauma." University of Alaska, March 2008. http://elders.uaa.alaska.edu/powerpoints/boarding-school_historical-trauma_3-08.pdf, accessed June 10, 2013.

Newhouse, David, Cora Voyageur, and Dan Beavon, eds., *Hidden in Plain Sight: Contributions of Aboriginal Peoples to Canadian Identity and Culture*. Toronto: University of Toronto Press, 2005.

Newman, Jason Charles. "'There Will Come a Day When White Men Will Not Rule Us': The Round Valley Indian Tribe and Federal Indian Policy, 1856–1934." PhD diss., University of California, Davis, 2004.

News from Indian Country. http://indiancountrynews.net, accessed June 10, 2013.

New-York Missionary Society. *A Sermon Delivered before the New York Missionary Society, to Which Are Added the Annual Report of the Board of Directors and Other Papers Relating to American Missions*. New York: New York Missionary Society, 1802.

———. *Report of the Directors of the New-York Missionary Society, Presented at the Annual Meeting, Held on Tuesday, April 7, 1812*. New York: New York Missionary Society, 1812.

Nicholas, M. A. "A Little School, a Reservation Divided: Quaker Education and Allegany Seneca Leadership in the Early American Republic." *American Indian Culture and Research Journal* 30, no. 3 (2006): 1–21.

Niezen, Ronald. *Spirit Wars: Native North American Religions in the Age of Nation Building.* Berkeley: University of California Press, 2000.

O'Neill, Colleen. *Working the Navajo Way: Labor and Culture in the Twentieth Century.* Lawrence: University of Kansas Press, 2005.

O'Reilly-Scanlon, Kathleen, Christine Crowe, and Angelina Weenie. "Pathways to Understanding: 'Wâhkôhtowin' as a Research Methodology." *McGill Journal of Education* 39, no. 1 (2004): 29–44.

Office of Federal Acknowledgment, Bureau of Indian Affairs. Historical Technical Report, Jena Band of Choctaw Indians. Federal Register 59, no. 209 (October 31, 1994).

Office of the Treaty Commissioner. *Treaty Implementation: Fulfilling the Covenant.* Saskatoon: Office of the Treaty Commissioner, 2007.

Ogilvie, M. H. *Religious Institutions and the Law in Canada,* 2nd ed. Toronto: Irwin Law, 2003.

Oliver, José R. "The Archaeological, Linguistic, and Ethnohistorical Evidence for the Expansion of Arawakan into Northwestern Venezuela and Northeastern Colombia." PhD diss., University of Illinois at Urbana-Champaign, 1989.

Omi, Michael, and Howard Winant. *Racial Formation in the United States from the 1960s to the 1990s.* 2nd ed. New York: Routledge, 1994.

Opinions Attorney General (1932–1934), Louisiana.

Osorio, Jonathan Kamakawiwo'ole. *Dismembering Lahui: A History of the Hawaiian Nation to 1887.* Honolulu: University of Hawai'i Press, 2002.

Osterhammel, Jurgen. *Colonialism: A Theoretical Overview.* Translated by Shelley L. Firsch. 2nd ed. Princeton, NJ: Markus Wiener Publishers, 2005.

Owners of the Water: Conflict and Collaboration over Rivers. DVD. Directed by Laura R. Graham, David Hernández Palmar, and Caimi Waiassé. Watertown, MA: Documentary Educational Resources, 2009.

The Oxford English Dictionary, 2nd ed., edited by John Simpson and Edmund Weiner. Oxford: Oxford University Press, 1989.

Parrish, Jasper. "The Story of Captain Jasper Parrish." In *Garland Library of Narratives of North American Indian Captivities*, edited by Wilcomb E. Washburn. New York: Garland Publishers, Inc., 1976.

Patrick, Christine S. "The Life and Times of Samuel Kirkland, 1741–1808: Missionary to the Oneida Indians, American Patriot, and Founder of Hamilton College." PhD diss., State University of New York at Buffalo, 1993.

Patterson, Victoria, DeAnna Barney, Skip Willits, and Les Lincoln, eds. *The Singing Feather: Tribal Remembrances from Round Valley.* Ukiah: Mendocino County Library, 1990.

Paxton, Katrina. "Learning Gender: Female Students at the Sherman Institute, 1907–1925." In *Boarding School Blues: Revisiting American Indian Educational Experiences,* edited by Clifford Trafzer, Jean Keller, and Lorene Sisquoc. Lincoln, NE: University of Nebraska Press, 2006.

Paz, Carmen Laura. "Las politicas indigenistas en el marco del nuevo ideal nacional (1953–1958)." *Espacio Abierto* 9, no. 3 (2000): 365–390.

Paz, Sarela. "Desandando los caminos de la interculturalidad: una aproximación a la educación intercultural bilingüe." In *Escuelas y procesos de cambio,* edited by Alejandra Ramírez, 125–150. Cochabamba: CESU, 2006.

Peacock, Thomas, and Marlene Wisuri. *Ojibwe Waasa Inaabidaa: We Look in All Directions*. Afton, MN: Afton Historical Society Press, 2002.

Pearce, Roy Harvey. *The Savages of America: A Study of the Indian and the Idea of Civilization*. Rev. ed. Baltimore: Johns Hopkins Press, 1965.

Pelikan, Jaroslav. *The Vindication of Tradition*. New Haven: Yale University Press, 1984.

Peña, Adrián Setién. *Realidad indígena venezolana*. Caracas: Fundación Centro Gumilla, 1999.

Penney, Jonathon W., and Robert J. Danay. "The Embarrassing Preamble? Understanding the 'Supremacy of God' and the *Charter*." (2006) 39 *U.B.C.L. Rev.* 287.

People v. Schocko, No. 97–06–003-ICW (Grand Traverse Band Tribal Ct., Oct. 21, 1999).

Perez Gonzalez, Zaida. "Reseña de 'Manual de lenguas indígenas de Venezuela'" de Esteban Emiliano Mosonyi y Jorge C. Mosonyi. *Boletin de lingüística* 17 (2002): 124–127.

Perrin Michel. "La littérature orale des guajiro." *L'Homme* 11, no. 2 (1971): 109–112.

"Petition of Sachems, Chiefs and Warriors of the Seneca, Onondaga, Cayuga and Tuscarora Nations for Prohibition of Sale of Ardent Spirits, January 20, 1808." Petitions, Correspondence and Reports Regarding Indians, 1783–1831, A1823, Albany, NY: New York State Archives.

Pickens, Alex L., and David Kemble, eds. *To Teach the Children: Historical Aspects of Education in Hawaii*. Honolulu: Bernice Pauahi Bishop Museum, 1982.

Pilkington, Doris. *Follow the Rabbit-Proof Fence*. Brisbane: University of Queensland Press, 1996.

Pilkington, Walter, ed. *The Journals of Samuel Kirkland: 18th Century Missionary to the Iroquois, Government Agent, Father of Hamilton College*. Clinton, NY: Hamilton College, 1980.

Piper v. Big Pine, 193 Cal. 664 (1924).

Pisani, Donald. *From Family Farm to Agribusiness: The Irrigation Crusade in California and the West, 1850–1931*. Berkeley: University of California Press, 1984.

Postema, Gerald J. "Implicit Law." In *Rediscovering Fuller: Essays on Implicit Law and Institutional Design*, edited by Willem J. Witteveen and Wibren van der Burg. Amsterdam: Amsterdam University Press, 1999.

Postema, Gerald J. "On the Moral Presence of Our Past." (1991) 36 *McGill L.J.* 1153.

Postero, Nancy. *Now We Are Citizens: Indigenous Politics in Postmulticultural Bolivia*. Palo Alto, CA: Stanford University Press, 2007.

Powless, Chief Irving. "Treaty Making." In *Treaty of Canandaigua, 1794: 200 Years of Treaty Relations between the Iroquois and the United States*, edited by Anna M. Schein and G. Peter Jemison, 15–34. Santa Fe: Clear Light Publishers, 2000.

Pratt, Mary Louise. *Imperial Eyes: Studies in Travel Writing and Transculturation*. Abingdon, UK: Routledge, 1992.

Proceedings of the Third Annual Meeting of the Lake Mohonk Conference of the Friends of the Indian, Held October 7 to 9, 1885. Philadelphia: Sherman & Co., Printers, 1886, 43.

Proctor, Thomas. "Narrative of the Journey of Col. Thomas Proctor to the Indians of the North-West." In *Pennsylvania Archives,* 2nd Series, edited by John B. and William H. Egle Linn, 4, no. 2, 552–622. Harrisburg, PA: B. F. Meyers, 1876.

PROEIB Andes ORG. n.d. http://www.proeibandes.org/, accessed June 10, 2013.

Promislow, Janna. "Toward a Legal History of the Fur Trade: Looking for Law at York Factory, 1714–1763." LL.M. thesis, Osgoode Hall Law School, Toronto, 2004.

Prucha, Francis Paul. *American Indian Policy in the Formative Years: The Indian Trade and Intercourse Acts, 1780–1834.* Lincoln, NE: University of Nebraska Press, 1970.

———. *The Great Father: The United States Government and the American Indians.* Abr. ed. Lincoln, NE: University of Nebraska Press, 1986.

Pukui, Mary Kawena. *'Ōlelo No'eau: Hawaiian Proverbs & Poetical Sayings.* Bernice P. Bishop Museum special publication, no. 71. Honolulu: Bishop Museum Press, 1983.

Pukui, Mary Kawena, E. W. Haertig, and Catherine A. Lee. *Nānā I Ke Kumu (Look to the Source),* vol. 1. Honolulu: Hui Hanai, an Auxiliary of the Queen Lili'uokalani Children's Center, 1972.

———. *Nānā I Ke Kumu (Look to the Source),* vol. 2. Honolulu: Hui Hanai, an Auxiliary of the Queen Lili'uokalani Children's Center, 1972.

Purich, Donald J. "Affirmative Action in Canadian Law Schools: The Native Student in Law School." (1986–1987) 51 *Sask. L. Rev.* 79.

Quijano, Aníbal. "Coloniality of Power, Eurocentrism, and Latin America." *Nepantla: Views from the South* 1, no. 3 (2000): 533–580.

Quispe, María Teresa, and Darío Moreno. "La educacíon intercultural bilingüe en un contexto de transformación social." *El estado ante la sociedad multiétnica y pluricultural: Políticas públicas y derechos de los pueblos indígenas en Venezuela (1999–2010),* edited by Luis Jesús Bello, 118–127, 2011.

R v. Gladue, [1999] 1 S.C.R. 688.

Rabbit-Proof Fence. Directed by Philip Noyce. Miramax, 2002. Film.

Racine v. Woods, [1983] 2 S.C.R. 173, 1 D.L.R. (4th) 193.

Radan, Peter, Denise Meyerson, and Rosalind F. Croucher, eds., *Law and Religion: God, the State, and the Common Law.* New York: Routledge, 2005.

Ramos, Alcida Rita. "Cutting Through State and Class: Sources and Strategies of Self-Representation in Latin America." In *Indigenous Movements, Self-Representation, and the State in Latin America,* edited by Kay B. Warren and Jean E. Jackson, 251–278. Austin: University of Texas Press, 2002.

Ramos Díaz, Martín. *Niños mayas, maestros criollos: Rebeldía y educación en los confines del trópico.* Mexico: Universidad de Quintana Roo, Fundación Oasis, Gobierno del Estado de Quintana Roo, 2001.

Rapoport, Amos. *The Meaning of the Built Environment.* Tucson: University of Arizona Press, 1990. First published 1982 by Sage Publications.

———. "Systems of Activities and Systems of Settings." In *Domestic Architecture and the Use of Space: An Interdisciplinary Cross-cultural Study,* edited by Susan Kent, 9–20. Cambridge: Cambridge University Press, 1990.

Rappaport, Joanne. *Intercultural Utopias: Public Intellectuals, Cultural Experimentation, and Ethnic Pluralism in Colombia.* Durham: Duke University Press, 2005.

Rawls, John. *Political Liberalism.* New York: Columbia University Press, 2005.

Ray, Arthur J., Jim Miller, and Frank Tough. *Bounty and Benevolence: A History of Saskatchewan Treaties.* Montreal: McGill-Queen's University Press, 2000.

Razor, Peter. *While the Locust Slept: A Memoir.* Saint Paul: Minnesota Historical Society Press, 2002.

Reel, Estelle. *Uniform Course of Study.* Washington, DC: Government Printing Office, 1901.

Reference re Same-Sex Marriage, [2004] 3 S.C.R. 698, 246 D.L.R. (4th) 193.

Reference re Secession of Quebec, [1998] 2 S.C.R. 217, 161 D.L.R. (4th) 385.

Reference re Section 24, B.N.A. Act, [1930] 1 D.L.R. 98 at 106–107, [1930] A.C. 124.

Regan, Paulette. *Unsettling the Settler Within: Indian Residential Schools, Truth Telling, and Reconciliation in Canada.* Vancouver: University of British Columbia Press, 2010.

Report of the Commissioner of Industrial and Vocational Education for the Year Ending June 30, 1914. California State Printing Office, 1914.

Research and Statistics Division, Department of Justice, Canada. *Review of the Nunavut Community Justice Program: Final Report.* Appendix I, with assistance from Scott Clark Consulting Inc., 2004. http://www.justice.gc.ca/eng/rp-pr/aj-ja/rr05_7/index.html, accessed June 10, 2013.

Reyhner, Jon Allan, and Jeanne M. Oyawin Eder. *American Indian Education: A History.* University of Oklahoma Press, 2006.

Rhoads, C. J., to Senator Huey Long, March 3, 1932, File 68776–1931–800, Part I, Record Group 75, National Archives.

Ripstein, Arthur. "Justice and Responsibility." (2004) 17 *Can. J.L. & Jur.* 361.

Roan, Chief Wayne. *Nature's Law.* Heritage Community Foundation. 2004. http://www.abheritage .ca/natureslaws/index2.html, accessed June 10, 2013.

Robie, Harry. "Red Jacket's Reply: Problems in the Verification of a Native American Speech Text." *New York Folklore* 12, no. 3–4 (1996): 99–117.

Robinson, William, as told by Walter Wright. *Men of Medeek,* 2nd ed. Kitimat, BC: Northern Sentinel Press, 1962.

Roe. v. Wade, 410 U.S. 113 (1973).

Roediger, David. *The Wages of Whiteness: Race and the Making of the American Working Class.* New York: Verso, 1991.

Rorty, Richard. "The Priority of Democracy to Philosophy." In *Philosophical Papers.* Vol. 1, *Objectivity, Relativism, and Truth.* Cambridge: Cambridge University Press, 1991.

Rothenberg, Paula S., ed. *White Privilege: Essential Readings on the Other Side of Racism.* New York: Worth Publishers, 2002.

Russell, Sally, and Bruce Levene. *Voices and Dreams: A Mendocino County Oral History.* Ukiah: Mendocino County Library, 1991.

Sai, David Keanu. "American Occupation of the Hawaiian State: A Century Unchecked." *Hawaiian Journal of Law and Politics* 1 (2004): 46–81.

———. "The American Occupation of the Hawaiian Kingdom: Beginning the Transition from Occupied to Restored State." PhD diss., University of Hawai'i at Manoa, 2008.

Salomon, Frank. *The Cord Keepers: Khipus and Cultural Life in a Peruvian Village.* Durham, NC: Duke University Press, 2004.

San Manuel v. National Labor Relations Board, 475 F. 3d 1306 (D.C. Cir. 2007).

Sanborn, J. W., ed. *A Long-Lost Speech of Red Jacket*. Friendship, NY: privately published, 1912.

Saul, John Ralston. *A Fair Country: Telling Truths about Canada*. Toronto: Viking Press, 2008.

Sault Ste. Marie Tribe of Chippewa Indians Tribal Code, Enforcement of Foreign Judgments, Chapter 86. http://www.saulttribe.com/images/stories/government/tribalcode/chaptr86 .pdf, accessed June 10, 2013.

Schlesinger, Rudolf, et al. *Comparative Law*. 4th ed. New York: Foundation Press, 1980.

Schneider, Khal. "Citizen Lives: California Indian Country, 1855–1940." PhD diss., University of California, Berkeley, 2006.

Schouls, Tim. *Shifting Boundaries: Aboriginal Identity, Pluralist Theory, and the Politics of Self-Government*. Vancouver: University of British Columbia Press, 2003.

Schutz, Albert J. *The Voices of Eden: A History of Hawaiian Language Studies*. Honolulu: University of Hawaii Press, 1994.

Seaver, James E. *A Narrative of the Life of Mrs. Mary Jemison*. Edited and with an introduction by June Namias. Norman: University of Oklahoma Press, 1992.

Second Census of the United States, 1800. M32. Microfilm reel 28. National Archives and Records Administration, Washington, DC.

Sennett, Richard, and Jonathan Cobb. *The Hidden Injuries of Class*. New York: Vintage Books, 1972.

Shanley, Mary Lyndon. *Feminism, Marriage, and the Law in Victorian England, 1850–1895*. Princeton: Princeton University Press, 1989.

Sheehan, Bernard W. *Seeds of Extinction: Jeffersonian Philanthropy and the American Indian*. Chapel Hill, NC: Published for the Institute of Early American History and Culture at Williamsburg, VA, 1973.

Sherman, Rachel. Producing the Superior Self: Strategic Comparison and Symbolic Boundaries among Luxury Hotel Workers. *Ethnography* 6 (2005): 131–158.

Sider, Gerald. *Lumbee Indian Histories: Race, Ethnicity, and Indian Identity in the Southern United States*. Cambridge: Cambridge University Press, 1993.

Silva, Noenoe K. *Aloha Betrayed: Native Hawaiian Resistance to American Colonialism*. Durham: Duke University Press, 2004.

Simon, Judith, and Linda Tuhiwai Smith, eds. *A Civilising Mission? Perceptions and Representations of the New Zealand Native Schools System*. Auckland: University of Auckland Press, 2001.

Simon, Judith, ed. *Nga Kura Maori: The Native Schools System, 1867–1969*. Auckland: Auckland University Press, 1998.

Smith, Andrea. *Conquest: Sexual Violence and American Indian Genocide*. Cambridge, MA: South End Press, 2005.

———. "American Studies without America: Native Feminisms and the Nation-State." *American Quarterly* 60, no. 2 (2008): 312.

———. "Heteropatriarchy and the Three Pillars of White Supremacy: Rethinking Women of Color Organizing." *The Color of Violence: The Incite! Anthology*. Cambridge: South End Press, 2006.

———. "Queer Theory and Native Studies: The Heteronormativity of Settler Colonialism." *GLQ: A Journal of Lesbian and Gay Studies* 16, no. 1 (2010): 41–68.

Smith, Paul Chaat. *Everything You Know about Indians Is Wrong*. Minneapolis: University of Minnesota Press, 2009.

Snipp, C. Matthew. "The Changing Political and Economic Status of the American Indians: From Captive Nations to Internal Colonies." *American Journal of Economics and Sociology* 45 (April 1986): 145–157.

Society of Friends of Pennsylvania and New Jersey. *A Sketch...for Promoting the Improvement and Gradual Civilization of the Indian Natives*. London, 1812. Reprint of 1805 report.

Southern Workman. "Incidents of Indian Life at Hampton. A Peep into the Girl's Rooms." 1879.

———. "Incidents of Indian Life at Hampton. Indian Girls' Account of Winona Lodge." November 1882.

Stavenhagen, Rodolfo. Report of the Special Rapporteur on the Situation of Human Rights and Fundamental Rights of Indigenous Peoples, E/CN.4/2004/80, para. 20, p. 9. The *United Nations Declaration on the Rights of Indigenous Peoples*, GA Res. 61/295, UN GAOR, 61st Sess. (2007).

Stephens, Sharon. "Introduction: Children and the Politics of Culture in 'Late Capitalism.'" In *Children and the Politics of Culture*, edited by S. Stephens, 3–48. Princeton: Princeton University Press, 1995.

Strickland, Rennard. *Fire and the Spirits: Cherokee Law from Clan to Court*. Norman, OK: University of Oklahoma Press, 1975.

Sturtevant, William C. "David and Dennis Cusick: Early Iroquois Realist Artists." *American Indian Art Magazine* 31, no. 2 (2006): 44–55.

Sunstein, Cass R. "'On Analogical Reasoning,' Commentary." (1993) 106 *Harv. L. Rev.* 741.

Suquamish Tribe, The. http://www.suquamish.org/HistoryCulture.aspx, accessed October 7, 2010.

Suttles, Wayne. "The Shed-Roof House." In *A Time of Gathering: Native Heritage in Washington State*, edited by Robin K. Wright, 212–222. Seattle: University of Washington Press for the Burke Museum, 1991.

Swatzler, David. *A Friend among the Senecas: The Quaker Mission to Cornplanter's People*. Mechanicsburg, PA: Stackpole Books, 2000.

Szasz, Margaret Connell. *Education and the American Indian: The Road to Self-Determination since 1928*, 3rd ed. Albuquerque: University of New Mexico Press, 1999.

———. *Indian Education in the American Colonies, 1607–1783*, 1st ed. Albuquerque: University of New Mexico Press, 1988.

Talbot, Edith Armstrong. *Samuel Chapman Armstrong: A Biographical Study*. New York: Doubleday, Page & Company, 1904.

Talks and Thoughts 3, no. 10 (April 1889): 1.

Talks and Thoughts 8, no. 6 (December 1893): 1–2.

Taylor, Solange. *Language-in-Education Planning: PROEIB Andes and the Consolidation of Bilingual Education Policies in Bolivia, Peru, and Chile*. Diss. in Educational Studies, Jesus College, Comparative and International Education, 2005.

Thomas, Jacob E., et al. *Great Law Workshop, January–February 1992*. Ohsweken, Six Nations Reserve: Sandpiper Press. Videocassette.

Thomas, Jake. *The Great Law*. VHS (Ten-Tape Series). Iroquoian Institution, 1992.

Tiro, Karim Michel. "The People of the Standing Stone: The Oneida Indian Nation from Revolution through Removal, 1765–1840." PhD diss. University of Pennsylvania, 1999.

Tooker, Elisabeth. "The League of the Iroquois: Its History, Politics, and Ritual." In Vol. 15, *Northeast* of *Handbook of North American Indians,* edited by Bruce G. Trigger, 418–441. Washington, DC: Smithsonian Institution, 1978.

Trask, Haunani-Kay. *From a Native Daughter: Colonialism and Sovereignty in Hawai'i.* Rev. ed. Honolulu: University of Hawaii Press, 1999.

———. "Fighting the Battle of Double Colonization: The View of a Hawaiian Feminist." Working Paper #52, Office of Women in International Development. East Lansing, MI: Office of Women in International Development, 1984.

———. "Settlers of Color and 'Immigrant' Hegemony: 'Locals' in Hawaii." *Amerasia Journal* 26, no. 2, (2000): 1–24.

Trennert, Robert A. "From Carlisle to Phoenix: The Rise and Fall of the Indian Outing System, 1878–1930." *Pacific Historical Review* 52 (August 1983): 267–291.

———. *The Phoenix Indian School: Forced Assimilation in Arizona, 1891–1935.* Norman: University of Oklahoma Press, 1988.

Tully, James. *Public Philosophy in a New Key: Democracy and Civic Freedom,* vol. 1. Cambridge: Cambridge University Press, 2008.

Turner, Dale. *This Is Not a Peace Pipe: Towards a Critical Indigenous Philosophy.* Toronto: University of Toronto Press, 2006.

Turner, Nancy J. *The Earth's Blanket: Traditional Teachings for Sustainable Living.* Vancouver: Douglas & McIntyre, 2005.

Valandra, Edward. "Rethinking Indigenous Underdevelopment in the United States." *Wicazo Sa Review* 12 (Autumn 1997): 111–142.

Van Cott, Donna Lee. "A Political Analysis of Legal Pluralism in Bolivia and Colombia." *Journal of Latin American Studies* 32 (2000): 207–234.

Vaughan, Mary Kay. *Cultural Politics in Revolution: Teachers, Peasants, and Schools in Mexico, 1930–1940.* Tucson: University of Arizona Press, 1997.

Vicariato Apostolico de Machiques, http://servidor-opsu.tach.ula.ve/alum/pd_4/vica_a_m/html /indive.html, accessed June 10, 2013.

Villalón, María E. *Educación para indígenas en Venezuela: Una crítica razonada,* pp. 6–9. CEVIAP 9. Caracas: Centro Venezolano de Investigaciones en Antropología y Población, 1994.

Wade, J. P. "First School for State Indians Held in LaSalle Parish; History of Tribe Near Jena Is Related." *Shreveport Times,* October 31, 1929.

Waganakising Odawa Tribal Code: Little Traverse Bay Bands of Odawa Indians, Title IX. Criminal Laws; Liquor Control. http://www.ltbbodawa-nsn.gov/TribalCode/TRIBAL%20CODE%20 121709%20REVISED%20DLB%20MASTER.pdf, accessed June 10, 2013.

Walker, Frances. In *Annual Report of the Secretary of the Interior on the Operations of the Department for the Year 1872.* Washington, DC: Government Printing Office, 1872.

Wall, Wendy. "Gender and the 'Citizen Indian.'" In *Writing the Range: Race, Class, and Culture in the Women's West,* edited by Elizabeth Jameson and Susan Armitage, 202–221. Norman: University of Oklahoma Press, 1997.

Wallace, Anthony F. C. *The Death and Rebirth of the Seneca.* New York: Knopf, 1970. Reprint, New York: Vintage Books, 1972.

Warman, Arturo. *Y venimos a contradecir.* Mexico City: Casa Chata, 1976.

Warren, Jonathan. *Racial Revolutions: Antiracism and Indian Resurgence in Brazil.* Durham, NC: Duke University Press, 2001.

Washinawatok-El Issa, Ingrid. In *Women of the Native Struggle: Portraits and Testimony of Native American Women*, edited by Ronnie Farley. New York: Orion Books, 1993.

Watson, Lawrence Craig. "Marriage and Sexual Adjustment in Guajiro Society." *Ethnology* 12 (1967): 153–161.

———. *Guajiro Personality and Urbanization.* Los Angeles: Latin American Center, University of California, 1968.

Watson-Franke, Maria Barbara. "Social Pawns or Social Powers: The Position of Guajiro Women." *Antropológica* 45 (1976): 19–39.

———. "To Learn for Tomorrow: Enculturation of Girls and Its Social Importance among the Guajiro of Venezuela." In *Enculturation in Latin America: An Anthology*, edited by Johannes Wilbert, 191–211. Latin American Center: University of California, Los Angeles, 1976.

Watt, Marilyn. "Federal Indian Policy and Tribal Development in Louisiana: The Jena Band of Choctaw." PhD diss., Pennsylvania State University, 1986.

Webber, Jeremy. "Legal Pluralism and Human Agency." (2006) 44 *Osgoode Hall L.J.* 167.

Westad, Odd Arne. *The Global Cold War: Third World Interventions and the Making of Our Times.* New York: Cambridge University Press, 2005.

Westerink, Diane. "Manual Training Movement." n.d. http://www.nd.edu/~rbarger/www7 /manualtr.html, accessed March 19, 2010.

Wexler, Laura. *Tender Violence: Domestic Visions in an Age of US Imperialism.* Chapel Hill: The University of North Carolina Press, 2000.

White, Richard. *The Roots of Dependency: Subsistence, Environment and Social Change among the Choctaws, Pawnees, and Navajos.* Lincoln, NE: University of Nebraska Press, 1988.

Whiu, Leah. "A Maori Woman's Experience of Feminist Legal Education in Aotearoa." (1994) 2 *Waikato L. Rev.* 161.

Wilbur, Ray Lyman, Secretary of the Interior. Response to T. H. Harris, Louisiana State Superintendent of Education, March 3, 1932, File 68776–1931–800, Part I, Record Group 75, National Archives.

Wilkinson, Norman B. "Robert Morris and the Treaty of Big Tree." *The Mississippi Valley Historical Review* 40, no. 2 (1953): 257–278.

Williams, Walter L. "Patterns in the History of the Remaining Southeastern Indians, 1840–1975." In *Southeastern Indians Since the Removal Era*, edited by Walter L. Williams, 193–210. Athens: University of Georgia, 1979.

Wilpert, Gregory. *Changing Venezuela by Taking Power: The History and Policies of the Chávez Government.* London and New York: Verso, 2007.

———. Chavez Announces Nationalization, Constitutional Reforms for Venezuela. http://www .reclaimthemedia.org/communications_rights/chavez_to_nationalize_venezuelan _telecommunications_energy_industres, Reclaim the Media, accessed May 21, 2013.

Wilson, Diane. *Beloved Child: A Dakota Way of Life.* St. Paul: Minnesota Historical Society Press, 2011.

Wist, Benjamin Othello. *A Century of Public Education in Hawaii, October 15, 1840–October 15, 1940.* Honolulu: The Hawaii Educational Review, 1940.

Wolfe, Patrick. "Land, Labor, and Difference: Elementary Structures of Race." *The American Historical Review* 106, no. 3 (2001): 866–905.

World Bank, The. http://microdata.worldbank.org/index.php/catalog/570, accessed June 10, 2013.

Yamamoto, Eric K. *Interracial Justice: Conflict and Reconciliation in Post–Civil Rights America.* New York: New York University Press, 1999.

Young, Brian. *The Politics of Codification: The Lower Canadian Civil Code of 1866.* Montreal: McGill-Queen's University Press, 1994.

Index

Australia: and history of colonial indigenous education, 9–10; race and indigenous educational policy in, 6

Aymara (Bolivia), 188–189, 198n22

Baca, Lawrence R., 14n10
Bahktin, Mikhail, 262n10
Barak, Aharon, 222n35
Baran, Paul, 92
Barker, Adam, 110n9
Barroso, Emelina, 229, 238
Bartell, Ernest, 87
Barth, Karl, 191–192, 195
Basham, Leilani, 32, 44n73
Basso, Keith, 3
Beamer, B. Kamanamaikalani, 41n28
Beatty, Willard W., 58
Behar, Ruth, 232
Benham, Maenette K. P., 24, 42n48
Beltrán, Luis, 252–253
Beyer, Carl Kalani, 42n49, 44n67
Big Tree, Treaty of (1797), 119, 129n24
bilingual education. See intercultural bilingual education; languages
Biloxi-Tunicas (Louisiana), 71n67
Bishop, Charles R., 17, 18, 19, 24, 25, 26, 30–36, 37, 39n5, 42n40, 42n48, 43n51, 43n57, 45n79, 45n81, 45–46n84–86, 46n94
Black, Cobey, 34
Blackhawk, Ned, 65n9
boarding schools: archival and anecdotal evidence of student-initiated arson in, 174n32; economic policy and Indian education in California from 1902 to 1945, 91–109; emphasis on in studies of American Indian education, 127n4; establishment and re-establishment of in Alaska, 138–139, 143, 144; experience of as metaphor, 267–283; land policy and establishment of, 4; regimentation and discipline of Indian bodies in, 172n4; and transformation of Native domestic homes and spaces, 148–172; and vocational training in rural Yucatán, 73–88, 198n24. See also education
Boarding School Seasons: American Indian Families, 1900–1940, 269
Bolívar, Simón, 251

Bolivia, indigenous education and politics of knowledge in, 177–196
Borrows, John, 13
Brave Bull, 165
Brave Heart-Jordan, Maria Yellow Horse, 271, 272, 283n8
Brazil, 72n75
Britton, June, 97
Brooks, James, 66n10
Brown vs. Board of Education of Topeka (1954), 143
Buffalo Creek (New York), 114–127
Buffalohead, Roger, 165
built environments, and architecture, 153, 155–156
Bureau of Fisheries, 140, 141
Bureau of Indian Affairs, 141, 269. See also Office of Indian Affairs
Burns, Allan, 83

"cabin," contrasted to "home" in photographic images, 159
Cáceres, Victor, 196
California, and indigenous boarding schools from 1902 to 1945, 6–7, 91–109
Campins, Luis Herrera, 233
Canada: and history of colonial indigenous education, 8–9; indigenous legal traditions and law schools in, 200–218, 226–227n76–77; and living tree as metaphor for legal fluidity, 223n53; and national dialogue on residential school history, 270, 279; and role of indigenous intellectuals in discussions about sovereignty, nationhood, and indigenous rights, 190–191; self-government and evolutionary nature of law in, 225n67
Canadian Charter of Rights and Freedoms, 217
Canandaigua (New York), 120
Canandaigua, Treaty of (1794), 125
Captain Jim (Havasupai), 168–169, 171
Carlisle Indian Industrial School (Pennsylvania), 103, 268, 270, 280
Carpio, Myla, 111n20
Carr, Curtis Thorpe, 157
Casa Del Estudiante Indigena (Mexico City), 11–12
Castellanos, M. Blanet, 11

Dalker, Fred, 67n26
Davin Report (1879), 8
Dawes, Henry, 91
Dawson, Alexander, 11
Dekanawida (Haudenosaunee), 116, 117
deliberation, as source of indigenous legal tradition in Canada, 205–206
Deloria, Philip, 11, 66n13, 275
Demientieff, Ivan, 138
Densmore, Christopher, 131n56
Department for Indigenous Affairs (Venezuela), 234, 262n18, 264n42
De Rouen, René Louis, 53
Diaz, Porfirio, 10
disease: impact of on Alaska Natives, 137–138; Ojibwe and influenza epidemic of 1918, 277
Dole, Sanford, 34
domains, use of term in debate on assimilation policy, 149, 173n10
domestication: and indigenous education at Kamehameha Schools for Native Hawaiians, 18–20, 25–30; use of term, 17. *See also* architecture; gender
Dorman, Ellen, 96
D'Suq'Wub (Washington), 150–152
Duncan, Myrtle, 103–104
Duncan, Victoria, 104

economics: and cost of indigenous boarding schools in Yucatán, 79–80; impact of modernization and global in Yucatán, 87–88; and indigenous boarding schools in California from 1902 to 1945, 91–109. *See also* Great Depression; labor; underdevelopment
Ecuador. *See* PROEIB
education, indigenous: as act of containment and of "retraining" of indigenous subjects, 88n4; distinct character of under Jim Crow in South, 48–65; exploration and comparison of regional histories as methodology for study of, 7–12; Haudenosaunee and debate with missionaries on nonindigenous education in early nineteenth century, 114–127; history of in Alaska, 133–145; indigenous legal traditions and law schools in Canada, 200–218; in Kamehameha Schools in Hawai'i and themes of domestication

and marriage, 16–38; new directions in comparative studies of, 12–14; overview of impact of colonialism on, 4–6; overview of issues of race and segregation in, 6–7; and politics of knowledge in Bolivia, 177–196; strategies of Flor Ángela Palmar Barroso for development of in Venezuela, 229–260; systems of before colonization, 2–4, 40n19. *See also* boarding schools; intercultural bilingual education; universities
Ellis, Clyde, 93
Ellis, Olive, 104
Emma, Queen (Hawai'i), 38n2
environment, as source of indigenous law in Canada, 203–205
environmental law, in Canada, 201, 220n19
Episcopal Church, 136
Escuela Básica Nacional La Resistencia (National Primary School of the Resistance, Venezuela), 248–249
essentialism, intercultural bilingual education in Andean region and theoretical critique of, 191–192, 195
Everwind, Alex, 276–277, 284n18
Eyre, Kāwika, 30

family, concept of domesticity and metaphor of, 18
Fanon, Frantz, 198–199n31
Farmer's Brother (Seneca), 114, 120, 130n40
Feld, Steven, 262n10
Feliz, Blanche, 99, 105
feminism, and critique of marriage, 20
Fenton, William N., 128n5, 128n7, 128n10
Fickinger, Paul, 59, 60
Flandreau Indian Boarding School (South Dakota), 273, 275, 280
Flathead (Montana), 3
Fletcher, Alice, 165
Foley, Neil, 71n65
For the Rights of All: Ending Jim Crow in Alaska (documentary), 147n31
Forsman, Leonard, 151
Fort Niagara (New York), 120
Foucault, Michel, 225n71
Frank, Andre Gunder, 92
Frazer, Ventha, 112n57
Freeman, Arvella, 102

Indian Home Building Fund, 165
Indian Reorganization Act of 1934 (IRA), 93, 107, 109
Indian Residential Schools Settlement Agreement (Canada, 2006), 270
Indian Self-Determination and Education Assistance Act (1975), 145, 146n10
indigeneity: and definition of "indigenous" in study of indigenous education, 11; and Program for Training in Intercultural Bilingual Education for Andean Countries in Bolivia, 188–193
indigenous philosophers, and significance of "word warriors" in Canada, 190–191
indio permitido ("authorized Indian"), 178
Industrial Surveys, of Indian households by boarding school system, 166–171, 175n61
Instituto Nacional Indigenista (National Indigenous Institute, INI), 75, 77
interactive distance learning, in Alaska, 145
intercultural bilingual education (IBE): and indigenous languages in Andean region, 181, 182, 183, 229–260; use of term, 261n7. *See also* languages; Program for Training in Intercultural Bilingual Education for Andean Countries
interculturalidad (interculturality), and indigenous education in Bolivia, 177–196
internados (boarding schools), 74, 75–77
internment camps, and Alaska Natives, 140
Inuit (Nunavut), 211–214, 227n77
Inupiat (Alaska), 139
Iverson, Peter, 93

Jackson, Sheldon, 136–137
Jacobs, Margaret, 6
Jamieson, Sara, 236, 242
Jamison, Eugene, 99, 100, 107, 109
Jamison, Eugene, Jr., 109
Jemison, Mary, 130n36
Jena Band of Choctaws (Louisiana), 51–65
Jennings, Francis, 66n10, 128n11
Jim Crow, and distinct character of Indian education under policies of in South, 48–65. *See also* segregation
Johnson, Horace, 106
Johnson-O'Malley Act (1934), 14n2, 57, 146n10

Johnston, Basil, 204, 269–270, 282
Johnston, Francis, 159
Johnston, John, 130n40
Johnston, William, 117, 130n40
Jones, Mary Jackson, 66n15, 72n72
Jones v. Ellis (1929), 142
Jorgenson, Joseph, 92
Juarez, Benito, 10

Kamehameha III, King, 22
Kamehameha V, King, 34
Kamehameha Schools (Hawai'i), 16–38
Kanahele, George S., 32, 33, 42–43n49, 45n79, 45n84, 46n89
Keahiolalo-Karasuda, RaeDeen, 41n28
Kekūanāo'a, Mataio, 22–24, 41n36
Kirkland, Samuel, 130n37
Kirstein, Leonard, 159, 162
knowledge: indigenous education and politics of in Bolivia, 177–196; oral transmission of before colonization, 2–4; and place of indigenous education at universities in Latin America, 198n25; Program for Training in Intercultural Bilingual Education for Andean Countries and alternative forms of in Bolivia, 190–191
Kramer, Karen L., 89–90n23
Krout, Mary H., 34, 46n94
Kuykendall, Ralph S., 40n23

labor: and economics of Indian education in California, 93, 97, 98, 100, 101, 104, 105, 108; and goals of manual education at Kamehameha Schools in Hawai'i, 26–30; and vocational training in indigenous boarding schools in Yucatán, 73–88. *See also* vocational training
Lakota, 3, 166, 271, 274
land tenure, and land policy: and allotment system, 91–92, 94–95, 96, 108, 275, 278; and establishment of off-reservation government boarding schools, 4; Native Hawaiians and loss of, 16; and speculation in late eighteenth-century New York, 119
Land Wars of 1860s (New Zealand), 9
languages: employment in Mexico and English, 85–86; gender in Hawaiian oral tradition and, 44n73; and intercultural bilingual education in South America, 181; and

politics: and ambiguous status of Alaska Natives, 134; impact of indigenous education in Bolivia on, 177–196; and marriages in Hawaiian kingdom, 33; and symbolic power of indigenous languages, 265n54

power, D'Suq'Wub in Washington state as expression of indigenous, 152

Pratt, Richard Henry, 91, 164

proclamations, as source of indigenous law in Canada, 206–207

Proctor, Thomas, 128n12

PROEIB. *See* Program for Training in Intercultural Bilingual Education for Andean Countries

Program for Training in Intercultural Bilingual Education for Andean Countries (PROEIB), 177–196

proletarianization, and economics of Indian education, 93

Proyecto Andino de Tecnologias Campesinas (PRATEC), 192

Prucha, Francis Paul, 117, 129n16

Pueblo, 152–153, 174n27

Pukui, Mary Kawena, 32, 40n26

Quakers, and missionaries, 123, 130n37, 154–155

Quipus (talking knots), 3

Rabbit-Proof Fence (film), 15n15

race: ambiguous position of Indians in US hierarchy of, 50; contemporary politics of in Brazilian context, 72n75; and debate over identity in PROEIB, 198–199n31; and discourse on black-white relations in South in Jim Crow era, 50; and formation as sociohistorical process, 65n6, 71n68; overview of issues in indigenous education, 6–7; and schools for Jena Choctaws in Louisiana, 55, 58, 60–64. *See also* ideology; racism; segregation

racism: anti-black among Indians in South in Jim Crow era, 58, 60–62; and assimilation policy of Australian government, 10; and development of public education in Alaska, 142; immigrant communities and minorities in US, 71n65. *See also* ideology; race; segregation

Rappaport, Joanne, 195

Rawls, John, 225n68

Razor, Peter, 274

Red Jacket (Seneca), 116, 118–119, 121–124, 128n8, 131n56

Red Lake Indian Reservation (Minnesota), 2, 269, 276–277, 280–281

regional histories, exploration and comparison of as methodology for study of indigenous education, 7–12

Regional Office of Indigenous Affairs (Oficina Regional de Asuntos Indígenas, Venezuela), 243, 262n18

religion. *See* missionaries; sacred sources

Removal policy (1830s-1840s), in American South, 49, 65n3

resistance: archival and anecdotal evidence of student-initiated arson in boarding schools and, 174n32; of Ojibwe to government construction of boarding school on Red Lake Reservation, 1–2, 280–282; of Round Valley Reservation (California) to indigenous boarding schools, 105

Rhoads, C. J., 54

Richardson, E. E., 52, 54, 55–56

Rivardi, John, 120

Rivera, Silvia, 177

Robertson, M. S., 57, 58, 59, 63, 68n36–37, 70n53

Robie, Harry, 131n56

Round Valley Indian Reservation (California), 92–109

Russia, and indigenous history of Alaska, 134, 135–136, 138, 145n2

Russian-American Company, 135

Russian Orthodox Church, 135–136

Ryan, Carson, 57, 69n53

sacred sources, of indigenous law in Canada, 202–203

Saginaw Chippewa Tribe (Michigan), 283

St. Joseph's Mission School (British Columbia), 155, 156

"Sandy Lake Tragedy" (Minnesota), 278

Santa Fe Indian School, 174n27

Sartre, Jean-Paul, 199n31

scholarships, to indigenous boarding schools in Yucatán, 79

schoolhouse, and built environment of Indian boarding schools, 155–156

Schroeder, Herb, 145

Schutz, Albert J., 21, 42n42

Second Great Awakening, 117

Secretaria de Educación Pública (Ministry of Education, or SEP), 75, 76

segregation: development of public education in Alaska compared to policies of in South, 141–143; local variations as applied to Indians in Jim Crow South, 49–50; overview of issues in indigenous education, 6–7; and schools for Jena Choctaws in Louisiana, 56, 61. *See also* Jim Crow; race; racism

Seneca (New York), 114, 116, 130n36–37, 154–155. *See also* Haudenosaunee

Seventh-day Adventist Church, 146n18

sexuality, disciplining of Hawaiian during colonization, 31–32, 35, 38

Sherman, Rachel, 90n34

Sherman Institute (California), 94, 95, 97, 98, 99, 100, 101, 103, 105, 107, 108

Silva, Noenoe K., 40n25

Simón Rodriguez Experimental University (Venezuela), 230, 259

slavery, of Alaska Natives by Russians, 135, 145n2

Sliffe, Helene, 56, 68n33

Smith, Andrea, 18, 42n46

Smith, Paul Chaat, 148

social mobility, and Maya view of wage work, 84, 85

social order, and indigenous legal system in Canada, 210–211

social work, and adverse effects of boarding school experience, 271

Society of Friends. *See* Quakers

South: and distinct character of Indian education under Jim Crow, 48–65; history of segregation compared to development of public education in Alaska, 141–143

South Dakota, 97

sovereignty: and Ojibway resistance to construction of government school on reservation, 1; role of indigenous intellectuals in Canadian discussions about nationhood, indigenous rights, and, 190–191

Spanish language: debates on exclusive use of in Latin America, 5; and intercultural bilingual education in Latin America, 186, 232, 233, 240. *See also* languages

Special Law for Intercultural Bilingual Education (Venezuela), 230

speeches, by Haudenosaunee orators, 115

stereotypes: and Indian anti-black racism in Jim Crow South, 61; of Indian "savagery" and white superiority, 66n13

Stevens, Isaac, 151

Stewart Indian School (Nevada), 94

Stillday, Eugene, 280

story telling: and indigenous legal tradition in Canada, 206, 220–221n24; symbolism of Windigo in Ojibwe, 284n22. *See also* oral tradition

subjectitivity. *See* conscious subjects

Suquamish (Washington), 150–152

Suttles, Wayne, 150

Swengel, Edward, 95

symbols: and boarding school experience in discourse on American colonialism, 268; Western architectural forms as, 149, 164

Szasz, Margaret Connell, 68n33, 69n43, 129n23

Thompson, Samuel H., 56

Thorpe, Jim, 280

Tiro, Karim Michel, 129n23

Tobeluk vs. Lind (1976), 143–144

Tomah Boarding School (Wisconsin), 276, 277

Tooker, Elisabeth, 128n10

tort law, in Canada, 201

Trade and Intercourse Act (1796), 117, 130n44

tradition, use of term in context of legal system in Canada, 202, 226n74. *See also* oral tradition

Trask, Haunani-Kay, 65n8

Trennert, Robert, 93–94

Truth and Reconciliation Commission (Canada), 270

Tully, James, 223n50, 225n69

Tunica (Louisiana), 68n36, 71n67

Turner, Dale, 190–191, 194

Turner, Nora, 103

Tuscarora (New York), 114

Tyonek decision (1992), 146n5

Ukaliannuk, Lucien, 213

underdevelopment, and Indian economies in nineteenth- and twentieth-century California, 92, 102, 107, 109n5

www.ingramcontent.com/pod-product-compliance
Lightning Source LLC
Chambersburg PA
CBHW071835270326
41929CB00013B/1999